SONAR POWER!

Scott R. Garrigus

SONAR Power!

Credits: Interior and Cover Design—Michelle Frey, Stephanie Japs, Cathie Tibbetts, and John Windhorst, DOV Graphics; Technical Editor—Michael Nickolas, Cakewalk; Index— Kevin Broccoli.

Library of Congress Catalog Number: 2001086928
ISBN: 1-929685-36-X

5   4   3   2

MUSKA&LIPMAN

Muska & Lipman Publishing
2645 Erie Avenue, Suite 41
Cincinnati, Ohio 45208
www.muskalipman.com
publisher@muskalipman.com

This book is composed in Melior, Columbia, Helvetica, and Courier typefaces using QuarkXpress 4.1.1, Adobe PhotoShop 5.5, and Adobe Illustrator 8.0. Created in Cincinnati, Ohio, in the United States of America.

About the Author

Scott R. Garrigus
www.garrigus.com

Scott R. Garrigus has been involved with music and computers since he was 12 years old. After graduating from high school, he went on to earn a B.A. in music performance with an emphasis in sound recording technology at UMass, Lowell. In 1993, he released his first instrumental album on cassette, entitled *Pieces Of Imagination*. In 1995, he began his professional writing career when his first article appeared in *Electronic Musician* magazine. In 2000, he authored his first book, *Cakewalk Power!* This was the first book to deal exclusively with the Cakewalk Pro Audio, Guitar Studio, and Home Studio software applications. In 2001, he completed his second book, *Sound Forge Power!,* which was the first book to deal exclusively with Sonic Foundry's Sound Forge audio editing software. Today, Garrigus continues to contribute articles to *Electronic Musician,* in addition to a number of other print and online publications, including *Digital Pro Sound, Keyboard,* CNET, and *Web Review.* He also publishes his own music technology e-zine, called *DigiFreq* (**www.digifreq.com**), which provides free news, reviews, tips and techniques for music technology users.

Dedication

To Mom, Dad, Babci, Dziadzi, Grandma, Grandpa, Mark, and Steve. Thanks for all your love and support. And to Ron, Claire, Ellie, Vinnie, and Ron Jr. for being there and making me feel like a part of your family.

Acknowledgments

My third book is here! I wasn't sure I'd make it through the writing process a third time. I certainly couldn't have made it this far in my writing career without the help of many wonderful people. I want to thank all my music technology friends who take the time to visit my Web site and to read my ramblings each month in the *DigiFreq* newsletter. DigiFreqers rule!

Thanks to all the Cakewalk users (many of whom are also DigiFreqers) for making Cakewalk software so successful and popular. This book wouldn't exist without your dedication and support. Thanks to the people at Cakewalk for creating SONAR and also for helping prepare and promote this book.

Thanks to the team at Muska & Lipman Publishing for putting out such a polished product.

And, as always, thank you, God for giving me the strength and determination to achieve my dreams.

Table of Contents

Introduction

This is the first book on the market that deals exclusively with Cakewalk Music Software's SONAR. You can find other Cakewalk-related and generic books about using computers to create and record music that may provide a small amount of information about SONAR, but none of them provides complete coverage of the product. Of course, SONAR comes with an excellent manual, but like most other manuals, it is meant only as a feature guide.

Instead of just describing the features of the program and how they work, I'm going to dig deep down into the software and show you exactly how to use the product with step-by-step examples and exercises that will help make your composing and recording sessions run more smoothly. I'll explain all of the features available, and I'll do it in a manner you can understand and use, right away.

So why should you listen to me? Well, SONAR is based on Cakewalk's Pro Audio product, and I've been using Pro Audio since it was spawned from the programming code of Cakewalk Professional. I've also written about Cakewalk products in numerous review articles for magazines such as *Electronic Musician*, *Keyboard*, and *Recording*. In addition, I've been working with the people at Cakewalk for quite some time now, learning all there is to know about SONAR, as well as testing the product during the beta process. And the people at Cakewalk have helped me develop much of the information in this book, making sure that everything is "officially" technically accurate. How's that for a seal of approval? Suffice it to say, I know my way around the product, and now I would like to share that knowledge with you.

I'm going to assume that SONAR is installed on your computer and that you know how to start the program. In addition, you should have at least skimmed through the manual that comes with the software and have all your external audio and MIDI gear set up already. I'm also going to assume that you know how to use your mouse for clicking, dragging, double-clicking, right-clicking, and so on. You should also know how to work with basic Windows features such as Windows Explorer and the

Windows Control Panel. And you should have access to the World Wide Web or perhaps a friend who does. Otherwise, all you need is a strong interest in learning how to get the most out of SONAR. Just leave the rest up to me, and I promise that you'll be working with SONAR like you never have before. You might even have some fun with it, too.

How This Book is Organized

You'll find that although I've tried to avoid overlapping content between this book and the manual that comes with SONAR, in some instances, this overlap just can't be avoided. I wanted to be sure to help you understand all the important features of the program, and doing so means including some basic explanations to begin with. For the most part, though, the information included in this book is more "how to" rather than "this feature does so-and-so."

Chapter 1, "MIDI and Digital Audio Basics," and Chapter 2, "Getting Started with SONAR," provide an introduction to computer music and the software. These chapters explain the importance of registration and how to find help, as well as the major features and more obscure parts of the software, and how they work together. You'll also find a brief description of the differences between SONAR and Pro Audio 9.

Chapter 3, "Customizing SONAR," shows you how to make SONAR work the way you want it to. This chapter explains program preferences and workspace customization, as well as how to find the optimal settings for MIDI and audio functionality.

In Chapter 4, "Working with Projects," you'll learn how to work with projects. This chapter includes step-by-step instructions for opening, closing, and saving existing projects. You'll also learn how to create new projects and how to make your own project templates.

Chapter 5, "Getting Around in SONAR," and Chapter 6, "Recording and Playback," describe how to navigate within SONAR and how to record and play back your projects. You'll find instructions on how to record and play MIDI, as well as audio, and you'll learn about recording multiple tracks at once. I'll explain the importance of the Now time and show you how to use the Go menu, search, and markers, as well as the Zoom features. After you read these chapters, you'll be making your way through SONAR like a pro.

In Chapter 7, "Editing Basics," and Chapter 8, "Exploring the Editing Tools," you're ready to dive into editing. First, I'll explain the basics to you, including tracks and clips, the Event Editor, and Piano Roll view. Then you can investigate the editing tools in more detail.

Chapter 9, "Composing with Loops," will show you how to use the new looping features and Loop Construction view found in SONAR. With these features, you can compose songs using nothing more than audio sample loops. The new looping features add similar functionality to SONAR as you would find in Sonic Foundry's ACID software.

Chapter 10, "Software Synthesis," also explores some of the new features provided in SONAR. Similar to the VST synth features that you find in Steinberg's Cubase software, SONAR gives you access to virtual synthesizer plug-ins. These plug-ins let you compose music with MIDI using software-based synthesizers rather than the synth in your sound card or your external MIDI keyboard.

Chapter 11, "Effects: The Really Cool Stuff," explains one of my favorite parts of SONAR. The things you can do with these tools are amazing. I'll cover both the MIDI and audio effects, and I'll show you how to use them in offline and real-time situations. I'll even share some cool presets I've developed, so you can use them in your own recording projects.

Chapter 12, "Mixing It Down," takes a look at mixing. I know that mixing music via software can be confusing sometimes. Nothing beats being able to just grab a fader on a hardware-based mixer, but after you read this chapter, you may find that with all the functionality that SONAR provides, mixing is actually easier, and you have more control when using an on-screen software mixer.

I've received many questions as to SONAR's capabilities in terms of music notation, so that's the topic I'll cover in Chapter 13, "Making Sheet Music." I'll explain all the tools you have at your disposal, as well as what you can and cannot do. Although SONAR doesn't provide full-fledged music notation features, you might be surprised at what you find here.

Chapter 14, "Studio Control with StudioWare and Sysx"; Chapter 15, "Advanced StudioWare Techniques"; Chapter 16, "CAL 101"; and Chapter 17, "Advanced CAL Techniques," jump into some of the more complicated features that SONAR offers. Don't worry if you think that StudioWare and CAL are out of your reach as a beginning user. Actually, you can use these features in plenty of ways even if you decide not to explore them fully. But just in case you're interested in learning more, I'm going to show you how to develop your own panels in StudioWare and your own scripts in CAL. By the time you finish reading, you won't know how you lived without them.

Finally, in Chapter 18, "Take Your SONAR Project to CD," I'll show you how to prepare your SONAR project and burn it onto CD.

My hope is that, by reading this book, you will learn how to master SONAR. And, along the way, if you have a little fun while you're at it, that's all the better.

Conventions Used in This Book

As you begin to read, you'll see that most of the information in this book is solid and useful. It contains very little fluff. I won't bore you with unrelated anecdotes or repetitious data. But to help guide you through all this material, I'll use several different conventions that highlight specific types of information that you should keep an eye out for.

TIP

Tips are extra information that you should know related to the current topic being discussed and, in some cases, include personal experiences and/or specific techniques not covered elsewhere.

CAUTION

Cautions highlight actions or commands that can make irreversible changes to your files or potentially cause problems in the future. Read them carefully because they may contain important information that can make the difference between keeping your files, software, and hardware safe, and you from losing a huge amount of work.

NOTE

Of course, sometimes you might like to know, but don't necessarily need to know, certain points about the current topic. Notes provide additional material to help you avoid problems or shed light on a feature or technology, and they also offer related advice.

Tell Us What You Think!

I have tested the information in this book and, to the best of my knowledge, the information is accurate. Of course, with all projects of this size you may find that a small number of mistakes may have crept in. If you find any errors or have suggestions for future editions, please let us know. Visit us at:

www.muskalipman.com/sonar.

1

MIDI and Digital Audio Basics

If you're anything like me, you want to get started right away learning all about SONAR. But if you don't understand the basic concepts and terms associated with computer music, you might have a hard time working your way through this book. So, just to give you a quick overview of the most significant aspects of music technology, this chapter will do the following:

► Define MIDI and explain how it works

► Define digital audio and explain how it works

► Explain the difference between MIDI and digital audio

Of course, this one chapter can't replace an entire book about the subject. If you want to learn more about MIDI and digital audio, plenty of extended resources are available. For example, there is an e-book called the *Desktop Music Handbook* available for free reading on the Web. You can find it at **http://www.cakewalk.com/Tips/Desktop.htm.**

What Is MIDI?

MIDI (which stands for Musical Instrument Digital Interface) is a special kind of computer language that lets electronic musical instruments (such as synthesizer keyboards) "talk" to computers. It works like this: Say you use a synthesizer keyboard as your musical instrument. Every key on the keyboard of your synthesizer has a corresponding electronic switch. When you press a key, its corresponding switch is activated and sends a signal to the computer chip inside your keyboard. The chip then sends the signal to the MIDI interface in your keyboard, which translates the signal into MIDI messages and sends those messages to the MIDI interface in your computer system.

NOTE

A *MIDI interface* is a device that is plugged into your computer allowing it to understand the MIDI language. Basically, you can think of the interface as a translator. When your electronic musical instrument sends out MIDI messages to your computer, the MIDI interface takes those messages and converts them into signals that your computer can understand.

The MIDI messages contain information telling your computer that a key was pressed (called a *Note On* message), which key it was (the name of the note represented by a number), along with how hard you hit the key (called the *MIDI velocity*). For example, if you press middle C on your keyboard, a Note On message is sent to your computer telling it that you pressed a key. Another message containing the number 60 is sent telling the computer that you pressed middle C. And a final message is sent containing a number from 1 to 127 (1 being very soft and 127 being very loud), which tells your computer how hard you hit the key.

Different MIDI messages represent all the performance controls on your keyboard. In addition to each key, MIDI messages represent the modulation wheel, pitch bend wheel, and other features. Your computer can store all the MIDI messages that are sent to it as you play your keyboard. The timing of your performance (how long it takes you to hit one key after another and how long you hold down each key) can be stored as well. Your computer can then send those MIDI messages back to your keyboard with the same timing, so that it seems like you are playing the music, but without touching the keys. The basic concept goes like this: You play a piece of music on your keyboard. Your performance is stored as instructions in your computer. Then those instructions are sent back to your keyboard from the computer, and you hear the piece of music played back exactly the same way you performed it, mistakes and all (see Figure 1.1).

Figure 1.1
This diagram shows how MIDI messages are recorded and played back with a computer.

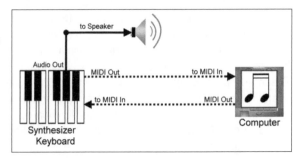

What Is Digital Audio?

Digital audio is the representation of sound as numbers. Recording sound as digital audio is similar to recording sound using a tape recorder, but slightly different. Let's say you have a microphone connected to your computer system. When you make a sound (such as singing a tune, playing a musical instrument, or even simply clapping your hands), the microphone "hears" it and converts the sound into an electronic signal. The microphone then sends the signal to the sound card in your computer, which translates the signal into numbers. These numbers are called *samples.*

NOTE

A *sound card* is a device that is plugged into your computer allowing it to understand the electronic signals of any audio device. Basically, you can think of the sound card as a translator. When an audio device (such as a microphone, electronic music instrument, CD player, or anything else that can output an audio signal) sends out signals to your computer, the sound card takes those signals and converts them into numbers that your computer can understand.

The samples contain information telling your computer how the recorded signal sounded at certain instants in time. The more samples used to represent the signal, the better the quality of the recorded sound. For example, to make a digital audio recording that has the same quality as audio on a CD, the computer needs to receive 44,100 samples for every second of sound that's recorded. The number of samples received per second is called the *sampling rate.*

The size of each individual sample also makes a difference in the quality of the recorded sound. This size is called the *bit depth.* The more bits used to represent a sample, the better the sound quality. For example, to make a digital audio recording with the same quality as audio on a CD, each sample has to be 16 bits in size.

NOTE

Computers use binary numerals to represent numbers. These binary numerals are called *bits*, and each bit can represent one of two numbers: 1 or 0. By combining more than one bit, computers can represent larger numbers. For instance, any number from 0 to 255 can be represented with 8 bits. With 16 bits, the range becomes 0 to 65,535.

Your computer can store all the samples that are sent to it. The timing of each sample is stored as well. Your computer can then send those samples back to the sound card with the same timing so that what you hear sounds exactly the same as what was recorded. The basic concept goes like this: Your sound card records an electronic signal from an audio device (such as a microphone or CD player). The sound card converts the signal into numbers called samples, which are stored in your computer. Then those samples are sent back to the sound card, which converts them back into an electronic signal. The signal is sent to your speakers (or other audio device), and you hear the sound exactly as it was recorded (see Figure 1.2).

Figure 1.2
This diagram shows how audio is converted into numbers so that it can be recorded and played back with a computer.

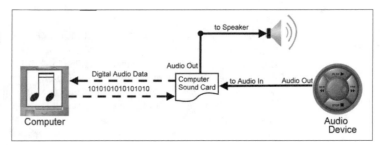

So, What's Really the Difference?

After reading the explanations of MIDI and digital audio, you might still be wondering what the difference is between them. Both processes involve signals being sent to the computer to be recorded and then the computer sending those signals back out to be played, right? Well, the point that you have to keep in mind is that, when you're recording MIDI data, you're not recording actual sound. You are recording only performance instructions. This concept is similar to a musician reading sheet music, with the sheet music representing MIDI data and the musician representing a computer. The musician (or computer) reads the sheet music (or MIDI data) and then stores it in memory. The musician then plays the music back via a musical instrument. Now what if the musician uses a different instrument to play back the music? The musical performance remains the same, but the sound changes. The same thing happens with MIDI data. A synthesizer keyboard can make all kinds of different sounds, but playing the same MIDI data back with the keyboard yields the exact same performance, no matter what.

When you're recording digital audio, you *are* recording actual sound. If you record a musical performance as digital audio, you cannot change the sound of that performance, as described earlier. And because of these differences, MIDI and digital audio have their advantages and disadvantages. Because MIDI is recorded as performance data and not actual sound, you can manipulate it much more easily than you can manipulate digital audio. For example, you can easily fix mistakes in your performance by simply changing the pitch of a note. And MIDI data can be translated into standard musical notation. Digital audio can't. On the other hand, MIDI can't be used to record anything that requires actual audio, such as sound effects or vocals. With digital audio, you can record any kind of sound whatsoever. And you can always be sure that your recording will sound exactly the same every time you play it back. With MIDI, you can't be sure of that because, although the MIDI data remains the same, the playback device or sound can be changed.

I hope that this description clears up some of the confusion you may have about MIDI and digital audio. You need to be familiar with a number of other related terms, but I will cover them in different areas of the book as I go along. For now, as long as you understand the difference between MIDI and digital audio, I can begin talking about the real reason you bought this book—how to use SONAR.

2

Getting Started with SONAR

Now that you have a basic understanding of the technology involved in making music with computers, I think you'll find working with SONAR more enjoyable. Ready to get started? This chapter will do the following:

▶ Tell you how to obtain the latest product update

▶ Explain the importance of registering your software

▶ Give you a quick tour of SONAR's major features

▶ Explain the differences between SONAR and Pro Audio

▶ Show you how to make a number of adjustments to your computer system to improve its performance

▶ Let you know where to look for help, if problems arise

What Version of SONAR Do You Have?

Since Cakewalk has decided to give a new name to its flagship product and start it off with a new version number (although the program is based on its predecessor, Pro Audio 9), you are more than likely working with SONAR 1.0. Of course, you still might not be using the latest version. Cakewalk is constantly fixing and improving the software. Any problems that you may experience might easily be remedied with an update. To find out exactly what version you're using, start SONAR, and click on Help > About Cakewalk. A dialog box similar to Figure 2.1 then appears, displaying your exact version number. You should then check to see whether a more recent update is available.

CHAPTER 2

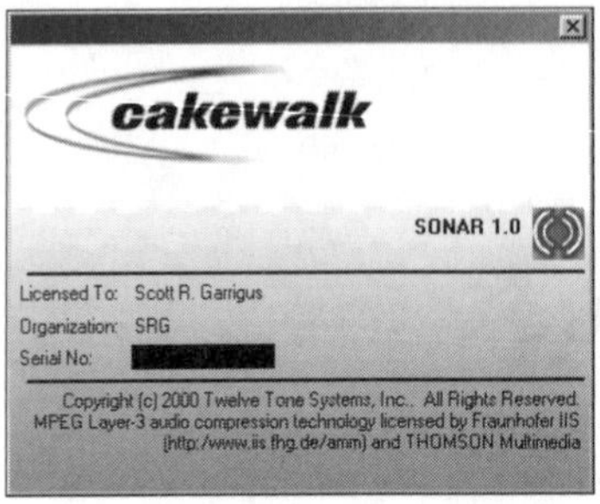

Figure 2.1
The About Cakewalk
dialog box shows the
program's current
version number.

Get the Latest Product Update

Although automatically receiving new product updates would be nice,
most companies (except maybe Microsoft) can't afford to send out CDs to
all their users every time they create updates. That's one of the reasons
the Internet has become such a wonderful tool. Sometimes the answer to
your problem is just a download away. Cakewalk provides a support area
on its Web site where you can get the latest updates for all of the
Cakewalk products. Just follow these steps to get the updates:

1. Log on to the Internet, start your Web browser, and type the following
    address: **http://www.cakewalk.com/download/**. This takes you to
    Cakewalk's Downloads page, as shown in Figure 2.2.

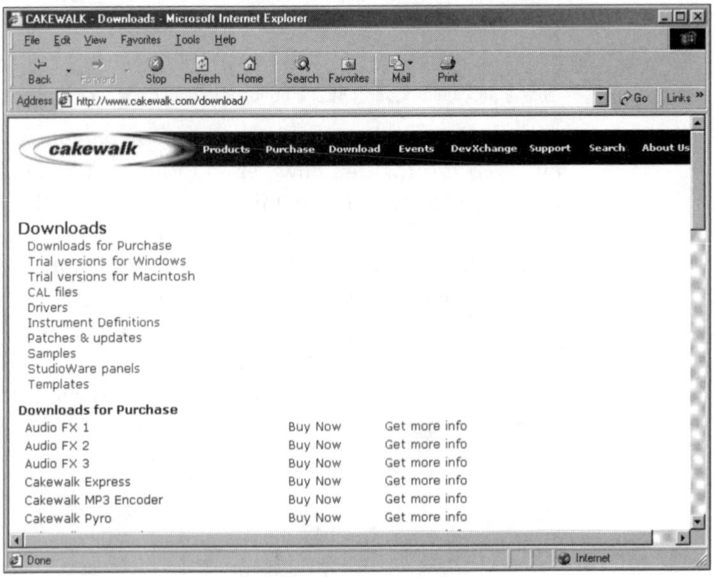

Figure 2.2
You can download
updates from the
Cakewalk Patches and
Updates support page.

2. In the section labeled Downloads, click on Patches & updates.

3. In the Patches & updates section, click on the line that says "Get the latest patch or update for your Cakewalk product." You then see a directory of folders. Double-click the SONAR folder to open it.

    If more than one update is available, simply compare your current version with the updates listed and select the appropriate one. For instance, if you have SONAR 1.01, you'll want the update that upgrades version 1.01 to the current version.

4. Create a temporary folder on your Windows desktop and download the update file to that folder.

5. Run the file, and your software is upgraded. That's all there is to upgrading.

NOTE

Think you've found a bug? Just because a software product is released to the public doesn't mean it's perfect. Improvements are always being made. That's why updates become available. If you have a problem with SONAR on a regular basis and you can reproduce that problem by performing the same steps each time, you may have found a bug in the software. Before you go spreading any rumors, first tell a friend about it and see whether he or she can reproduce the problem on his or her computer system. If so, then you should drop an e-mail to Cakewalk at **support@cakewalk.com** and let the people there know about the problem. The staff may already be aware of the bug and be working on a fix for it. But then again, they may not, and although your diligence won't make you famous, you'll feel good knowing that you may have saved your fellow SONAR users from a lot of frustration. Really, you will.

CHAPTER 2

Register Your Software

Do you think registering your software is important? If not, think again. First and foremost, if you don't register your software, Cakewalk won't provide you with technical support. You'll be sorry if you run into a problem that causes you to lose some of your precious work, and the only thing between you and your sanity is the people at Cakewalk. If you're a techno-wizard, and this situation doesn't worry you, that's great. But there's something else you may not have thought about. What if your hard drive crashes, and you need to reinstall all your software applications, including SONAR? And at the same time, what if you can't find the jewel case that your SONAR CD came in? Yes, the jewel case, not the CD. Why is it significant? Because the jewel case has a little sticker with a very important number printed on it—your CD-KEY. Without that number, you can't install SONAR. So, now who you gonna call? Yeah, that's right. By the way, your product serial number is important, too.

Remember to send in that registration card! And just to be safe, you might want to check with Cakewalk to make sure your information is on file. You just do the following:

1. Find your CD jewel case and look on the back to make sure your CD-KEY is printed there.

2. Find your product serial number, either by looking on the detachable part of your registration card or by starting SONAR and selecting Help > About Cakewalk.

3. Call Cakewalk at 888-CAKEWALK or 617-441-7870 (USA) and make sure that you're registered. Also check to see that your correct address and phone number are in the system.

Now you can rest easy in knowing that help is just a phone call or e-mail away.

> **TIP**
>
> To prevent yourself from losing your CD-KEY or serial number, you might want to write them on your SONAR CD. Be sure to use an indelible pen and write the numbers on the top (the side with the printed material) of the CD. Don't write on the shiny side. You also might want to write down the numbers in a second location, just in case. I like to keep track of all the serial numbers for my software applications in a simple text file. I have a list containing the names, CD-KEYs (if available), and serial numbers of all the important software installed on my computer system. I also include the current version number and company contact information for each product. Then, if I ever run into a problem, I just refer to the list. By the way, you might also want to print the text file each time you update it. If your hard drive crashes, the text file won't do you any good since you won't be able to access it.

Take a Quick Tour of SONAR

Because SONAR is such a powerful application, you can use it for a variety of different tasks. They include composing music, developing computer game music and sounds, producing compact discs, creating audio for the World Wide Web, and even scoring films and videos. SONAR provides a number of features to support all these endeavors and more. As a matter of fact, you can use SONAR as the central piece of "equipment" in your studio because it allows you to control all your music gear from your computer via on-screen control panels. However you decide to use SONAR, you'll find plenty of flexibility and power in the tools provided.

Projects

In SONAR, all your music data for a single body of work is organized as a *project*. A project can be anything from a Top 40 song or a 30-second radio spot to a full-length symphonic score, such as a movie soundtrack. Along with the music data, all of SONAR's settings for a single work are stored in the project as well. A project is saved on disk as a single file with a .WRK or .BUN file name extension. The difference between the two file types is that a work (WRK) file stores only MIDI data and project settings, whereas a bundle (BUN) file also includes any audio data within a project. (For more information, see Chapter 4.)

Tracks, Clips, and Events

The music data within a project is organized into units called *tracks*, *clips*, and *events*. Events, which are the smallest units, consist of single pieces of data, such as one note played on a MIDI keyboard. Clips are groups of events. They can be anything from a simple MIDI melody to an entire vocal performance recorded as audio. And tracks are used to store clips. For example, a pop song project might contain seven tracks of music data—six for the instruments and one for the vocal performance. Each track can contain any number of clips that might represent one long performance or different parts of a performance. And SONAR gives you unlimited tracks. The only limitation is the speed of your CPU and the amount of memory (RAM) you have in your computer. I'll talk more about tracks, clips, and events in Chapter 7.

Track View

To work with the data in a project, you have to use the tools called *views* in SONAR. Views are like windows that let you see and manipulate the data in a project in a variety of ways. The most important is the Track view, shown in Figure 2.3.

Figure 2.3
The Track view is the main window used to work with a project in SONAR.

CHAPTER 2

In this window, you can see all the tracks that are available in a project. You also can view and edit all the basic track settings, as well as all the clips contained in each track. I'll talk about the Track view extensively in a number of different chapters in the book.

NOTE

If you have used Cakewalk software in the past, particularly if you upgraded to SONAR from Pro Audio, Guitar Studio, or Home Studio, then you'll notice that the Audio view is no longer available. Actually, the Audio view features are still provided in SONAR, but now the Track view doubles as the Audio view.

Staff View

In the Staff view, you can work with the MIDI data in your project as standard music notation. By selecting one or more MIDI tracks in the Track view and opening the Staff view, you can see your music just as if it were notes on a printed page, as in Figure 2.4

Figure 2.4
In the Staff view, you can see and edit your MIDI data as standard music notation.

Using the Staff view, you also can edit your music as notation by adding, changing, or deleting notes. Special notation functions such as dynamics markings, percussion parts, and guitar chord symbols are included, too. You can notate anything from a single one-staff melody to an entire 24-part musical score. I'll talk about using the Staff view in Chapter 13.

Piano Roll View

Although the Staff view is great for traditional music editing, it doesn't allow you to access expressive MIDI data, such as note velocity or pitch bend controller messages. For that data, you can use the Piano Roll view. This view displays notes as they might appear on a player-piano roll, as shown in Figure 2.5.

Figure 2.5
The Piano Roll view gives you access to both note and MIDI controller messages.

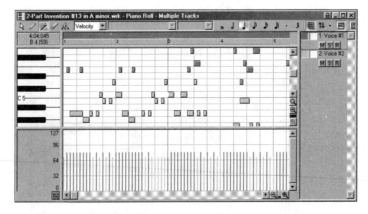

You can change note pitch and duration by simply dragging on the rectangular representations. But more importantly, you can view and edit MIDI controller messages graphically with the mouse instead of having to deal with raw numbers. For more details about the Piano Roll view, see Chapter 7.

Event List View

If you really want precise control over the data in your project, the Event List view is the tool for the job. The Event List view shows each individual event in a track (or the entire project) as special keywords and numbers in a list, as shown in Figure 2.6.

Trk	HMSF	MBT	Ch	Kind	Data		
4	00:00:01:16	3:02:424	12	Wheel	0		
4	00:00:01:16	3:02:427	12	Wheel	-1536		
4	00:00:01:16	3:02:430	12	Wheel	0		
4	00:00:01:16	3:02:432	12	Wheel	-896		
4	00:00:01:16	3:02:440	12	Wheel	0		
4	00:00:01:16	3:02:457	12	Note	E 6	62	288
4	00:00:01:16	3:02:467	12	Wheel	896		
4	00:00:01:16	3:02:472	12	Wheel	0		
4	00:00:01:20	4:01:228	12	Note	D 6	64	263
4	00:00:01:24	4:01:475	12	Note	E 6	71	279
4	00:00:01:28	4:02:236	12	Note	D 6	56	265
4	00:00:02:02	4:02:472	12	Note	B 5	65	282
4	00:00:02:06	5:01:230	12	Note	D 6	65	252
4	00:00:02:10	5:01:475	12	Note	A 5	74	259
4	00:00:02:14	5:02:231	12	Note	D 6	74	246
4	00:00:02:17	5:02:468	12	Note	G 5	76	270
4	00:00:02:21	6:01:242	12	Note	F#5	71	252
4	00:00:02:25	6:02:002	12	Note	E 5	66	249
4	00:00:02:29	6:02:220	12	Note	D 5	69	241
4	00:00:03:03	6:02:473	12	Note	G 5	74	305
4	00:00:03:10	7:01:456	12	Note	G 5	82	278
4	00:00:03:15	7:02:230	12	Note	F#5	85	218

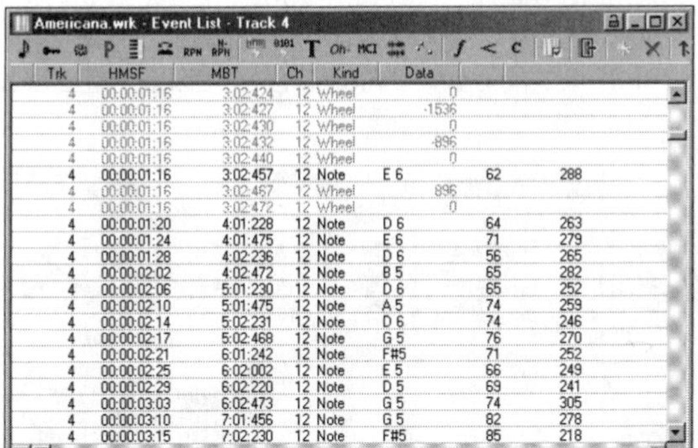

Figure 2.6
For really precise editing tasks, the Event List view gives you access to the individual events in a project.

Using this view is similar to looking at the raw MIDI data that is recorded from your MIDI keyboard or controller. You can edit the characteristics of single notes and MIDI controller messages by typing in data. You'll probably use the Piano Roll view more often, but it's nice to know the Event List view is available if you need it. I'll talk more about the Event List view in Chapter 7.

Loop Construction View

One of the new features in SONAR, the Loop Construction view, gives you an easy way to create your own sample loops. These loops, which are digital audio clips designed to be played over and over again, can be used to construct entire songs. While you're working with the Loop Construction view, you see the sound wave of your loop, as in Figure 2.7.

Figure 2.7
The Loop Construction view is a special editing tool for creating sample loops.

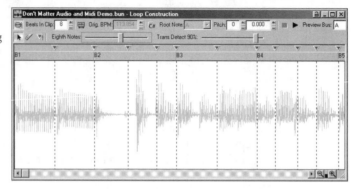

Not only does the Loop Construction view allow you to create your own sample loops, but you can even use ACID-compatible loops, like the loops found in Sonic Foundry's ACID software. In Chapter 9, I'll get into more detail about the Loop Construction view.

Console View

When you're ready to mix all your MIDI and audio tracks down to a single stereo file, you can use the Console view. This tool is made to look and function like a real recording studio mixing console, as you can see in Figure 2.8.

Figure 2.8
The Console view looks and functions similar to a real recording studio mixing console.

You can use the Console view to adjust the panning and volume for each track in a project. As a matter of fact, you can use the Console view in place of the Track view for adjusting track settings and recording new tracks. And just like on a real mixing console, you can monitor volume levels via on-screen meters and mute and solo individual or groups of tracks. I'll talk more about the Console view in Chapter 6, Chapter 11, and Chapter 12.

StudioWare and CAL

Two of the most advanced features provided by SONAR are StudioWare and CAL (Cakewalk Application Language). Even though these features seem complicated, they're actually quite easy to use. Sure, if you really want to dive in and master these features, they can get complex, but for the most part, they are accessible to even the most timid user. What's more, when you start using StudioWare and CAL, you won't want to stop. Separately, StudioWare allows you to design on-screen panels to manipulate MIDI data and control your MIDI gear, and CAL allows you to create macros or small programs so that you can automate the different tasks you perform within SONAR. You can use StudioWare and CAL together to build your own editing tools within SONAR. You can even create programs that will make music automatically for you. These two features alone have quite a bit of power, so I'll talk a lot more about them in Chapter 14, Chapter 15, Chapter 16, and Chapter 17.

Examine the Differences between SONAR and Pro Audio

Since SONAR is based on the same programming code as Pro Audio, you'll notice that many of SONAR's features are the same as in Pro Audio, but there are many new features as well. Among the key features that make up SONAR are new WavePipe software synthesizers—called DX instruments or DXi—DirectX 8 audio effects automation, a new Loop Construction view for creating and manipulating audio loops, and a redesigned Track view for more efficient recording and editing sessions.

SONAR's new WavePipe 2.0 technology not only gives you better audio recording and playback performance, but it also allows you to use software synthesizers similar to the ones you find in Steinberg's Cubase VST application. The SONAR soft synths use the latest Microsoft DirectX technology, giving you responsive playback when using WDM drivers and output through DirectX audio effects. And because SONAR supports DirectX 8, you can now automate individual effects parameters.

CHAPTER 2

As I mentioned earlier, the new Loop Construction view lets you create and edit your own sample loops. You can then stretch, pitch-shift, and adjust the tempo of the loops just like in Sonic Foundry's ACID software. And if you already have a collection of ACID loops, SONAR will let you load up and work with those as well.

The Track view has been changed significantly. Not only does it provide the functions of the old Track view, but it doubles as an audio editor by providing the functions of the old Audio view, too. In addition, the Track view gives you access to many of the same controls for each track in your project that you would find in the Console view, including signal level meters. Suffice it to say, you'll be spending a lot of time with the Track view.

If you don't understand some of the things I've been talking about here, don't worry. I'll be going over all of the features found in SONAR in detail throughout the remaining chapters.

Set Up Your System for Better Performance

Cakewalk specifies a system with a 4400 MHz processor and 64 MB of random access memory (RAM) as the basic requirements to run SONAR.

Of course, you also need a Windows-compatible MIDI interface and/or sound card. If your computer system lives up to (or surpasses) these specifications, simply installing SONAR is more than likely all you'll need to do to get up and running with the software. If you really want to get the best performance from SONAR, however, you can make a number of adjustments to your computer system that will allow you to squeeze as much power out of it as possible. Depending on your computer's specifications, these changes may even allow you to play back a few more simultaneous digital audio tracks or apply more real-time effects. (See Chapter 11 for more information.)

Microprocessor

You can't do much to tweak your computer's central processing unit (CPU), aside from maybe upgrading it to a newer chip or buying a whole new computer system. Suffice it to say, the newer and faster your CPU, the better your computer system and SONAR will perform. From oldest to newest, the order of available chips goes something like this:

Pentium, Pentium with MMX, Pentium Pro, Pentium II, Pentium III, and Pentium 4 (being the latest at the time of this writing).

Of course, although having the best chip available is nice, that doesn't mean you need it. You can also get away with using different brands such as AMD or Cyrix, but they tend to be less powerful. For instance, the AMD K6 is similar to a Pentium with MMX at the same clock speed. Also, a Cyrix chip is usually less powerful than a standard Pentium running at a speed of about two-thirds of the Cyrix. Recently, however, AMD has come out with new chips that compare in performance with the Pentium. These include the Athlon and Duron. You still need to be careful here, though, because some sound cards are not compatible with AMD processors. Be sure to check for compatibility issues before you purchase a new computer system or sound card. Basically, you can apply more real-time effects at once with a more powerful CPU. SONAR will run more smoothly as well.

> **TIP**
>
> If you're really adventurous, you can try overclocking your CPU, but I wouldn't recommend it. (Overclocking means making the CPU run faster than its rated speed.) If you're not careful, you could end up destroying your computer system. But with the right tweaks, it is sometimes possible to make your computer run faster. You might even be inclined to building your own PC. If you're interested, check out this article posted at Prorec.com: **http://www.prorec.com/prorec/articles.nsf/articles/ E674C87E2991AA3F862568E9006D7D10.**

If you would like to test just how much of your CPU power is used when you perform different tasks with your computer, Windows provides a nifty utility called the System Monitor. Just follow these steps to use it:

1. Click the Start button and choose Programs > Accessories > System Tools > System Monitor to see if the System Monitor is installed. If the System Monitor isn't installed, open the Windows Control Panel, double-click on Add/Remove Programs, and select the Windows Setup tab in the Add/Remove Programs Properties dialog box. Then select Accessories from the list, click on the Details button, select System Monitor from the resulting list, and click on the OK buttons to close the dialog boxes. Windows then installs the System Monitor.

CHAPTER 2

2. Open the System Monitor by clicking the Start button and then selecting Programs > Accessories > System Tools > System Monitor. The program should look similar to Figure 2.9.

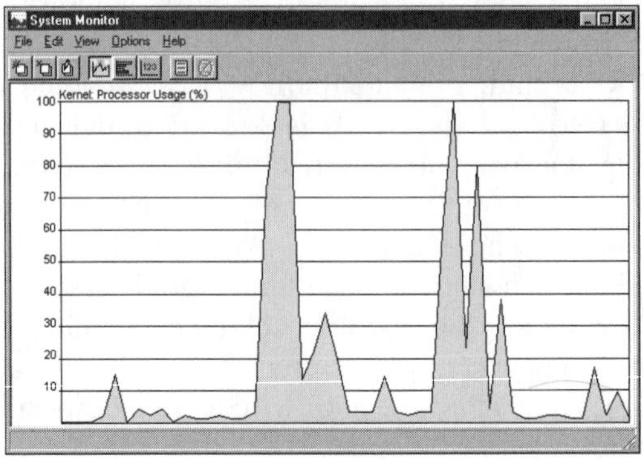

Figure 2.9
The Windows System Monitor accessory monitors your CPU usage.

3. Select Edit > Add Item. In the resulting dialog box, click on Kernel in the Category list. Then click on Processor Usage in the Item list, and click the OK button.

4. Depending on the current settings, you may see a line chart, bar chart, or numerical chart. You can select the different displays via the View menu.

Now, as you use your computer, the System Monitor will continuously show the changes in your CPU power usage.

System Memory (RAM)

You probably already know this point, but the more memory you have installed in your computer, the better. This is especially true for large applications such as SONAR. Even though Cakewalk lists 64 MB in the system requirements, you would be better off with 128 MB of RAM. Not only does increased memory allow your system to run more smoothly, it makes the system run faster, too. With more RAM available, Windows is less likely to have to access virtual memory.

Virtual Memory

To fool your computer into thinking it has more RAM than it really does, Windows uses part of your hard disk space as *virtual memory*. Every time you start your system, Windows creates a "swap file" on your hard drive. This "swap file" grows and shrinks as you perform different tasks with your computer. Whenever you try to use more RAM than is installed in your system, Windows stores the excess data in the "swap file." For example, if you have 32 MB of RAM in your system, and you run four different programs at once that each take up 16 MB of RAM, technically, two of those applications shouldn't be able to run. However, Windows simply uses virtual memory to handle that extra 32 MB load. Because virtual memory uses your hard disk for storage, and your hard disk provides much slower access than your system's RAM, all that "swap file" processing makes your computer run more slowly. That's why your system runs faster with more RAM installed.

Hard Disk Drive

The speed of your hard drive is one of the single most important factors in determining how many audio tracks you'll be able to use during playback with SONAR. Hard drives can be connected to a computer using different types of interfaces: SCSI, IDE, and E-IDE. In terms of performance, SCSI is better than IDE, but a good E-IDE drive can be almost as good as SCSI. A few specifications to look out for are average seek time (which should be as low as possible, preferably 9 milliseconds or less), rotation speed (which should be as high as possible, the average being 5,400 rpm), and sustained data transfer rate (which should also be as high as possible, with at least 5 MB per second being a good start). One other factor to avoid is hard disk controller cards that connect via an ISA expansion slot inside your computer. A PCI-based connection is much better. By the way, using the System Monitor, you can test your hard drive performance the same way you can test CPU usage (explained earlier).

Aside from your upgrading to a new hard drive, one Windows tweak might get you a little more speed from your current drive. It's a setting for DMA access for your hard drive controller. This setting gives your hard drive direct access to your computer's memory. This way, the data doesn't have to be processed by the CPU first and thus provides a bit more speed. If your hard drive supports DMA, you can activate it like this:

1. Open the Windows Control Panel, double-click on System, and click on the Device Manager tab in the System Properties dialog box.
2. Under Disk Drives in the list of devices, select your hard disk drive. It might read something like "Generic IDE Disk."
3. Click on the Properties button, and then click on the Settings tab in the hard disk drive's Properties dialog box. The dialog box should look similar to Figure 2.10.

CHAPTER 2

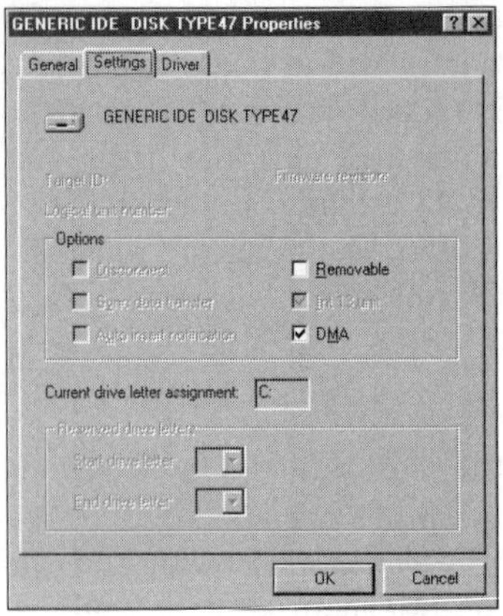

Figure 2.10
This generic hard disk drive Properties dialog box shows the hard drive settings.

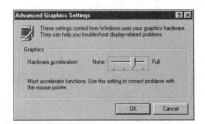

4.   Select DMA in the Options section and then click on the OK buttons to close the dialog boxes.

After Windows restarts, your hard drive will access the computer's memory directly, which may or may not provide a noticeable speed increase.

Video Card

Believe it or not, your video card can have an effect on your computer system's performance. First, hardware video acceleration can cause problems with audio playback. If you have a PCI-based video card, and your audio is sometimes plagued with clicks, pops, or other anomalies, these sounds could mean that your hardware video acceleration is set too high. Try dragging a program window around on the screen while your computer is playing digital audio tracks. Does this action affect the audio? If so, you can try reducing or disabling hardware video acceleration to remedy the problem. To do so, just follow these steps:

1.   Open the Windows Control Panel and double-click on System.

2.   In the System Properties dialog box, click on the Performance tab. Then click on the Graphics button under Advanced Settings.

3.   In the Advanced Graphics Settings dialog box, drag the Hardware Acceleration slider to the left, to either reduce or disable hardware video acceleration. The dialog box should look similar to Figure 2.11.

Figure 2.11
The amount of hardware video acceleration is set via the Advanced Graphics Settings dialog box.

4. You may or may not have to disable hardware video acceleration altogether. You'll have to experiment to see what works best for your system. After you set the slider, click the OK buttons to close the dialog boxes.

After Windows restarts, your new settings will take effect. If you have a newer computer system with an AGP-based graphics card, you shouldn't have to worry about hardware video acceleration problems. AGP-based cards can access the system memory directly without having to deal with the PCI bus; thus, they don't usually exhibit the problems I mentioned earlier.

Other video-related settings that can affect the performance of your system include screen savers, video resolution, and video color depth. Basically, when you're doing any processor-intensive work with your computer, you should disable your screen saver. Even when the screen saver isn't showing anything on the screen, it sits in the background monitoring your system for activity and thus takes up processor time. Plus, some screen savers have no regard for what your computer is currently doing, and they become active right in the middle of a recording session, ruining that great vocal track. To turn off your screen saver, do the following:

1. Right-click anywhere on the Windows desktop and select Properties from the pop-up menu.

2. Select the Screen Saver tab in the Display Properties dialog box.

3. Select None from the drop-down list in the Screen Saver settings section (see Figure 2.12) and then click the OK button.

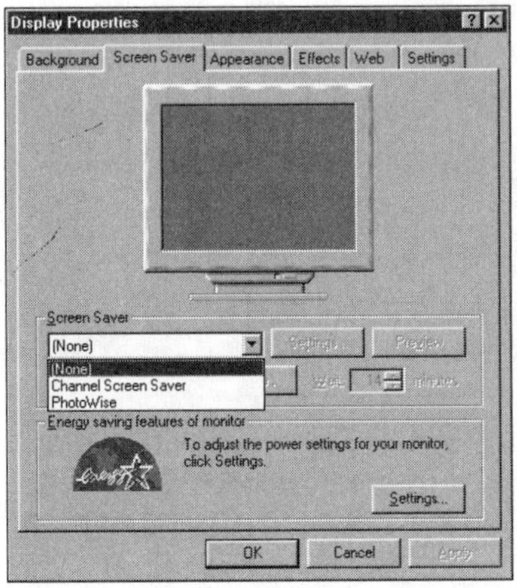

Figure 2.12
In the Display Properties dialog box, you can set many different Windows parameters, including the screen saver.

CHAPTER 2

Video resolution and video color depth affect how precise your computer monitor displays graphics. A higher color depth means more colors will be displayed, and a higher resolution means the sharper the image will be. But the higher the resolution and the higher the color depth, the harder your computer has to work. High settings can slow down your computer quite a bit, especially if you have an older CPU and an older video card. Your best bet is to use a resolution of 800×600 and a depth of 256 colors. You really don't need anything more than that, although using a higher resolution allows you to fit more MIDI/audio tracks on the screen at once. A higher resolution is also nicer when you're working with music notation. You can experiment with higher settings to see how they affect your system. Reducing the color depth is more important than reducing the resolution, though. To change the color depth and resolution, do the following:

1. Right-click anywhere on the Windows desktop and select Properties from the pop-up menu.

2. Select the Settings tab in the Display Properties dialog box.

3. From the drop-down list in the Colors section (see Figure 2.13), select 256 Colors. Then drag the slider in the Screen Area section to the left until it reads 800 by 600 pixels. After you've set the slider, click the OK button.

Figure 2.13
In the Display Properties dialog box, you can set many different Windows parameters, including the video resolution and color depth.

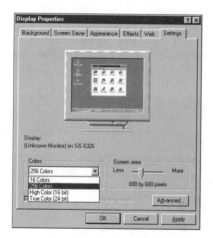

Windows may or may not restart automatically (depending on the version you're using), but when you're done, your monitor will show the new resolution and color depth settings. Getting used to the new settings might take awhile if you've been using higher settings all along, but don't worry, you'll live. And I think you'll like how much snappier Windows reacts.

TIP

For additional tips on dealing with video cards, check out this Web page: **http://www.cakewalk.com/Support/VideocardTips.html.**

Network Card

If you have your computer hooked up to a network, you should either use a different computer system for audio recording or temporarily disable your network card when you're using SONAR. Network activity is notorious for stealing CPU cycles at critical times, and this can slow down your system quite a bit. The easiest way to remove your computer from the network is simply to unplug your network cable. However, you can get even better performance if you disable your network card like this:

1. Open the Windows Control Panel, double-click on System, and click on the Device Manager tab in the System Properties dialog box.

2. Under Network Adapters in the list of devices, select your network card. The name will probably reflect the name of the product. An example might be "EZ-Link USB Adapter."

3. Click on the Properties button to open your network card's Properties dialog box. The dialog box should look similar to Figure 2.14.

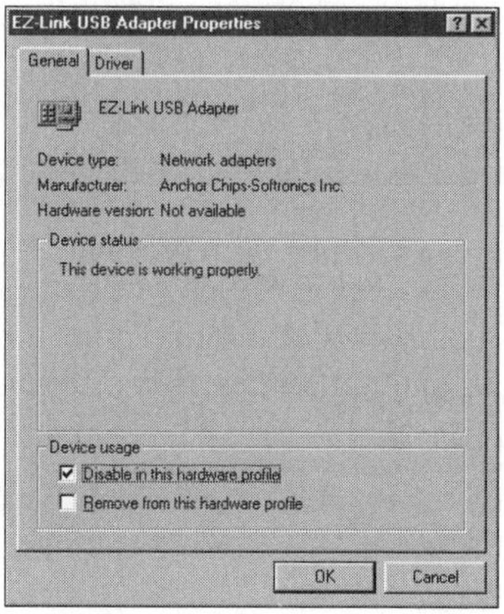

Figure 2.14
This sample network card Properties dialog box shows the status of the device.

CHAPTER 2

4.   Select Disable in this hardware profile in the Device usage section and then click on the OK button to close the dialog box.

Windows disables your network card without your having to restart. Then you can simply close the System Properties dialog box, and you're done.

Sound Card

As far as sound cards are concerned, there are a couple of things that you should know. PCI-based sound cards perform much better than older ISA-based sound cards. The newer PCI-based cards usually include more advanced audio circuitry, which is designed to take more of the audio processing workload off your computer's CPU. It's also nice to have a card that supports the DirectSound features of Microsoft's DirectX technology. This type of card provides greater application compatibility and sometimes better performance, too.

In addition, SONAR supports a new Microsoft technology called WDM (Windows Driver Model). If you have a sound card that has WDM drivers, SONAR will give you much better performance in terms of audio latency. Basically, latency is a form of audio delay that occurs when a software program like SONAR can't "communicate" with your sound card fast enough while processing audio data, which results in an audible delay. This only occurs with features that use real-time processing, though. In SONAR, these include input monitor and real-time DXi performance. I'll talk more about latency in Chapter 3, input monitoring in Chapter 6, and DXis in Chapter 10. In the meantime, when looking for a sound card, be sure to ask the manufacturer if the card comes with WDM drivers. If not, that's okay, but you won't get the proper performance from the input monitoring or real-time DXi performance features in SONAR.

TIP

For a list of sound card manufacturers who currently support (or plan to support in the future) WDM technology, check out this Web page: **http://www.cakewalk.com/Products/SR/WDM.html.**

TIP

For really in-depth technical information about WDM, check out this Web page: **http://www.microsoft.com/HWDEV/desinit/wdm.htm.**

NOTE

One of the most common questions I get from readers is, "What sound card should I buy?" There are so many different sound cards on the market, providing so many different features, that I can't simply recommend one or the other. I can, however, tell you what features to look for so that you can make an educated choice.

I've already mentioned that you should look for a PCI-based, DirectX-compatible sound card. You should also be aware of the types of connections that sound cards supply. The typical sound card provides a number of different audio inputs and outputs including line level, microphone level, and speaker. Line level inputs and outputs are used to transfer sound from cassette decks, radios, electronic keyboards, or any other standard audio device. Microphones generate a very small audio level by themselves, so they need a special input of their own, which is connected to an internal preamplifier on the sound card. Speakers also need their own special connector with a built-in amplifier in order to produce a decent amount of volume. Some high-end sound cards also offer digital inputs and outputs. These special connectors let you attach the sound card directly to compatible devices such as some CD players and DAT (digital audio tape) decks. Using these connections gives you the best possible sound, because audio signals stay in the digital domain and don't need to be converted into analog signals. You should also be aware that connectors come in a variety of forms. Low-cost cards usually provide the same 1/8-inch jacks used for headphones on boom boxes. For better quality, there are 1/4-inch, RCA, or XLR jacks. Connections can also be balanced or unbalanced. Balanced connections provide shielding to protect the audio signal against RFI (radio frequency interference). Unbalanced connections don't provide any type of protection.

If you want to be able to record more than one audio track at once, you'll need a card with multiple audio connections. Most average sound cards internally mix all of their audio sources down to one stereo signal, but other, higher-end (more expensive) cards let you record each device separately on its own discreet stereo channel. This capability is much more desirable in a music recording studio, but not everyone needs it. You'll also want to look for a card with full-duplex capabilities. This means the card can record and play back audio simultaneously. This is opposed to a half-duplex card, which can perform only one function at a time.

A good quality audio signal is something that everybody desires. During recording, the sampling rate (which I talked about in Chapter 1) plays a big part in the quality of the audio signal. Suffice it to say, the higher the sampling rate that a sound card can handle, the better the sound quality. The sampling rate of a CD is 44.1 kHz (44,100 samples per second) and all sound cards on the market support this. Professional cards can hit 48 kHz or higher. Bit resolution (which I also talked about in Chapter 1) is a factor in determining digital sound quality as well. The more bits you have to represent your signal, the better it will sound. The CD standard is 16 bits, which is supported by all sound cards. Some cards (again, mostly high-end) go up to 20, 22, or even 24 bits.

(continued on next page)

CHAPTER 2

NOTE (Continued)

Two other measurements you need to look out for are signal-to-noise ratio and frequency response. As with the other measurements mentioned here, the higher the better. Since all electronic devices produce some amount of noise, the signal-to-noise ratio of a sound card tells you how much higher the signal strength is compared to the amount of internal noise made by the sound card. The bigger the number, the quieter the card. A good signal-to-noise measurement is about 90 dB or higher. Frequency response is actually a range of numbers, which is based on the capabilities of human hearing. The frequency response of human hearing is approximately 20 Hz to 20 kHz. A good sound card will encompass at least that range, maybe even more.

If you want to purchase a sound card with a built-in MIDI synthesizer, there are a number of additional features you should know about. Early sound cards supported synthesizers based on FM (frequency modulation) synthesis. Unfortunately, this method wasn't much of a step up from the basic beeps and boops of a PC speaker. Even though FM works well with organ and bell-type sounds, it fails miserably when trying to portray any other type of instrument. Fortunately, today's sound cards use a technology called *wavetable synthesis*. This process can provide some very realistic sounds. The reason for this realism lies in the fact that a wavetable synthesizer plays back pre-recorded real-life instruments and sounds. When the synthesizer receives a MIDI "noteon" message, instead of creating a sound electronically from scratch (as with FM), it plays back a small digital recording, which can be anything from the sound of a piano to the effect of ducks quacking. The only drawback to wavetable synthesis is that the samples need to be kept small since they are stored in RAM (random access memory) or ROM (read-only memory). Suffice it to say, the bigger the wavetable RAM or ROM your card comes with, the better. A good number to look for is about 2 MB.

You'll also want to take into account the degree of playback control over the wavetable samples that a card provides. All sound cards today support General MIDI (GM), which is a set of guidelines specifying 128 pre-set sounds that all GM-compatible synths must have and the memory location (or MIDI program number) of those sounds. This ensures that if a sound card is told to play program number 37, it will always call up a slap electric bass sound rather than a soprano saxophone. Unlike professional synthesizers, however, GM doesn't support any kind of sound parameter programming. That's where the GS and XG formats come in. The Roland GS format expands on the GM standard by offering additional sounds along with sound-programming control over a few synthesis parameters. Yamaha's XG format goes even further by requiring three separate effects processors, more than a dozen programmable synthesis parameters (such as the brightness of a sound), and more than 100 sets of 128 sounds each. So be sure to get a card that supports GS, XG, or both.

By following these guidelines, and taking some time to research your purchase, you should be able to find the right sound card to fit your needs. Good luck!

Set Up Your Cakewalk Hardware Profile

Of course, making many of the previously mentioned changes to your computer system every time you want to use SONAR and then changing them back for normal system use can be a major hassle. Luckily, Windows includes a handy feature called Hardware Profiles. You can think of Hardware Profiles as Windows presets, similar to synthesizer or audio effects gear presets. Using the Hardware Profiles feature, you can store a number of Windows configuration settings under a unique name and then recall those settings when you start your computer system. So, for instance, you can have a profile to set up your hardware for normal system use, another profile for computer gaming, yet another profile for audio recording, and so on. Creating Hardware Profiles is very simple, too; you just do the following:

1. Open the Windows Control Panel, double-click on System, and click on the Hardware Profiles tab in the System Properties dialog box. The dialog box should look similar to Figure 2.15.

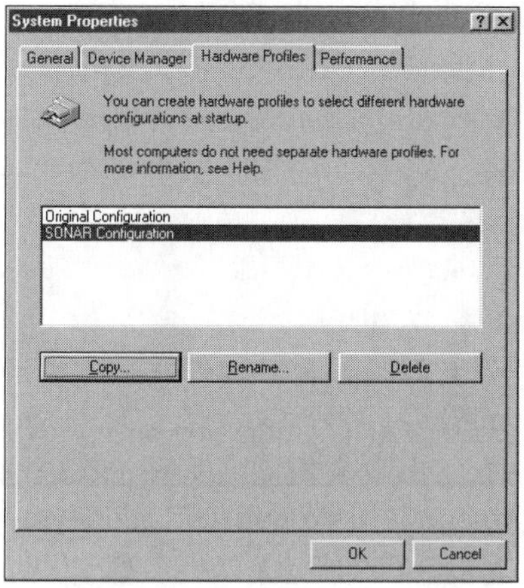

Figure 2.15
The Hardware Profiles tab of the System Properties dialog box shows the different hardware configurations.

2. More than likely a default profile called "Original Configuration" will be listed. This configuration holds your current system settings. Click on it to select it.

3. Click on the Copy button to make a copy of the Original Configuration profile.

4. In the Copy Profile dialog box, type a new name for the new profile— something like SONAR Configuration. Then click on the OK buttons to close both dialog boxes.

5. Restart your computer. At startup, your system will ask you to choose a hardware profile. Select SONAR Configuration.

6. Go through the list of tweaks that I described earlier, such as the hard drive DMA setting, video acceleration setting, and so on.

Now, the next time you start Windows, you can choose a system configuration to fit your needs for that computing session. The only setting from the list of tweaks that isn't saved in a Hardware Profile is the screen saver setting. You have to change it manually each time. Yeah, I know it's a bummer. Personally, I always leave the screen saver disabled. If I know I'm going to be away from the computer for more than fifteen minutes, I just turn off the monitor.

TIP

With all this talk about computer system specifications, I thought you might be interested to know about the computer system I use to run SONAR. I picked all of the components myself and had Aberdeen, Inc. (**www.aberdeeninc.com**) build the base system for me. The system components are as follows:

▶ ABIT BE6-II Pentium III ATX motherboard

▶ Intel Pentium III processor 700 MHz w/256 K L2

▶ Pentium III heatsink with cooling fan

▶ 256 MEG SDRAM 168-pin DIMM PC100 memory

▶ Promise Ultra66 PCI IDE Controller

▶ Teac 3.5 1.44 MB floppy drive

▶ WD Expert WD205BA hard drive 20.5 GB 9ms 7200rpm Ultra/66

▶ Addtronics Super Tower ATX 8x5.25/3x3.5 300W ATX

I added the following components myself:

▶ Creative Encore 6X PC-DVD drive

▶ Ricoh MP7060A CD-RW drive

▶ Diamond Stealth III S540 video card

▶ Sound Blaster Live! sound card

In addition, I usually use a high-end audio interface for recording, but because I review many different products for *Electronic Musician* magazine, this component changes from time to time.

Find Help When You Need It

Cakewalk provides a number of ways for you to find help when you're having a problem with SONAR. The two most obvious places to look are the user's guide and the SONAR Help file. Actually, these two sources contain basically the same information, but with the Help file, you can perform a search to find something really specific. At the first signs of trouble, you should go through the included troubleshooting information. If you can't find an answer to your problem there, then you can pay a visit to the Cakewalk Web site.

The support page of the Cakewalk Web site (**http://www.cakewalk.com/Support/**) contains a ton of helpful information, including FAQs (lists of frequently asked questions and their answers) and technical documents that provide details on a number of Cakewalk-related topics. You should check them first. If you still can't find an answer to your problem, the next place to look is in the Cakewalk newsgroups (**http://www.cakewalk.com/Support/newsgroups.html**). In the newsgroups, you can trade tips, advice, and information with other Cakewalk product users. And many times, you'll find that someone has had the same problem you're having, and he or she has already found a solution. You can also find a very active Discussion area on my own Web site (**http://www.garrigus.com/**). Isn't sharing great? Also, be sure to check out Appendix D, "Cakewalk Resources on the Web," at the end of this book for even more helpful information.

Of course, you can also contact Cakewalk Technical Support directly. You can either e-mail your questions to **support@cakewalk.com**, or you can call 617-441-7891 (USA). Currently, the hours are Monday through Friday from 10 a.m. to 6 p.m. Eastern time. Tech Support also offers extended hours on Thursday till 10 p.m. But remember, to receive technical support, you have to be a registered user. If you call or send e-mail, you'll be asked for your serial number. As I said before, remember to send in that registration card! You'll be a much happier camper, er…Cakewalker.

CHAPTER 2

3

Customizing SONAR

As the old Yiddish proverb goes, "Everyone is kneaded out of the same dough, but not baked in the same oven." The point I'm trying to make is that, although we all may be SONAR users, it doesn't mean we like to work with the product in the same exact way. I have my way of doing things, and you probably have your own way. Luckily, SONAR provides a number of settings so that you can make the program conform to your own way of working. In this chapter, you'll learn the following:

▶ How to organize all the different files associated with SONAR

▶ How to customize the program's workspace, including colors, toolbars, window layouts, and key bindings

▶ How to set up all the MIDI parameters

▶ How to find the optimal audio settings

Organize Your Files

As you work with SONAR, you'll be dealing with many different types of files. They include project files, StudioWare files, CAL files, and so on. By default, SONAR places all these files in the same location on your hard drive: the Program Files\Cakewalk\SONAR 1 folder. This location may be fine with you, but personally I like to have everything neatly organized in its own place on my hard drive. (A bit obsessive-compulsive perhaps, but hey, I can always find what I'm looking for, right?) My other reason for not liking the default scenario is that the SONAR program files are in that folder, too. Everything is just mixed up in one huge folder, which makes it difficult to back up important project files and so on. (By the way, I'll be talking about backing up files in Appendix B, "Backing Up Your Project Files.")

CHAPTER 3

My Documents

What I like to do is keep all my important files in the My Documents folder on my hard drive. And I'm not just talking about SONAR files, although that's what I'll be discussing here. By keeping them together, I can easily back up all my important files in one fell swoop by simply making a copy of the My Documents folder. In case you're wondering, the My Documents folder is set up automatically by Windows when you install it. Keeping all your important files in a single location was initially Microsoft's idea. You don't have to go along with it, but it really does work.

To make sure all your files aren't mixed together within the My Documents folder, you can create a number of subfolders—one for each of the different file categories. SONAR has ten different categories of files associated with it. The best way I've found to organize them is as follows:

1. Open the Windows Explorer. Then locate and open the My Documents folder on your hard drive.

2. Create a new subfolder by right-clicking within the My Documents folder and selecting New > Folder from the pop-up menus. Name the new folder "SONAR."

3. Open the SONAR folder, and create ten new subfolders with the following names:

    ► Songs
    ► Templates
    ► CAL Files
    ► Window layouts
    ► Wave files
    ► Video files
    ► Sysx files
    ► Play list
    ► Groove Quantize
    ► StudioWare

When you're finished, the file structure should look similar to what's shown in Figure 3.1. Don't worry about all the different file types. I'll talk about them throughout the book when appropriate.

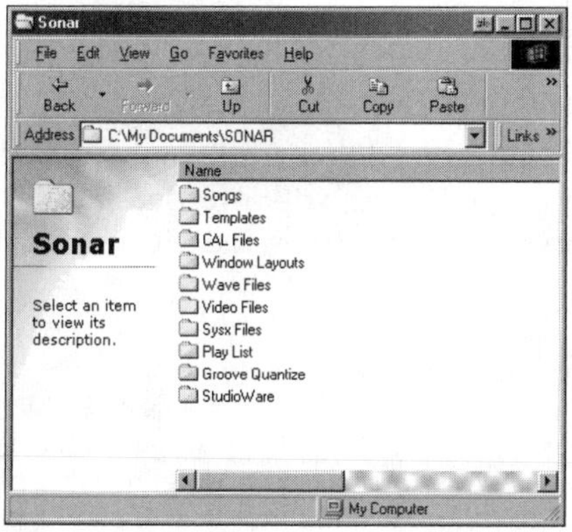

Figure 3.1
Your SONAR subfolders should look like this within the My Documents folder.

Put Everything in Its Place

Now that you have your folders organized, you can move all your existing files to the appropriate locations. Follow these steps to do so:

1. Open the Windows Explorer. Then locate and open the Program Files\Cakewalk\SONAR 1 folder on your hard drive.

2. Take a look at Table 3.1.

Table 3.1
SONAR File Type Extensions and Their Assigned My Documents Folder Locations.

File Extension	Folder Location
.MID	Songs
.WRK	Songs
.BUN	Songs
.TPL	Templates
.CAL	CAL Files
.CakewalkWindowLayout	Window Layouts
.WAV	Wave Files
.RA	Wave Files
.ASF	Wave Files
.MP3	Wave Files
.AVI	Video Files
.MPG	Video Files
.MOV	Video Files
.SYX	Sysx Files
.SET	Play List
.GRV	Groove Quantize
.CakewalkStudioWare	StudioWare

CHAPTER 3

3. Find all the files with the extensions shown in the first column of Table 3.1 and move them to the appropriate folders, as shown in the second column of Table 3.1.

4. Take each row one at a time until you've gone through all the file types. For example, start with row one and find all files with an .MID extension; then move them to the My Documents\SONAR\Songs folder.

NOTE

Notice that although you set up folders for only ten file categories, quite a few more file types are listed in Table 3.1. More file types exist because some of SONAR's files come in different forms even though they belong to the same category. For instance, project files can come in the form of MIDI (.MID) files, Work (.WRK) files, and Bundle (.BUN) files. I'll explain the differences in Chapter 4.

Isn't it nice to have everything neatly organized and in its proper place? Believe me, you'll appreciate it in the long run. But you're still not quite finished.

Location, Location, Location

After you've created your folders and moved all your files, you need to let SONAR know about the new locations. If you don't, and you try loading one of your project files, you might get an error message because SONAR won't be able to locate some of the project's accompanying files. Here's what you need to do:

1. In SONAR, select Options > Global.

2. In the Global Options dialog box, select the Folders tab. You then see a list of ten folder locations, as shown in Figure 3.2.

Figure 3.2
You can set folder locations in SONAR's Global Options dialog box.

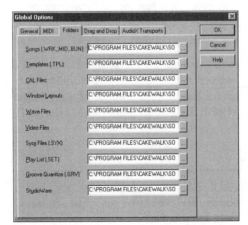

3. For each of the file categories, you need to type or use the browse button to locate the new folder location. As an example, for the Songs category, type "C:\My Documents\SONAR\Songs." Be sure to substitute for the letter C the appropriate letter that represents your hard drive if it's different.

4. Click on the OK button. From now on, SONAR will know where to look for each of the different file types and will automatically open the appropriate folder when you open a project file, for instance.

TIP

In addition to the ten file types I discussed earlier, SONAR actually deals with two other types of files as well. These are data files and picture files. Whenever you record audio data using SONAR, the program creates temporary data files (in the WAV file format) to hold the audio data for your project. These data files are stored in the data directory. SONAR also creates picture files for the audio data in your project, which hold "drawings" of the audio waveforms. Initially, the data files are stored in the Program Files\Cakewalk\SONAR 1\Audio Data directory, and the picture files are stored in the Program Files\Cakewalk\SONAR 1\Picture Cache directory on your hard drive. You can change these storage locations by choosing Options > Audio to open the Audio Options dialog box and clicking on the Advanced tab. You'll notice the Data Directory and Picture Directory parameters at the top of the box. If you have only one hard drive in your computer system, you should probably just leave these directories at their default locations. If you have two hard drives in your system, you can get better performance out of SONAR if you keep your SONAR program files on one drive and put your data and picture files on another drive. You might even want to move your entire My Documents folder to the second drive. That way you have all your program files on one drive and all your data files on another drive. This is an extra safeguard in case your first hard drive ever crashes.

The Workspace

Not only can you change the way SONAR handles files, but you also can change the way SONAR looks and the way it responds to your commands. By customizing the SONAR workspace, you can increase your efficiency with the program and make it more comfortable to work with. Some of the adjustments you can make are to the colors, toolbars, window layouts, and key bindings.

CHAPTER 3

Colors

SONAR allows you to change the colors of almost every element on the screen within the program. I haven't found much use for making color changes, though. The default colors that the program ships with work just fine for me. However, you might find a different set of colors more pleasant to work with, or maybe you can see some colors better than others. Changing the colors SONAR uses is simple—follow these steps:

1. In SONAR, select Options > Colors. The Colors dialog box then appears, as shown in Figure 3.3.

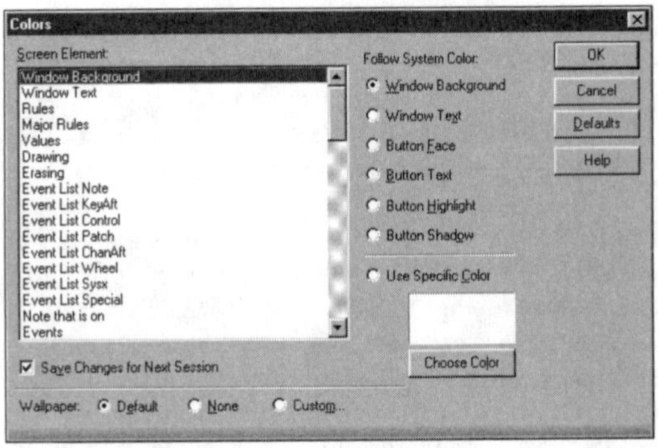

Figure 3.3
In the Colors dialog box, you can change the appearance of SONAR to your liking.

2. On the left side of the dialog box is a list of all the screen elements you can change. To change the color of an element, select it.

3. Select how you want that screen element to look by choosing a color from the right side of the dialog box. You can have the color of the element follow the color of some of the default Windows element colors, or you can use a specific color.

4. You can also change the background wallpaper of the SONAR workspace by choosing one of the options at the bottom of the Colors dialog box. If you choose the Custom option, you can even load your own Windows bitmap (.BMP) file for display. Loading your own file is not very useful, but it can be fun.

5. When you've completed your changes, just click on the OK button.

Toolbars

To increase your productivity, SONAR provides a number of toolbars for quick access to many of its major functions. So, instead of having to click through a series of menus, you can simply click on a single toolbar button. Toolbars are available for standard file access functions, recording and playback controls, and so on.

SONAR allows you to change the look and position of its toolbars, as well as determine whether they are visible. Why wouldn't you want to have all the toolbars on the screen all the time? Because they can clutter up the workspace and get in the way while you're working on a project.

Change Their Position

Just as with most toolbars in other Windows programs, you can dock these toolbars to the top or the bottom of the SONAR workspace by dragging and dropping them with the mouse. SONAR doesn't allow you to dock them to the sides of the workspace, though. And if you drop a toolbar anywhere within the workspace, it becomes a little floating window, as shown in Figure 3.4.

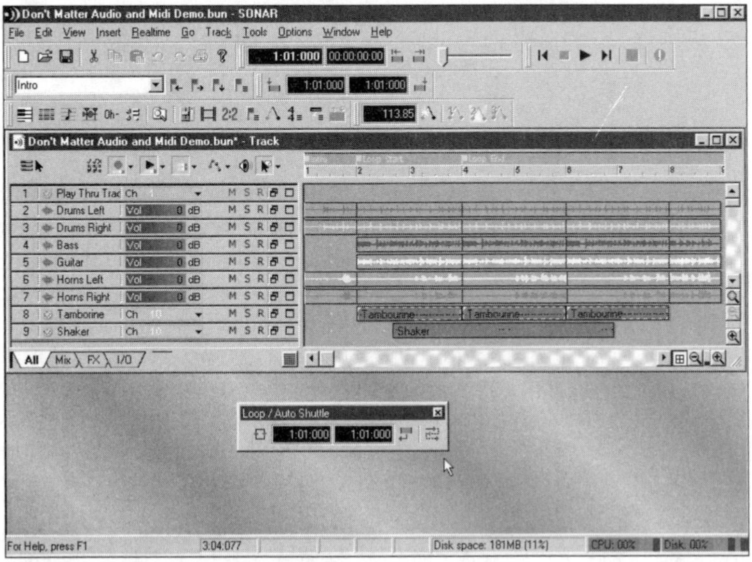

Figure 3.4
Toolbars can be docked at the top or bottom of the SONAR workspace. They can also reside anywhere else within the workspace as small floating windows.

Change Their Appearance

To change the appearance of the toolbars, you need to access the Toolbars dialog box. Just choose View > Toolbars, and the Toolbars dialog box will appear, as shown in Figure 3.5.

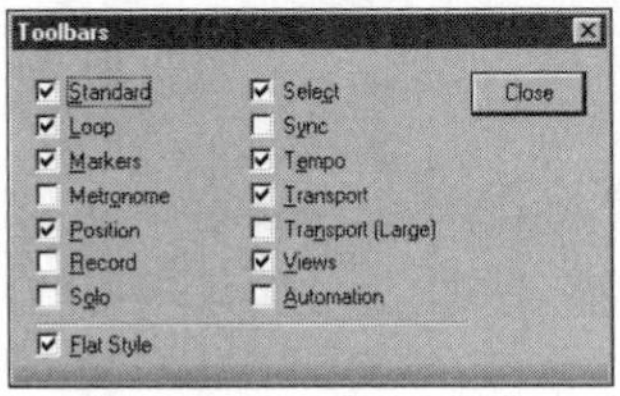

Figure 3.5
Using the Toolbars dialog box, you can change the appearance of SONAR's toolbars.

By placing or removing the check mark next to each selection, you control whether the associated toolbar will be visible. For example, if you remove the check mark in the box next to the Standard selection, the Standard File Functions toolbar will disappear. You can also have the buttons in the toolbars either appear flat or similar to 3D by changing the Flat Style selection at the bottom of the Toolbars dialog box.

NOTE

The only thing that disappoints me about SONAR's toolbars is that you can't customize them in any other ways. For instance, you can't change which buttons appear in each toolbar, and you can't create your own specialized toolbars for rapid access to the features you use most often. Plus, no toolbars are available for any of the editing functions within the program. Well, guess what? I found a way around this little dilemma by utilizing StudioWare. I'll tell you all about it in Chapter 15.

Window Layouts

As you're working on a project in SONAR, you need to use many of the views described in Chapter 2. When you want to save the project, the size and position of the view windows are saved along with it. This capability is nice, because you can pick up exactly where you left off the next time you open the project. As you get more experienced with SONAR, you'll probably find that having the views set up in certain configurations helps your recording sessions go more smoothly. For instance, you might like having the Track view positioned at the top of the workspace, with the Staff view and the Piano Roll view positioned underneath it, as shown in Figure 3.6.

Figure 3.6
The size and position of all views are saved along with a project.

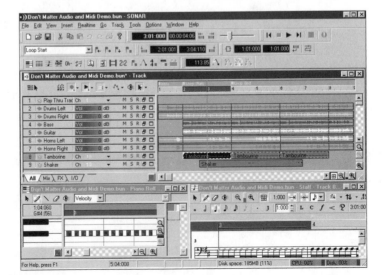

What if you come up with a few favorite configurations that you like to use during different stages of the same project? Or what if you want to use those configurations on a different project? That's where window layouts come in. Using window layouts, you can save the current size and position of the view windows as a layout file. Then you can later load the saved layout and apply it to any open project. You can also update a saved layout, delete it, or rename it. You do so by using the Window Layouts dialog box.

Create a Layout

You create a window layout like this:

1. Arrange the views in the workspace in the positions and sizes that you would like them to be saved. You also must decide whether you want certain views to be open.

2. Select View > Layouts to open the Window Layouts dialog box, as shown in Figure 3.7.

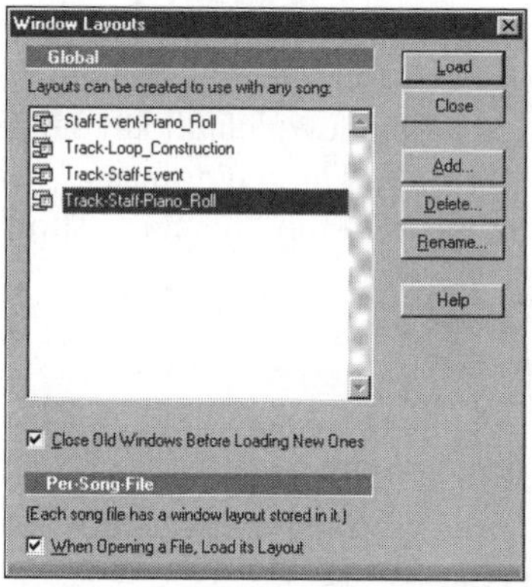

Figure 3.7
You can create new layouts by using the Window Layouts dialog box.

Window Layouts
Global
Layouts can be created to use with any song:
Staff-Event-Piano_Roll
Track-Loop_Construction
Track-Staff-Event
Track-Staff-Piano_Roll
☑ Close Old Windows Before Loading New Ones
Per-Song-File
(Each song file has a window layout stored in it.)
☑ When Opening a File, Load its Layout

Buttons: Load, Close, Add..., Delete..., Rename..., Help

3. Click on the Add button and type a name for the new layout in the New Global Layout dialog box that appears.

> **TIP**
>
> I've found that giving a descriptive name to each layout helps me when I want to load them. For example, I include the names of each open View in the name of the layout. If I have the Track, Staff, and Piano Roll views open in the layout, I name it "Track-Staff-Piano_Roll."

4. Click on the OK button, and your new layout is then listed in the Window Layouts dialog box.

CHAPTER 3

5.   From here, you can rename or delete a layout in the list. You can also load a layout by selecting it from the list and clicking on the Load button.

6.   When you're finished, click on the Close button.

Layout Options

The Window Layouts dialog box contains two optional settings that let you control how layouts are loaded. The Close Old Windows Before Loading New Ones option determines whether any views you have currently open in the workspace will be closed when you load a new layout. The When Opening a File, Load its Layout option determines whether SONAR will load the accompanying layout when a project is opened. I like to keep both of these options activated.

Key Bindings

One of the most useful customization features that SONAR provides is key bindings. Like toolbars, they give you quick access to most of SONAR's features. Instead of having to click through a series of menus, you can simply press a key combination on your computer's keyboard. Initially, SONAR ships with a few default key bindings for opening and saving a project, for example. These bindings are displayed next to their assigned menu functions, as in the File menu shown in Figure 3.8.

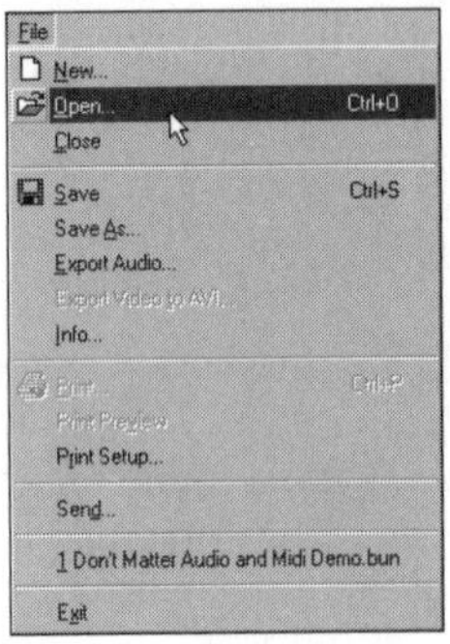

Figure 3.8
Initially, the key binding for opening a project is Ctrl+O.

The wonderful thing about key bindings is that if you don't like them, you can change them. You also can create new ones for functions that don't already have them preassigned. There's only one limitation: a maximum of sixty-two key bindings. You can work around this limitation, however; I'll talk about that later in this chapter. The available computer keyboard combinations include the following:

▶ The Ctrl key in combination with any letter of the alphabet

▶ Any function key (F1 through F12)

▶ The Ctrl key in combination with any function key

▶ The Shift key in combination with any function key

Create Your Own Key Bindings

You can easily create your own key bindings and change existing ones. Here's how:

1. Select Options > Key Bindings to open the Key Bindings dialog box, as shown in Figure 3.9.

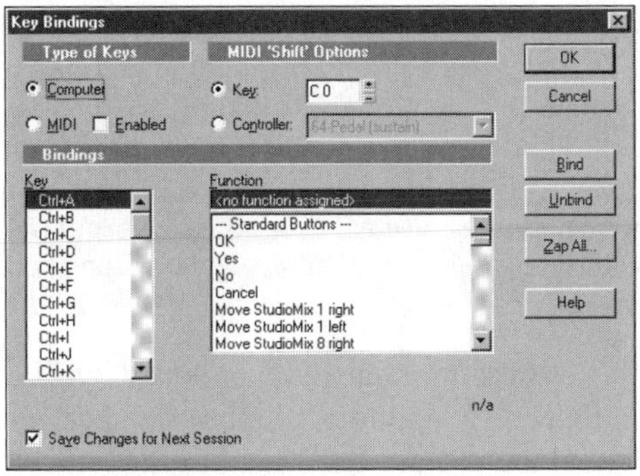

Figure 3.9
You can set key combinations in the Key Bindings dialog box.

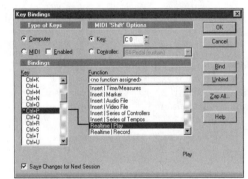

2. In the Function list under the Bindings section of the dialog box, select the SONAR function that you want to bind to a key combination.

3. In the Key list, select the key combination that you want to bind to the selected function.

4. Click on the Bind button. You then see a connection created, as shown in Figure 3.10.

Figure 3.10
A connection between a function and key combination is made when you click on the Bind button.

CHAPTER 3

5. As I mentioned before, you can create up to sixty-two key bindings. You can also remove single key bindings by using the Unbind button. And if you want to get rid of them all, just click on the Zap All button.

6. When you're done, click on the OK button.

CAUTION

Near the bottom of the Key Bindings dialog box is the Save Changes for Next Session option. When you select it, any key bindings you create will be saved so that you can use them every time you run SONAR. If this option is not selected, you will lose any changes you make when you exit the program. By default, this option is selected. I suggest you keep it that way, unless for some reason you just need a few temporary key bindings during a recording session.

After you've created (or changed) some key bindings, you'll notice the changes in SONAR's menus. As I mentioned earlier, the key bindings are displayed next to their assigned menu functions.

MIDI Key Bindings

Remember when I mentioned that you can get around the limit of the sixty-two available key bindings? This is it: MIDI key bindings. You can assign the keys on your MIDI keyboard synthesizer or controller as key bindings to execute functions within SONAR. (Cool, huh?) For example, you can assign the File > New function in SONAR to the middle C key on your keyboard. Then, when you press middle C, SONAR opens the New Project File dialog box.

TIP

If your studio is set up so that your computer isn't located next to your MIDI keyboard or controller, using MIDI Key Bindings is a great way to still have access to SONAR. For example, if you want to be able to start and stop recording of SONAR via your MIDI keyboard, you can just assign one MIDI Key Binding along with the "shift" key or controller to the Realtime > Play function and another MIDI key binding along with the "shift" key or controller to the Realtime > Stop function.

You create MIDI key bindings the same way you create computer keyboard bindings, as discussed earlier. The only difference is that you have to select MIDI as the Type of Keys option in the Key Bindings dialog box and make sure to activate MIDI key bindings by selecting the Enabled option, as shown in Figure 3.11. Also, when you select a key combination in the Key list, you select musical keys rather than computer keyboard keys.

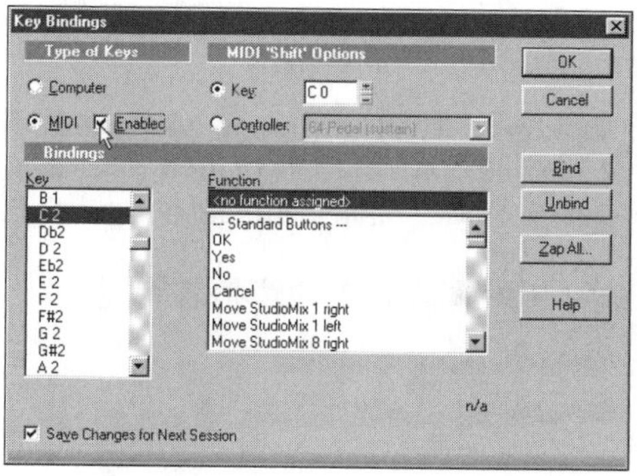

Figure 3.11
You select MIDI as
the Type of Keys
option to active MIDI
key bindings.

In addition, to prevent the MIDI key bindings from activating while
you're performing, you need to set up a "shift" key or controller to turn
the MIDI key bindings on and off. Under MIDI Shift Options in the Key
Bindings dialog box, you can assign a MIDI key or controller message to
act as a sort of "on/off switch." When you want to use a MIDI key
binding, activate the "shift" key or controller first to tell SONAR you're
about to use a MIDI key binding.

MIDI Settings

Even though SONAR does a good job of setting up all its MIDI options
during installation, it's still a good idea for you to go through them to
make sure everything is the way you want it to be. You might be
surprised at how much control you have over how SONAR handles MIDI
data. Not only can you designate which MIDI devices the program will
use, you can also determine what types of MIDI data will be recorded or
not and optimize MIDI playback.

MIDI Devices

The first time you run SONAR, it scans your computer system to see
whether you have a MIDI interface installed. SONAR prompts you to
select the available MIDI ports that you want to use, but you can always
change your selections later.

> **NOTE**
>
> As explained in Chapter 1, a *MIDI interface* is a device that is plugged into
> your computer allowing it to understand the MIDI language. Every MIDI
> interface has at least two connections on it, called *MIDI ports*. One is the MIDI
> In port, which is used to receive MIDI data. The other is the MIDI Out port,
> which is used to send MIDI data. Some of the more sophisticated MIDI
> interfaces on the market have multiple pairs of MIDI ports. For instance, I use a
> Music Quest 8Port/SE, which has eight MIDI In and Out ports. Having all these
> ports allows me to connect more than one MIDI instrument to my computer.

CHAPTER 3

To see what MIDI ports SONAR is using and to designate which ports you want to use, do the following:

1. Select Options > MIDI Devices to open the MIDI Ports dialog box. This dialog box contains lists of all the input MIDI ports and output MIDI ports that you have available. For an example, see Figure 3.12.

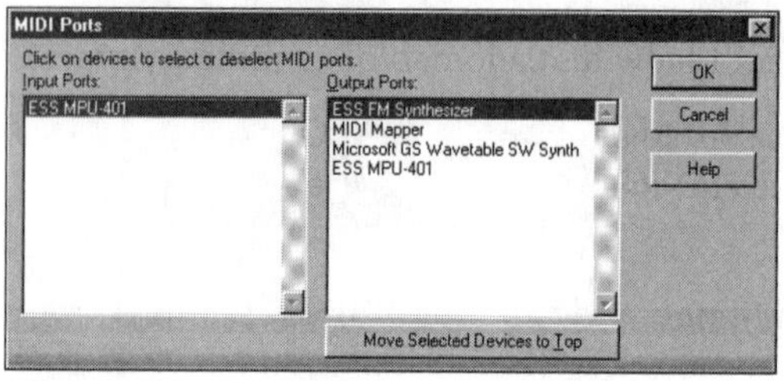

Figure 3.12
The MIDI Ports dialog box lists all the available input and output MIDI ports.

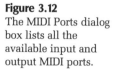

2. Simply select the input and output ports that you want to be able to access for use within SONAR.

3. When you're finished, click on the OK button.

All the ports selected here will be available in the Track Properties dialog box, which I'll talk about in Chapter 4.

Global MIDI Options

SONAR provides a number of different MIDI options, some of which are global, and others that are project oriented. The project-oriented options (which I'll talk about in Chapter 4) are saved and loaded along with project files. The global options remain the same no matter which project is currently open.

Filter Out MIDI Messages

The global MIDI options allow you to select the types of MIDI messages that you want to record in SONAR. Sometimes you might not want certain MIDI data to be included in your recordings. For example, if your MIDI keyboard sends channel aftertouch messages or key aftertouch messages, you might want to filter them out. These types of messages are very resource-intensive and can sometimes bog down your synthesizer with too much data.

NOTE

There are seven types of MIDI messages, each providing different kinds of functionality within the MIDI language. These categories include notes, key aftertouch, channel aftertouch, controllers, program changes, pitch bend, and system exclusive.

The notes category pertains to MIDI Note On and MIDI Note Off messages. Whenever you press a key on your MIDI keyboard, a MIDI Note On message is sent. When you let the key go, a MIDI Note Off message is sent.

On some MIDI keyboards, in addition to hitting the keys, you can press and hold them down to apply varying degrees of pressure. This pressure is called aftertouch. Depending on how the synthesizer is programmed, aftertouch lets you control how loud it is or even how it sounds. Aftertouch comes in both key and channel varieties. Key aftertouch allows you to have different pressure levels for each individual key on the keyboard. Channel aftertouch restricts you to a single pressure level over the entire range of the keyboard.

A wide range of controller MIDI messages is available. Basically, these messages give you control over different aspects of your MIDI synthesizer or device. Some controller messages let you control volume, whereas others let you control the position of a synthesizer sound in the stereo field. However, far too many are available to discuss them all here.

Program changes (also called patch changes) let you select from the many different sounds available in a MIDI synthesizer. For example, a program change #1 MIDI message might activate a piano sound in your synthesizer, and program change #10 might activate a glockenspiel sound.

Pitch bend messages allow you to temporarily alter the tuning of your MIDI instrument. Many MIDI keyboards have a lever or a wheel that lets you control pitch bend. Moving this wheel makes the instrument send out pitch bend (also called pitch wheel) messages.

System exclusive messages pertain to special MIDI data that is (as the name implies) exclusive to the instrument sending and receiving it. For instance, the manufacturer of a MIDI synthesizer might include special functions in the product that can't be controlled via standard MIDI messages. By using system exclusive messages, the manufacturer gives you access to these special functions but still keeps the product compatible with the MIDI language.

For more in-depth information about MIDI and the different types of messages available, you should read a book dedicated specifically to the subject. One of my favorites is *MIDI for Musicians* by Craig Anderton (Music Sales Corp, 1998, ISBN 0-8256-1050-8).

By default, SONAR has notes, controllers, program changes, pitch bend, and system exclusive messages activated, and it has key aftertouch and channel aftertouch deactivated. If you want to change these settings, though, you can do the following:

1. Select Options > Global to open the Global Options dialog box.
2. Click on the MIDI tab at the top of the dialog box.

3. Under the Record section, select the types of MIDI messages that you want to allow SONAR to record, as shown in Figure 3.13.

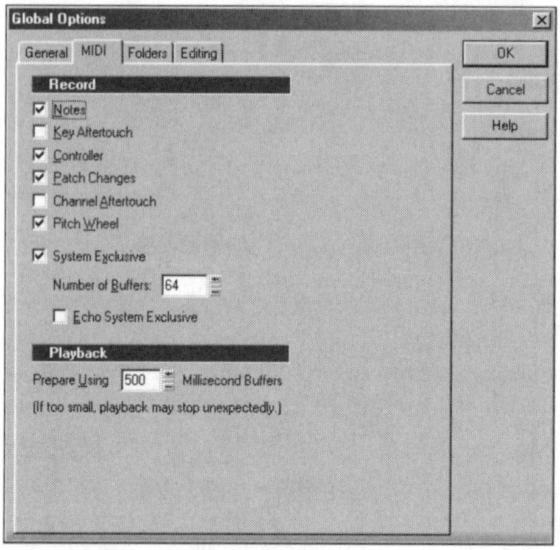

Figure 3.13
You can determine the types of MIDI messages SONAR will be allowed to record.

4. Click on the OK button when you're finished.

Optimize MIDI Playback

To get smooth and consistent playback of MIDI data, SONAR uses a buffer (a temporary storage area) to hold the data before it gets sent out through the MIDI interface. This buffer keeps the data from getting backed up, which can cause erratic playback or even stop playback altogether. The buffer also helps to control playback latency. Whenever you change a parameter in SONAR while a project is playing, a slight delay always occurs between the time you make the adjustment and when you hear the results. That's called *latency*.

The Global Options dialog box contains a setting that allows you to adjust the size of SONAR's MIDI playback buffer. If the buffer is set too low, it can cause erratic playback, and if it is set too high, it can cause noticeable latency. By default, the buffer size is set to 500 milliseconds. This setting should be fine in most cases. However, you might want to experiment to find an even better setting. The trick is to find the lowest setting without affecting playback. I've been able to get away with a setting of 100 (on a Pentium II/300 computer system), so depending on the speed of your computer system, you might want to try that. You can change the buffer size like this:

1. Select Options > Global to open the Global Options dialog box.
2. Click on the MIDI tab at the top of the dialog box.
3. Under the Playback section, type the new buffer size.
4. Click on the OK button when you're finished.

Instrument Definitions

Most MIDI instruments today provide a bank of sounds compatible with the General MIDI standard. At the same time, most instruments also provide additional sounds as well as other features that aren't defined by General MIDI. Some older MIDI instruments don't support General MIDI at all. To let you work more efficiently with these instruments, SONAR provides instrument definitions.

> **NOTE**
>
> Sounds in a MIDI instrument are stored as a group of parameter settings called a *patch*, and patches are stored in groups called *banks*. A MIDI instrument can have up to 16,384 banks of 128 patches each. This means that a MIDI instrument can theoretically contain up to 2,097,152 different sounds, although most don't.
>
> With such a large potential for diversity, MIDI instruments from one manufacturer usually don't provide the same functionality as instruments from another manufacturer. This point is important, because MIDI data is ambiguous. The same data can be played back using any MIDI instrument, but that doesn't mean it will sound the same. Different instruments contain different sounds, and they interpret MIDI differently as well.
>
> To remedy the problem, General MIDI was created.
>
> *General MIDI (GM)* is a set of rules applied to the MIDI language that standardize the types of sounds contained in a MIDI instrument (along with their patch numbers) and how different MIDI controller messages are interpreted. Most modern MIDI instruments provide a special bank of GM sounds and a GM operating mode. When running in GM mode, different MIDI instruments respond to the same MIDI data in the same way. So, MIDI data played back on one instrument is guaranteed to sound the same when played on any other instrument.

Using instrument definitions, you can "tell" SONAR all about the features and capabilities provided by each of the MIDI instruments in your studio. This information includes the name of each patch, the range of notes supported by each patch, the MIDI controller messages that are supported, which registered parameter numbers (RPNs) and non-registered parameter numbers (NRPNs) are supported, and the bank select method used. Basically, instrument definitions allow you to refer to the patches in your MIDI instruments by name rather than number when you're assigning sounds to tracks in SONAR. (I'll talk more about this subject in Chapter 4.) The same applies for musical note names and MIDI controller message names.

CHAPTER 3

Set Up Your Instruments

SONAR includes a number of predefined instrument definitions so that you can simply assign them without having to go through the process of creating your own. You can assign instrument definitions to each of the MIDI ports on your MIDI interface. You can also assign them to the individual MIDI channels (1 through 16).

NOTE

The MIDI language provides sixteen different channels of performance data over a single MIDI port connection. MIDI instruments can be set to receive MIDI data on a single channel, if need be. This means you can control up to sixteen different MIDI instruments (each with its own unique sound) even if they are all connected to the same MIDI port on your MIDI interface. In addition, most MIDI instruments are capable of playing more than one sound at a time. This means the instrument is *multitimbral*. If you assign a different sound to each of the sixteen MIDI channels, a single MIDI instrument can play sixteen different sounds simultaneously.

To assign instrument definitions to each of the MIDI ports and channels in your setup, follow these steps:

1. Select Options > Instruments to open the Assign Instruments dialog box, as shown in Figure 3.14.

Figure 3.14
You can assign instrument definitions in the Assign Instruments dialog box.

Assign Instruments		
Select one or more Port/Channel destinations, then click on an Instrument.		OK
Port/Channel	Uses Instrument:	Cancel
1: ESS FM Synthesizer / 1	<default>	Define...
1: ESS FM Synthesizer / 2	General MIDI	
1: ESS FM Synthesizer / 3	General MIDI Drums	Help
1: ESS FM Synthesizer / 4	Generic (Patches 0..127)	
1: ESS FM Synthesizer / 5	Generic (Patches 1..128)	
1: ESS FM Synthesizer / 6	Roland GS	
1: ESS FM Synthesizer / 7	Roland GS Drumsets	
1: ESS FM Synthesizer / 8	SoundFont Device	
1: ESS FM Synthesizer / 9	Yamaha XG	
1: ESS FM Synthesizer / 10	Yamaha XG Drum Kits	
1: ESS FM Synthesizer / 11		
1: ESS FM Synthesizer / 12		
1: ESS FM Synthesizer / 13		
1: ESS FM Synthesizer / 14		
1: ESS FM Synthesizer / 15		
1: ESS FM Synthesizer / 16	☑ Save Changes for Next Session	

2. From the list on the left, select the MIDI port(s) and/or MIDI channel(s) to which you want to assign definitions.

3. From the list on the right, select the instrument definition you want to use. For example, if you're going to use the MIDI instrument that's connected to the selected port in General MIDI mode, choose the General MIDI Instrument Definition.

CAUTION

Near the bottom of the Assign Instruments dialog box is the Save Changes for Next Session option. When you select it, any assignments you create will be saved so that you can use them every time you run SONAR. If this option is not selected, you will lose any changes you make when you exit the program. I suggest you select this option, unless for some reason you change the configuration of your studio for each new recording session.

4.   Click on the OK button when you're finished.

Now SONAR will know the capabilities of your MIDI instrument or instruments and act appropriately when you access different features, such as editing MIDI controller messages (which I'll talk about in Chapter 7).

Take the Easy Way Out

If you don't see a specific instrument definition for your MIDI instrument listed in the Assign Instruments dialog box, SONAR allows you to import more of them. The program ships with a large collection of additional instrument definitions that cover many of the MIDI instruments on the market from manufacturers, such as Alesis, E-mu, Ensoniq, General Music, Korg, Kurzweil, Roland, and Yamaha. The instrument definitions are stored in files with .INS extensions. For example, the Yamaha instrument definitions are stored in the file YAMAHA.INS. Importing these files is simple; just do the following:

1.   Select Options > Instruments to open the Assign Instruments dialog box.

2.   Click on the Define button to open the Define Instruments and Names dialog box, as shown in Figure 3.15.

Figure 3.15
The Define Instruments and Names dialog box allows you to import additional instrument definitions.

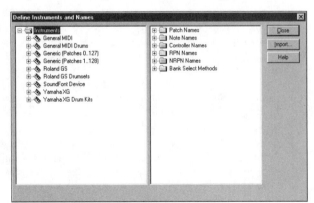

CHAPTER 3

3. Click on the Import button to open the Import Instrument Definitions dialog box and select the .INS file that you want to import. For example, if your MIDI instrument is manufactured by Roland, select the ROLAND.INS file.

4. When SONAR displays a list of the instrument definitions contained in that file, select the one(s) you want and click on the OK button. Your selections are then listed under Instruments in the Define Instruments and Names dialog box.

5. Click on the Close button, and you then see your selections listed under Uses Instrument in the Assign Instruments dialog box.

6. Click on the OK button when you're finished.

If you still can't find an instrument definition for your MIDI instrument from the extensive collection included with SONAR, you can download even more from the Internet. Cakewalk provides a download section on its Web site (**http://www.cakewalk.com/download/**) where you can pick up additional instrument definition files. Other sites on the Web supply them, too. For more details, take a look at Appendix D, "Cakewalk Resources on the Web."

Create Your Own

More than likely, you'll find instrument definitions for all your MIDI equipment either included with SONAR or available for download from the Internet. On the off chance that you don't, though, SONAR allows you to create your own. Creating your own instrument definitions can be a bit complicated, because you must have a good knowledge of the MIDI language and you need to be able to read the MIDI implementation charts that come with your instruments.

NOTE

The MIDI language contains more than one hundred different messages for conveying musical information, and a MIDI instrument isn't required to be able to send or recognize all of them. A MIDI instrument needs to transmit and receive only the messages that are relevant to the features it provides. It can ignore all the other messages. Therefore, manufacturers include MIDI implementation charts with all their products.

A MIDI implementation chart lists all the types of MIDI messages that are transmitted and recognized by its accompanying MIDI instrument. The chart includes the note range of the instrument, what MIDI controller messages it supports, whether it supports system exclusive messages, and more.

To give you an idea of how to read a simple MIDI implementation chart and how to create a basic instrument definition, let's go through the process step-by-step:

1. Select Options > Instruments to open the Assign Instruments dialog box.

2. Click on the Define button to open the Define Instruments and Names dialog box.

3. Take a look at Table 3.2, which shows the MIDI implementation chart for an E-mu PROformance Plus Stereo Piano MIDI instrument.

Table 3.2
E-mu PROformance Plus MIDI Implementation Chart.

MIDI Command	Transmitted	Received	Comments
Note On	No	Yes	
Note Off	No	Yes	
Pitch Wheel	No	Yes	
Program Change	No	Yes	0-31
Overflow Mode	Yes	Yes	
Channel Pressure	No	No	
Poly Key Pressure	No	No	
Control Change	No	Yes	PWH, #1, #7
Sustain Footswitch	No	Yes	#64
Sostenuto Footswitch	No	Yes	#66
Soft Footswitch	No	Yes	#67
Split Footswitch	No	Yes	#70
All Notes Off	No	Yes	
Omni Mode	No	No	
Poly Mode	No	No	
Mono Mode	No	No	
System Exclusives	No	No	

4. Right-click on Instruments on the left side of the Define Instruments and Names dialog box, and select Add Instrument from the pop-up menu.

5. Type a name for the new instrument. For this example, type "E-mu PROformance Plus."

CHAPTER 3

6. Open the new instrument by clicking on the + (plus) box next to it, as shown in Figure 3.16.

Figure 3.16
This dialog box shows a new instrument definition.

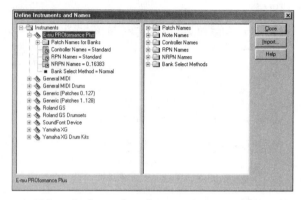

7. Take a look at what the new instrument contains. SONAR automatically creates the standard settings needed. Because the E-mu PROformance Plus doesn't support bank select messages, RPNs, or NRPNs, you don't need to change them. The PROformance supports the standard MIDI controllers, too, so you don't have to change them either. You do need to change the patch names, though.

8. Open the Patch Names for Banks folder in the E-mu PROformance Plus instrument by clicking on the + (plus) box next to it. You should see General MIDI listed there. Because this instrument doesn't support GM, you need to change that name.

9. To change the General MIDI patch names list, you first need to create a new patch names list specifically for the PROformance by right-clicking on the Patch Names folder on the right side of the Define Instruments and Names dialog box.

10. Select Add Patch Names List from the pop-up menu, and type a name for the new list. In this case, type "E-mu PROformance Plus."

11. The PROformance manual shows all the patch names for the instrument (numbers 0 to 31). To add those names to the new patch name list, right-click on the list and select Add Patch Name from the pop-up menu.

12. Type a name for the first patch (in this case, "Dark Grand") and press the Enter key on your computer keyboard. Because this is just an example, you can leave the list as is, but if you were to add all the names to the list, it would look something like Figure 3.17.

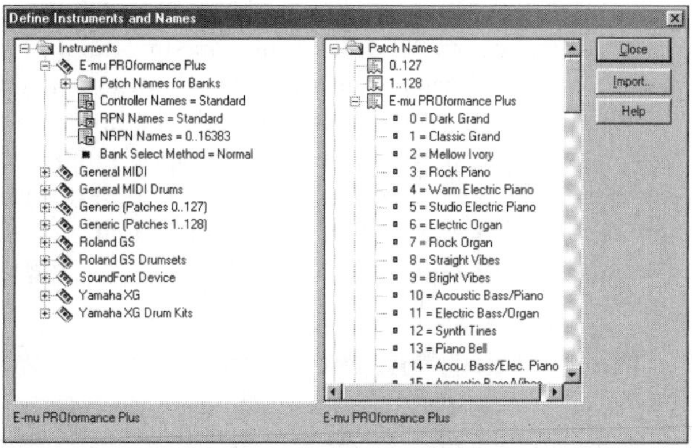

Figure 3.17
This dialog box shows a patch name list for the E-mu PROformance Plus.

13. Drag and drop the E-mu PROformance Plus patch names list on to the General MIDI list in the E-mu PROformance Plus Instrument Definition.

14. In the Bank Number dialog box, enter the number of the bank that you want to be used for this set of patch names. Click OK. The patch names list for the instrument is then changed.

15. Click on the Close button and then click on the OK button to finish.

This set of steps was actually a very simplified demonstration on how to create your own instrument definition. If the controller names needed to be changed or the instrument supported RPNs or NRPNs, you would create and edit those lists in the same way you do a patch name list. It's doubtful that you'll ever need to create your own instrument definitions, because SONAR comes with a large number of them (as well as more being available for download on the Internet), but just in case, you can find more details in the SONAR User's Guide.

Optimal Audio Settings

When SONAR plays back digital audio on your computer, it puts a lot of stress on the system. Remember when I talked about digital audio in Chapter 1? A CD-quality digital audio recording requires 44,100 numbers (samples) to be processed every second. During playback, most of your computer's processing power is used solely for that purpose. Depending on the power of your system, this processing can make the response of some of SONAR's controls a bit sluggish, in particular the Console view controls. For example, if you adjust the volume of a digital audio track in the Console view during playback, you might experience a slight delay between the time you make the adjustment and the time you hear the results. As I mentioned above, this period is called latency, and you'll want as little of it as possible occurring during your sessions.

CHAPTER 3

SONAR provides a number of different advanced settings that enable you to reduce latency. The first time you start the program, it attempts to make some educated guesses as to what these settings should be, and although these settings usually work just fine, you might still be able to squeeze better performance out of your computer system. However, adjusting these settings can be tricky, and, unfortunately, there are no set rules. There are, however, some general guidelines you can follow to optimize your audio settings for the best possible performance.

The Latency Slider

The single most important adjustment you can make is to the Latency slider, and it's pretty simple to use. The lower you set it, the lower the latency; and the higher you set it, the higher the latency. It can't be that simple though, can it? No, I'm afraid not. By lowering the Latency slider, you also run the risk of making playback unstable. If you set the Latency slider too low, you might hear dropouts or glitches or playback may even stop altogether. And the lower you set the Latency slider, the fewer digital audio tracks you can play at the same time.

To find the right setting, you have to experiment with a number of different projects. For those projects with only a small number of digital audio tracks, you might be able to get away with a very low Latency slider setting. As an example, on my Pentium II/300, I was able to play a project with six digital audio tracks while having the Latency slider set as low as it could go. For projects with a large number of digital audio tracks, you might have to raise the Latency slider and put up with a bit of latency while you work. To set the Latency slider, follow these steps:

1. Select Options > Audio to open the Audio Options dialog box.

2. Click on the General tab. The Latency slider is located in the Mixing Latency section, as shown in Figure 3.18.

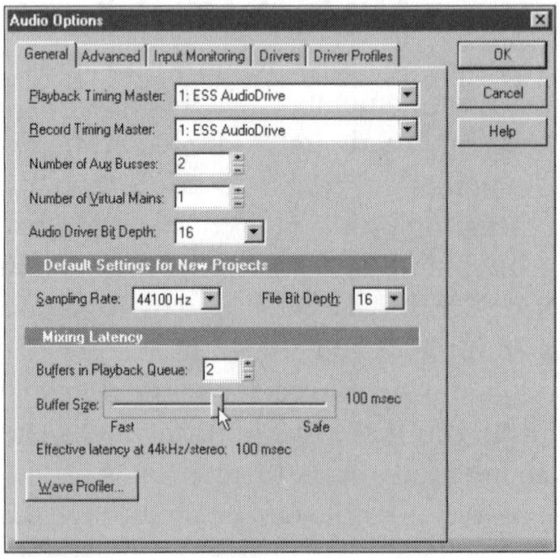

Figure 3.18
In the Audio Options dialog box, you can adjust the Latency slider.

3. Click and drag the Latency slider to the left to lower latency. Click and drag the Latency slider to the right to raise latency. On average, I like to keep it set at about 62.5 msec (milliseconds).

4. Click on the OK button when you're finished.

Queue Buffers and Buffer Size

Two other settings that affect latency and audio performance are the number of buffers in the playback queue and the I/O (input/output) buffer size. Like the Latency slider, if they are set too low, you can experience dropouts or glitches during playback. And higher settings mean more latency. Again, you need to experiment with the settings. I've found that values of 4 for the number of Buffers In Playback Queue and 64 for the I/O Buffer Size work quite well. If you want to change them, you can do the following:

1. Select Options > Audio to open the Audio Options dialog box.

2. Click on the General tab. The Buffers In Playback Queue setting is located in the Mixing Latency section, as shown in Figure 3.19.

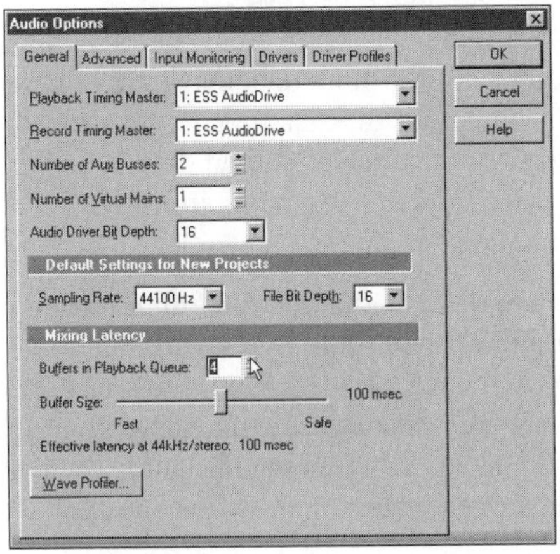

Figure 3.19
In this dialog box, you can set the Buffers In Playback Queue setting.

3. Type the new value.

4. Click on the Advanced tab. The I/O Buffer Size setting is located in the File System section, as shown in Figure 3.20.

CHAPTER 3

Figure 3.20
In this dialog box,
you can set the I/O
Buffer Size setting.

5. Type the new value.

6. Click on the OK button when you're finished.

Read and Write Caching

When your computer sets aside a part of its memory to hold recently read or written information from a disk drive, this process is known as *disk caching*. Windows uses disk caching to help speed up read and write operations to your disk drives. When data is read or written to disk as a continuous stream (like with digital audio), disk caching can actually slow things down.

SONAR has two options that let you either enable or disable disk caching while the program is running. By default, SONAR keeps disk caching disabled. If you have a large amount of memory in your computer (such as 128 MB or more), disk caching may actually improve performance. If you would like to see whether enabling this option makes any difference with your computer system, follow these steps:

1. Select Options > Audio to open the Audio Options dialog box.

2. Click on the Advanced tab. The Enable Read Caching and Enable Write Caching settings are located in the File System section, as shown in Figure 3.21.

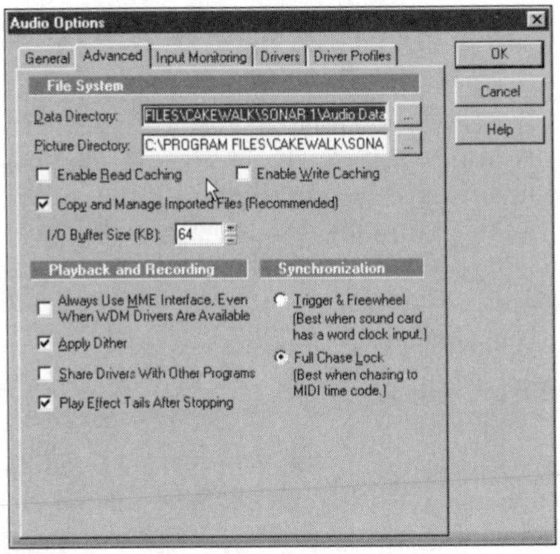

Figure 3.21
In this dialog box, you can set the Enable Read Caching and Enable Write Caching settings.

3. Click on each setting to activate it.

4. Click on the OK button when you're finished.

DMA and the Wave Profiler

A device that can read your computer's memory directly without getting the CPU involved is said to support direct memory access (DMA). A sound card is such a device. SONAR uses the DMA settings of your sound card to ensure that MIDI and digital audio tracks within a project play in synchronization with one another. When you first run SONAR, it scans your sound card to automatically determine the DMA settings. These settings are listed in the Audio Options dialog box under the Driver Profiles tab. Leave these settings alone! In all but the most extreme cases, it won't do you any good to change them. And if you're having excessive problems with MIDI and audio playback, you should contact Cakewalk Technical Support.

If you accidentally change the DMA settings (or just can't help yourself from seeing what will happen if you do), you can easily have SONAR scan your sound card again to bring the original settings back. Here's how to do so:

1. Select Options > Audio to open the Audio Options dialog box.

2. Click on the General tab.

3. Click on the Wave Profiler button at the bottom of the dialog box. SONAR then scans your sound card and resets its DMA settings.

4. Click on the OK button to close the Audio Options dialog box.

CHAPTER 3

TIP

If you're still using Pro Audio 8 or Pro Audio 9, you should upgrade. Audio performance in SONAR has been improved tremendously. Some of the settings have changed, too. For instance, Pro Audio 8 doesn't have a Latency slider. And even with optimal settings, Pro Audio 8 still exhibits some latency. But just in case you don't plan to upgrade, let me give you some general guidelines for optimizing the audio settings in Pro Audio 8 (Pro Audio 9 has the same settings as SONAR, which were discussed earlier in the chapter):

1. Keep both the Enable Read Caching and Enable Write Caching parameters deactivated. Unless you have an older computer system, these settings can hurt Pro Audio's performance.

2. You can leave the File I/O Buffers and I/O Buffer Size settings to their defaults of 32 and 64, respectively. These settings are directly related to the speed of your hard disk drive and have more to do with consistent playback than they do with latency. If you get hiccups during playback, you might want to increase the I/O Buffer Size settings, but more than likely the default settings will be fine.

3. Set the Wave Queue Buffers to 3. Anything less, and Pro Audio probably won't be able to commence playback. This parameter depends on the speed of your CPU, which is directly related to the latency issue. I have found 3 to be a good setting for my system. Anything more is pretty much wasting memory, but if you have a slower system, you might need to increase the setting to 4 or so.

4. The Wave Buffer Size is also directly related to latency. The higher the value, the larger the latency; the lower the value, the smaller the latency. You also have to be careful not to set the buffer too low, because a smaller buffer size value also reduces the number of audio tracks you can have playing at once, as well as the number of real-time effects that can be used simultaneously. I've found 32 to be a good setting for my system. It allows me to have 20 or so audio tracks going at once, and the latency is very small.

5. Leave the DMA settings for your sound card at their default. If you accidentally alter them, use Pro Audio's Wave Profiler feature to have them automatically determined again.

4

Working with Projects

As I mentioned in Chapter 2, a project is SONAR's way of representing a song or any other musical body of work. A project holds all your music data, including MIDI and/or audio, along with a number of program settings. You can't do anything in SONAR without first creating a new project or opening an existing one. So, in this chapter, I'm going to talk all about projects, including the following topics:

▶ How to open an existing project

▶ How to create a new project

▶ How to create your own templates

▶ How to save a project

Opening Projects

Every time you start SONAR, it presents you with the SONAR Quick Start dialog box (see Figure 4.1). From here, you have the choice of opening an existing project, opening a project that you recently worked with, or creating a new one.

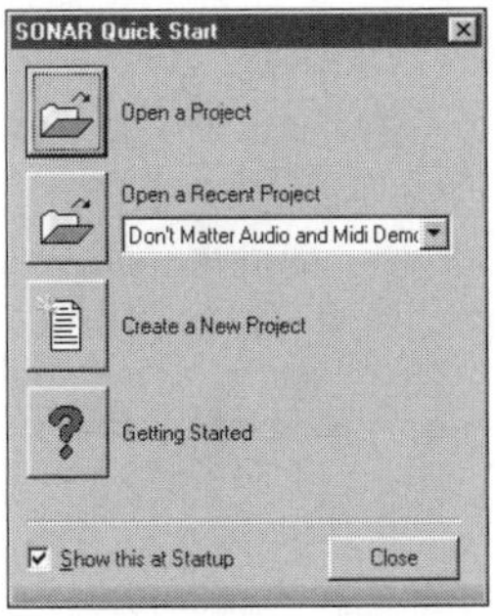

Figure 4.1
The SONAR Quick Start dialog box appears when you start SONAR.

If you choose to open an existing project, SONAR displays a standard file selection dialog box so you can select the project you want to load. If you've set up your My Documents folders as described in Chapter 3, the file dialog will initially display the contents of your Songs folder. Of course, you can examine other disk locations just as you would when loading a file in any other Windows application.

By choosing the Open A Recent Project option in the SONAR Quick Start dialog box, you can open a project that you've previously worked with. You simply select the project from the drop-down list and then click on the folder button next to the list. SONAR keeps track of the last eight projects you've worked with. When you open a ninth, the project on the bottom of the list is bumped off—not killed or deleted, just removed from the list.

You also can open an existing or recent project by using SONAR's standard menu functions. To open an existing project, just select File > Open. To open a recent project, select the File menu and then click on the name of the project you want to open from the list on the bottom half of the menu (see Figure 4.2).

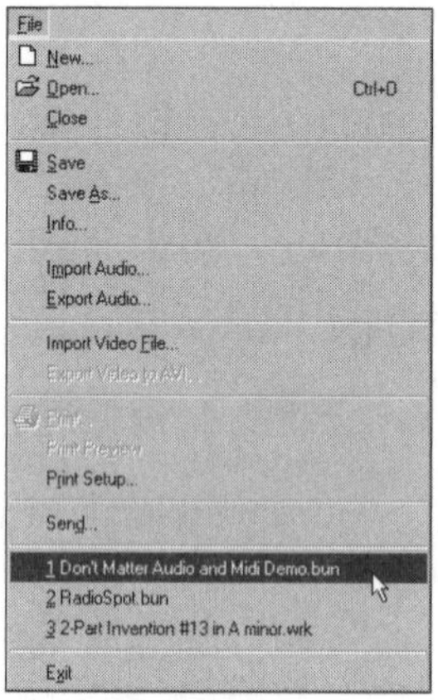

Figure 4.2
You can use the File menu to open an existing or recent project.

File	
New...	
Open...	Ctrl+O
Close	
Save	
Save As...	
Info...	
Import Audio...	
Export Audio...	
Import Video File...	
Export Video (AVI)...	
Print	
Print Preview	
Print Setup...	
Send...	
1 Don't Matter Audio and Midi Demo.bun	
2 RadioSpot.bun	
3 2-Part Invention #13 in A minor.wrk	
Exit	

TIP

Personally, I find it easier to use the standard menu functions to open a project. To keep the dialog from popping up every time you start SONAR, make sure the Show this at Startup check box at the bottom of the box is not selected (see Figure 4.1). You can do the same thing with the Tip of the Day dialog box.

Create a New Project

To create a new project, you can select the appropriate option in the SONAR Quick Start dialog box, or you can choose File > New from SONAR's menu. Whichever method you use, SONAR then displays the New Project File dialog box (see Figure 4.3).

Figure 4.3
You choose from the New Project File dialog box to start a new project.

From here, you need to choose a template upon which to base your new project. After you make your selection, SONAR creates a new project complete with predefined settings that reflect the template you selected.

What's a Template?

A template is a special type of file upon which new projects are based. You can think of templates as sort of predefined projects. Templates contain the settings for all the parameters in a project. Templates enable you to quickly and easily set up a new project for a particular type of musical session. For example, if you need to record a rock song with guitar, organ, bass, and drums, you could get a head start on your project by using SONAR's Rock Quartet template. You can also use templates to set up SONAR for different kinds of studio configurations or if you need to work with a particular MIDI instrument.

SONAR ships with more than thirty different templates that represent a wide range of recording situations. You can use a template called Normal to start a new project totally from scratch. And if you don't find what you need from the templates included with SONAR, you can always create your own.

Create Your Own Template

Any parameters that are saved in a project can also be saved as a template. To create your own template, you simply do the following:

1. Select File > New, and choose the Normal template. Choosing this template creates a new, blank project for you, ready to be filled.

2. Set SONAR's parameters to reflect the type of template you want to create.

3. Select File > Save As to display the Save As dialog box (see Figure 4.4).

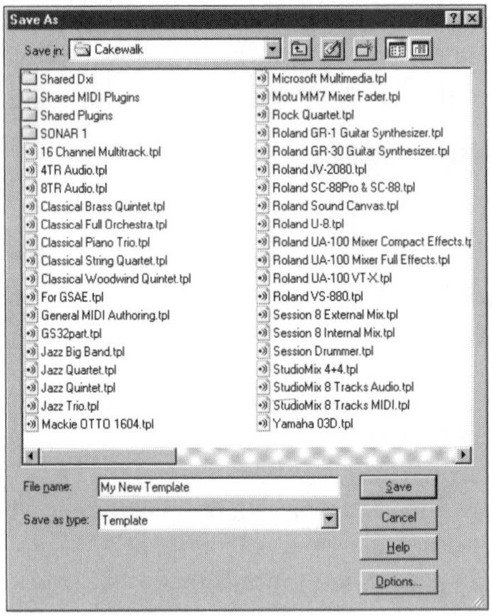

Figure 4.4
You can give your new template a name in the Save As dialog box.

4. Choose Template from the Save As Type drop-down list.

5. Enter a name for your new template in the File Name field and click on the Save button.

The next time you want to create a new project, your template will be listed along with the rest in the New Project File dialog box.

> **TIP**
>
> If you bypass the SONAR Quick Start dialog box—either by disabling it (as I mentioned earlier) or by clicking on its Close button, SONAR automatically creates an empty, new project for you every time you start the program. This project is based on the Normal template, which is saved as the NORMAL.TPL file. If you would like to have SONAR configured in a particular way every time you run the program, simply create a new template and save it as the NORMAL.TPL file. Now SONAR will automatically load your special template during startup. Be sure to make a copy of the NORMAL.TPL file and rename it to something like BLANK.TPL, in case you ever want to create an empty new project.

But what parameters do you need to set when you're creating a new template? Let's go through them one at a time, shall we?

Track Configuration and Parameters

Before you start recording any MIDI or audio data in SONAR, you have to set up your tracks in the Track view. You need to add tracks and tell SONAR the types of tracks (MIDI or audio) they are going to be by right-clicking within the Track pane of the Track view and choosing either Insert Audio Track or Insert MIDI Track from the pop-up menu (see Figure 4.5). You can continue doing this until you have all the tracks you need for your template.

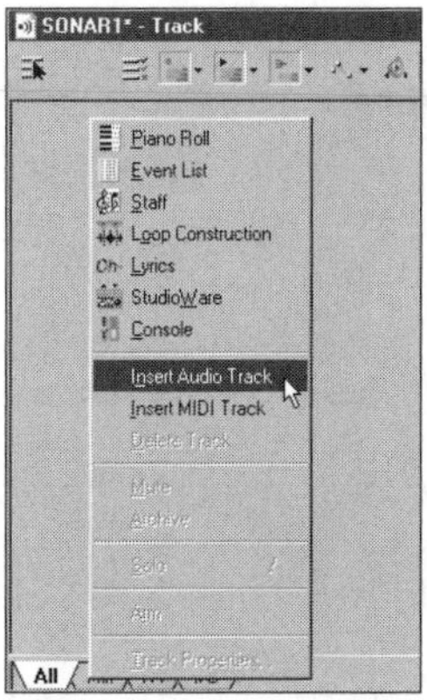

Figure 4.5
Add new tracks to your template using the Track pane of the Track view.

In addition to adding new tracks, you also need to set up the accompanying parameters for each. These parameters include the name, channel, bank, patch, volume, pan, key offset, velocity offset, time offset, input, and output.

> **NOTE**
>
> When you look in the Track view, you'll notice there are some additional parameters available for adjustment. These parameters are not usually set up when creating a template, so I will cover them later in the book.

All of these parameters can be changed directly within the Track view (see Figure 4.6), but you can also access some of them via the Track Properties dialog box (see Figure 4.7). Because you can change all of the parameters within the Track view, just using that method most of the time is easiest. The only time you might need to use the Track Properties dialog box is if you want to add a descriptive comment to a track or when you want to access the Patch browser (I'll talk more about this later). To access the Track Properties dialog box, right-click on the track you want to change and select Track Properties from the pop-up menu.

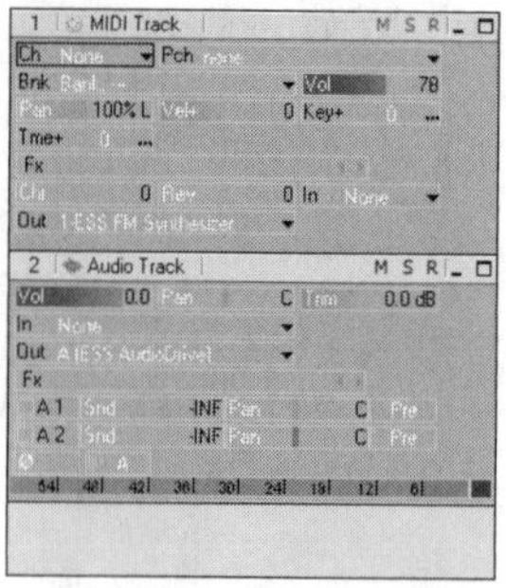

Figure 4.6
All track parameters
can be changed within
the Track view.

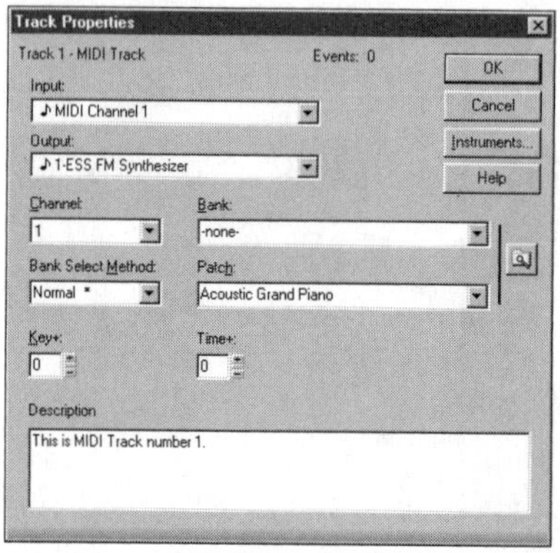

Figure 4.7
Some track parameters
are available within
the Track Properties
dialog box.

Name

To name a track, double-click within its Name field in the Track view.
Then type something and press the Enter key on your computer keyboard
when you're done. That's all there is to it. A track name can be anything
from a short, simple word like *Drums* to a longer, descriptive phrase such
as *Background Vocals (Left Channel)*.

Channel (Ch)

This parameter is for MIDI tracks only. It tells SONAR what MIDI channel
you want it to use to play back the data in a track. To change this
parameter, just click on the *Ch* drop-down list and choose a channel.

Bank (Bnk)

Also for MIDI tracks only, the bank parameter tells SONAR which bank of
sounds you want to use in your MIDI instrument. To change this
parameter, just click on the *Bnk* drop-down list and choose a bank.

Patch (Pch)

Also for MIDI tracks only, the patch parameter tells SONAR which patch
(or sound) you want to use from the bank in your MIDI instrument. To
choose a patch, click on the *Pch* drop-down list. If you've set up your
instrument definitions as described in Chapter 3, you should see the
names of the patches for your MIDI instrument in the *Pch* drop-down list.

CHAPTER 4

TIP

You can also choose patches for a track using the Patch Browser. Just right-click on the Pch parameter of a MIDI track to open the Patch Browser dialog box (see Figure 4.8).

You will see a list of all the patches available from the instrument definitions you set up earlier. To search for a particular patch, type some text into the Show Patches Containing the Text parameter. To choose a patch, select it from the list. Then click OK.

Figure 4.8
Use the Patch Browser as an alternative for assigning patches to a track.

Volume (Vol)

The volume parameter sets the initial loudness level of a track. That's basically all there is to it. You can set the volume by clicking and dragging within the *Vol* parameter. Drag to the left to lower the volume. Drag to the right to raise the volume. You can also change the volume numerically by clicking the *Vol* parameter to highlight it, pressing F2 on your computer keyboard, typing in a new value, and pressing Enter. The value can range from 0 (off) to 127 (maximum) for MIDI tracks, and −INF to +6 dB for audio tracks.

Pan (Pan)

The pan parameter determines where the sound of a track will be heard in the sound field between two stereo speakers. You can make it so the sound will play out of the left speaker, the right speaker, or anywhere in between. That is called *panning*. You can set the pan by clicking and dragging within the *Pan* parameter. Drag to the left to pan the track to the left. Drag to the right to pan the track to the right. You can also change the pan numerically by clicking the *Pan* parameter to highlight it, pressing F2 on your computer keyboard, typing in a new value, and pressing Enter. The value can range from −127 (100 percent left) to +127 (100 percent right). A value of 0 is dead center. Pan works on both MIDI and audio tracks.

Key Offset (Key+)

The key offset parameter (which works only with MIDI tracks) lets you transpose the MIDI notes in a track during playback. It doesn't change the data that's actually recorded into the track. If you know that you're going to want the notes in a track transposed after they've been recorded though, setting up this parameter in your template can be useful. To set the key offset, double-click the *Key+* parameter to activate it. Then type in a new value and press Enter. The *Key+* value can range from -127 to $+127$, with each number representing a semitone (or half-step). For example, a value of -12 would transpose the notes down an octave, and a value of +12 would transpose them up an octave. A value of 0 means no transposition will be applied.

Velocity Offset (Vel+)

The velocity offset parameter (which works only with MIDI tracks) is similar to the key offset parameter, except instead of transposing MIDI notes during playback, it raises or lowers the MIDI velocity of each note in a track by adding or subtracting a number from -127 to $+127$. Again, the data that's actually recorded into the track isn't changed. You can set the velocity offset by clicking and dragging within the *Vel+* parameter. Drag left to lower the value. Drag right to raise the value. You can also change the velocity offset numerically by clicking the *Vel+* parameter to highlight it, pressing F2 on your computer keyboard, typing in a new value, and pressing Enter.

Time Offset (Tme+)

When you record a MIDI performance in SONAR, the timing of your performance is recorded along with the notes, and so on. Each MIDI event is "stamped" with an exact start time, which is measured in measures, beats, and clock ticks. The time offset parameter is similar to key offset and velocity offset, except that it adds or subtracts an offset value to the start time of the events in a MIDI track. Just as with key offset and velocity offset, the data that's actually recorded into the track isn't changed. The offset occurs only during playback, and you can set it back to zero to hear your original performance.

The time offset is useful if you want to make a track play a little faster or slower than the rest of the tracks, in case the performance is rushed or late. To change it, just double-click on the *Tme+* parameter to activate it. Then type in the number of clock ticks by which you want the events in the track to be offset and press Enter.

Input (In)

The input parameter lets SONAR know where the data for that track is going to be recorded from, whether it be an audio track or a MIDI track. To set the Input for an audio track, choose one of the inputs from your sound card in the *In* drop-down list. For example, if you have a Sound

Blaster Live card, your choices would be Left SB Live Wave In, Right SB Live Wave In, or Stereo SB Live Wave In. If you pick either the left or right choices, that means the track would record audio from either the left or right input on your sound card. If you pick the Stereo choice, the track would record audio from both inputs at the same time, making it a stereo audio track.

Setting the input parameter for a MIDI track is a bit different. Because MIDI has sixteen different channels, you can choose to record data using any one of those channels. Just make sure that your MIDI instrument is set to the same channel that you choose as your input, or your performance won't be recorded. You can also use the MIDI Omni setting. This setting allows SONAR to record data on all sixteen channels at the same time, so no matter what channel your MIDI instrument is set on, the data coming from it will be recorded. But if you're using multiple instruments with each set to a different channel, you're better off just setting the correct channel in each of the tracks right from the start.

Output (Out)

The output parameter tells SONAR which MIDI port or sound card output you want it to use to play back the data in a track. If the track is MIDI, you can select a MIDI port from the Out drop-down list. If the track is audio, you can select a sound card output from the Out drop-down list.

> **TIP**
> You can also change the properties for multiple tracks simultaneously. Just select the tracks you would like to adjust by Ctrl-clicking or Shift-clicking the appropriate Track numbers in the Track view. Then choose Track > Property > and the property you would like to change.

Timebase

Just like all sequencing software, SONAR uses clock ticks to keep track of the timing of your MIDI performance. Most of the time, you see them as measures and beats, because the program translates the clock ticks automatically. For each measure or beat, hundreds of clock ticks occur. The number of clock ticks that happen within a beat are called *pulses per quarter note* (*PPQ*) or the *timebase*. The timebase determines the resolution or accuracy of your MIDI timing data.

For example, if you want to use eighth-note septuplets (seven eighth notes per quarter note) in your performance, you have to use a Timebase that is divisible by 7 (such as 168 PPQ); otherwise, SONAR cannot record the septuplets accurately. By default, SONAR uses a timebase of 960 PPQ, which means every quarter note is represented by 960 clock ticks. The timebase can be set anywhere from 48 to 960 PPQ. To set the timebase, follow these steps:

1. Select Options > Project to open the Project Options dialog box (see Figure 4.9).

Figure 4.9
You can set the timebase in the Project Options dialog box.

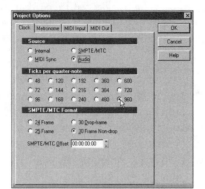

2. Click on the Clock tab.

3. Choose the timebase you would like to use from the selections in the Ticks Per Quarter-Note section.

4. Click on the OK button.

System Exclusive Banks

SONAR includes a System Exclusive (Sysx) librarian which lets you store MIDI System Exclusive messages in up to 256 banks (or storage areas). All the data in the librarian is saved along with a project. This means that each project can hold its own unique library of Sysx data. This capability can be very useful when you're putting together templates for special MIDI recording situations. Because the Sysx librarian is a significant part of SONAR, I'm going to talk about it in more detail in Chapter 14. I just wanted to be sure to mention it here so that you know that data contained in the librarian is saved along with your Template.

File Information and Comments

SONAR allows you to save description information in a project, including title, subtitle, instructions, author, copyright, keywords, and comments. This information can be useful—especially when you're creating a template—to remind yourself exactly what is contained in the file. To add information to a project, do the following:

1. Select File > Info to open the File Info window (see Figure 4.10).

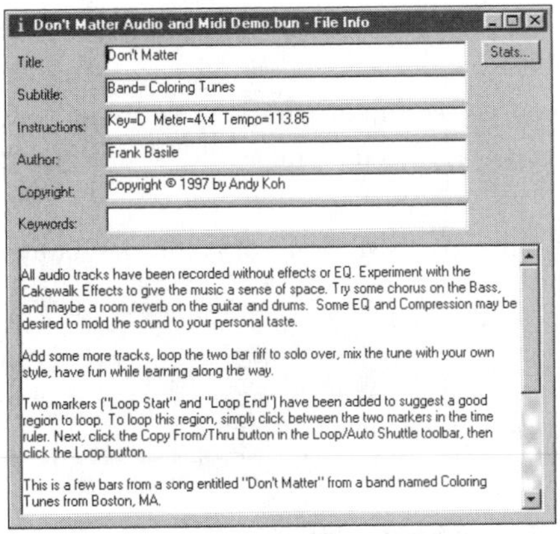

Figure 4.10
You can use the File Info window to add description information to your project or template.

2. Type the appropriate information in each of the fields. By the way, the information you enter in the Title, Subtitle, Instructions, Author, and Copyright fields will appear in the Staff view and on your music notation printouts (see Chapter 13).

3. Close the File Info window when you're finished.

The information that you entered is then included in the project or template file when you save it.

> **TIP**
>
> If you plan to share your project or template files with others, and you want them to follow special instructions you've included in the File Info window (or you just want to be sure they see your copyright notice), you can have the File Info window displayed automatically when the file is opened. Just save the project or template while the File Info window is still open.

Tempo, Meter, and Key

Every piece of music needs to have a tempo, meter (time signature), and key, so of course SONAR allows you to set and save these parameters within a project or template.

Set the Tempo

You can set the tempo for your piece like this:

1. Select View > Toolbars to make sure the Tempo Toolbar is visible (see Figure 4.11).

Figure 4.11
To set the tempo for a project, you need to use the Tempo toolbar.

2. Click on the Tempo display in the Tempo toolbar. The Tempo is then highlighted.

3. Type a new value for the tempo. The value ranges from 8.00 to 250.00. You can also use the + and − spin controls to adjust the tempo with the mouse.

4. Press the Enter key on your computer keyboard to set the tempo.

NOTE

For more information about changing the tempo in an existing project (and how that affects audio data), see Chapter 7.

Set the Meter (Time Signature) and Key (Key Signature)

Because a piece of music can have multiple time signatures and key signatures throughout, SONAR allows you to add multiple meters and keys to a project. For the purpose of creating a template, though, you'll more than likely just want to set the initial meter and key. To do so, follow these steps:

1. Select View > Meter/Key to open the Meter/Key View (see Figure 4.12).

Figure 4.12
You can add multiple time and key signatures to a project in the Meter/Key view.

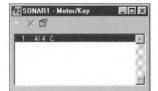

2. Double-click on the first (and for purposes of this example, the only one that should be there) Meter/Key change in the list to open the Meter/Key Signature dialog box (see Figure 4.13). Or click on the Insert button.

Figure 4.13
In the Meter/Key Signature dialog box, you can edit individual meter/key changes in the Meter/Key view.

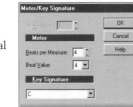

3. Enter the Beats Per Measure and the Beat Value you want to use. For example, if your song is in 6/8 time, you would change the Beats Per Measure to 6 and the Beat Value to 8.

4. Choose a key from the Key Signature drop-down list. For example, if your song is in the key of A, choose 3 Sharps (A).

5. Click on OK, and then close the Meter/Key view.

Other Parameters

A few other parameters are saved along with projects and templates, including synchronization settings, MIDI echo, metronome, record mode, and punch in/out times. But you'll usually set these parameters while you're working on a project, not beforehand. So, I'll talk more about them later in Chapter 6. For the purpose of creating a template, you can just let them be saved at their default values.

TIP

A template can also contain MIDI data and audio data. This data can be useful, for instance, if you have some favorite drum grooves or melodic phrases that you like to use frequently in your projects. Simply store these tidbits as clips in one of the tracks. When you save the template, the MIDI and/or audio data is saved along with it. Then, whenever you create a new project with that template, the MIDI and/or audio data will be ready and waiting for you to use.

Save Your Project

When it comes time to save your SONAR project, do the following:

1. Select File > Save As to open the Save As dialog box.

2. Choose the type of project file you want to save from the Save As Type drop-down list.

3. Enter a name for the file and click on the Save button.

The only thing you really have to decide (besides the name of the file) is the type of the file.

Project File Types

Projects can be saved as three different types of files: MIDI (.MID), Work (.WRK), and Bundle (.BUN).

MIDI Files

If you ever need to collaborate on a project with someone who owns a sequencing application other than SONAR, you should save your project as a MIDI (.MID) file. A MIDI file is a standard type of file that can be used to transfer musical data between different music software applications. Most music programs on the market today can load and

CHAPTER 4

save MIDI files. The problem with MIDI files, however, is that they can store only MIDI data; they can't hold audio data. And none of SONAR's settings are saved within a MIDI file either. So, if you're working on a project alone, or everyone else in your song-writing group uses SONAR, you don't need to deal with MIDI files. Of course, MIDI files can be useful in other circumstances, such as composing music for multimedia or sharing your music with others via the Internet.

Work Files

If you're working on a project that contains only MIDI data and no audio data, then you should save the project as a work (.WRK) file. Work files store all the MIDI data in a project, plus all the parameter settings (which you learned about earlier in this chapter) for the project. Work files do not store audio data.

Bundle Files

For those projects that contain both MIDI and audio data, you should save them as bundle (.BUN) files. If you use a bundle file, you can store all the data in a project (MIDI data, audio data, and project parameter settings) into a single file. Having a single file makes it very easy to keep track of all the data in a project plus make a backup of the project for easy recovery in case something goes wrong. I'll talk more about backing up your project files in Appendix B, "Backing Up Your Project Files."

TIP

SONAR has an Auto Save feature that automatically saves your data to a special backup file at fixed time intervals or every time a certain number of changes have been made to the project. Using this feature is a great way to keep your data safe in case a power outage occurs or you make a huge mistake that you can't undo. To activate Auto Save, do the following:

1. Select Options > Global to open the Global Options dialog box. Then click on the General tab.

2. For the option Auto-save Every 0 Minutes or 0 Changes, set either the number of minutes or the number of changes that need to occur between each time SONAR will do an automatic save of your project.

3. If you want to disable Auto Save, set both the minute and changes values back to zero.

4. Click on the OK button.

During an automatic save, SONAR saves your project in a special file with a different name. If your project is named "myproject.wrk," for example, SONAR does an automatic save to a file named "auto save version of myproject.wrk." If you ever need to recover your project, you can just open the special Auto Save file and then save it under the original filename.

5

Getting Around
in SONAR

CHAPTER 5

To record, play, and edit your music in SONAR, you have to know how to navigate your way through the data in your project. As you learned in Chapter 2, SONAR includes a number of tools that allow you to examine and manipulate your data. They are the Track, Piano Roll, Staff, and Event views. Although each of these views provides a different way to edit your data, they all share some common means of control. In other words, even though your data appears (and is edited) differently in each view, you access the data in a similar manner no matter what view you use. A little confused? Don't worry, you'll understand exactly what I mean after I finish describing the following topics:

▶ How to use the Now time
▶ How to use the Go menu
▶ How to set place marks in your project
▶ How to search for specific music data in your project

The Now Time

You learned a little about timing in Chapter 1 and Chapter 3. Essentially, you learned that in addition to the musical data itself, the timing of your performance is stored during recording. What this means is that SONAR keeps track of exactly when you play each note on your MIDI keyboard during a performance, and it stores those notes along with a *timestamp* (a timing value) containing the measure, beat, and clock tick when each note occurred.

To give you access to your data in a project, SONAR provides a feature known as the *Now time*. The Now time is essentially a pointer that indicates your current time location within a project. For example, the beginning of a project has a Now time of 1:01:000 (measure, beat, tick), which is the first beat of the first measure. If you want to view the data at the second beat of the tenth measure, for example, you have to set the Now time to 10:02:000. And, of course, you can get more precise by specifying clock ticks, such as in a Now time of 5:03:045, which would be the forty-fifth clock tick of the third beat in the fifth measure.

The Now time is also updated in real-time, which means that it changes constantly during recording or playback of a project. So, for example, as you play your project, the Now time counts along and shows you the current measure, beat, and tick while you listen to your music.

Show Me the Now Time

You can view the Now time in several different ways. Numerically, the Now time is displayed in the Position toolbar (see Figure 5.1).

Figure 5.1
You can view the Now time in the Position toolbar.

You can also use the Transport toolbar to view the Now time (see Figure 5.2). For more information about toolbars, see Chapter 3.

Figure 5.2
The Now time is displayed in the Transport toolbar as well.

In either toolbar, you'll notice that the Now time is shown as measures, beats, and ticks. But each toolbar has an additional numeric display. This display is also the Now time, shown as hours, minutes, seconds, and frames (known as SMPTE).

NOTE

SMPTE (which stands for the Society of Motion Picture and Television Engineers) is a special timing code used for synchronizing audio and video data, although it can be used for other purposes, too. The technology was originally developed by NASA because it needed a really accurate way to keep track of space mission data. In SONAR, you can use SMPTE to keep track of the timing of your project. SONAR automatically converts the measures, beats, and ticks in a project to the hours, minutes, seconds, and frames format used by SMPTE. The frames parameter comes from the fact that SMPTE is used extensively with video, film, and television. Video is created by recording a series of still picture frames very quickly. When these frames are played back, you see them as a moving picture. SMPTE can be used to time video data accurately right down to a single frame. Every second of video data usually has 30 frames, but the number depends on the format of the data. You'll learn more details about using SMPTE in Chapter 6. For now, just know that you can view and set the Now time of your project either in measures, beats, and ticks or in hours, minutes, seconds, and frames.

TIP

If you're like me, and you have some of your MIDI instruments set up in your home studio a fair distance away from your computer, you might have trouble reading the very tiny Now time display in either of the Position or Transport toolbars. To remedy this situation, Cakewalk has included the Big Time view in SONAR. Basically, it displays the Now time as large numbers on your computer screen (see Figure 5.3). The Big Time view has its own window, so you can position it anywhere within the SONAR workspace. You can change the size of the Big Time view by dragging any of its corners, just like you would with any window in Windows. To toggle the time format between measures, beats, ticks, and SMPTE, just click inside the Big Time view window. You can also change the font and the color of the display by right-clicking in the window and then making your selections in the standard Windows Font dialog box.

Figure 5.3
Using the Big Time view, you can display the Now time in varying fonts and sizes on your computer screen.

In addition to being displayed numerically, the Now time is displayed graphically within any of SONAR's view windows. In the Track, Piano Roll, and Staff views, the Now time is displayed as a vertical line cursor that extends from the top to the bottom of the view. As the Now time changes—either from being set manually or in real-time during playback or recording—the cursor in each of the views follows along in perfect sync and indicates graphically the place in the project the Now time is currently pointing. To demonstrate what I mean, try the following:

1. Select File > Open and load one of the sample project files that comes included with SONAR. For this example, choose 80's Rock.wrk (see Figure 5.4).

Figure 5.4
This screen shows the layout of the 80's Rock.wrk sample project.

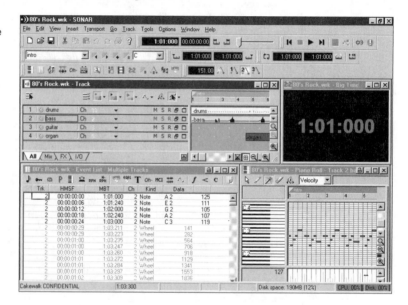

2. Select Realtime > Play or just click on the Play button in the Transport toolbar to start playing the project.

3. Look at the Track view. See the Now time cursor moving across the track display as the music plays?

4. Look at the Piano Roll view. The same thing is happening, right? Notice the row of numbers just above the place where the Now time cursor is moving; this is the Time Ruler. Every view has one (except the Event view, which I'll talk about later). The Time Ruler displays the measure numbers in the current project. By lining up the top of the Now time cursor with the Time Ruler in any of the views, you can get a quick estimate of the current Now time.

5. Look at the Event view. It's different from all the other views because it shows the data as one long list instead of displaying data from left to right. And instead of a vertical line, it shows the Now time cursor as a small red box. While a project plays, the Now time cursor in the Event view moves down the list, and it marks the same exact place in the project as all the other view cursors do. Everything is synchronized to the Now time.

Set the Now Time

As you've just seen, the Now time changes automatically as a project is played, but you can also set the Now time manually while a project isn't playing. SONAR gives you this capability so that you can access different parts of your project for editing, which I'll talk about in Chapter 7.

Numerically

Changing the Now time is easy. If you would like to set the Now time to a precise numerical value, you can simply type it into the display on the Position toolbar. Here's how:

1. If you want to set the Now time using measures, beats, and ticks, click on the measures, beats, and ticks display in the Position toolbar. The display becomes highlighted (see Figure 5.5).

Figure 5.5
You can change the Now time by clicking on the display to highlight it.

2. Type the measures, beats, and ticks value you want to use, and press Enter on your computer keyboard.

TIP

If you want to quickly set the Now time to a particular measure or beat, you don't have to enter all the numerical values. For example, to set the Now time to measure two, type 2. That's it. Or to set the Now time to measure five, beat three, type 5:3 or 5 spacebar 3. To specify ticks, you must enter something for all the values.

3. If you want to set the Now time using hours, minutes, seconds, and frames, click on the SMPTE display in the Position toolbar. The display then becomes highlighted (see Figure 5.6).

Figure 5.6
You can change the
Now time by specifying
SMPTE time code
values, too.

4. Type the hours, minutes, seconds, and frames value you want to use and press Enter on your computer keyboard.

> **TIP**
>
> Just as with the measures, beats, and ticks, if you want to quickly set the Now time to a particular hour, minute, or second, you don't have to enter all the numerical values. For example, to set the Now time to two minutes, type 0:2. That's it. Or to set the Now time to five minutes, three seconds, type 0:5:3. To specify frames, you must enter something for all the values.

Graphically

Remember when I described the Time Rulers in each of the views in the "The Now Time Cursor" section? Well, you can quickly change the Now time by simply clicking on any of the Time Rulers. For example, you can do the following:

1. As you did earlier, select File > Open and load one of the sample project files that comes included with SONAR. For this example, choose 80's Rock.wrk.

2. Click on the Time Ruler in the Track view. See how the Now time changes?

3. Click on the Time Ruler in the Piano Roll view. Same result, right? Depending on where you click on the Time Ruler, the Now time changes to the appropriate value within the measure that you click.

TIP

You might notice that when you click on the Time Ruler in any of the views, the Now time is automatically set to the first beat of the nearest measure. This happens because of SONAR's Snap to Grid feature. Snap to Grid automatically snaps the Now time cursor to the nearest predefined value when you try to set it via a Time Ruler. This feature makes it easy to do quick and precise settings. Without Snap to Grid, setting the Now time accurately using a Time Ruler can be difficult.

Each view (except the Event view) in SONAR has its own separate Snap to Grid, but the feature is set in the same manner no matter which view you're using. To activate or deactivate the Snap to Grid in a view, just click on the Snap to Grid button (see Figure 5.7). To set a Snap to Grid interval, right-click on the Snap to Grid button to display the Snap to Grid dialog box (see Figure 5.8). Now select a resolution by choosing a note duration from the list, typing a time value to use, or selecting a standard resolution such as events, markers, or clip boundaries. After you're finished setting the Snap to Grid, click on the Time Ruler, and you'll notice that the Now time cursor snaps to the resolution that you've chosen.

Figure 5.7
The Snap to Grid button controls whether the Snap to Grid feature is on or off.

Figure 5.8
You can set the Snap to Grid via the Snap to Grid dialog box.

4. As before, the Event view works a little differently. Here, you can simply click on any event in the list, and the Now time changes to the exact timing value of that event.

The Position Slider

Another quick way to set the Now time graphically is to use the Position slider. The slider is part of the Position toolbar (see Figure 5.9). To use the slider, just click and drag it. Also, if you click to the left or right of the slider, the Now Time updates one measure at a time. That's it.

Figure 5.9
You can drag the Position Slider left or right to decrease or increase the Now time, respectively.

The Go Menu

In addition to allowing you to set the Now time numerically and graphically, SONAR provides a few special functions that let you quickly change the Now time to some musically related points in a project. All these functions are a part of the Go menu. To activate them, simply select the Go menu and choose the appropriate function. Following is a list of the functions along with explanations for each of them:

Go-Time

Go-Time allows you to change the Now time numerically by entering a measure, beat, and tick value. It works in exactly the same way as the measure, beat, and tick display in the Position toolbar. The only difference is that Go-Time opens a dialog box.

Go-From and Go-Thru

When editing data in SONAR, you first need to select the data that you want to work with. It's the same as in any computer program that lets you work with data. For instance, if you want to delete some text in a word processor, you first select the data to highlight it, and then you delete it.

Well, if you have some data in your project currently selected, you can quickly set the Now time to the time that corresponds with the beginning (called the From time) or the end (called the Thru time) of the selection using the Go-From and Go-Thru functions, respectively. You'll learn more details about selecting data in Chapter 7.

Go-Beginning and Go-End

The Go-Beginning and Go-End functions are pretty self-explanatory. Simply put, they allow you to set the Now time to the time that corresponds with the beginning or the end of a project.

Go-Previous Measure and Go-Next Measure

As with Go-Beginning and Go-End, Go-Previous Measure and Go-Next Measure are self-explanatory. They let you quickly set the Now time to the time that corresponds to the first beat of the previous measure or the first beat of the next measure relative to the current Now time. In other words, if the Now time is set at 5:01:000 (beat one of measure five), selecting Go-Previous Measure changes it to 4:01:000 (beat one of measure four), and selecting Go-Next Measure changes it to 6:01:000 (beat one of measure six).

NOTE

If the Now time is set to something like 5:01:050, Go-Previous Measure actually changes it to the first beat of the current measure, which in this case would be 5:01:000. I'm not sure why, but that's how it works.

Go-Previous Marker and Go-Next Marker

The Go-Previous Marker and Go-Next Marker functions work in a similar manner as the Go-Previous Measure and Go-Next Measure functions. Go-Previous Marker and Go-Next Marker let you quickly set the Now time to the time that corresponds to the closest previous marker or next marker relative to the current Now time. Of course, because I haven't told you about markers yet, you're probably wondering what I mean. So, let's talk about markers, shall we?

Markers, Oh My!

All the methods for setting the Now time that I've described so far have either been based on numbers or predefined musical designations such as measures, beats, or the beginning and ending of a project. These methods are all fine when you already have the music for your project written out so you know exactly where everything occurs ahead of time, but what if you're creating a song from scratch simply by recording the parts on the fly? In a case like that, being able to put names to certain locations within a project would be very helpful, and that's exactly what markers allow you to do.

With markers, you can assign a name to any exact point in time (in either measures, beats, and ticks or SMPTE) in a project. They're great for designating the places where the verses and choruses start and end within a song. And they make it very easy for you to jump to any point within a project that you specify simply by name.

Make Your Mark(ers)

Creating markers is a simple process. Essentially, you just need to set the Now time to the measure, beat, and tick at which you want to place the marker in the project, activate the marker dialog box, and type in a name. Activating the marker dialog box is the key here, because you can do so in a number of different ways. To create a marker, you just do the following:

1. Set the Now time to the measure, beat, and tick or the SMPTE time at which you want to place the marker in the project. As you learned earlier, you can set it either numerically or graphically.

2. Select Insert > Marker to open the Marker dialog box (see Figure 5.10). You can also open the Marker dialog box by pressing F11 on your computer keyboard; holding the Ctrl key on your computer keyboard and clicking just above the Time Ruler (the Marker section) in the Track, Staff, or Piano Roll views; right-clicking in a Time Ruler; clicking on the Insert Marker button in the Markers toolbar; or clicking on the Insert Marker button in the Markers view. (I'll describe the Markers toolbar and view later in this chapter.)

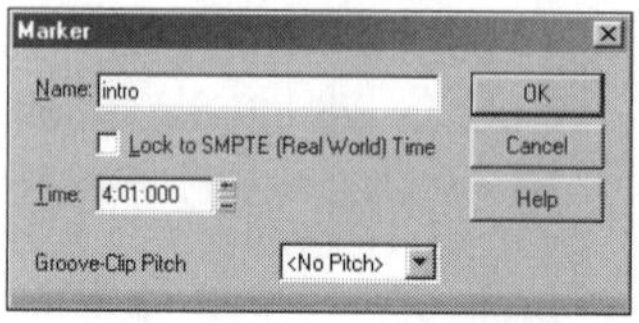

Figure 5.10
Using the Marker dialog box, you can create a marker.

Marker	☒
Name: intro	OK
☐ Lock to SMPTE (Real World) Time	Cancel
Time: 4:01:000 ⬍	Help
Groove-Clip Pitch <No Pitch> ▾	

3. Type a name for the marker.

4. If you want the marker to be assigned to a measure/beat/tick value, you don't need to do anything more. The measure/beat/tick time of the marker is shown in the middle of the Marker dialog box.

5. If you want the marker to be assigned to a SMPTE time, activate the Lock To SMPTE (Real World) Time option.

NOTE

If you use the Lock To SMPTE (Real World) Time value, your marker is assigned an exact hour/minute/second/frame value. It retains that value no matter what. So, even if you change the tempo of the project, the marker keeps the same time value, although its measure/beat/tick location may change because of the tempo. This feature is especially handy when you're putting music and sound to video, when you need to have cues that always happen at an exact moment within the project.

By leaving a marker assigned to a measure/beat/tick value, however, you can be sure that it will always occur at that measure, beat, and tick even if you change the tempo of the project.

6. Click on OK.

When you're finished, your marker (with its name) is added to the marker section, just above the Time Ruler in the Track, Staff, and Piano Roll views.

> **TIP**
>
> Usually, you add markers to a project while no real-time activity is going on, but you can also add markers while a project is playing. Simply press the F11 key on your computer keyboard, and SONAR creates a marker at the current Now time. The new marker is automatically assigned a temporary name, which you can later change.

Edit the Markers

Editing existing markers is just as easy as creating new ones. You can change their names and times, make copies of them, and delete them.

Name Change

To change the name of a marker, follow these steps:

1. Right-click on the marker in the Marker section of the Time Ruler in one of the views to open the Marker dialog box. Alternatively, select View > Markers to open the Markers view (see Figure 5.11) and double-click on the marker in the list to open the Marker dialog box.

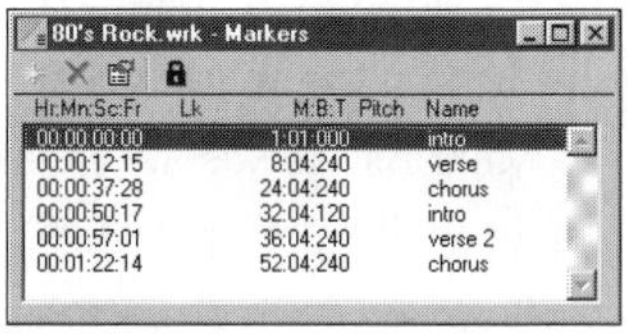

Figure 5.11
The Markers view displays a list of all the markers in a project.

Hr:Mn:Sc:Fr	Lk	M:B:T	Pitch	Name
00:00:00:00		1:01:000		intro
00:00:12:15		8:04:240		verse
00:00:37:28		24:04:240		chorus
00:00:50:17		32:04:120		intro
00:00:57:01		36:04:240		verse 2
00:01:22:14		52:04:240		chorus

2. Type a new name for the marker.
3. Click on OK.

Time Change

Follow these steps to change the time value of a marker numerically:

1. Right-click on the marker in the Marker section of the Time Ruler in one of the views to open the Marker dialog box. Alternatively, select View > Markers to open the Markers view and double-click on the marker in the list to open the Marker dialog box.
2. Type a new measure/beat/tick value for the marker. If you want to use an SMPTE value, activate the Lock To SMPTE (Real World) Time option and then type a new hour/minute/second/frame value for the marker.
3. Click on OK.

You can also change the time value of a marker graphically by simply dragging the marker within the Marker section of the Time Ruler in one of the views with your mouse. Drag the marker to the left to decrease its time value or drag it to the right to increase its time value. Simple, no?

Make a Copy

To make a copy of a marker, follow these steps:

1. Hold down the Ctrl key on your computer keyboard.
2. Click and drag a marker in the Marker section of the Time Ruler in one of the views to a new time location.
3. Release the Ctrl key and mouse button. SONAR displays the marker dialog box.
4. Enter a name for the marker. You can also change the time by typing a new value, if you'd like. The time value is initially set to the time corresponding to the location on the Time Ruler to which you dragged the marker.
5. Click on OK.

Delete a Marker

You can delete a marker in one of two ways, either directly in the Track, Staff, or Piano Roll views or via the Marker view. Here's the exact procedure:

1. If you want to use the Track, Staff, or Piano Roll views, click and hold the left mouse button on the marker that you want to delete.
2. If you want to use the Markers view, select View > Markers to open the Markers view. Then select the marker that you want to delete from the list.
3. Press the Delete key on your computer keyboard.

TIP

To prevent your markers from being edited, you can lock them into position. Just open the Markers view, select the marker or markers you want to lock, and click on the Lock button (the button with the picture of a little lock on it). To unlock a marker, the procedure is the same.

Navigate with Markers

Of course, what good would creating markers do you if you couldn't use them to navigate through the data in your project? What's more, all you need to do is select the name of a marker, and the Now time is automatically set to the exact time of that marker. You can jump to a specific marker in a project in two different ways: either by using the Markers view or the Markers toolbar.

Use the Markers View

To jump to a specific marker using the Markers view, do the following:

1. Select View > Markers to open the Markers view.

2. Select the marker that you want to jump to from the list. SONAR then sets the Now time to the time corresponding to that marker, and the Track, Staff, Piano Roll, and Event views jump to that time.

Use the Markers Toolbar

To jump to a specific marker using the Markers toolbar, just select the marker from the Markers toolbar drop-down list (see Figure 5.12).

Figure 5.12
Using the Markers toolbar, you can quickly set the Now time to any marker by simply selecting a name from a list.

SONAR sets the Now time to the time corresponding to that marker, and the Track, Staff, Piano Roll, and Event views jump to that time.

> **TIP**
>
> One other quick way to jump to a specific marker in a project is to select the Now time in the Position toolbar and then press the F5 key on your computer keyboard to bring up a list of all the markers in the current project. Select a marker from the list and click on OK. The Now time is automatically set to the time corresponding to that marker.

Where, Oh Where?

Until now, I have been describing how to navigate through the data in a project by somehow specifying the Now time, with the result being that you go to a specific point within the project. Well, what happens when you don't know the exact position in a project you want to move to? For instance, out of all the data in all the tracks in your project, suppose you need to set the Now time to the first occurrence of the note middle C? Instead of playing the project and trying to listen for the note, or looking through each and every track manually, you can use SONAR's Go-Search function.

CHAPTER 5

Go-Search allows you to automatically examine all the data in your project and find any MIDI events that have certain attributes that you specify. Upon finding the first event of the specified type, Go-Search sets the Now time to the time corresponding with that event. This function is very useful for finding significant points within a project and placing markers there or for precision editing tasks, which (as you've probably guessed by now) you'll learn more about later in Chapter 8. In the meantime, you can find specific MIDI events using the Go-Search function like this:

1. Select Go > Beginning to set the Now time to the beginning of the project. If you don't take this step, Go-Search begins looking at your data starting at the current Now time, not at the beginning of the project. This means that if the Now time is currently set to 10:01:000, Go-Search does not look at any of the data contained in the first nine measures.

2. Select Go > Search to open the Event Filter–Search dialog box (see Figure 5.13).

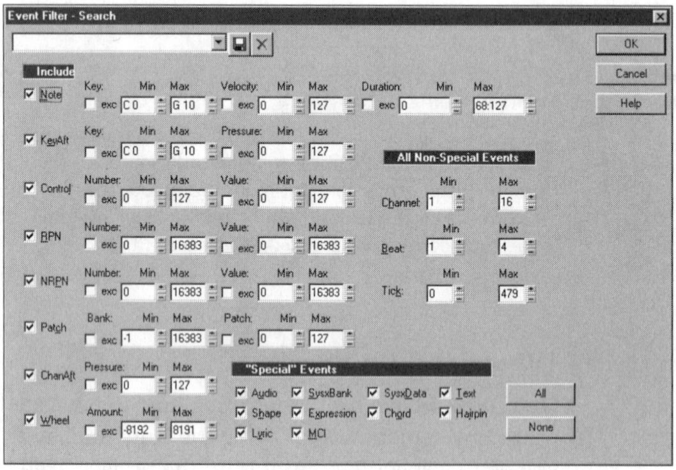

Figure 5.13
In the Event Filter–Search dialog box, you specify the criteria for your search.

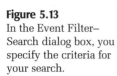

3. Select the criteria for your search. Don't let all the settings in the Event Filter–Search dialog box intimidate you. They aren't very complicated to use. Basically, all you need to do is select the types of MIDI events that you would like to include in your search. For instance, if you want to look for MIDI note and pitch wheel events (but nothing else), deselect all the event types except for note and wheel.

TIP

By the way, whenever you open the Event Filter–Search dialog box, it automatically has all event types selected. To quickly deselect all event types, click on the None button. The All button does the exact opposite.

After you select all your event types, you need to set the ranges for each of the parameters. For example, say you want to look for any MIDI note events between the pitches of C5 and G7 and with a velocity between 50 and 80. To do so, simply set the Note Key minimum parameter to C5, the Note Key maximum to G7, the Note Velocity minimum parameter to 50, and the Note Velocity maximum parameter to 80. You can also specify a range of durations (note length) if you'd like. Each event type has its own unique set of parameter ranges: Key aftertouch has key and pressure parameters, patch change has bank and patch number parameters, and so on. You can also set up searches that are a little more complicated by excluding ranges of parameters. If you select the Exclude option next to any of the parameter range settings, the search excludes event types with that specific parameter range. For example, if you want to search for MIDI note events that do not fall within the range of C5 and G7, you set up the minimum and maximum parameters, as in the earlier example, and you activate the Key Exclude option.

Using the Event Filter–Search dialog box, you can specify "Special" Events, too, such as Audio, System Exclusive, Text, and Chord events. These "Special" Events don't include any additional parameter settings, though, so Go-Search simply finds any events of that kind within the data of your project. And lastly, you can choose to set a range of MIDI channels, beats, or ticks to search within. They are called Non-Special Events.

TIP

Because setting these search criteria every time you need to find specific data in a project can be tedious, it would be nice if you could save the settings for future use, wouldn't it? Well, you can. Just type a name in the Preset box at the top of the Event Filter–Search dialog box and click on the Save button (the button with the little disk icon on it). All your current search criteria settings are then saved under that name. The next time you use Go-Search, you can simply select the name from the Preset box drop-down list, and all your previous settings will be loaded. You can save as many Presets as you'd like, and if you ever want to delete one, just select it from the list and click on the Delete button (the button with the red X on it).

4.   Click on OK.

CHAPTER 5

SONAR searches through the data in your project, finds the first event that falls under the search parameters that you specified, and then sets the Now time to the time that corresponds to that event. If you want to quickly apply that same search again to find the next event with the same criteria, select Go > Search Next. SONAR continues the search (beginning at the current Now time), finds the next event that falls under the search parameters you specified, and then sets the Now time to the time that corresponds to that event, and so on. Here's another fact you should be aware of: If you first select some of the data in your project, the search is conducted only on that selected data, not all the data in the project.

The Go-Search Challenge

So, do you think that you now have a good understanding of how the Go-Search function works? To test you on what you've learned, I've put together a little search challenge. First, read the challenge, and then see whether you can set up the Event Filter–Search dialog options appropriately. When you think you've got it, take a look at the answer to see how you did.

A Simple Search

Find the first MIDI note event in the project that falls between the pitches of F4 and D7 and that has a velocity between 40 and 70. Also, restrict the search to MIDI Channel 2 only.

Here's the answer:

1. Select Go > Beginning to set the Now time to the beginning of the project.

2. Select Go > Search to open the Event Filter–Search dialog box.

3. Click on the None button to clear all settings.

4. Select the MIDI note event type.

5. Set the Note Key minimum parameter to F4.

6. Set the Note Key maximum parameter to D7.

7. Set the Note Velocity minimum parameter to 40.

8. Set the Note Velocity maximum parameter to 70.

9. Set the Non-Special Event Channel minimum parameter to 2.

10. Set the Non-Special Event Channel maximum parameter to 2.

11. Click on OK.

Did you get it right? If so, congratulations! I threw that MIDI channel restriction in there to make it a little more confusing. Setting both the minimum and maximum Channel parameters to the same number restricts the search to that MIDI channel. In this case, it was 2. If you didn't get quite the right settings, don't worry. With a little practice, you'll be able to easily master this feature.

6

Recording
and Playback

In this chapter, you get to the meat and potatoes (or the beans and rice, if you're a vegetarian) portion of the product—the main ingredient in the SONAR recipe, so to speak. Being able to record and play your music with SONAR turns your computer into a full-fledged recording studio. Without these features, SONAR would just be a glorified music data editor/processor. So, if you're going to memorize one chapter in the book, this should be it. You'll probably use the recording and playback features of SONAR most often. Therefore, I'm going to devote separate sections of the chapter to each way you can possibly record data in SONAR. The topics include the following:

▶ Reviewing the parameters that need to be set prior to recording

▶ Learning how to record and play MIDI tracks

▶ Learning how to record and play audio tracks

▶ Learning how to record multiple tracks at once

▶ Recording new tracks automatically using looping

▶ Correcting mistakes using punch in and punch out

▶ Recording MIDI one note at a time

▶ Using importing instead of recording

▶ Learning what synchronization is and how to use it

Preliminary Parameters

In Chapter 4, you learned about a number of parameters you can save to define a project template. Some of those parameters are related to recording, including track parameters, timebase, tempo, meter, and key. I'll mention these parameters throughout this chapter, but I won't go into detail on how to change them. If you need to refresh your memory, take a look at Chapter 4 again.

In addition to these parameters, you need to be aware of a few others before doing any recording in SONAR. I didn't describe them in Chapter 4 because you usually set these parameters while working on a project, not beforehand when creating a template.

Metronome

If you've ever taken music lessons, you know what a *metronome* is. It's a device that makes a sound for each beat in each measure of a piece of music. You simply set the tempo you want, and the metronome sounds each beat accurately and precisely. You use this device to help you play in time with the correct rhythm. In SONAR, the metronome feature helps you to keep the right time so that your music data is stored at the right measure and beat within the project.

The metronome feature in SONAR is electronic (of course), and it's a bit more sophisticated than what you might find in a handheld unit. First of all, the tempo for the metronome is the same as the tempo setting for the project, so when you set the project tempo, you're also setting the metronome tempo. Normally, you would just have to turn the metronome on and off, but in SONAR, you need to set several other parameters before using the metronome feature. You can access these parameters by selecting Options > Project to open the Project Options dialog box and then clicking on the Metronome tab (see Figure 6.1).

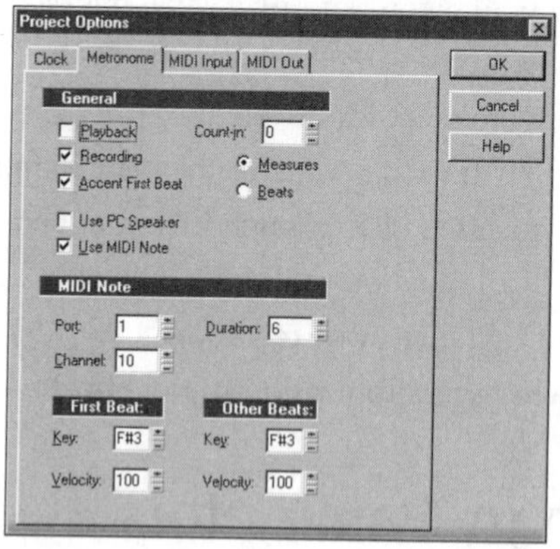

Figure 6.1
In the Project Options dialog box, you can access the metronome parameters.

General

In the General section of the Project Options dialog box, you can determine whether the metronome will sound during playback, recording, or both by activating the Playback and Recording options. The Accent First Beat option determines whether the metronome will sound the first beat of each measure a little louder than the others. You can also select whether the metronome will use your computer's built-in speaker or one of your MIDI instruments to make its sound by activating the Use PC Speaker or Use MIDI Note options (I'll talk more about this last option shortly). You have to activate one of them; otherwise, the metronome won't make any sound at all.

Count-in

Using the Count-in option in the General section, you can get the feel of the tempo before SONAR starts recording your performance. Depending on how you set it, the metronome will sound a number of beats or measures before recording begins. For example, if your project is set for a 4/4 meter, and you set the Count-in option to 1 Measures, the metronome will sound four beats before SONAR begins recording.

MIDI Note

If you select the Use MIDI Note option in the General section of the Project Options dialog box, the settings in the MIDI Note section determine which MIDI instrument is used to make the metronome sound and which note is used for the first beat and remaining beats of each measure. The settings are reasonably self-explanatory. Using Port and Channel, you can set the MIDI port and channel that your MIDI instrument uses. Duration determines how long each metronome "beep" will sound. The duration is measured in ticks, so if you use the default timebase of 120 ticks per quarter note, a duration of 15 would be equivalent to a thirty-second note.

You can set the pitch (key) and loudness (velocity) of the first beat and remaining beats in each measure by using the First Beat and Other Beats options. If you want the first beat of each measure to be accented, you should set the velocity a little higher in the First Beat Velocity option. For example, you could set it to 127 and set the Other Beats Velocity to 110. Also, if your MIDI instrument is General MIDI-compatible and you set the Channel option to 10, you can use a percussion instrument for the metronome sound. I like to use a rimshot sound.

MIDI Echo

Some MIDI instruments do not provide any way for you to play them (such as a built-in keyboard) except by sending them MIDI messages. These instruments are called modules. To play a module, you need to trigger the module's sounds by playing another instrument, such as a MIDI keyboard. By connecting the MIDI Out from the MIDI keyboard to the MIDI In of the module, you can play the sounds in the module by performing on the keyboard.

CHAPTER 6

But what if you want to record your performance using SONAR? In this case, you would have to connect the MIDI Out from the keyboard to the MIDI In of your computer. This means you would no longer be sending MIDI messages from the keyboard to the module, so how would you hear your performance? You could connect the MIDI Out from your computer to the MIDI In of the module, but the MIDI messages from the keyboard would still go directly to the computer and not the module. To remedy this situation, SONAR includes a feature called MIDI echo.

Basically, MIDI echo takes the MIDI messages from your computer's MIDI input(s) and sends the messages back out to your computer's MIDI output(s). You can control which MIDI channels the data is echoed from and which ports and channels the data is echoed to. You can access these parameters by selecting Options > Project to open the Project Options dialog box and then clicking on the MIDI Input tab (see Figure 6.2).

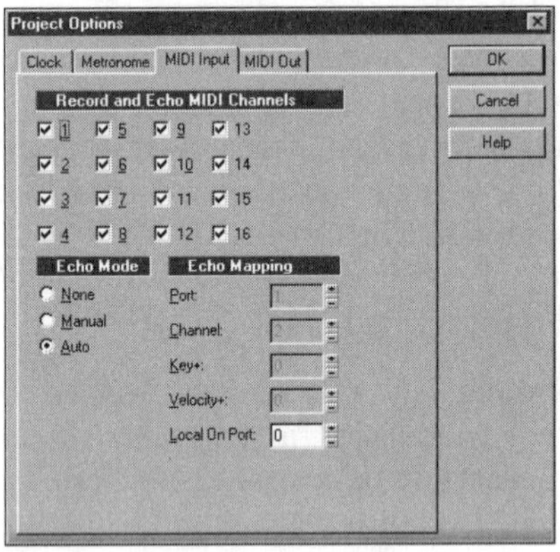

Figure 6.2
In the Project Options dialog box, you also can access the MIDI echo parameters.

Record and Echo MIDI Channels

In the Record and Echo MIDI Channels section of the Project Options dialog box, you can choose which MIDI channels data will be echoed from. You usually should just keep all the channels activated, because these options also control which MIDI channels you can record data from. For example, if you deactivate option 1, you cannot record data from MIDI Channel 1.

Echo Mode and Echo Mapping

If you don't want to use MIDI echo, select None in the Echo Mode section of the dialog box. If you want to specify which port and channel the incoming data will be echoed to, select Manual and then make your settings in the Echo Mapping section. More than likely, you'll want to leave the Echo Mode set to Auto, though. In this mode, the port and channel to which the currently selected track in the Track view are set determine which port and channel the MIDI data is echoed to. Using

Auto works out to be easier, because you might have a number of different modules in your studio. Instead of manually changing the MIDI echo settings each time you want to work with a different module, you can have them changed automatically simply by setting up a new track in the Track view.

NOTE

One other MIDI echo option is rarely needed, but you should be aware of it. It's the Local On Port option. When you use one MIDI instrument (master) to play another (slave), pressing a key on the master instrument not only plays a sound on the slave, but also on the master. Most of the time, you'll want only the slave instrument to make sounds. To remedy this situation, you can turn off the sounds in the master instrument by using the Local On feature. All modern instruments have it. SONAR attempts to automatically set this feature every time you start it up, but sometimes it might not work (especially if you have an older instrument). If your instrument doesn't support the Local On feature, you can set the Local On Port option to block MIDI echo for a specified MIDI Port. I doubt that you'll have to use this option, so you can just keep it set to zero, unless you run across the double-note problem.

Sampling Rate and Bit Depth

You learned about the meanings of the terms *sampling rate* and *bit depth* in Chapter 1. SONAR lets you set the sampling rate and bit depth used for the audio data that you record. Depending on the sophistication of your sound card, you can set the sampling rate up to 96,000 Hz and the bit depth up to 24-bit.

So what settings should you use? Well, the higher the sampling rate and bit depth, the better the quality of your recorded audio. Higher settings also put more strain on your computer system, however, and the data take up more memory and hard disk space. Plus, if your input signal is already bad (if you use a low-end microphone to record your vocals, for instance), higher settings won't make it sound any better.

In my opinion, if your computer has enough power, memory, and hard disk space, then you should use the highest settings your sound card will support. Using these settings will ensure that you get the best-quality recording. The only problem to watch out for is if you plan to put your music on CD. In that case, the audio needs to have a sampling rate of 44,100 Hz and a bit depth of 16-bit.

CHAPTER 6

NOTE

In order to store music on a CD, the audio data is required to have a sampling rate of 44,100 Hz and a bit depth of 16. These values cannot be higher or lower. They must be exact. Of course, you can start off by recording your audio with different settings. For example, if your computer has a limited amount of memory or hard disk space, you may want to use smaller values. I wouldn't recommend this, though, unless it's absolutely necessary, because lower values mean lower quality audio. You can also record using higher values, which actually raises the quality of your audio data. When it comes time to put the audio on CD, however, you must convert the sampling rate and bit depth to the values mentioned above.

Using SONAR's Change Audio Format feature, you can convert the bit depth of the audio in your project. Just select Tools > Change Audio Format to access it. Unfortunately, the Change Audio Format feature only lets you convert between 16- and 24-bit. For any other bit depth values (and to convert the sampling rate) you will need to use a separate digital audio editing application, such as Sonic Foundry's Sound Forge (**www.sonicfoundry.com**), Syntrillium's Cool Edit (**www.syntrillium.com**), or Steinberg's WaveLab (**www.steinberg.net**).

To access these parameters, select Options > Audio to open the Audio Options dialog box and then click on the General tab (see Figure 6.3).

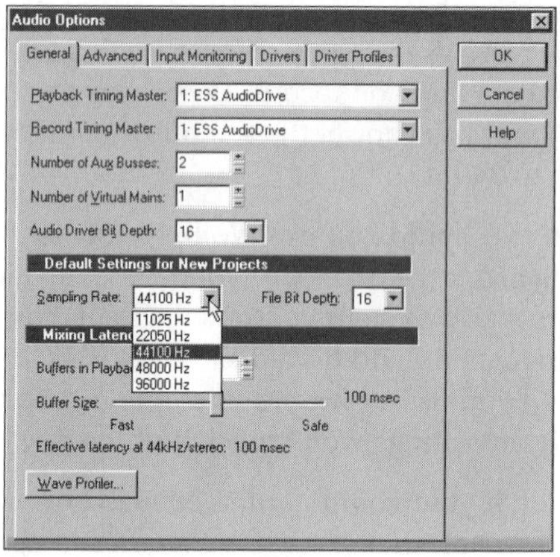

Figure 6.3
In the Audio Options dialog box, you can access the sampling rate and file bit depth parameters.

In the Default Settings for New Projects section, you can make your selections in the Sampling Rate and File Bit Depth drop-down lists.

Input Monitoring

When recording an audio track, you usually want to listen to your performance as it's being recorded. In the past, due to the limitations of sound card drivers, you would be able to listen only to the "dry" version of your performance. This means that you would have to listen to your performance without any effects applied. With the input monitoring feature, however, SONAR allows you to listen to your performance with effects applied as it's being recorded. This can be especially useful, for example, when recording vocals where it's customary to let the singer hear a little echo or reverberation during his or her performance. If you're not sure what I'm talking about, don't worry. I'll cover effects in more detail in Chapter 11.

To activate input monitoring for your sound card, choose Options > Audio to open the Audio Options dialog box. Then click the Input Monitoring tab (see Figure 6.4).

Figure 6.4
In the Audio Options dialog box, you can activate input monitoring for your sound card.

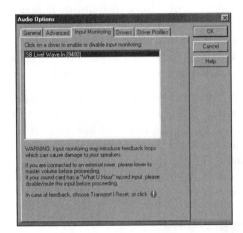

To activate input monitoring for your sound card(s), just select the driver(s) in the list. Then click OK.

CAUTION

Input monitoring may cause a feedback loop between your sound card input(s) and output(s). This happens, for example, when the signal coming out of a speaker is fed back into a microphone and the sound keeps looping and building up into a very loud signal. This feedback looping can damage your speakers. To be safe, you might want to turn the volume down on your speaker system before you activate input monitoring. If you hear feedback, deactivate input monitoring by clicking Input Monitoring tab in the Audio Options box and then clicking on the driver.

For a possible solution to your feedback problem, check the Windows Mixer settings for your sound card. Some sound cards have a monitoring feature that should be turned off when you are using input monitoring. For instance, if you have a Sound Blaster Live card, open the Record Controls in the Windows Mixer and make sure you are not using the "What U Hear" option as your recording input.

CHAPTER 6

Record Mode

When you record MIDI or audio data into an empty track, SONAR simply places that data into the track within a new clip. (In Chapter 2, you learned how SONAR stores data as events, which are stored within clips, which in turn are stored within tracks.) When you record data into a track that already contains data, what happens to that existing data?

SONAR provides two different recording modes (actually, there are three, but I'll talk about Auto Punch later in the chapter), both of which provide a different means of dealing with existing data. The Sound on Sound mode mixes the new data with the existing data. So, for example, if you record a vocal part into a track that already contains music, you hear both the vocal and the music when you play back that track. The Overwrite mode replaces the existing data with the new data. So, in this example, the music is erased, and the vocal takes its place. Then, when you try to play the Track, you hear only the vocal.

Keep in mind that you need to deal with recording modes only when you're recording data into a track that already contains data. More than likely, you won't be doing that very much because SONAR allows you to record an unlimited number of tracks, and you can easily place each part of your song on a separate track. If you do need to set the recording mode, however, just select Transport > Record Options to open the Record Options dialog box (see Figure 6.5).

Figure 6.5
In the Record Options dialog box, you can set the recording mode.

In the Recording Mode section, select either Sound on Sound or Overwrite and click on OK.

MIDI Track Recording and Playback

Believe it or not, you now have the knowledge needed to start recording in SONAR. Nothing is really complicated about the process, but you should follow a number of steps to make sure that everything occurs smoothly. Here and in the following sections, I'll show you step by step how to record MIDI tracks, audio tracks, and multiple tracks at once. First, let's tackle MIDI tracks. To get started, do the following:

1. Create a new project or open an existing one. If you use a template to create a new project, you might be able to skip some of the following steps, but you should probably run through them anyway, just in case.

2. Set the meter and key signature for the project. The default settings are 4/4 and the key of C Major.

3. Set the metronome and tempo parameters. The default tempo for a new project is 100 beats per minute.

4. Set the timebase for the project. The default setting is 960 PPQ (pulses per quarter note). More often than not, you won't have to change this setting.

5. Set the recording mode. Unless you plan to record data to a track that already contains data, you can skip this step. The default recording mode is Sound on Sound.

6. Add a new MIDI track to the Track view and adjust the track's properties. For more information about track properties and how to set them, refer to Chapter 4.

7. Arm the track for recording to let SONAR know that you want to record data on the track. Right after the name parameter in the Track view, you'll see three buttons labeled M, S, and R. Click on the R button to arm the track for recording (see Figure 6.6).

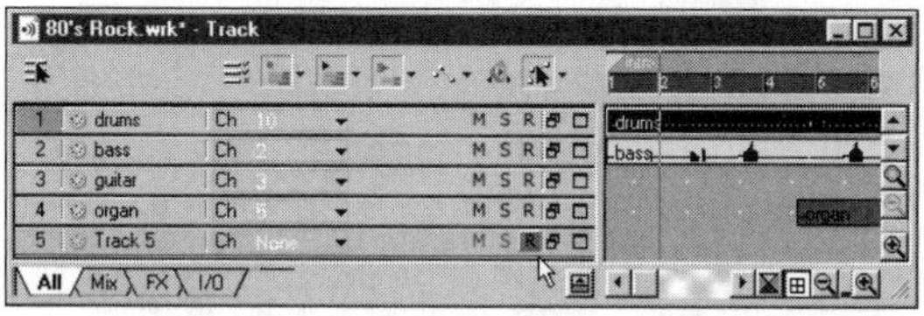

Figure 6.6
You arm a track for recording by clicking on its associated R button in the Track view.

8. Set the Now time to the point in the project where you would like the recording to begin. Most of the time, it will be the very beginning of the project, but SONAR provides the flexibility of letting you record data to a track starting at any measure, beat, or tick within a project.

9. Select Transport > Record to start recording. (You can also press the R key on your computer keyboard or click on the Record button in the Transport toolbar.) If you set a Count-in, the metronome will first count the number of beats you entered, and then SONAR will begin recording.

10. Perform the material you want to record.

CHAPTER 6

11. After you finish performing, select Transport > Stop to stop recording. (You can also press the spacebar on your computer keyboard or click on the Stop button in the Transport toolbar.) SONAR creates a new clip in the track containing the MIDI data you just recorded (see Figure 6.7).

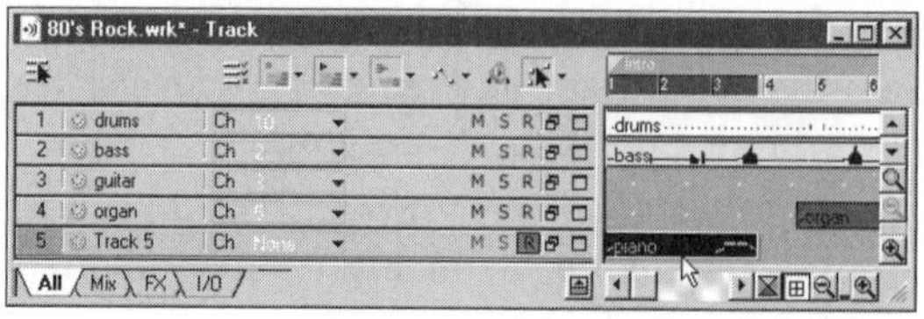

Figure 6.7
After you've finished recording, SONAR creates a new clip in the track representing the MIDI data.

12. Listen to your performance by setting the Now time back to its original position and selecting Transport > Play. (You can also press the spacebar on your computer keyboard or click on the Play button in the Transport toolbar.) If you don't like the performance, you can erase it by selecting Edit > Undo Recording. Then go back to Step 8, and try recording again.

NOTE

SONAR provides an Undo feature that allows you to reverse any action that you take while working on a project. You're probably familiar with this feature, because it can be found in most applications that allow you to manipulate data, such as word processing software and so on. SONAR goes a bit further, however, by providing an Undo History feature. This feature logs every step you take while working on a project and allows you to undo each step all the way back to the beginning of your current session. The Undo History is not saved, though, so as soon as you close a project, you lose the ability to undo any changes. To access the Undo History, just select Edit > History to open the Undo History dialog box (see Figure 6.8). You then see a list of all the tasks you've done during the current session. To go back to a certain point in the session, just select a task in the list and click on OK. SONAR undoes any tasks performed after the task you selected. SONAR can keep track of as many as 2,147,483,647 tasks, the maximum number of which you can set in the Maximum Undo Levels parameter of the Undo History dialog box. Remember, though, the more tasks SONAR keeps track of, the more memory and hard disk space it needs.

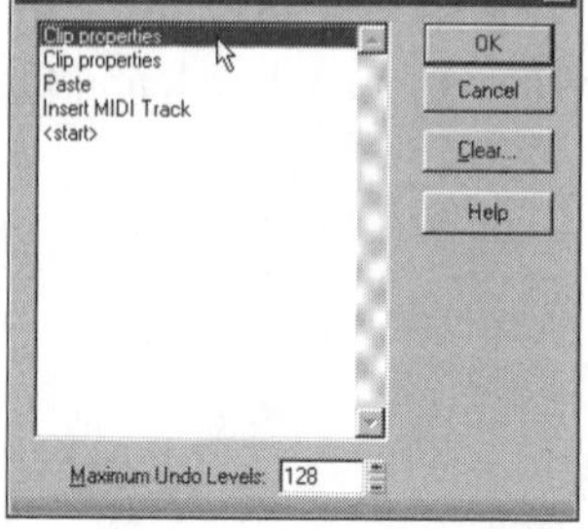

Figure 6.8
Using the Undo History dialog box, you can reverse your actions.

TIP

If you find that your performance for the most part is good except for only a few trouble spots, you might want to try fixing the mistakes by editing the MIDI notes rather than using Undo and then performing the whole thing all over again. You'll learn how to edit MIDI data in Chapter 7.

13. After you've recorded a performance you like, disarm the track by clicking on its R button again. By disarming the track, you won't accidentally record over the data while you're recording any additional tracks.

14. Go back to Step 6, and record any additional tracks that you would like to add to the project. While you're recording the new track(s), you will hear the previously recorded track(s) being played back. Because you can hear these tracks, you might want to turn off the metronome and just follow the music of the previous tracks as you perform the material for the new ones.

CAUTION

Be sure to save your project after each successful track recording. This step isn't really mandatory, but it's a good precautionary measure, because you never know when your computer may decide to crash on you. Rather than lose that really great performance you just recorded, quickly select File > Save (or press Ctrl+S on your computer keyboard) so you can rest easy in knowing that your data is safe.

Audio Track Recording and Playback

Recording audio tracks in SONAR is very similar to recording MIDI tracks, but, of course, because the nature of the data is different, you need to take a few additional steps. Here's the step-by-step process for recording audio tracks:

1. Create a new project or open an existing one. If you use a template to create a new project, you might be able to skip some of the following steps, but you should probably run through them anyway, just in case.

2. Set the meter and key signature for the project. The default settings are 4/4 and the key of C Major.

3. Set the metronome and tempo parameters. The default tempo for a new project is 100 beats per minute.

CHAPTER 6

4. Set the timebase for the project. The default setting is 960 PPQ (pulses per quarter note). More often than not, you won't have to change this setting.

5. Set the recording mode. Unless you plan to record data to a track that already contains data, you can skip this step. The default recording mode is Sound on Sound.

6. Set the sampling rate and the file bit depth for the project.

7. Add a new audio track to the Track view and adjust the track's properties. For more information about these properties and how to set them, refer to Chapter 4.

8. If you want to hear effects added to your performance while you're recording, activate input monitoring for your sound card. Then add effects to your track by right-clicking on the *Fx* parameter (located in the Track pane along with all the other track parameters) and choosing Audio Effects > Cakewalk > (the effect you would like to add). I'll talk more about effects in Chapter 11.

9. Arm the track for recording to let SONAR know that you want to record data on the track. Right after the name parameter in the Track view, you'll see three buttons labeled M, S, and R. Click on the R button to arm the track for recording.

10. After you arm the track, you'll notice the meter (shown right below all the other track parameters) light up (see Figure 6.9). This meter displays the level of the audio input for your sound card in decibels.

Figure 6.9
Each audio track has a meter showing its input signal level in decibels.

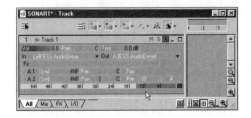

NOTE

Decibel is a very complicated term to describe. The most basic explanation would be that a decibel is a unit of measurement used to determine the loudness of sound. In SONAR, the audio meters can range from −90 dB (soft) to 0 dB (loud). To change the display range of a meter, right-click on it and choose a new setting from the pop-up menu. For now, that's really all you need to know.

11. Set the audio input level for your sound card so that it's not too loud but also not too soft. To do so, you have to use the software mixer that came with your sound card. In the Windows taskbar, you should see a small, yellow speaker icon. Double-click on the speaker icon to open your sound card mixer. Then select Options > Properties to open the sound card mixer Properties dialog box. In the Adjust Volume For section, select Recording, make sure all boxes below are checked, and click on OK to display the recording controls for your sound card mixer (see Figure 6.10).

Figure 6.10
You use your sound card mixer to adjust the input levels for your sound card.

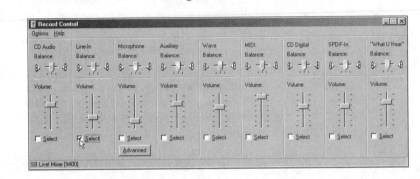

12. For the set of controls labeled Line-In, activate the Select option. This option tells your sound card that you want to record audio using its line-input connection. If you want to use a different connection (such as microphone or internal CD player), you need to use the set of controls associated with that connection.

NOTE

These steps show how to use a standard Windows sound card for recording. You may have a sound card that uses a different method for setting audio input levels. In that case, you need to read the documentation for your sound card to find out how to use it correctly.

13. When you have access to the input level controls for your sound card, begin your performance, playing at the loudest level at which you plan to record. As you play, the meter for the track will light up, displaying the sound level of your performance. You should adjust the input level so that, when you play the loudest part of your performance, the meter does *not* turn red. If it turns red, you have overloaded the input, and if you record at that level, your audio signal will be distorted. When you play the loudest part of your performance, if the meter lights up anywhere between −6dB and −3dB, then you have a good input level setting.

CHAPTER 6

14. After you finish setting your input level, close the sound card mixer. Next, set the Now time to the point in the project where you would like the recording to begin. Most of the time, it will be the very beginning of the project, but SONAR provides the flexibility of letting you record data to a track starting at any measure, beat, or tick within a project.

15. Select Transport > Record to start recording. (You can also press the R key on your computer keyboard or click on the Record button in the Transport toolbar.) If you set a Count-in, the metronome will first count the number of beats you entered, and then SONAR will begin recording.

16. Perform the material that you want to record.

17. After you finish performing, select Transport > Stop to stop recording. (You can also press the spacebar on your computer keyboard or click on the Stop button in the Transport toolbar.) SONAR creates a new clip in the track containing the audio data you just recorded (see Figure 6.11).

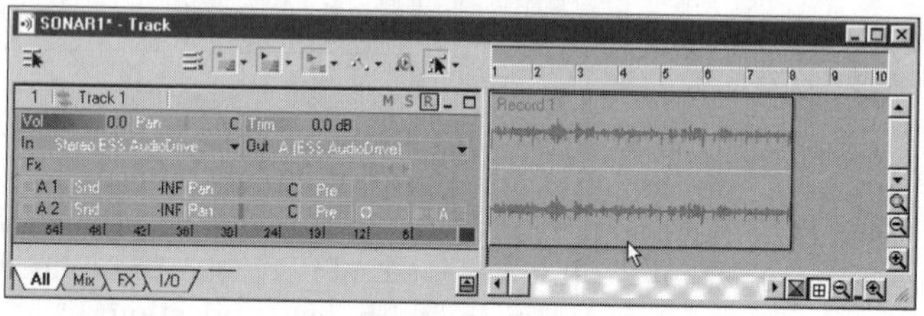

Figure 6.11
After you've finished recording, SONAR creates a new clip in the track representing the audio data.

18. Listen to your performance by setting the Now time back to its original position and selecting Transport > Play to start playback. (You can also press the spacebar on your computer keyboard or click on the Play button in the Transport toolbar.) If you don't like the performance, erase it by selecting Edit > Undo Recording. Then go back to Step 14 and try recording again.

19. After you've recorded a performance you like, disarm the track by clicking on its R button again. By disarming the track, you won't accidentally record over the data while you're recording any additional tracks.

20. Go back to Step 7 and record any additional tracks that you would like to add to the project. While you're recording the new track(s), you will hear the previously recorded track(s) playing back. Therefore, you might want to turn off the metronome and just follow the music of the previous tracks as you perform the material for the new ones.

TIP

If you have your home studio set up within a single room containing all your equipment (including your computer) and you are recording audio tracks using a microphone, the microphone will pick up the background noise made by your electronic devices (including the fan inside your computer). To remedy this situation, you might want to set up your microphone and one of your MIDI instruments in a different room, while keeping them connected to your computer via longer cables. Then you can set up some MIDI key bindings (you learned about them in Chapter 3) so that you can control SONAR remotely. This way, when you record the audio from your microphone, it won't pick up all that background noise.

Multiple Track Recording and Playback

If you have more than one MIDI input on your MIDI interface or more than one audio input on your sound card, you can record to multiple tracks simultaneously. Recording multiple tracks works well when you need to record a whole band of musicians. Instead of having each musician play individually (which can sometimes ruin the "groove"), you can record everyone's part at once (which usually makes the song flow much better).

To record multiple tracks, just follow the same instructions I outlined earlier for recording MIDI and audio tracks. The only difference is that you must set up and arm more than one track. When you start recording, the MIDI or audio data from each musician will be recorded to separate tracks simultaneously.

NOTE

When setting the input property for multiple MIDI tracks, SONAR doesn't allow you to select specific MIDI input ports. If you want to record more than one MIDI track at once, you must set the input property of each track to a different MIDI channel. You also have to be sure that each MIDI instrument is set to send data on a specific MIDI channel. If you have more than one instrument sending data on the same channel, the data from both instruments will be recorded on the same track.

CHAPTER 6

TIP

Even if you're using a basic sound card to record audio, you can still record two different audio tracks at once. You can do so because your sound card has a stereo input. This means you can use the left and right audio channels separately to record two individual tracks. When you set up the tracks prior to recording, just select the Input for one track to be the left audio channel of your sound card and the input for the other track to be the right audio channel of your sound card. You also might need a special audio cable. Most basic sound cards provide only one stereo input connection at a 1/8-inch size. The cable you will need is called a Y-adapter audio cable with a stereo 1/8-inch mini plug to phono plugs (or connections). You should be able to find the cable at your local Radio Shack.

Loop Recording

If you plan to add a vocal track or an instrumental track (such as a guitar solo) to your project—something that may require more than one try to get right—you might want to use *loop recording* instead of recording and undoing a single track over and over again manually. Loop recording allows you to record several tracks, one right after the other, without having to stop in between each one. Here's how it works:

1. If you want to record MIDI tracks, follow steps 1 through 7 in the "MIDI Track Recording and Playback" section presented earlier in this chapter. If you want to record audio tracks, follow steps 1 through 13 in the "Audio Track Recording and Playback" section earlier in this chapter.

2. Set the Now time to the point in the project where you want looping to begin. Then select Transport > Loop And Auto Shuttle to open the Loop/Auto Shuttle dialog box (see Figure 6.12). Press F5 on your computer keyboard to bring up the Markers dialog box. Select the Marker named <Now > from the list and click on OK to set the Start time where the looping will begin.

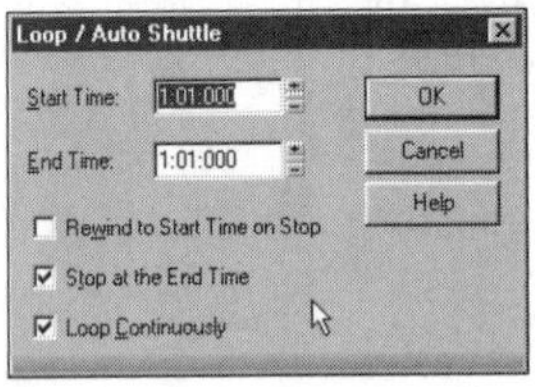

Figure 6.12
In the Loop/Auto Shuttle dialog box, you can set the loop recording parameters for SONAR.

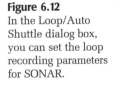

3. Type an End time for the loop using measure, beat, and tick values. Then activate the Stop at the End Time and Loop Continuously options and click on OK. Setting these options tells SONAR that, when you start recording, it will begin at the Loop Start Time, continue to the Loop End Time, and then loop back to the Start time to cycle through the loop over and over again, until you stop it.

TIP

You can also use the Loop toolbar to set the parameters for looping. Refer to Chapter 3 for more information about toolbars.

4. Select Transport > Record Options to open the Record Options dialog box. In the Loop Recording section, select either Store Takes in a Single Track or Store Takes in Separate Tracks. The first option stores each performance in the same track but in different clips stacked on top of each other. The second option stores each performance in a different track, automatically setting the same track parameters as the one you began with. I like to use the second option because it's more flexible, especially when I want to edit the data I just recorded. So, for this example, choose the Store Takes in Separate Tracks option. You can experiment with the other option later if you'd like.

5. Select Transport > Record to start recording. (You can also press the R key on your computer keyboard or click on the Record button in the Transport toolbar.) If you set a Count-in, the metronome will first count the number of beats you entered, and then SONAR will begin recording.

6. Perform the material you want to record as many times as you require to get a good take.

7. After you finish performing, select Transport > Stop to stop recording. (You can also press the spacebar on your computer keyboard or click on the Stop button in the Transport toolbar.) SONAR creates a new track containing the data you just recorded for every loop you cycled through (see Figure 6.13).

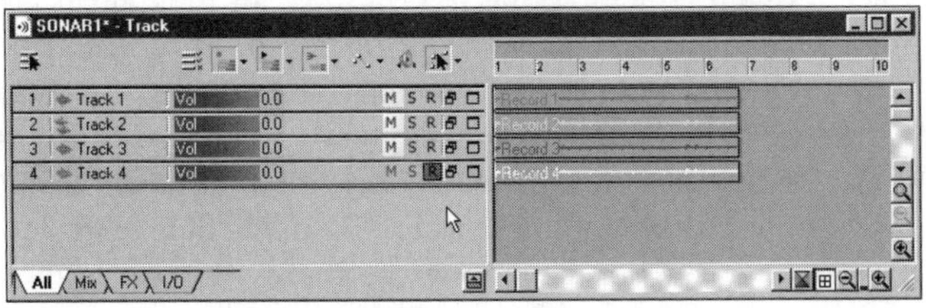

Figure 6.13
For every loop you record, SONAR creates a new track containing each individual performance.

CHAPTER 6

8.   Each track (except for the current one) is disarmed and muted. To listen to any of your performances, turn off looping by selecting Transport > Loop and Auto Shuttle to open the Loop/Auto Shuttle dialog box. Deactivate the Stop at the End Time option and click on OK. Set the Now time back to its original position and select Transport > Play to start playback. (You can also press the spacebar on your computer keyboard or click on the Play button in the Transport toolbar.) To listen to one of the recorded tracks, unmute it by clicking on the M button next to its name parameter in the Track view.

9.   After you've found a performance that you like and want to keep, delete the others by selecting the track (click on the appropriate track number on the left side of the Track view) and then select Track > Delete. If you want to select more than one track at once, just hold down the Ctrl key on your computer keyboard while you're selecting track numbers.

TIP

Instead of deleting all the extra tracks you created during looping, you might want to keep them for use later. You can do so by using SONAR's Archive feature. By archiving tracks, you store them within the current project, but they become "invisible" to SONAR. This means that when you play your project, the archived tracks will not play. As a matter of fact, archiving tracks helps to increase SONAR's performance because it doesn't process the tracks at all when they are archived. To archive a track, just right-click on its track number and select Archive from the pop-up menu. You'll notice that the track's Mute button turns into an A (Archive) button. This change in the button name shows that the track is archived. You can still make changes to the track (and the data in it), but SONAR will not play the track.

Punch Recording

When you make a mistake while recording MIDI data, it's usually no big deal, because you can easily make corrections (such as changing the pitch of a note) with SONAR's various editing tools (see Chapter 7). But what about when you're recording audio? Sure, you can edit the data by cutting and pasting sections or processing it with effects, but you can't edit the pitch of a single note or make any other precision corrections like you can with MIDI data. So, with audio, you have to record your performance all over again. By using SONAR's punch recording feature, however, you have to rerecord only the part of the performance you messed up, leaving the good parts alone.

Using punch recording, you can set up SONAR to automatically start recording and stop recording at precise times during a project. You therefore can record over certain parts of your performance without having to redo the whole thing. Punching is very similar to regular audio track recording, but with a few differences. Here's the step-by-step procedure:

1. Say you want to correct some mistakes on an audio track you just recorded. To get started, make sure the track is still armed for recording (its R button is red).

2. Activate punch recording by selecting Transport > Record Options to open the Record Options dialog box (see Figure 6.14). In the Recording Mode section, select Auto Punch. Then, for the Punch In Time, type the measure, beat, and tick at which you want SONAR to begin recording. For the Punch Out Time, type the measure, beat, and tick at which you want SONAR to stop recording. The section of the track that falls between the Punch In Time and the Punch Out Time should contain the part of your performance in which you made the mistakes.

TIP

For a quick way to set the Punch In and Out times, just click and drag in the Time Ruler of the Track view to make a data selection, then right-click in Time Ruler and choose Set Punch Points from the pop-up menu. For more information on selecting data, read chapters 7 and 8.

Figure 6.14
You use the Record Options dialog box to set the recording mode to Auto Punch and to set the Punch In and Punch Out times.

3. Set the Now time to the point in the project before the Punch In Time where you would like playback to begin. You might want to start from the very beginning of the project or just a few measures before the Punch In Time. However long it takes you to get into the groove of the performance is how far ahead of the Punch In Time you should set the Now time.

CHAPTER 6

4. Select Transport > Record to start recording. (You can also press the R key on your computer keyboard or click on the Record button in the Transport toolbar.) If you set a Count-in, the metronome will first count the number of beats you entered, and then SONAR will begin playback.

5. Play along with the existing material, exactly as you did before when you first recorded the track. When SONAR reaches the Punch-In Time, it will automatically start recording the new part of your performance.

6. When the Now time has passed the Punch Out Time, SONAR will stop recording, and you can select Transport > Stop to stop SONAR. (You can also press the spacebar on your computer keyboard or click on the Stop button in the Transport toolbar.) SONAR replaces any existing material between the Punch In Time and the Punch Out Time with the new material you just played. As long as you didn't make any mistakes this time, your track will now be fixed.

7. Listen to your performance by setting the Now time back to its original position and selecting Transport > Play to start playback. (You can also press the spacebar on your computer keyboard or click on the Play button in the Transport toolbar.) If you don't like the performance, you can erase it by selecting Edit > Undo Recording. Then go back to Step 3 and try recording again.

Step Recording

Even though you may be an accomplished musician, more than likely, you have one main instrument you're good at playing. If that instrument is the keyboard, that skill puts you ahead of some other musicians, because the keyboard is one of the easiest instruments to use to record a MIDI performance. You can use other MIDI instruments, such as MIDI woodwind instruments, MIDI drums, and MIDI guitars, but those instruments tend to be very expensive. And if you learn to play a wind instrument or the drums or a guitar, you probably have a real instrument of that kind, not a MIDI one. This puts you at a bit of a disadvantage when you're trying to record MIDI tracks. However, SONAR provides a feature called step recording that allows you to record a MIDI track one note at a time without your having to worry about the timing of your performance.

In other words, you select the type of note you want to enter (such as a quarter note or a sixteenth note), and then you press one or more keys on your MIDI keyboard. SONAR then records those notes into the track with the timing you selected. You can also enter the measure, beat, and tick at which you want the notes to occur. Here's how the step recording feature works:

1. Follow steps 1 through 8 in the "MIDI Track Recording and Playback" section, earlier in this chapter.

2. Select Transport > Step Record to open the Step Record dialog box (see Figure 6.15).

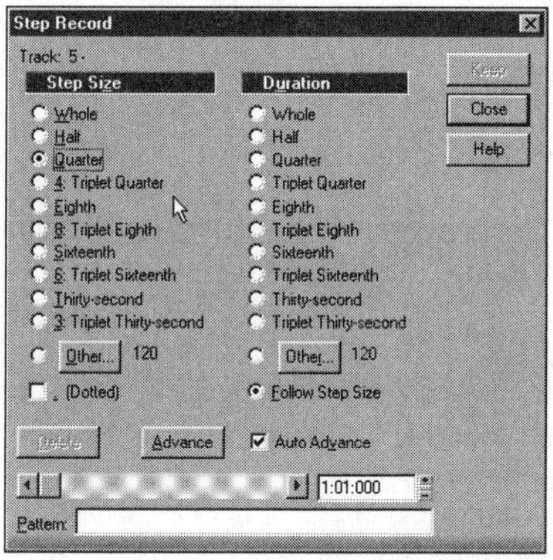

Figure 6.15
Using the Step Record dialog box, you can record MIDI data to a track without having to worry about the timing of your performance.

3. In the Step Size section, enter the size of the note you want to record. For example, if you want to record a quarter note, select Quarter.

4. In the Duration section, you can set the length of the note independent of the step size. More often than not, though, you'll want the duration to be the same as the step size. To make things easier, you can set the Duration to Follow Step Size, so that both values will be the same and you won't have to bother selecting a duration.

5. To record the note, press a key on your MIDI instrument. For example, if you want to record a middle C to the track, press middle C on your MIDI instrument. By the way, you can also press more than one key at a time if you want to record a chord. For example, if you want to record a C major chord, press the C, E, and G keys on your MIDI instrument at the same time.

CHAPTER 6

6.   SONAR records the data to the track and (if the Auto Advance option is activated, which it is by default) moves the Now time forward by the step size amount (which is a quarter note in this example). If the Auto Advance option isn't activated, you have to click on the Advance button to move the Now time manually. Also, if you want to record a rest instead of a note, you have to click on the Advance button. This way, SONAR will move the Now time ahead by the step size amount without recording anything.

7.   To change the Now time manually, just enter a new value into the field shown below the Auto Advance option. To move forward or backward by a step, click on the arrows on the scroll bar shown next to the Now time. Also, if you want to delete the most recent step, click on the Delete button.

TIP

If you need to record many repeating patterns, you might want to use the Pattern option in the Step Record dialog box. In the Pattern box, you can enter a pattern of beats that SONAR will follow automatically so that you don't have to click on the Advance button at all, even for rests. For example, if you need to record a pattern with notes on the first two beats, a rest on the third beat, and another note on the fourth beat, you enter 12R4 in the Pattern box. Now, when you start to record the pattern, you simply press keys on your MIDI instrument for beats 1 and 2, SONAR advances past beat 3 because it is a rest, and then you press another key for beat 4. Then you keep repeating the same routine over and over again until you get to the point in your music where you no longer need to repeat the same rhythmic pattern. I know this process sounds a bit complicated, but if you play with it for a while, you'll get the hang of it.

8.   When you're finished recording, click on the Keep button to keep the data and have SONAR add it to the track. Alternatively, you can click on the Close button to discard the data you just recorded.

9.   Listen to your performance by setting the Now time back to its original position and selecting Transport > Play to start playback. (You can also press the spacebar on your computer keyboard or click on the Play button in the Transport toolbar.) If you don't like the performance, you can erase it by selecting Edit > Undo Recording. Then go back to Step 2 and try recording again.

TIP

As an alternative to the step recording feature, you might want to try using the Staff view. With the Staff view, you can still enter your MIDI data one note at a time without worrying about performance timing. Plus, the Staff view allows you to enter and edit your data using standard music notation. I'll describe this feature in more detail in Chapter 13.

Importing

One other way you can get MIDI and audio data into a project is to import it rather than record it. SONAR allows you to import data from audio files, MIDI files, and other project files. Why would you want to import files? Well, you may have a great drum track in a project or a MIDI file that you would like to use in another project. You might also want to use sample loops for some of the material in your audio tracks (I'll talk about sample loops in Chapter 9). Importing material is actually very easy.

Importing from Project and MIDI Files

Importing data from a project or a MIDI file into another project is just a matter of copying and pasting, as shown in the following steps. To get started, just do the following:

1. Open the project or MIDI file from which you want to copy data.
2. In the Track view, select the clip(s) that you want to copy. You can also select an entire track or a number of whole tracks to copy.
3. Select Edit > Copy to open the Copy dialog box (see Figure 6.16). Make sure the Events in Tracks option is activated and then click on OK.

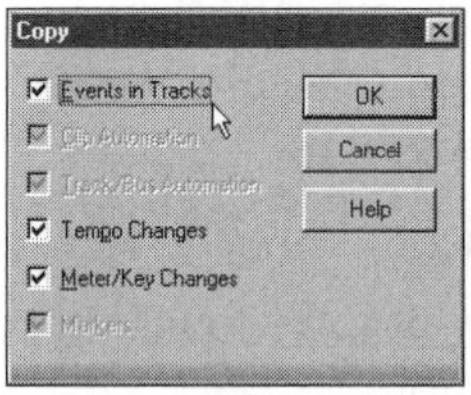

Figure 6.16
Using the Copy dialog box, you can copy data within a project or from one project into another project.

4. Open the project to which you want to paste the data.
5. In the Track view, select the track where you want to start pasting the data. If you copied more than one track, the first copied track will be pasted to the selected track and the other copied tracks will be pasted to consecutive tracks after the selected one.
6. Set the Now time to the point in the track you would like the data to be pasted.

CHAPTER 6

7. Select Edit > Paste to open the Paste dialog box (see Figure 6.17). You don't have to change any of the parameters here (I'll go over them in more detail in Chapter 8). Click on OK.

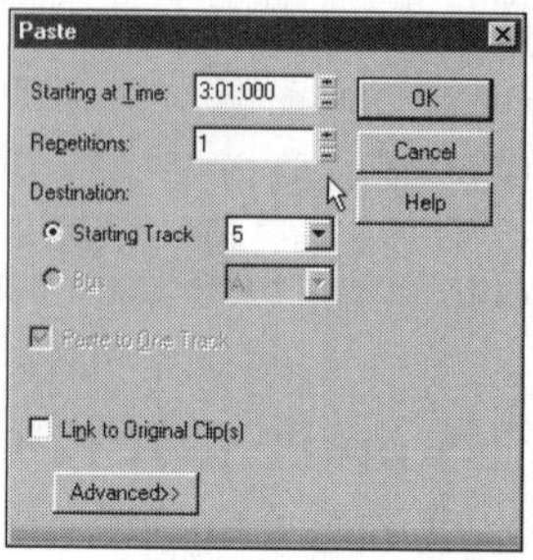

Figure 6.17
The Paste dialog box takes any previously copied data and places it where you specify.

SONAR copies the data you selected from the first project or MIDI file and places a copy of the data into the second project within the tracks and at the Now time you specify. In addition to reusing your own material, you can share material with a friend this way.

Importing Audio Files

You learned about audio files in Chapter 3. SONAR allows you to import .WAV, .MP3, .AIF, .ASF, and .AU audio files. This is important because at some time you might record some audio using another program, and you might want to use that data within one of your SONAR projects. Doing so is really simple; just follow these steps:

1. Select the track to which you want to import the audio file.
2. Set the Now time to the point in the track that the file should be placed.
3. Select Filet > Import Audio to open the Open dialog box.
4. Choose the audio file you want to import.
5. If you want to listen to the file before you import it, click on the Play button.
6. If the audio file is a stereo audio file, you can have either the left and right channels merged into one track or split between two different tracks (starting with the one you selected). To have the file split, activate the Stereo Split option.
7. Click on Open.

SONAR then imports the file and inserts it into the track(s) you selected at the Now time you specified.

Synchronization

One other aspect related to recording that you should know about is *synchronization*. This subject is fairly complicated and a bit beyond the scope of this book, but you might need to utilize synchronization in two somewhat popular situations. So, I'll cover a few of the basics and explain how to use synchronization in those two particular situations.

Basics

All music is based on time. Without time, there is no music. To record and play music data, SONAR needs a timing reference. It uses this reference to determine the exact measure, beat, and tick at which an event should be stored during recording or at which it should be played. When you work with SONAR alone, it uses one of two different clock sources as its reference: either the clock built into your computer (internal) or the clock built into your sound card (audio). By default, SONAR uses the internal clock as its timing reference. Because the internal clock cannot be used if you have audio data in your project, SONAR automatically changes the clock to audio when a track's source is set to an audio input or when a audio file is inserted into the project. So, the built-in clock on your sound card provides the timing for all the data that you record into a project, and it allows SONAR to keep all the tracks synchronized during playback. This is internal synchronization.

Sometimes, though, you might need to synchronize SONAR externally with another piece of equipment. For example, if you have a drum machine (a special type of MIDI instrument that plays only drum sounds) containing some special songs that you programmed into it, you might like to have the data in your current SONAR project play along with the data contained in the drum machine. You would have to synchronize SONAR to the drum machine. In this situation, the drum machine would be known as the *master* device, and SONAR would be the *slave* device. The master would send messages to the slave, telling it when to start and stop playback and what tempo to use so that they can stay in sync with one another. To accomplish this, you need to use what is called MIDI Sync.

MIDI Sync

MIDI Sync is a special set of MIDI messages that allow you to synchronize MIDI devices to one another. These messages include Start (telling a slave device to start playback at the beginning of the song), Stop (telling a slave device to stop playback), Continue (telling a slave device to continue playback from the current location in the song—the Now time in SONAR), Song Position Pointer or SPP (telling a slave device to jump to a specific time position in the song—the Now time in SONAR), and Clock (a steady pulse of ticks sent to the slave device telling it the speed of the current tempo of the song).

CHAPTER 6

To synchronize SONAR with an external MIDI device using MIDI Sync, follow these steps:

1. Configure your drum machine (or other MIDI device you want to use as the master) to transmit MIDI Sync messages. You'll have to refer to the user's guide for your device on how to do so.

2. In SONAR, open the project that you want to synchronize. Then select Options > Project to open the Project Options dialog box and click on the Clock tab (see Figure 6.18).

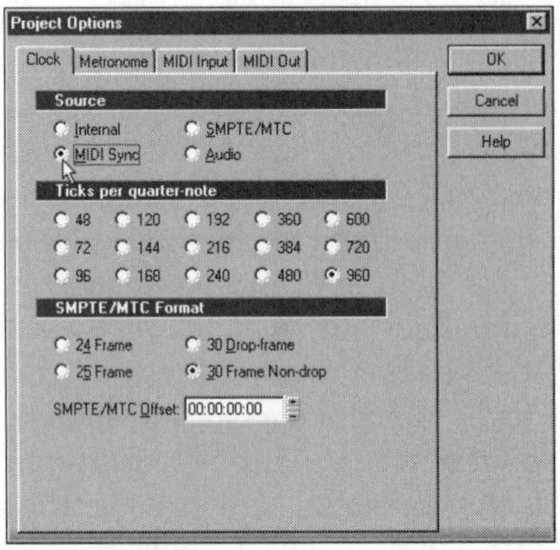

Figure 6.18
Using the Project Options dialog box, you can configure SONAR for synchronization.

3. In the Source section, click on the MIDI Sync option and click on OK.

4. Follow the steps outlined earlier for recording or playing MIDI tracks, but when you activate recording or playback, SONAR won't respond right away. Instead, it will display a message that says "Waiting for MIDI Sync."

5. After you see this message, start playback on your master device. It will then send a Start message to SONAR, and both the device and SONAR will play through the song in sync with one another. In the case of the drum machine, you will hear it play its sounds in time with the music being played by SONAR.

6. To stop playback, don't use the commands in SONAR; instead, stop playback from the master device. It will send SONAR a Stop message, and SONAR will stop at the same time automatically.

While working with SONAR via MIDI Sync, just remember to start, stop, and navigate through the project using the master device instead of SONAR. Otherwise, all the other steps for recording and playback are the same.

NOTE

You cannot record or play audio tracks in SONAR while using MIDI Sync. If you have some previously recorded MIDI data stored in a drum machine (or other MIDI device) that you want to use in your SONAR project, first use MIDI Sync to transfer that data into SONAR. Then use the drum machine (or other MIDI device) as a playback device.

SMPTE/MIDI Time Code

You might need to use synchronization when you're composing music to video. Here, though, the synchronization method is different because a VCR is not a MIDI device, so MIDI Sync won't work. Instead, you have to use SMPTE/MIDI Time Code. You learned a little about SMPTE in Chapter 5, so you know that it is a timing reference that counts hours, minutes, seconds, and frames (as in video frames). But you didn't really learn how it works.

NOTE

In addition to video, SMPTE/MIDI Time Code is often used to synchronize a sequencer to an external multitrack tape recorder or DAT (digital audio tape) deck. The procedure for doing so (explained below) is the same.

SMPTE is a complex audio signal that is recorded onto a tape track (in the case of video, it's recorded onto one of the stereo audio tracks) using a time code generator. This signal represents the absolute amount of time over the length of the tape in hours, minutes, seconds, and frames. A sequencer (such as SONAR) reading the code can be synchronized to any exact moment along the length of the entire tape recording. In this case, the VCR would be the master, and SONAR would be the slave. When you play the tape in the VCR, SONAR will play the current project in sync to the exact hour, minute, second, and frame.

Reading the time code from tape requires a SMPTE converter, which translates the SMPTE code into MTC (MIDI Time Code). The MIDI Time Code is read by the MIDI Interface and sent to the sequencer (SONAR). MIDI Time Code is the equivalent of SMPTE, except that it exists as special MIDI messages rather than an audio signal. As SONAR receives MTC, it calculates the exact measure, beat, and tick that corresponds to the exact time reading. This means you can start playback anywhere along the tape, and SONAR will begin playing or recording MIDI or audio data at precisely the right point in the current project in perfect sync.

CHAPTER 6

As an example, say you need to compose some music to video. This video could be your own or a video from a client. To synchronize SONAR to the video, you need to follow these steps:

1. If the video is your own, you need to add SMPTE time code to it using a SMPTE generator. This process is called *striping*. I won't go into the details of doing that here. You'll need to purchase a SMPTE generator and read the instructions in the included manual on how to stripe SMPTE to tape. If the video is from a client, he or she will probably stripe the tape before sending it to you.

TIP

You also need a SMPTE converter to read the time code from the tape. If you have a professional MIDI Interface attached to your computer, it may provide SMPTE generating and converting capabilities. Check the user's manual to be sure. You might be able to save yourself some money. I use a Music Quest 8Port/SE MIDI Interface from Opcode (**www.opcode.com**), and it includes multiple MIDI ports as well as SMPTE capabilities.

2. In SONAR, open the project you want to synchronize. Then select Options > Project to open the Project Options dialog box and click on the Clock tab.

3. In the SMPTE/MTC Format section, you need to select a frame rate for the time code. If you're composing music to your own video, just use the default selection, 30 Frame Non-Drop. If you're composing music for a client, he or she should let you know what frame rate you need to use.

NOTE

Different types of video material use different tape speeds for recording. The frame rate corresponds to how many frames per second are used to record the video to tape. For film, 24 frames per second is used. For video, several different rates are used depending on whether the video is recorded in color or black-and-white and so on. For more information about frame rates, you should consult the user's guide for your SMPTE generating/reading device.

4. You might also need to enter a SMPTE/MTC Offset in hours, minutes, seconds, and frames. Whether you need to enter an Offset depends on whether the video material starts at the very beginning of the time code stripe, which is a value of 00:00:00:00.

NOTE

When you stripe a tape with SMPTE, the time code always starts with a value of 00 hours, 00 minutes, 00 seconds, and 00 frames. However, the actual video material on the tape may start a bit later, say at 00 hours, 01 minutes, 20 seconds, 00 frames. If that's the case (and your client should let you know this fact), you need to enter an Offset of 00:01:20:00 into SONAR so that SONAR will begin playing the project at that time rather than at the initial time code value.

5. After you finish entering the settings, click on OK.

6. Now you can follow the steps outlined earlier for recording or playing MIDI tracks, but when you activate recording or playback, SONAR won't respond right away. Instead, it will display a message saying "Waiting for 30 Frame" (or whatever frame rate you selected).

7. After you see this message, start playback on your master device (in this case, start the tape playing in the VCR). It will then send SMPTE code to SONAR, and both the device and SONAR will play through the song in sync with one another. In the case of the VCR, you will see it play the video in time with the music that is being played by SONAR.

8. To stop playback, don't use the commands in SONAR; instead, stop playback from the master device.

TIP

If you would rather control playback from the master device (the VCR) entirely without having to first start it in SONAR, select Transport > Loop and Auto Shuttle to display the Loop/Auto Shuttle dialog box. Then activate the Loop Continuously option and click on OK.

A little confused? Well, as I said, synchronization is a complicated subject. You'll find a little more information in the SONAR User's Guide and the Help files, but it isn't any easier to understand than the information I've provided here. Your best bet is to experiment as much as possible with synchronization and get a good beginner's book on audio recording. Knowing how to utilize synchronization is worthwhile if a situation that requires it ever arises.

CHAPTER 6

7

Editing Basics

After you've finished recording all your tracks, it's time to do some editing. Actually, if you're like me, you might end up doing some editing during the recording process. This is especially true for MIDI tracks, because it's so easy to fix the pitch or timing of a note quickly if you happen to make a mistake or two. You'll do most of your editing after the fact, though, and SONAR provides a number of different tools to get the job done. I briefly described these features in Chapter 2, but in this chapter, I'll go into more detail about the following:

▶ Dealing with tracks and clips in the Track view

▶ Editing MIDI note and controller messages in the Piano Roll view

▶ Editing audio data in the Track view

▶ Editing individual events in the Event List view

▶ Changing the tempo via the Tempo view

CAUTION

Before you do any kind of editing to your recently recorded material, I suggest you make a backup of your project file. This way, if you totally mess things up during the editing process, you'll still have your raw recorded tracks to fall back on. Take a look at Appendix B, "Backing Up Your Project Files," for more information.

Arranging with the Track View

The first part of the editing process has to do with arranging the material in your project. Of course, you can do any kind of editing at any time you like. You don't have to follow exactly what I say, but it's just logical to start with arranging. Basically, this step involves rearranging the tracks and clips in your project so that they provide a better representation of the song you're trying to create. For example, after listening to the project a few times, you might find that the guitar part in the second verse sounds better in the first verse, or you might want the vocal to come in a little earlier during the chorus. You can accomplish these (and many other) feats by manipulating your tracks and clips.

Dealing with Tracks

You already learned how to work with the Track view in terms of setting up track properties, navigating within SONAR, and recording new tracks. However, I haven't talked about actually manipulating the tracks themselves and the data within them. Manipulating includes selecting, sorting, inserting, and otherwise changing your original data.

Scrolling

As you already know, the Track view consists of two areas: The Track pane (on the left) shows the track properties and the Clips pane (on the right) shows the track data. The Clips pane contains scroll bars (see Figure 7.1). These scroll bars work the same as scroll bars in any standard Windows application. You either click on the arrows to move the display, or you click and drag the scroll bars to move the display.

Figure 7.1
Using the scroll bars, you can access additional information that doesn't fit on the screen.

The horizontal scroll bar allows you to display all the data within all the tracks. As you scroll to the right, the measure numbers on the Time Ruler increase. Scrolling doesn't change the Now time, though (as you learned in Chapter 5). A vertical scroll bar affects both the Track and Clips pane areas. As you move the bar up or down, the different tracks within the project are displayed, starting from 1 (at the top of the list).

In addition to the Track view, scroll bars are available in all the other views. In the Piano Roll view, you can scroll horizontally to display the data in a track similar to the clips in the Track view. You also can scroll vertically to display different MIDI note ranges. The Event List view is the oddball, because it only lets you scroll vertically to display all the events within a track as one long list. I'll describe the different views later in this chapter.

CHAPTER 7

Zooming

The Track view (as well as other views, except the Event List view) also provides zooming functions. Using these functions, you can magnify the data in a track in case you want to do some really precise editing. If you take a look at the bottom-right corner of the Track view (see Figure 7.2), you'll notice two sets of buttons (one along the bottom and one along the side) that have little pictures of magnifying glasses on them.

Figure 7.2
The zoom features reside in the bottom-right corner of the view.

Using the buttons along the bottom, you can magnify the track data horizontally. So, by clicking on the Zoom In button (the button with the magnifying glass with a + sign shown on it), the clips grow bigger in size horizontally and give you a more detailed look at the data they contain. Clicking on the Zoom Out button, of course, does the opposite. And the same buttons along the side of the Track view perform the same functions, except that they affect the display vertically. You'll also notice that as you zoom in vertically, the track parameters will be shown beneath each track in the Track pane. In addition, you'll notice a little gauge in between each set of zoom buttons. These gauges show you the current level of magnification being used.

> **TIP**
>
> Click and hold the mouse on either zoom gauge, and up pops a zoom meter. You can use the meter to quickly set the zoom level by dragging your mouse (see Figure 7.3). 
>
> **Figure 7.3**
> You can also change the zoom level via the Zoom meters.

In addition to the Zoom In and Zoom Out buttons on the right side of the view, you'll find another button with an empty magnifying glass shown on it. This button activates the Zoom tool. You can use this tool to select a range of data and just zoom in on that selection. To use it, simply do the following:

1. Click on the Zoom tool button.

2. Move your mouse pointer within the Clips pane, and it turns into a magnifying glass.

3.   Click and drag anywhere within the area to select some data (see Figure 7.4).

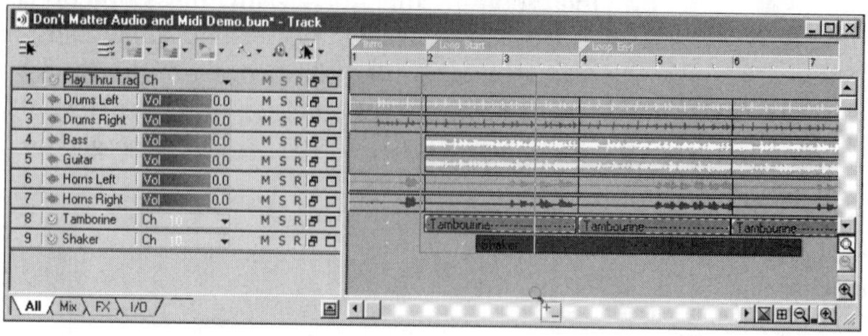

Figure 7.4
You just click and drag to make a selection with the Zoom tool.

4.   Release the mouse button. SONAR then zooms in on the selection (both horizontally and vertically, depending on how you drag the mouse), and your mouse pointer returns to normal.

You have to click on the Zoom tool button every time you want to use it.

Selecting

To manipulate your tracks in a project for editing, you have to be able to select them. In Chapter 6, I mentioned how to select a single track: You simply click on the track number of the track you want to select. But sometimes you might want to have more than one track selected at one time. You also might need a quick way to select all the tracks in your project. Or after going through the trouble of selecting a number of tracks, you might want to deselect one or two while keeping the others selected. You accomplish these tasks as follows:

▶   To select more than one track, hold down the Ctrl key on your computer keyboard as you click on the Track numbers.

▶   To select all tracks in a project, select Edit > Select > All.

▶   To deselect all tracks in a project, select Edit > Select > None.

▶   To deselect a track while keeping others selected, just hold down the Ctrl key on your computer keyboard as you click on the track number.

By the way, all these procedures also work in the other views. The only difference is the items being selected. Just remember that to select a single item, you simply click on it. To select more than one item, you hold down the Ctrl key on your computer keyboard as you click. To select all or none of the items, you choose Edit > Select. Some special selection features are also available, but I'll talk about them later in this chapter and in Chapter 8.

Sorting

You can change the order in which the tracks appear in a couple of different ways. Being able to sort the tracks can be useful if you want to keep related tracks together in the track list. For instance, you might want to keep all the percussion tracks or all the vocal tracks together. It's easier to work on your song when the tracks are grouped together in this way— at least, it is for me.

Click and Drag

The easiest way to move a track within a list is simply to drag it to a new location. Just move your mouse pointer over the little icon next to the name parameter of the track you want to move and then click and drag it anywhere within the list. When you release your mouse button, the track moves to the new location and takes on a new track number.

Track Sort

You also can use the Track Sort function to sort tracks in the list based on the track properties. You use this function as follows:

1.   Select Track > Sort to open the Sort Tracks dialog box (see Figure 7.5).

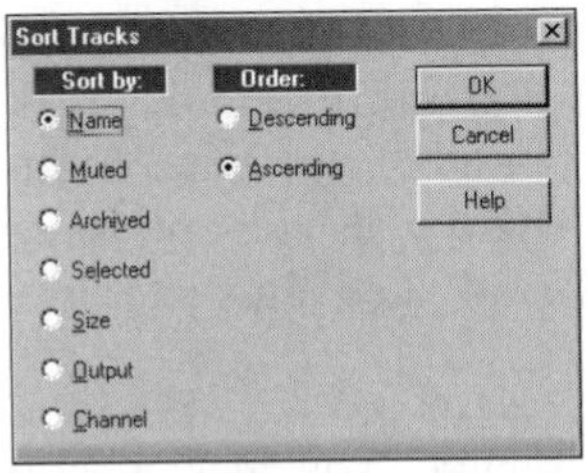

Figure 7.5
Using the Sort Tracks dialog box, you can rearrange the tracks in the Track view.

2.   In the Sort by section, select the track property by which you want to sort the tracks.

3.   In the Order section, select whether you want the tracks to be sorted in ascending or descending order.

4.   Click on OK.

SONAR then sorts the tracks according to the settings you specified. And remember, the track numbers for the tracks are changed as well, because the tracks have been moved to new locations within the list. Each track maintains its parameter settings and data, though.

Inserting

If you ever need to insert a new track in between two existing tracks within the list, you can do the following:

1.   Right-click on the track number of the track above which you want to insert a new track.

2. From the pop-up menu, select Insert Audio Track or Insert MIDI Track, depending on the type of track you need.

SONAR moves the current track down one location in the list and inserts a new track at the location you clicked on. For example, if you right-click on Track 2 and select Insert MIDI Track, SONAR moves Track 2 (and all the tracks below it) down by one and inserts a new MIDI track at number 2 in the list.

Cloning

If you ever need to make a copy of a track, you can do the following:

1. Select the track you want to copy.

2. Select Track > Clone to open the Clone dialog box (see Figure 7.6).

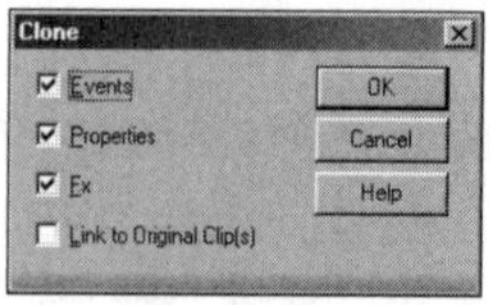

Figure 7.6
You can make a copy
of a track by using
the Clone dialog box.

3. You can choose to copy the events within the track, the track properties, the effects (Fx) assigned to the track (I'll talk more about effects in Chapter 11), or all of the above. Simply activate the appropriate options. There is also an option for preserving linked clips (I'll talk more about linked clips later in this chapter).

4. Click OK.

SONAR makes a copy of the track you selected and adds it to the bottom of the track list. If you want to move the track to a new location in the list, you can do so as explained earlier.

Erasing

Getting rid of tracks that you no longer need is very easy. Simply select the track, and select Track > Delete. But SONAR also provides another erasing function that's a little more flexible. Instead of erasing the track entirely, it allows you to delete all the data in the track while keeping the track properties intact. To do so, just select the Track, and then choose Track > Wipe. Nothing could be easier.

Hiding

If you click on the Track Manager button in the toolbar at the top of the Track view (see Figure 7.7), you can access the Track Manager. Using the Track Manager, you can hide tracks in the Track view. To hide tracks, do the following:

Figure 7.7
Click the Track
Manager button in
the Track view to open
the Track Manager.

1. Click on the Track Manager button to open the Track Manager (see Figure 7.8). You will see a list of all the tracks in the Track view. You will also see some other items (aux bus, mains, etc.). Don't worry about those for now. I'll talk more about them in Chapter 12.

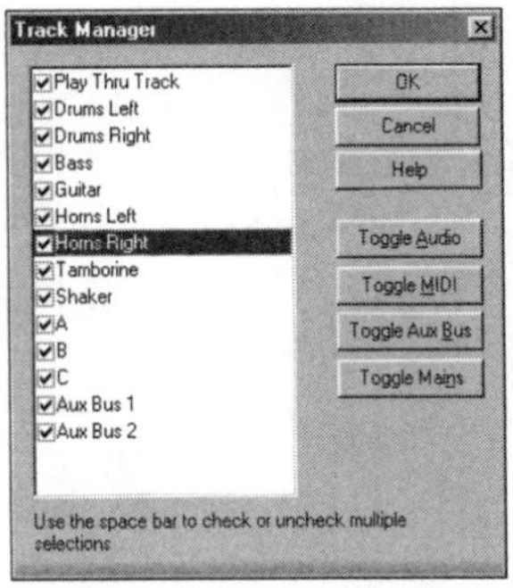

Figure 7.8
Use the Track Manager
to hide tracks in the
Track view.

2. To hide an individual track, click to remove the check mark next to that track in the list. Then click OK.

3. To hide a group of tracks (such as all the audio tracks or all the MIDI tracks), click on the appropriate button—Toggle Audio, Toggle MIDI— to select the appropriate group. Then press the spacebar on your computer keyboard to remove the check marks. Finally, click OK.

Of course, you can also make tracks appear again by doing the opposite of the preceding procedures. These changes to the Track view are in appearance only. They don't affect what you hear during playback. For example, if you hide an audio track that outputs data during playback, you still hear that data even if you hide the track. Hiding tracks can come in handy when you want to work only on a certain group of tracks at a time and you don't want to be distracted or overwhelmed by the number of controls being displayed.

TIP
You can quickly hide a single track by right-clicking on its track number and choosing Hide Track from the pop-up menu. To make the track visible again, however, you need to use the Track Manager.

Dealing with Clips

Unless you insert, copy, or erase tracks in your project, you're not actually doing any kind of data manipulation. If you move a track in the track list or sort the tracks, that doesn't change the data within them. To make changes to the data within your project, you have to manipulate the clips within the tracks.

Clip Properties

For organizational purposes, SONAR allows you to change the way clips are displayed. To change the properties, you can right-click on a clip and select Clip Properties from the pop-up menu to open the Clip Properties dialog box (see Figure 7.9). Here, you can assign a name to the clip (which doesn't have to be the same name as the track in which the clip resides) and the color of the clip.

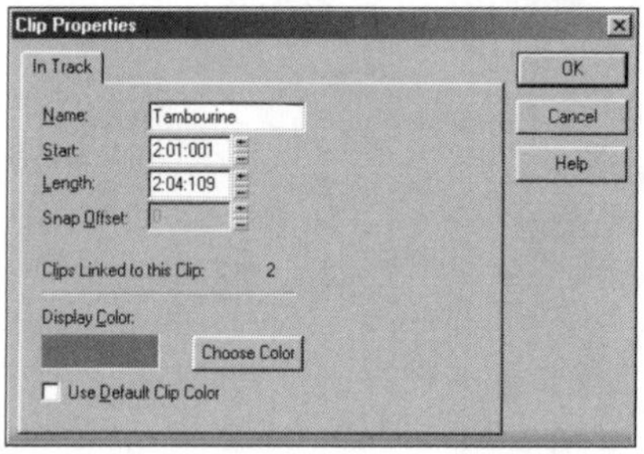

Figure 7.9
To change the name
or color of a clip, you
use the Clip Properties
dialog box.

The name and the color of a clip don't affect the data within your project, but you can also change the start time of the clip in this dialog box. This is the position within the project at which the clip begins. If you enter a new start time for the clip, the clip is moved within the track to the new time and, during playback, SONAR will play the clip at the new time as well. This move does change the data within your project.

View Options

You can also change whether the names you assign to clips will be displayed and whether clips will be displayed with a graphical representation of the data they contain. In other words, if a clip contains audio data, it shows a drawing of what the sound wave for the audio data might look like. For MIDI data, the clip shows a mini piano roll display.

To change these options, just right-click anywhere within the Clips pane and select View Options from the pop-up menu to display the Track view Options dialog box (see Figure 7.10). Activate the appropriate options (Display Clip Names and Display Clip Contents) and click on OK.

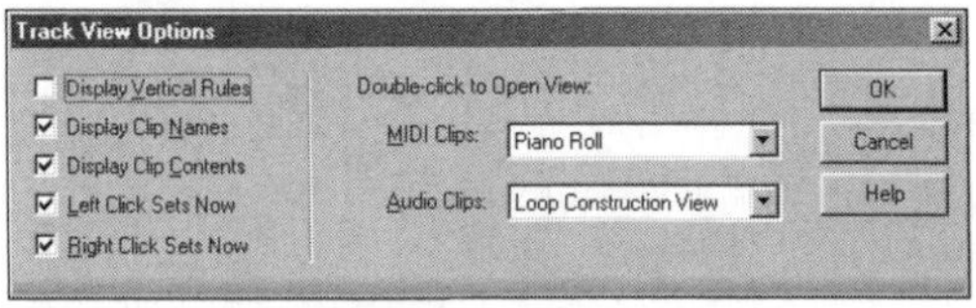

Figure 7.10
Using the Track view Options dialog box, you can show or hide clip names and contents.

Using the Track view Options dialog box, you also can specify whether left-clicking or right-clicking will change the Now time (the Left Click Sets Now or Right Click Sets Now options), whether to display vertical rule lines for the Time Ruler (Display Vertical Rules option), and which views open automatically when you double-click on a MIDI or audio clip.

Selecting

You select clips the same way you select tracks. To select a single clip, click on it. To select more than one clip, hold down the Ctrl key on your computer keyboard while clicking on the clips you want to select. You know the rest.

There is one additional selection method that doesn't apply to tracks, and that method is selecting only a portion of a clip. This procedure is known as working with partial clips. This capability is useful when you want to split a clip into smaller clips or combine a clip with another one to make a larger clip. I'll describe this topic in more detail later in this chapter.

To select only part of clip, hold down the Alt key on your computer keyboard and drag your mouse pointer across the clip to select a part of it. You can also drag across several clips (or even over several tracks) to make a partial selection of multiple clips.

NOTE
When you're making selections or moving data, the start and end times of your selections or data are affected by the Snap to Grid. You learned how to use the Snap to Grid feature in Chapter 5.

Splitting and Combining

Using partial selections, you can combine and split clips into new, smaller or larger clips. Combining clips is very easy. Just select the clips you want to combine and choose Edit > Bounce to Clip(s). SONAR then creates one new clip from the old, selected ones.

Bounce To Track(s)

The problem with the Bounce to Clip(s) function is that it works only on clips that are on the same track. If you want to combine clips from different tracks, you have to use the Bounce to Track(s) function as follows:

NOTE

The Bounce to Track(s) function also has a limitation: It works only with audio tracks.

1. Select the clips you want to combine.

2. Choose Edit > Bounce to Track(s) to open the Bounce to Track(s) dialog box (see Figure 7.11).

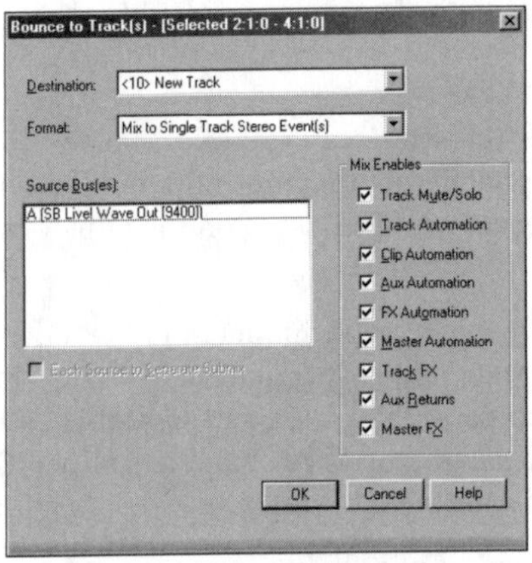

Figure 7.11
Use the Bounce to Track(s) function to combine clips from multiple tracks.

3. Since you are combining clips from multiple tracks into one clip, the new clip has to reside on a single track. In the Destination drop-down list, choose the track on which you want your new combined clip to reside.

4. The Bounce to Track(s) function lets you determine the format of your new clip. In the Format drop-down list, choose the format you would like to use. Choose Mix to Single Track Stereo Event(s) to create a single stereo track from your combined clips. Choose Mix to Separate Left and Right Tracks to create two new tracks, each holding the left and right stereo channels of your new audio data respectively. Choose Mix Stereo Content to Mono to create a single mono track from your combined clips.

5. In the Source Bus(es) section, choose the output of your sound card that you would like SONAR to use when combining your clips.

6. In the Mix Enables section, activate the automation and effects options you would like to have included in the new clip from the clips being combined. You should usually keep all these options activated. I'll talk more about effects and automation in chapters 11 and 12.

7. Click OK.

SONAR combines all your clips into one new clip and puts it in the track you specified.

The Split Function

SONAR also enables you to split clips using its Split function. It works like this:

1. Select the Clip(s) that you want to split.

2. Choose Edit > Split to open the Split Clips dialog box (see Figure 7.12).

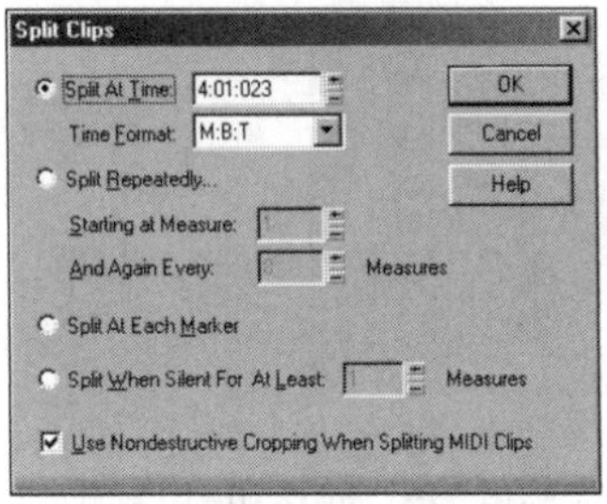

Figure 7.12
Using the Split Clips dialog box, you can split clips into new, smaller clips in a variety of ways.

3. Choose the Split option you want to use. The Split At Time option lets you split a clip at a certain measure, beat, or tick. The Split Repeatedly option lets you split a clip into a bunch of smaller clips instead of just two new smaller ones. Just enter at what measure you want the first split to occur and at how many measures you want each consecutive split to occur after that. For example, if you have a clip that begins at measure 2 and ends at measure 7, and you want to create three two-bar clips out of it, enter 2 for the starting measure and 2 for the split interval. The Split at Each Marker option lets you split clips according to the markers you set up in the Track view. You learned about markers in Chapter 5. Finally, the Split When Silent For At Least option lets you split clips at any place where silence occurs within them. You can set the interval of silence that SONAR has to look for by entering a number of measures.

4. Click on OK.

Moving and Copying

You can also change the arrangement of your data by moving and copying clips to new locations, either within the same tracks or into other tracks. One way to move a clip is to use the Clip Properties dialog box and enter a new start time for the clip. You can also move a clip by simply clicking and dragging it to a new location with your mouse. As long as the track you're dragging the clip into doesn't contain any other existing clips, you have nothing to worry about. SONAR simply moves the clip to its new location.

If the track contains existing data, though, SONAR asks how you want the data to be handled by displaying the Drag and Drop Options dialog box (see Figure 7.13). You then have to choose one of three options: Blend Old and New, Replace Old with New, or Slide Over Old to Make Room.

Figure 7.13
If you move a clip within a track that contains existing material, SONAR displays the Drag and Drop Options dialog box.

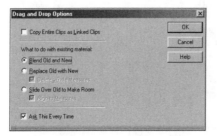

If you choose the Blend Old and New option, the clip you're moving simply overlaps any existing clips. This means that the clips remain separate, but they overlap so that, during playback, the data in the overlapping sections play simultaneously. If you choose the Replace Old with New option, the overlapping portion of the clip you are moving replaces (which means erases and takes the place of) the portion of the clip being overlapped. If you choose the Slide Over Old to Make Room option, the start times of any existing clips are simply changed to make room for the new clip. So, during playback, the new clip plays at the time it was placed at, and the existing clips play a little later, depending on how much their start times had to be changed.

If you would rather copy a clip instead of just moving it, you can use SONAR's Copy, Cut, and Paste functions. Actually, using the Cut function is the same as moving a clip. If you use the Copy function, though, you can keep the original clip in its place and put a copy of it in the new location. This procedure works as follows:

1. Select the clip(s) you want to copy.
2. Select Edit > Copy to open the Copy dialog box (see Figure 7.14).

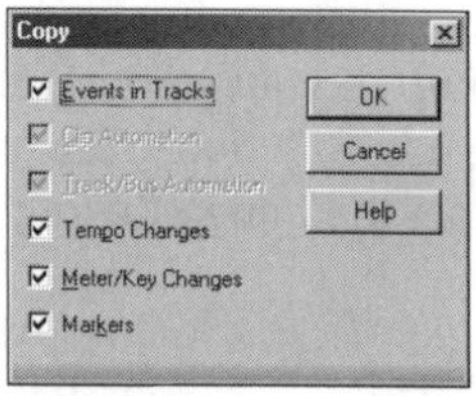

Figure 7.14
To copy clips, you use the Copy dialog box.

CHAPTER 7

3.   Choose the type(s) of data you want to copy. Usually, you should choose the Events in Tracks option.

4.   Click on OK.

5.   Click on the track number of the track into which you want to copy the clip(s).

6.   Set the Now time to the point within the track at which you want to place the clip(s).

7.   Select Edit > Paste to open the Paste dialog box. Then click on the Advanced button to open the Advanced Paste dialog box (see Figure 7.15).

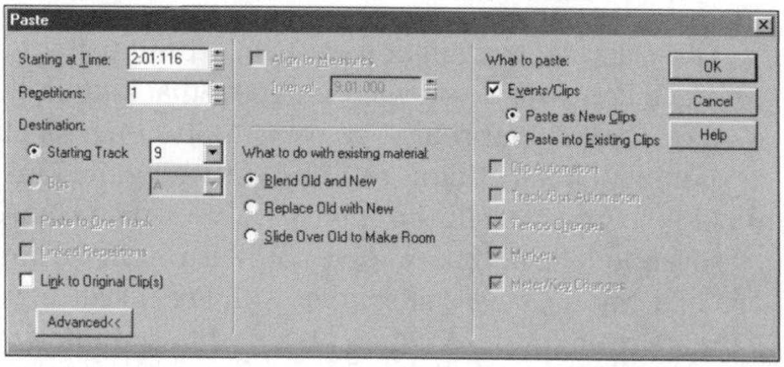

Figure 7.15
Clicking on the Advanced button will open the Advanced Paste dialog box.

8.   Choose the options you want to use. Most of these options are self-explanatory. Setting the Starting at Time option is the same as setting the Now time in Step 6. Setting the Starting Track option is the same as setting the Track in Step 5. The Repetitions option simply lets you create more than one copy of the clip if you want. I've already talked about the options listed under What to do with existing material. The only new ones are the Paste as New Clips and Paste into Existing Clips options. The Paste as New Clips option creates a new clip and then follows the overlapping rules that you choose with the What to do with existing material options. The Paste into Existing Clips option, however, merges the clip that you are copying with any existing clips that it overlaps. You end up with material from both clips merged into one.

9.   Click on OK.

If some of these options sound a little confusing, just experiment with them a bit. Make an extra backup of your project, and then use it to go wild with the copying and pasting functions. Try every possible combination, and soon you'll get the hang of using them.

> **TIP**
> You can also quickly copy a clip by holding down the CTRL key on your computer keyboard and clicking and dragging the clip to a new location. A copy of the clip is made and placed at the new location.

Linked Clips

You may have noticed a few other options in the Paste dialog boxes—namely, the Linked Repetitions and Link to Original Clips options. These options deal with a special feature in SONAR called linked clips. Using this feature, you can link copies of a clip to each other so that any changes you make to one clip will affect the others that are linked to it. This way, you can easily create repeating patterns and then make changes to the patterns later.

For example, you might have a cool drum pattern in a clip that takes up one measure and you want to repeat that pattern through the first eight measures of your song. You can simply copy the clip and then paste it (setting the Repetitions to 7 and activating the Linked Repetitions and Link to Original Clips options). SONAR then copies your clip and pastes seven identical, linked copies of it. If you make any changes to one of the clips, these changes affect them all. For instance, you can change the snare drum from sounding on beat 2 to sounding on beat 3 in one of the clips, and the change happens in all of them. Linked clips is a very fun, cool, and time-saving feature.

If you ever want to unlink linked clips, just follow these steps:

1. Select the clips you want to unlink. You don't have to unlink all linked clips in a group. For example, if you have four linked clips, you can select two of them to unlink, and the two that you leave unselected remain linked.

2. Right-click on one of the selected clips and select Unlink from the pop-up menu to open the Unlink Clips dialog box.

3. Choose an unlink option. The New Linked Group option unlinks the selected clips from the other clips but keeps them linked to each other. The Independent, Not Linked At All option totally unlinks the clips from any others.

4. Click on OK.

Linked clips are shown with dotted outlines in the Clips pane of the Track view. When you unlink them, they appear as normal clips again.

Erasing

Deleting any clips that you no longer need is an easy process; just follow these steps:

1. Select the clips you want to delete.

2. Select Edit > Delete to open the Delete dialog box (see Figure 7.16).

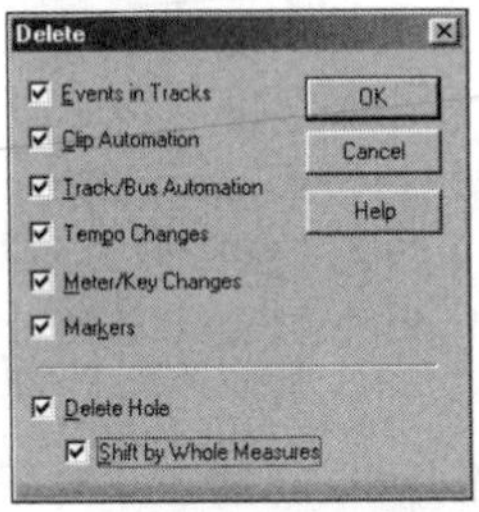

Figure 7.16
In the Delete dialog box, you can determine the type of data you want to erase.

3. Make sure the Events in Tracks option is activated.

4. If you want to have SONAR remove the space that's created when you delete the clip(s), activate the Delete Hole option. SONAR moves any other existing clips in the track backward (toward the beginning of the project) by the amount of time opened when you delete the clip(s). Just give it a try, and you'll see what I mean.

5. Click on OK.

Inserting

Instead of manipulating existing data, you sometimes might need to introduce silent parts into your project. You can do so by using SONAR's Insert > Time/Measures feature. This feature allows you to insert blank space in the form of measures, ticks, seconds, or frames. You also can insert the space either into the whole project or into selected tracks. It works like this:

1. Select Edit > Select > None to clear any currently selected data in the project.

2. If you want to insert space into the whole project, skip to Step 3. Otherwise, select the track(s) into which you want to insert space.

3. Set the Now time to the point in the track(s) or project at which you want the space inserted.

4. Select Insert > Time/Measures to open the Insert Time/Measures dialog box (see Figure 7.17).

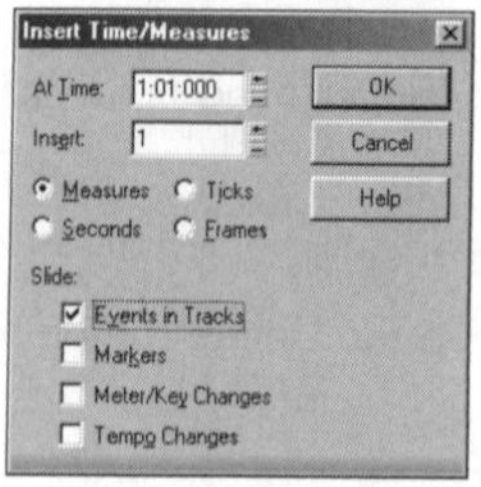

Figure 7.17
In the Insert Time/Measures dialog box, you can insert blank space into selected tracks or the entire project.

5. The At Time parameter reflects the current Now time. Type a new time here, or make adjustments if you'd like.

6. For the Insert parameter, type the number of units of blank space you want to have inserted.

7. Select the type of unit you want to have inserted. You can choose to insert measures, ticks, seconds, or frames.

8. In the Slide section, choose the types of data that will be affected by the insert process. The types of data you select will be moved to make room for the new blank space. Of course, you'll almost always want to have the Events in Tracks option activated. When you're inserting space into selected tracks, the Events in Tracks option is usually the only one you want to have activated. When you're inserting space into the entire project, on the other hand, you'll more than likely want to have all the options activated.

9. Click on OK.

SONAR then inserts the number of measures, ticks, seconds, or frames you typed into the Insert parameter at the Now time you specified. It also moves the types of data you selected by sliding the data forward in time (toward the end of the project). So, for instance, if you inserted a measure of blank space into the entire project at measure 2, then all the data in all the tracks starting at measure 2 is shifted forward by one measure. Whatever data was in measure 2 is now in measure 3, and any data that was in measure 3 is in measure 4, and so on.

Slip Editing

Up until now, all of the editing functions I've described in this chapter work by making permanent changes to the MIDI and audio data in your clips and tracks. This is called *destructive processing*, because it "destroys" the original data by modifying (or overwriting) it according to any editing that you apply.

> **NOTE**
>
> As you know, you can remove any destructive processing done to your data by using SONAR's Undo function. You can also load a saved copy of your project containing the original data. But neither of these restoration methods is as convenient as using nondestructive processing.

In contrast to destructive processing, SONAR also includes some editing functions (called *slip editing* functions) that provide *nondestructive* processing. The slip editing functions are nondestructive because they don't apply any permanent changes to your data. Instead, they are applied only during playback, letting you hear the results while leaving your original data intact.

The slip editing functions can be used to crop the beginning or end of a clip, shift the contents of a clip, or shift-crop the beginning or end of a clip.

Cropping a Clip

To crop the beginning or end of a clip, do the following:

1. If you want to crop the beginning of a clip, position your mouse over the left end of the clip until the cursor turns into a square (see Figure 7.18).

Figure 7.18
Position your mouse over the left end of the clip to crop the beginning.

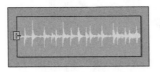

2. Click and drag your mouse toward the right so that the clip changes length, as shown in Figure 7.19.

Figure 7.19
Click and drag to the right to shorten the clip from the beginning.

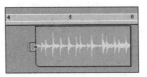

CHAPTER 7

3. If you want to crop the end of a clip, follow steps 1 and 2 but adjust the right end of the clip rather than the left end, so that it looks like what is shown in Figure 7.20.

Figure 7.20
Click and drag the right end of the clip to crop the end.

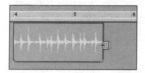

When you crop a clip, the data that is cropped is not deleted. Instead, the data is masked so that you will not hear it during playback. So, if you crop the first two beats in a one-measure clip, those first two beats will not sound during playback. And if you crop the last two beats in a one-measure clip, those last two beats will not sound during playback.

NOTE

When you crop a clip, the length of the clip is altered. The space where the cropped data used to be will be filled with silence during playback. So, you may need to make some adjustments to the position of your clips within your tracks.

Shifting a Clip

Instead of cropping a clip (and thus changing its length) you can also shift the data inside a clip without changing the length of the clip. To shift a clip, do the following:

1. Press and hold the Alt+Shift keys on your computer keyboard.
2. Position your mouse over the middle of the clip until the cursor turns into a square (see Figure 7.21).

Figure 7.21
To shift a clip, position your mouse in the middle of the clip.

3. Click and drag to the left to shift the data in the clip toward the beginning of the clip.
4. Click and drag to the right to shift the data in the clip toward the end of the clip.

When you shift a clip, the data in the beginning or end of the clip is cropped, but the length of the clip is not altered, as shown in Figure 7.22.

Figure 7.22
Shifting a clip still crops the data but doesn't alter the length of the clip.

Shift-Cropping a Clip

Shift-cropping is a combination of the aforementioned functions. When you shift-crop a clip, the data in the clip is shifted and the length of the clip is altered. To shift-crop a clip, do the following:

1. Press and hold the Alt+Shift keys on your computer keyboard.
2. Position your mouse over the left or right end of the clip (depending on whether you want to shift-crop the beginning or end of the clip) until the cursor turns into a square.
3. Click and drag to the left or right to alter the length of the clip and shift the data inside the clip at the same time.

The slip editing functions can be very powerful alternatives to cutting and pasting. Since the data from the clips isn't deleted, you can edit the clips at any time to specify what portions of their data will sound during playback. So, for example, if you have a clip that contains a vocal phrase and the first word in the phrase isn't quite right, you can crop it. But later on, if you decide that the word actually sounded good, just uncrop it and, like magic, your data is restored.

TIP

SONAR provides some additional non-destructive editing functions called *envelopes*. I'll talk more about envelopes in Chapter 12.

Audio Editing

Although SONAR provides separate views for precise editing of MIDI data, it doesn't provide a dedicated view for editing audio data. Instead, the Track view doubles as an audio editor. To edit audio in the Track view, you simply use all of the functions described previously in this chapter to edit any audio clips in your tracks. There are some other, more sophisticated functions available for editing audio data that I'll describe in Chapter 8.

There are, however, a couple things you should keep in mind while editing audio in the Track view.

Audio Waveforms

When examining audio clips, you'll notice that they display the audio waveforms corresponding to the audio data inside them.

NOTE

An *audio waveform* is a graphical representation of sound. Let me try to explain using the cup and string analogy. Remember when you were a kid, and you set up your own intercom system between your bedroom and your tree house using nothing but a couple of paper cups and a long piece of string? You poked a hole in the bottom of each cup and then tied one end of the string to one cup and the other end of the string to the other cup. Your friend would be in the tree house with one of the cups, and you would be in your bedroom with the other. As you talked into your cup, your friend could hear you by putting his cup to his ear, and vice versa. Why did it work?

Well, when you talked into the cup, the sound of your voice vibrated the bottom of the cup, making it act like a microphone. This movement, in turn, vibrated the string up and down, and the string carried the vibrations to the other cup. This movement made the bottom of that cup vibrate so that it acted like a speaker, thus letting your friend hear what you said. If it were possible for you to freeze the string while it was in motion and then zoom in on it so you could see the vibrations, it would look similar to the audio waveforms shown in Figure 7.23.

As you can see, a waveform shows up and down movements just like a vibrating string. A line, called the *zero axis,* runs horizontally through the center of the waveform. The zero axis represents the point in a waveform at which there are no vibrations or there is no sound, so the value of the audio data at the zero axis is the number zero (also known as *zero amplitude*). When a waveform moves above or below the zero axis, vibrations occur, and thus there is sound. The amplitude value of a waveform in these places depends on how high above or how low below the zero axis the waveform is at a certain point in time (shown on the Time Ruler).

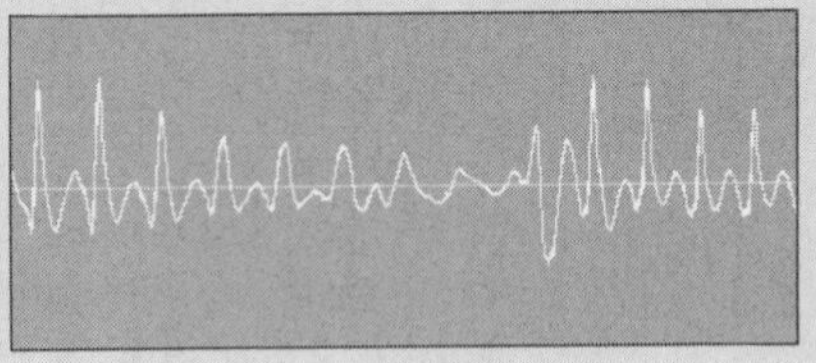

Figure 7.23
An audio waveform
is similar to that of a
vibrating string if you
could freeze and zoom
in on it to observe the
vibrations.

Snap to Zero Crossing

Another thing to keep in mind is that you need to make sure to edit your audio data at zero crossings in the waveform to avoid noisy pops or clicks. You can do so by activating the Snap to Audio Zero Crossings feature, which you access via the Snap to Grid dialog box. Just open the Snap to Grid dialog box by right-clicking on the Snap to Grid button at the bottom of the Track view and then put a check mark next to the Snap to Audio Zero Crossings option.

The Snap to Audio Zero Crossings feature (when activated) makes sure that, when you make a selection or perform an edit, your selections or edits fall on zero crossings in the audio waveform.

NOTE

Remember the description of the zero axis? Well, any point in an audio waveform that lands on the zero axis is called a *zero crossing*. It's called that because, as the waveform moves up and down, it crosses over the zero axis.

Why is it important that your selections and edits line up with zero crossings? Because a zero crossing is a point in the audio waveform at which no sound is being made, it provides a perfect spot at which to edit the waveform— for example, when you're cutting and pasting pieces of audio. If you edit an audio waveform at a point where it's either above or below the zero axis, you might introduce glitches, which can come in the form of audible pops and clicks. You get these glitches because you cut at a moment when sound is being produced. You also get them because, when you're pasting pieces of audio together, you cannot guarantee that the ends of each waveform will line up perfectly (except, of course, if they both are at zero crossings).

Practice Arrangement

Before you move on to the next part of the chapter, I thought you might like to try out some of the arranging techniques I just described. You can use one of the sample projects that comes supplied with SONAR to practice a few of the techniques and make that project sound a bit different by simply manipulating its tracks and clips. Just follow these steps:

1. Open the sample project called Ballad #1.wrk. Because you'll be working only with the tracks and clips in the project, close all of the open views except the Track view.

2. Save the project under a new name using File > Save As so that you don't ruin the original project file. Just type something like Practice Arrangement.wrk for the filename.

3. Play through the project once so you can hear what it sounds like before you make any changes.

CHAPTER 7

4. The first couple of changes you're going to make are to both the beginning and end of the song. I don't particularly like the ending, and I think the beginning needs a little more excitement. So, for this example, you can move the last clips in Tracks 1, 2, 3, and 6 to the beginning of those tracks. First, select the clips (see Figure 7.24).

Figure 7.24
Select the last clips in Tracks 1, 2, 3, and 6.

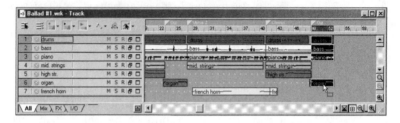

5. Choose Edit > Cut to open the Cut dialog box. Make sure the Events in Tracks option is activated. If you want to move the marker, just keep the Markers option activated, too. Then click on OK. SONAR temporarily removes those clips from the project.

6. To add the clips back into the project, but at the beginning, set the Now time to the beginning of the project.

7. Choose Edit > Paste to open the Paste dialog box. If only the basic Paste dialog box is displayed, click on the Advanced button to open the Advanced Paste dialog box.

8. Make sure the Repetitions parameter is set to 1 and the Starting at Track parameter is set to 1.

9. In the What to do with existing material section, activate the Slide Over Old to Make Room option. In the What to paste section, make sure the Events/Clips and the Paste as New Clips options are activated. Then click on OK.

   SONAR takes the clips you removed from the end of the project and inserts them into the beginning of the project. It also moves any existing clips in Tracks 1, 2, 3, and 6 forward in time (see Figure 7.25).

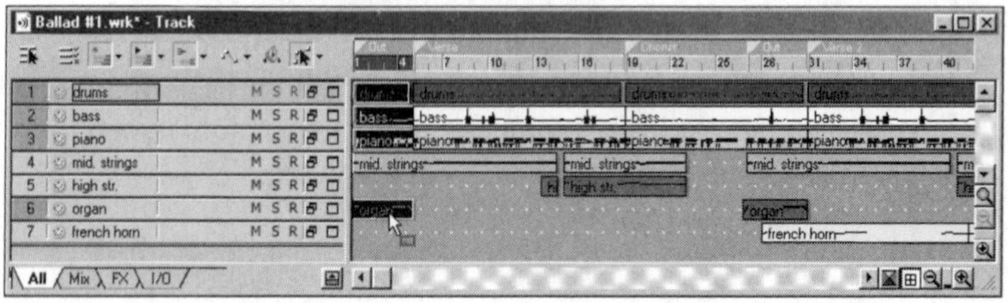

Figure 7.25
The clips from Tracks 1, 2, 3, and 6 at the end of the project have been moved to the beginning of the project.

CHAPTER 7

10. Try playing the project again to see what it sounds like now. Something isn't quite right, is it? When you pasted the material at the beginning of Tracks 1, 2, 3, and 6, the existing material in those tracks was moved forward, but the material in Tracks 4, 5, and 7 stayed in the same place. So now the music in those tracks doesn't line up correctly with the others. You have to move that material forward by four measures so that the music sounds the way it's supposed to. First, select Edit > Select > None to remove any current track and clips selections.

11. Select Tracks 4, 5, and 7. Be sure to select the entire tracks, not just the individual clips within them.

12. Click and drag the first clip in Track 4 four measures forward in time. This action opens the Drag and Drop Options dialog box. Be sure the Slide Over Old to Make Room and Align to Measures options are activated. Then click on OK. SONAR moves all the clips in Tracks 4, 5, and 7 forward four measures, and now everything is aligned correctly.

TIP

If you have trouble moving the clips exactly four measures, try activating the Snap to Grid feature in the Track view. I talked about the Snap to Grid feature in Chapter 5.

13. One last change you need to make is at the end of Track 6. When you removed the last clip in that track, a very tiny clip that was meant as an intro to that last clip was left behind. Because you've changed the ending, though, you no longer need that intro clip, so just delete it.

14. Set the Now time to the beginning of the project and start playback.

See how powerful the arranging features in SONAR are? With only a few simple changes, you've given this song a much nicer beginning and ending, and you didn't even have to add any new material. Of course, you could have made even more changes to make the song sound radically different, but I'll leave that to you to experiment with. Remember, you can't ruin anything, because you have the original project file saved to disk. This one is a practice file, so you can arrange to your heart's content. You might also want to try some arranging techniques on some of the other sample files included with SONAR.

Using the Piano Roll View

By manipulating the tracks and clips in your project, you can change the overall structure, but to fix single-note mistakes and make smaller changes, you need to do some precision editing. You do so by selecting individual or multiple tracks or clips in the Track view and then using the view menu to open the data within one of the other available views. For editing MIDI data, that would be the Piano Roll view. (You also can edit MIDI data as standard music notation in the Staff view, which I'll talk about in Chapter 13.)

Using the Piano Roll view (see Figure 7.26), you can add, edit, and delete MIDI note and controller data within your MIDI tracks. Looking somewhat like a player piano roll, the Piano Roll view represents notes as colored rectangles on a grid display with the pitches of the notes designated by an on-screen music keyboard.

Figure 7.26
The Piano Roll view resembles that of the old player piano rolls used in the late 1800s and early 1900s.

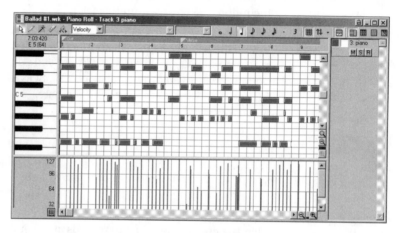

More precisely, the Piano Roll view consists of five major sections: the toolbar (located at the top of the view, containing all the view's related controls), the Note pane (located in the center of the view, displaying the notes in the currently selected track), the Keyboard pane (located on the left of the view, displaying the pitch values of the notes shown in the Note pane), the Controller pane (located at the bottom of the view, displaying the MIDI controller data in the currently selected track), and the Track pane (located at the right of the view, showing a list of all the tracks currently being displayed—the Piano Roll view can display the data from more than one track at one time).

You'll also notice that the Piano Roll view has scroll bars and zoom tools just like the Track view. These tools work the same way as they do in the Track view. In addition, a Snap to Grid function is represented by the Grid button in the toolbar. Other similarities are the marker area and the Time Ruler, which are located just above the Note pane. Basically, you can use the Piano Roll view to edit and view the data within the MIDI tracks of your project in more detail.

You can open the view in three different ways:

▶ In the Track view, select the track(s) you want to edit and then choose View > Piano Roll.

▶ In the Track view, right-click on a track or clip and choose View > Piano Roll from the pop-up menu.

▶ In the Track view, double-click on a MIDI clip in the Clips pane.

Whichever method you choose, SONAR then opens the Piano Roll view and displays the data from the track(s) you selected.

Working with Multiple Tracks

If you select more than one track to be displayed at one time, the Piano Roll view shows the data from each track using a unique color. For example, the notes and controllers from one track may be shown as yellow, and the data from another track may be shown as blue.

> **NOTE**
>
> The one exception to the use of track colors is that tracks with numbers ending in the same digit (that is, 1, 11, 21, and so on) must all share the same color. There's no way around this. You can change the color used by each number group, however, by using the Colors dialog box, which you access by selecting Options > Colors. You learned how to customize SONAR's colors in Chapter 3.

Each track is also listed in the Track pane with a set of individual controls (see Figure 7.27).

Figure 7.27
The data from multiple tracks is shown with different colors, and each track is listed in the Track pane.

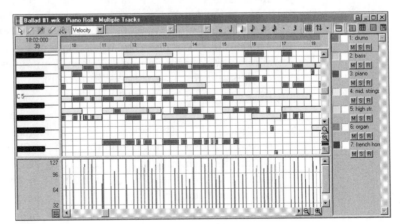

The Track Pane

When you open the Piano Roll view, the names and numbers of the tracks you selected are listed in the Track pane. For convenience, the associated Mute, Solo, and Record buttons for each track are also provided. Plus, you'll notice two other controls available for each track in the list:

▶ **Mask Selection**—The white button shown next to each track in the Track pane is the Mask Selection button. This button determines whether the notes for its associated track can be edited. When the button is white, the notes appear in color in the Note pane, and they can be edited. When the button is gray, the notes appear gray in the Note pane, and they cannot be edited. Clicking on the Mask Selection button toggles it on and off.

▶ **Show/Hide Track**—The button shown to the left of the Mask Selection button is the Show/Hide Track button. This button determines whether the notes for its associated track will be displayed in the Note pane. When the button is in color (which is the same color as the notes for that track), the notes are shown in the Note pane. When the button is white, the notes are not shown in the Note pane. Clicking on the Show/Hide Track button toggles it on and off.

The Track Tools

In addition to the Track pane controls, six other track-related controls are located in the toolbar. They are the last six buttons in the toolbar, at the right side of the Piano Roll view:

▶ **Invert Tracks**—The first button in the group (going from right to left) is the Invert Tracks button. Clicking on this button toggles the Show/Hide Track buttons for each of the tracks in the Track pane. This means that if one track has its Show/Hide Track button on and another track has its button off, clicking on the Invert Tracks button turns off the first track's Show/Hide button and turns on the second track's Show/Hide button. It toggles the current state of each Show/Hide Track button.

▶ **No Tracks**—The next button over in the toolbar is the No Tracks button. Clicking on this button turns off the Show/Hide Track buttons for each track in the Track List pane. No matter what state each Show/Hide Track button is in (either on or off), the No Track button turns them all off.

▶ **All Tracks**—The next button over in the toolbar is the All Tracks button. This button is the exact opposite of the No Tracks button. Clicking on the All Tracks button turns on the Show/Hide Track buttons for each track in the Track List pane.

▶ **Show/Hide Track Pane**—The next button over in the toolbar is the Show/Hide Track Pane button. Clicking on this button simply toggles between having the Track pane open or closed.

▶ **Show/Hide Controller Pane**—The next button over in the toolbar is the Show/Hide Controller Pane. Clicking on this button simply toggles between having the Controller pane open or closed. I'll talk more about the Controller pane later in this chapter.

▶ **Pick Tracks**—While you have the Piano Roll view open, you might want to add or remove some of the tracks in the Track pane. Instead of having to close the Piano Roll view, select other tracks in the Track view and then open the Piano Roll view again, you can use the Pick Tracks feature.

Clicking on the Pick Tracks button (the next button over from the Show/Hide Controller Pane button in the toolbar) opens the Pick Tracks dialog box. This box displays a list of all the tracks in your project. You can select one or more tracks from the list. (Hold down the Ctrl key on your computer keyboard to select multiple tracks.) After you click on the OK button, the tracks that you selected are listed in the Track pane, and the notes in those tracks are shown in the Note pane.

TIP

If you have two or more tracks that contain the same exact notes, those notes overlap one another in the Note pane. What determines which track's notes are on top is the order of the tracks in the Track pane. For example, if Track 4 is listed above Track 2 in the Track pane, the data from Track 4 overlaps the data from Track 2 in the Note pane. If you want to change this order (meaning you want the data from Track 2 to overlap the data from Track 4), you can click and drag the Track listing in the Track pane to a new position in the list.

Dealing with Notes

When you open a MIDI track in the Piano Roll view, the notes in that track are displayed in the Note pane. Each note is represented by a colored rectangle. The horizontal location of a note designates its Start time when you line up the left side of the rectangle with the numbers in the Time Ruler, and the vertical location of a note designates its pitch when you line up the whole rectangle with the keys in the Keyboard pane. The length of the rectangle designates the duration of the note (for instance, quarter note, eighth note, and so on).

NOTE

In one instance, the notes in the Note pane and the keys in the Keyboard pane appear differently. If you open the Piano Roll view for a track that uses a MIDI channel that has been assigned to a percussion instrument, instead of keys in the Keyboard pane, you'll see percussion instrument names. And instead of rectangles in the Note pane, you'll see small colored diamonds (see Figure 7.28). This mode is known as the Drum Mode. The colored diamonds still represent notes, but because there's no use for duration (or note length) when dealing with percussion, the diamonds all appear the same size. Also, instead of changing the pitch of a note when you move its diamond up or down in the Note pane, the actual instrument for that Note changes, according to the instrument names displayed in the Keyboard pane. Recall the description of assigning instruments and Instrument Definitions in Chapter 3. If you need to manually activate Drum Mode in the Piano Roll view, you can right-click in the Keyboard pane to open the Note Names dialog box. Just select the Use These Note Names Instead option to change the Keyboard pane display.

Figure 7.28
In Drum Mode, you can use the Piano Roll view to edit percussion tracks in a more intuitive manner.

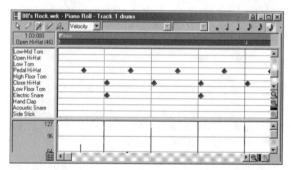

You can add new notes to a track or edit the existing ones using the tools represented by the first five buttons in the toolbar (from left to right on the left side of the Piano Roll view).

Selecting

The first button in the toolbar represents the Select tool. Using this tool, you can select notes for further manipulation, such as deleting, copying, moving, and so on. Essentially, you select notes the same way you select clips in the Track view. To select a single note, click on it. To select more than one note, hold down the Ctrl key on your computer keyboard while clicking on the notes you want to select. You know the rest.

One additional selection method involves the Keyboard pane. To select all the notes of a certain pitch, you can click on one of the keys in the Keyboard pane. You can also drag your mouse pointer across several keys to select the notes of a number of different pitches.

CHAPTER 7

Editing

After you've made a selection, you can copy, cut, paste, move, and delete the notes the same way you do with clips in the Track view. You can also edit notes individually by using the Draw tool. The second button in the toolbar represents the Draw tool. Using this tool, you can add (which I'll describe shortly) and edit the notes in the Note pane.

To change the Start time of a note, simply drag the left edge of its rectangle left or right. This action moves it to a different horizontal location along the Time Ruler.

To change the pitch of a note, simply drag the middle of its rectangle up or down. This action moves it to a different vertical location along the Keyboard pane.

To change the duration of a note, simply drag the right edge of its rectangle left or right. This action changes the length of the rectangle and thus the duration of the note.

Of course, sometimes you might want to make more precise changes to a note. You can do so by using the Note Properties dialog box. Just right-click on a note to open the Note Properties dialog box (see Figure 7.29).

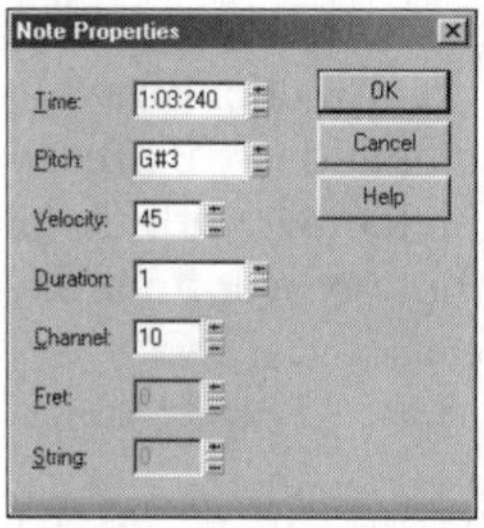

Figure 7.29
In the Note Properties dialog box, you can make precise changes to a note in the Piano Roll view.

In the Note Properties dialog box, you can make precise changes to the Start time, pitch, velocity, duration, and MIDI channel of an individual note by typing numerical values. If you're wondering about the fret and string parameters, I'll describe them in Chapter 13.

Drawing (or Adding)

In addition to editing, the Draw tool allows you to add notes to a track by literally drawing them in. To do so, just follow these steps:

1. Select the Draw tool by clicking on its toolbar button.

2. Select a duration for the new note(s). If you look a little further over in the toolbar, you'll notice a number of buttons with note values shown on them. Clicking on these buttons determines the duration for your new note(s). For example, if you click on the Quarter Note button, the duration is set to a quarter note. You'll also see two additional buttons: one representing a dotted note and another representing a triplet note. So, if you want your notes to be dotted or triplets, click on one of those buttons as well.

3. Click anywhere within the Note pane at the point at which you want to place the new note(s). Remember, the horizontal position of the note determines its Start time, and the vertical position of the note determines its pitch.

Erasing

Even though you can select and delete notes (as I described earlier), the Piano Roll view includes an Erase tool for added convenience. To use it, just select the Erase tool and then click on any note(s) in the Note pane that you want to delete. You can also click and drag the Erase tool over a number of notes to erase them all at once. By the way, the Erase tool is represented by the button in the toolbar with the picture of an eraser shown on it. It is not the next button over from the Draw tool. I'll describe that other tool later.

Scrubbing

When you're editing the data in a track, the procedure usually involves making your edits and then playing back the project to hear how the changes sound. However, playing back very small sections can be a bit difficult, especially when you're working with a fast tempo. To remedy this situation, SONAR provides a Scrub tool.

Using the Scrub tool, you can drag your mouse pointer over the data in the Piano Roll view and hear what it sounds like. To use it, simply select the Scrub tool by clicking on its button in the toolbar (the one with the small yellow speaker shown on it). Then click and drag your mouse pointer over the data in the Note pane. Dragging left to right plays the data forward (what would normally happen during playback), and dragging right to left enables you to hear the data played in reverse. This capability can be useful for testing very short (one or two measure) sections.

CHAPTER 7

TIP

Instead of using the Scrub tool, you might want to try a more useful technique for hearing what your changes sound like. Did you know that you can edit the data in your project as it's being played back? Of course, it's a bit difficult to edit anything while SONAR is scrolling the display as the project plays. I like to work on a small section of a project at a time. I set up a section of the project to loop over and over, and as SONAR is playing the data, I make any changes I think might be needed. Because the data is being played back while I edit, I can instantly hear what the changes sound like. This procedure is much easier than having to keep going back and forth, making changes and manually starting and stopping playback. You learned about looping in Chapter 6. By the way, you can use any of the views to edit your data while SONAR is playing a project. This tip is not just for the Piano Roll view.

Dealing with Controllers

When you open a MIDI track in the Piano Roll view, in addition to the notes in the Note pane, SONAR displays the MIDI controller data for that track in the Controller pane (see Figure 7.30). Because there are many different types of MIDI controller messages, to help you avoid confusion, the Piano Roll view displays only one type at a time. You can tell the type of MIDI controller that's being displayed by looking at the Control Type drop-down lists located in the toolbar right next to the Scrub tool button. The first list shows the type of controller being displayed. The second list shows the number of the controller being displayed. And the third list shows the MIDI channel being used for that controller. You can change the values for any of these lists by simply clicking on them and selecting a new value from the list that pops-up. Initially, MIDI Note Velocity is shown when you open the Piano Roll view.

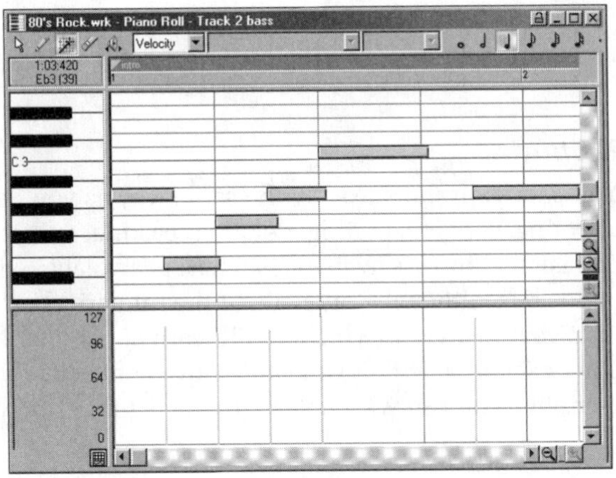

Figure 7.30
MIDI Controller data for a track is displayed in the Controller pane when you open the Piano Roll view.

Each controller is represented by a colored line that runs from the bottom of the Controller pane toward the top. The height of the line designates the value of the controller according to the ruler on the left side of the Controller pane. This ruler gives you a reference to go by for determining the value of a controller; it usually runs from 0 to 127, starting at the bottom of the Controller pane and going all the way to the top. The values can be different according to the type of controller being edited. The horizontal location of a controller designates its Start time according to the Time Ruler at the top of the Piano Roll view.

NOTE

In one instance, the controllers in the Controller pane and the ruler values appear differently. If you select the pitch wheel event type for editing, you'll notice that, instead of originating at the bottom of the Controller pane, the controllers start at the center and extend either up or down (see Figure 7.31). They do so because values for the pitch wheel range from −8192 to 0 to +8191, which you can see in the ruler values. Other than that, pitch wheel events are handled exactly the same as any other types.

Figure 7.31
The pitch wheel is the one exception to how controllers are displayed in the Controller pane.

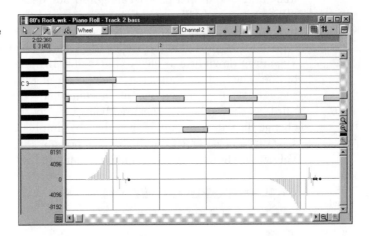

Editing

You edit controllers exactly the same way as you do notes in terms of selecting, copying, cutting, deleting, pasting, and so on. Unfortunately, no precision editing is available such as is available with the Note Properties dialog box, although you can edit the numerical values of controllers via the Event List view (which you'll learn about later in the chapter). One other exception is that you can't move controllers by simply dragging them like you can with notes. You have to cut and paste them instead.

Erasing and Scrubbing

The Eraser and Scrub tools work with controllers exactly the same as they do with notes.

CHAPTER 7

Drawing

You add controllers pretty much in the same way you add notes, but with a couple of exceptions. When you're using the Draw tool, in addition to clicking in the pane to add a single controller, you can also click and drag within the pane to add a whole series of controllers at once.

In addition, you can use another tool, called the Draw Line tool (its button is located right next to the Draw tool button in the Toolbar), to create a smooth series of controllers starting at one value and smoothly increasing or decreasing to another value. Without this tool, it's a bit difficult to achieve the same effect by drawing freely with the Draw tool. To use the Draw Line tool, you just click anywhere within the Controller pane at the controller value you want to begin with and then drag either to the left or right within the pane to draw a line that ends at a different time and a different value. When you release the mouse button, SONAR adds a smooth series of controller values from the first point to the second point in the pane.

CAUTION

If you draw over existing controller values in the Controller pane, the existing values are deleted and replaced with the new values that you have added.

Inserting

SONAR provides one other way to add a smooth series of controller values to your tracks: the Insert Series of Controllers function. I find using the Draw Line tool in the Piano Roll view much more intuitive, but if you need to add controllers over a very long span of time, the Insert Series of Controllers function can be useful. You use it as follows:

1. Select the track to which you want to add the controller values. You can do so either in the Piano Roll view or the Track view.

2. Select Insert > Series of Controllers to open the Insert Series of Controllers dialog box (see Figure 7.32).

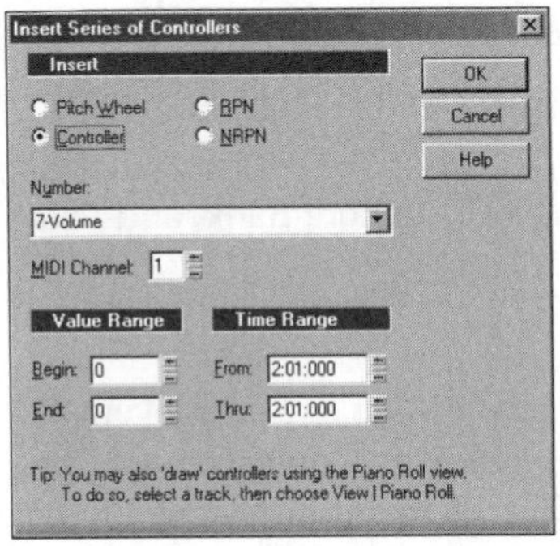

Figure 7.32
Using the Insert Series of Controllers dialog box, you can add a series of controllers that change smoothly from one value to another.

3. In the Insert section, choose the type of controller you want to add, the number of the controller (if appropriate), and the MIDI channel you want the controller to use.

4. In the Value Range section, type numbers for the begin and end parameters. These numbers determine the values of the controller over the range of the series. For example, if you're using a volume controller type, you can have an instrument get louder over time by typing in a small value for Begin and a larger value for End. If you want the instrument to get softer over time, you type a larger value for Begin and a smaller value for End.

5. In the Time Range section, type the measure, beat, and tick values for the location in the project where you want the series of controllers to be inserted.

TIP

You can also set the Time Range parameters before you open the Insert Series of Controllers dialog box by dragging your mouse pointer over the Time Ruler in either the Piano Roll view or the Track view. This action sets up a selection within the project that is automatically used to set the From and Thru values of the Time Range parameters.

Bank/Patch Change

The one type of data that the Piano Roll view doesn't allow you to manipulate is the bank/patch change. This type of event is useful when you want the sound of your MIDI instrument to change automatically during playback of your project. SONAR provides an Insert Bank/Patch Change function that you can use in case you need it.

Utilizing the Insert Bank/Patch Change function is very simple. You just do the following:

1. Click on the name of the track in the Track pane into which you want to insert the bank/patch change.

2. Set the Now time to the measure, beat, and tick at which you want the bank/patch change to occur.

3. Select Insert > Bank/Patch Change to open the Bank/Patch Change dialog box.

4. Choose a Bank Select Method, Bank, and Patch from the appropriate drop-down lists.

5. Click on OK.

SONAR then inserts a bank/patch change event in the track at the Now time you specified. By the way, you can insert (and also edit) bank/patch change events by using the Event List view; I'll describe that task later in this chapter.

Using the Event List View

For the most precise data editing (meaning individual events and their properties), you have to use the Event List view (see Figure 7.33). Using this view, you can add, edit, and delete any kind of event in any track within the entire project. The Event List view doesn't resemble any of the other views; instead of providing a graphical representation of your data, it provides a numerical representation, which you can edit and view. The Event List view displays events as one long list of columns and rows (similar to that of a spreadsheet). Each row holds the data for a single event, and the event's different properties are separated by columns.

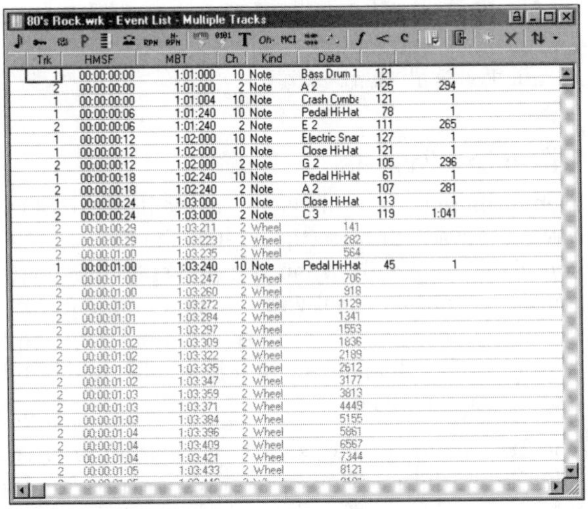

Figure 7.33
You can use the Event List view to edit events numerically using a spreadsheet-like format.

You can use the first column in the list to select events (which I'll describe later). The second column (titled Trk) shows the track number in which an event is stored. The third column (titled HMSF) shows the start time of an event as hours, minutes, seconds, and frames. The fourth column (titled MBT) also shows the start time of an event, but as measures, beats, and ticks. If an event is a MIDI event, the fifth column (titled Ch) shows the MIDI channel to which that event is assigned. The sixth column (titled Kind) shows the type of data an event holds (for example, a MIDI note event or an audio event). The seventh column (titled Data) actually spans across the seventh, eighth, and ninth columns (the last three), and these columns hold the data values associated with each event. For instance, for a MIDI note event, the seventh column would hold the pitch, the eighth column would hold the velocity, and the ninth column would hold the duration for the note.

Because the Event List view doesn't have any graphical data to contend with, it doesn't provide any Snap to Grid, Zoom, Time Ruler, or Marker features. It does allow you to scroll the list up and down and left and right so that you can access all the events shown. It also provides a toolbar full of buttons (which I'll describe later). One button that you'll recognize, though, is the Pick Tracks button. Just as with the other views, the Event List view allows you to display the data from multiple tracks at once.

Opening the View

You open the Event List view via the Track view. You simply select one or more tracks and then either select View > Event List or right-click on one of the selected tracks and choose View > Event List from the pop-up menu. That's all there is to it.

Filtering Events

Many different types of events are available in SONAR, and sometimes having to wade through them all in the Event List view can get a bit confusing, especially when you're displaying the data from multiple tracks. To help you deal with the problem, the Event List view allows you to filter out each of the event types from being displayed. This filtering does not affect the data at all; it just helps to unclutter the list display if that's what you need.

The first eighteen buttons in the toolbar represent different event types. Initially, all these buttons are set so that all event types are shown in the list when you open the Event List view. By clicking on a button, you can filter out its associated event type from the list. You can click as many of the buttons as you like to filter out multiple types of events. Clicking on a button again turns off its associated event type filter so that the events can be shown in the list again. To see the type of event each button is associated with, just hover your mouse pointer over a button until the pop-up text appears showing the name of the event type.

The Event Manager

If you find it easier to deal with the event types by name rather than by using the buttons, you can use the Event Manager. Just click on the Event Manager button on the toolbar (the one with the check mark shown on it) to open the Event Manager dialog box (see Figure 7.34).

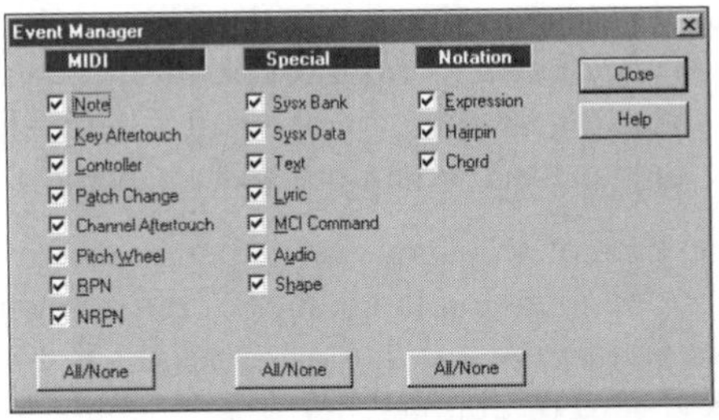

Figure 7.34
You can use the
Event Manager dialog
box to filter Event
types by name.

Event Manager		
MIDI	**Special**	**Notation**

☑ Note   ☑ Sysx Bank   ☑ Expression
☑ Key Aftertouch   ☑ Sysx Data   ☑ Harpin
☑ Controller   ☑ Text   ☑ Chord
☑ Patch Change   ☑ Lyric
☑ Channel Aftertouch ☑ MCI Command
☑ Pitch Wheel   ☑ Audio
☑ RPN   ☑ Shape
☑ NRPN

All/None   All/None   All/None

Close   Help

Initially, all the event types are activated so that they will be displayed
in the list. To filter out a certain type, just click on it to remove its
check mark. You can also use the All/None buttons to quickly activate
or deactivate groups of event types. Click on the Close button when
you're done.

TIP

You can also filter out event types by simply right-clicking anywhere within
the Event List and then selecting an event type from the pop-up list.

Editing Events

If you've ever used a spreadsheet application, you'll be right at home
with editing events in the Event List view. To navigate through the list,
you use the arrow keys on your computer keyboard. These keys move a
small, rectangular cursor through the list. This cursor represents the Now
time. As you move the cursor up and down through the list, the Now
time changes to reflect the time of the event upon which the cursor is
positioned. You can also move the cursor (which I'll call the Now time
cursor from now on) left and right to access the different event
parameters.

Changing

To change an event parameter, just position the Now time cursor over the
parameter, type a new value, and then press the Enter key on your
computer keyboard to accept the new value.

TIP

You can also change an event parameter by double-clicking on it and then
clicking on the little plus or minus buttons that appear to increase or decrease
the value, respectively.

CHAPTER 7

You can change the start time in the HMSF or MBT columns, the MIDI channel, the type of event, and most or all of the values in the data columns, depending on the type of event you're editing. The only thing you can't change is the track number of an event.

Changing the type of an event via the parameter in the Kind column is a bit different from changing the values of the other parameters. Instead of typing a new value, you either must press the Enter key on your computer keyboard or double-click the parameter. This action opens the Kind of Event dialog box (see Figure 7.35). The Kind of Event dialog box displays a list of all the event types available. Select the type of event you want to use and then click on OK.

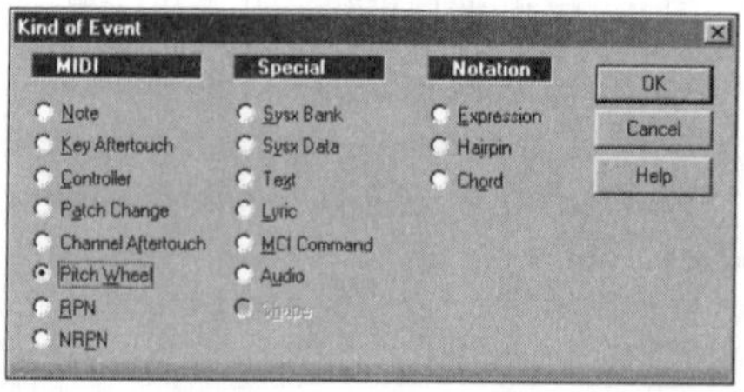

Figure 7.35
You use the Kind of Event dialog box to change the type of an event.

Kind of Event

MIDI: Note, Key Aftertouch, Controller, Patch Change, Channel Aftertouch, Pitch Wheel, RPN, NRPN

Special: Sysx Bank, Sysx Data, Text, Lyric, MCI Command, Audio

Notation: Expression, Hairpin, Chord

OK   Cancel   Help

Selecting

If you ever need to copy, cut, or paste events in the Event List view, you have to select them first. To select a single event, just click in the first column of the row representing the event. You can also select more than one event by dragging your mouse pointer within the first column of the list. If you want to remove a selection, click or drag a second time.

Inserting

You can also add new events to the list by using the Insert function. It works as follows:

1. Position the Now time cursor at the point in the list at which you want to insert a new event.

TIP

Setting the position of the Now time cursor in the Event List view isn't very intuitive. Because the list gives you such a specific close-up look at your data, it's sometimes hard to tell where in your project the Now time cursor is pointing. You might find it easier using one of the other views (such as the Track view or the Piano Roll view) to position the Now time cursor. That way, you get a graphical representation of your project and a better feel for the placement of the cursor. Then you can simply switch to the Event view, and the cursor will be positioned exactly (or at least very close) to the point where you want to insert the new event.

2. Either press the Insert key on your computer keyboard or click on the Insert Event button in the toolbar (the one with the bright yellow star shown on it). SONAR creates a new event in the list using the same parameter values as the event upon which the Now time was positioned.

3. Edit the event parameters.

> **TIP**
>
> When you're changing the type of event using the Kind parameter, the values in the Data columns change according to the type of event you choose. For a list of all the types of events available, along with all their associated parameters, look in the SONAR help file under Editing MIDI Events and Controllers > The Event List View > Event List Buttons And Overview.

Special Events

Two types of Events in SONAR can be accessed only via the Event List view. You can't manipulate them in any of the other views. The first one, called a text event, allows you to add notes to the data in your project. I'm not talking about musical notes, I'm talking about text notes—you know, like those little sticky notes you have plastered all over your studio. Text events can act as little reminders to yourself in case you need to keep track of some kind of special information in certain parts of your project. I've never had a lot of use for text events, but it's nice to know they're available if I need them.

The other type of special event is called the MCIcmd event, or the Windows Media Control Interface (MCI) command event. You can use the MCIcmd event to control the multimedia-related hardware and software in your computer system. For example, by setting the type of an event to MCIcmd and setting the event's Data parameter to PLAY CDAUDIO, you can make the audio CD inside your CD-ROM drive start to play. You can also use MCIcmd events to play audio files, video files, and more. But the problem is that none of these files can be synchronized to the music in your project, so you can't really use these events for too many things. In addition, the subject of MCI commands can be complex and are well beyond the scope of this chapter. If you want to find more information, take a look at the following area on the Microsoft Web site: **http://msdn.microsoft.com/library/psdk/multimed/mci_7vvt.htm**.

Deleting

Erasing events from the list is as easy as it gets. Just move the Now time cursor to the row of the event you want to remove and then click on the Delete Event button in the toolbar (the one with the big red X shown on it). You can also press the Delete key on your computer keyboard.

If you want to delete more than one event at once, select the events you want to remove and then select Edit > Cut to open the Cut dialog box. The parameters in this dialog box work the same way as described in the Track view section of this chapter.

Playing

If you want to quickly preview the event you're currently editing, you can have SONAR play back that single event by holding down the Shift key on your computer keyboard and then pressing the spacebar. If you continue holding the Shift key, each press of the spacebar scrolls down through the list and plays each event. This capability is especially useful for testing MIDI note events.

TIP

You can print a hard copy reference of the Event List if you have a printer connected to your computer system). While the Event List view is open, just select File > Print to print a copy of the list. You can also preview the list before printing it by choosing File > Print Preview.

Using the Tempo View

You learned how to set the initial tempo for a project by using the Tempo toolbar in Chapter 4. But, in addition to the initial project tempo, you can also have the tempo change automatically during playback. To allow you to specify tempo changes within a project, SONAR provides the Tempo view (see Figure 7.36). The Tempo view has some similarities to the Piano Roll view in that it displays a graphical representation of the data you need to manipulate—in this case, tempo. The Tempo view shows the tempo as a line graph with the horizontal axis denoting time (via the Time Ruler) and the vertical axis denoting tempo value.

Figure 7.36
The Tempo view displays the tempo in a project as a line graph.

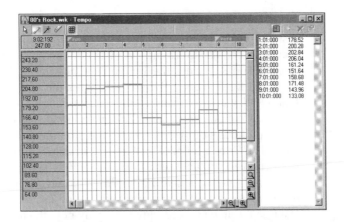

CHAPTER 7

More precisely, the Tempo view consists of three major sections: the toolbar (located at the top of the view, containing all the view's related controls), the Tempo pane (located in the main part of the view, displaying all the tempo changes in the project as a line graph), and the Tempo Change pane (located at the right of the view, showing a list of all the tempo changes within the project). Because tempo affects the whole project, no track selection tools are available here.

Because the Tempo view shows tempo changes graphically, it has scroll bars and zoom tools just like in the Piano Roll view. And, of course, these tools work the same here. In addition, this view provides a Snap to Grid function, which is represented by the Grid button in the toolbar. The Tempo view also contains a marker area and a Time Ruler located just above the Tempo pane. Along the left of the Tempo pane are the tempo measurements, which are used to show the value of the tempo changes displayed in the line graph.

Opening the View

To open the Tempo view, simply select View > Tempo. You don't need to select a track or clip or anything else. For a new project (or a project that doesn't contain any tempo changes), the Tempo view displays a straight horizontal line located vertically on the graph at the tempo measurement value that corresponds to the current tempo setting for the project. So, for instance, if your project has a main tempo of 100, then the line is shown at a tempo measurement of 100 on the graph. In addition to the horizontal line, a single entry in the Tempo Change pane shows the measure, beat, and tick at which the tempo event occurs, along with the tempo value itself. In this example, it is 1:01:000 for the measure, beat, and tick, and 100 for the tempo value.

Editing

Just as you can edit controller messages graphically in the Piano Roll view, you can use the Tempo view to edit tempo changes. Also, just as in the Piano Roll view, the Tempo view provides Select, Draw, Draw Line, and Erase tools. All these tools work the same way they do in the Piano Roll View. You can use the Select tool to select individual and groups of tempo changes by clicking and dragging. Using the Draw tool, you can literally draw in tempo changes on the line graph in the Tempo pane. The Draw Line tool enables you to create smooth tempo changes from one value to another by clicking and dragging. And using the Erase tool, you can erase single and multiple tempo changes by clicking and dragging. As you draw and erase within the Tempo pane, the line graph changes its shape accordingly to display how the tempo will change over time as the project plays. An increase in the tempo (*accelerando*, in musical terms) is shown as an incline in the line graph, and a decrease in tempo (*diminuendo*, in musical terms) is shown as a decline in the line graph.

The Tempo Change Pane

As I mentioned earlier, tempo changes are also listed numerically in the Tempo Change pane. Luckily, you can edit them here, too. I find it easier and more accurate to add and edit tempo changes via the Tempo Change pane rather than draw them in.

Inserting

To add a new tempo change to the list, do the following:

1. Set the Now time to the measure, beat, and tick at which you want the tempo change to occur.

2. Click on the Insert Tempo button in the toolbar (the one with the bright yellow star shown on it) to open the Tempo dialog box (see Figure 7.37).

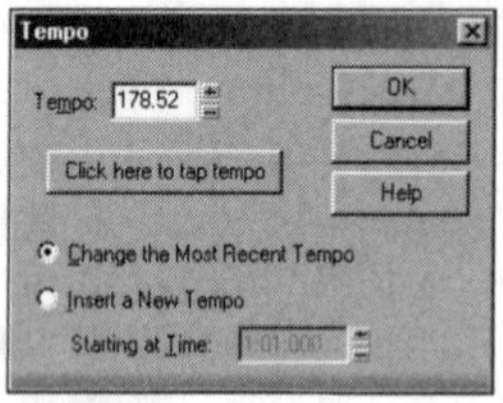

Figure 7.37
In the Tempo dialog box, you can add and edit tempo events.

3. Enter a value for the tempo parameter. You can also tap out a tempo by clicking on the Click here to tap tempo button. When you click repeatedly on the button, SONAR measures the time between each click and calculates the tempo at which you're clicking. It then enters the value into the tempo parameter automatically.

> **TIP**
>
> Instead of using your mouse to click on the Click here to tap tempo button, you might find it easier (and more accurate) to use the spacebar on your computer keyboard. Click on the button with your mouse once just to highlight it and then use your spacebar to tap out a tempo value.

4. Make sure the Insert a New Tempo option is activated.

5. You shouldn't have to enter a value for the Starting at Time parameter because you set the Now time earlier. However, you can change it here if you'd like.

6. Click on OK.

SONAR adds the new tempo change and displays it in the Tempo Change pane as well as on the graph in the Tempo pane.

Deleting and Editing

You can also edit or remove a tempo change from the list by using the appropriate toolbar buttons. First, select the tempo change you want to edit or delete by clicking on it in the list. If you want to delete the tempo change, click on the Delete Tempo button in the toolbar (the one with the big red X shown on it). If you want to edit the tempo change, click on the Tempo Properties button in the toolbar (the very last button at the right end of the toolbar). This action opens the Tempo dialog box. Make any changes necessary, as per the same settings I described for inserting a new tempo change.

Using the Tempo Commands

In addition to the Tempo view (and the Tempo toolbar), SONAR provides two other tempo-related functions. The Insert Tempo Change function works the same as adding a new tempo change in the Tempo Change pane in the Tempo view. However, this function can be used from within any of the other views. To access it, just select Insert > Tempo Change to open the Tempo dialog box (which you learned about earlier).

SONAR also provides a function that allows you to insert a series of tempos so that you can have the tempo change smoothly from one value to another over time. Using it is similar to using the Draw Line tool in the Tempo view, but here you specify your values numerically. You use this function as follows:

1. Select Insert > Series of Tempos to open the Insert Series of Tempos dialog box (see Figure 7.38).

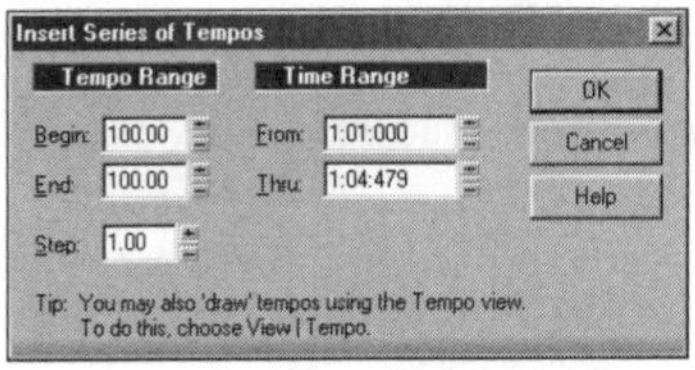

Figure 7.38
You can change the tempo smoothly from one value to another by using the Insert Series of Tempos dialog box.

2. In the Tempo Range section, enter a beginning and an ending value for the range of tempos to be inserted.

3. In the Time Range section, enter a beginning and an ending value for the range of time in your project in which you want the tempo changes to occur.

TIP

If you make a selection by dragging your mouse pointer in the Time Ruler of the Track view, for instance, before you select Insert > Series of Tempos, the Time Range values in the Insert Series of Tempos dialog box are set according to your selection. This shortcut makes it easier to see where in your project the tempo changes will be inserted.

4. For the Step parameter, enter a beat and tick value for how often you want a tempo change to be inserted within the Time Range you specified. For example, if you enter a value of 1.00, then the Insert Series of Tempos function will insert a new tempo change at every beat within the Time Range you specified.

5. Click OK.

SONAR then inserts a smooth series of tempo changes starting and ending with the Tempo Range values you specified within the time range you specified. Any existing tempo changes are overwritten.

8

Exploring the Editing Tools

In Chapter 7, you learned about some of the essential editing features found in SONAR, including all the views (and the tools they provide), as well as how to manipulate your data via copy, cut, paste, move, delete, and so on. Although these features provide a lot of power, you might be asking yourself, "Is that all there is?" Not likely! In addition to its fundamental tools, SONAR provides a full arsenal of sophisticated editing features. Some can be used to process audio data, some to process MIDI data, and some to process both kinds of data. One aspect they all have in common, however, is that they can be accessed within more than one view (similar to the copy, cut, and paste functions). Of course, as you learned previously, for MIDI data, you'll be using the Track, Piano Roll, Staff, and Event views, and for audio data, you'll be using the Track view.

This chapter covers the following:

▶ Advanced data selection

▶ Changing the loudness of audio clips

▶ Equalization

▶ Quantization

▶ Transposition

▶ Various advanced timing features

Advanced Data Selection

As you learned in the preceding chapter, you can select the data in your project within each of the views by using some basic clicking and dragging techniques. SONAR also provides some more sophisticated data selection features that enable you to use time as well as individual event properties for more precise editing.

By Time

If you ever need to select a range of data within a project that is based on time rather than data that is neatly tucked away into individual clips, you can select Edit > Select > By Time to do so. For example, say you need to copy the data in Track 8 that falls between the range of 4:2:010 (measure, beat, tick) and 13:3:050. But what if that data is stored in multiple clips within that range, and the clips don't neatly start and end at the beginning and ending times that you specified? That's the kind of situation for which this feature is useful. It works like this:

1. Choose Edit > Select > By Time to open the Select by Time dialog box (see Figure 8.1).

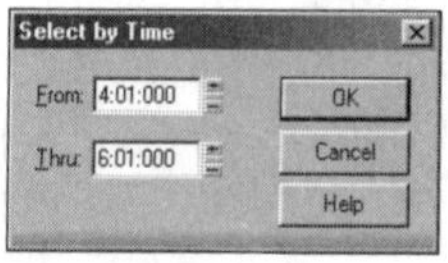

Figure 8.1

You can use the Select by Time dialog box to define a time range within your project in which data will be selected for editing.

2. Type the beginning (From) and ending (Thru) measure, beat, and tick values to define the range of time you want to select. Then click on OK. You use this dialog box to select a range of time within your project, but it doesn't select any actual data. For that, you need to select the track(s) you want to edit.

3. In the Track view, select the track(s) containing the data you want to edit.

SONAR selects the data within the clips within the tracks within the time range you specified so that you can edit it by using copy, cut, and the other features that you'll learn about in this chapter.

TIP

You can also make time selections within any of the views by simply clicking and dragging on the Time Ruler or by ALT dragging within a clip (you learned about this approach in Chapter 7), but by choosing Edit > Select > By Time, you can make more precise selections because you can enter the exact numerical values for the measures, beats, and ticks that define the range.

By Filter

For really precise editing tasks, you can choose Edit > Select > By Filter. Using this approach, you can refine a selection that you've already made with any of the other methods discussed previously. For instance, if you select some clips or tracks in the Track view, you can then choose Edit >

Select > By Filter to zero in (so to speak) your selection even further to the individual events within those clips and tracks based on their event properties.

Say you have a MIDI track in which you want to change all the notes with a pitch of C4 to C5. You can easily select only those notes by choosing Edit > Select > By Filter and then change their pitch by using the Transpose feature (which you'll learn about later). All the C4 pitches are then changed to C5, but none of the other notes in the track are affected. This feature works as follows:

1. Select the clip(s), track(s), or set of events you want to use as your initial selection. You can select clips and tracks in the Track view or a group of events in the Piano Roll view, Event view, or Staff view.

2. Choose Edit > Select > By Filter to open the Event Filter–Select Some dialog box (see Figure 8.2).

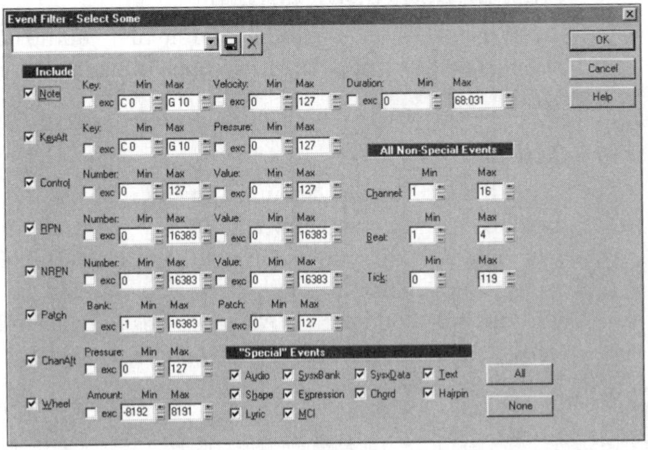

Figure 8.2
You can use the Event Filter–Select Some dialog box to set the criteria for the type of data you want to have selected.

3. Does this dialog box look familiar? The Event Filter–Select Some dialog box is the same as the Event Filter–Search dialog box, which you learned about in Chapter 5. The same information about how to use all the options applies here, so go ahead and set the options as you'd like.

TIP

As with the Event Filter–Search dialog box, the Event Filter–Select Some dialog box enables you to save presets for instant access to your favorite settings. By the way, presets are also available in many of the features that you'll learn about later in this chapter. I described how to use them in Chapter 5.

4. Click on OK.

SONAR searches through the data in your initial selection, finds the events that fall under the filter parameters you specified, and then selects those events while leaving any other events alone. If you want to refine your selection even further, just choose Edit > Select > By Filter again on the previous selection results.

Advanced Audio Editing

By using the cut, copy, paste, and slip editing tools in the Track view, you can manipulate the data in your audio tracks in a variety of ways. SONAR also provides a number of advanced features you can use to adjust the volume, apply equalization, and even reverse the data within audio clips. You access all these features by choosing Edit > Audio.

Adjusting Audio Volume

If you ever need to adjust the volume of an audio clip, you can use a number of different SONAR features to increase or decrease the volume of your data.

3dB Louder

Using the 3dB Louder feature, you can increase the volume of audio data by 3 dB each time you apply it. So, if you want to increase the volume of your data by 6 dB, you can apply the 3dB Louder feature to it twice. To use it, simply select the audio data you want to change and choose Edit > Audio > 3dB Louder. SONAR processes the data and you can see the results via the higher amplitude value(s) in the audio waveform(s).

CAUTION

Remember the description about setting your input level during the recording process in Chapter 6? I mentioned that you have to be careful not to set the level too high because it could overload the input and cause your audio to be distorted. Well, when you're raising the volume of audio data, you also have to watch out not to raise it too high. Setting it too high can cause clipping. Clipping occurs when SONAR attempts to raise the amplitude of audio data higher than 100 percent. The top and bottom of the waveform become clipped, and when you play the audio, it sounds distorted. So, be careful when using the 3dB Louder feature. Be sure to keep an eye on the amplitude levels of your audio waveforms, and also be sure to listen to your audio data right after you increase its volume to see if it sounds okay. If you hear distortion, then use Undo to remove the volume change.

3dB Quieter

The 3dB Quieter feature works in the same way as the 3dB Louder feature except that it decreases the volume of audio data by 3 dB.

> **CAUTION**
>
> You also have to be careful when using the 3dB Quieter feature—not because you might introduce distortion into the audio, but because every time you use it, it degrades the audio slightly. For instance, if you use the 3dB Quieter feature to lower the volume of audio data and then use the 3dB Louder feature to raise the volume, the quality of the audio will not be the same as it was originally. This difference is due to the limitations of processing digital audio signals, a subject that is a bit complex to explain here. More than likely, though, you won't be able to hear the difference in quality, because it really is only a slight degradation, so you don't need to worry about it too much.

Normalize

Like the 3dB Louder feature, the Normalize feature also raises the volume of audio, but in a different way. Instead of just simply raising the volume, Normalize first scans the audio waveform to find its highest amplitude level. It subtracts that amplitude level from the maximum level, which is 100 percent. Normalize then takes that value and uses it to increase the volume of the audio data. So, when all is said and done, the highest amplitude in the waveform is 100 percent, and all the other amplitude values are increased.

In other words, if an audio waveform has its highest amplitude value at 80 percent, Normalize subtracts that value from 100 percent to get 20 percent. It then increases the volume of the audio data by 20 percent so that the highest amplitude value is 100 percent, and all the other amplitude values are 20 percent higher. Basically, you can use Normalize to raise the volume of audio data to the highest it can be without causing any clipping.

To use Normalize, simply select the audio data, and choose Edit > Audio > Normalize.

> **CAUTION**
>
> You knew this caution was coming, didn't you? When you use the Normalize feature, just like the 3dB Louder and 3dB Quieter features, you have to be careful. If you raise the volume of audio data to its maximum, you can easily introduce clipping to the signal if you process it later with some of the other editing or effects features in SONAR. Usually, you should use the Normalize feature only after you know you're not going to do any more processing on that particular audio data. Then again, you probably shouldn't even use the Normalize feature at all (see the tip at the end of the "Crossfade" section).

CHAPTER 8

Fade

If you want to get a little more creative with your volume changes, you can build much more complex volume changes by using the Fade/Envelope feature as follows:

NOTE

A *fade-in* is a gradual and smooth increase from a low volume (loudness) to a higher volume. This increase in volume is also called a *crescendo* in musical terms. A *fade-out* is the exact opposite—a gradual and smooth decrease from a higher volume to a lower volume. In musical terms, this decrease in volume is called a *decrescendo*.

1. Select the audio data to which you want to apply the fade. Then choose Edit > Audio > Fade/Envelope to open the Fade/Envelope dialog box (see Figure 8.3). The dialog box displays a graph. The left side of the graph displays amplitude values, 0 to 100 percent from bottom to top. Inside the graph is a line, which represents the fade that will be applied to your selected audio data. If you look at the line from left to right, the left end of the line represents the beginning of your audio data selection and the right end of the line represents the end of your audio data selection. When you first open the dialog box, the line runs from the bottom left to the top right of the graph. If you leave it this way, a straight linear fade-in is applied to your audio data, because, as you look at the graph, the left end of the line is set at 0 percent, and the right end of the line is set at 100 percent. So, the volume of the audio data would begin at 0 percent and fade all the way up to 100 percent. See how it works?

Figure 8.3
You can use the Fade/Envelope dialog box to apply complex fades to your audio data.

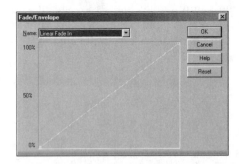

2. You can change the shape of the fade line in one of two ways. You can simply select one of the six available presets from the drop-down list at the top of the dialog box. Alternatively, you can change the fade line graphically by clicking and dragging the small squares at the ends of the line. These squares are called Nodes.

3. If you want to create some really complex fades, you can add more Nodes by clicking anywhere on the fade line. The more Nodes you add, the more flexibility you have in changing the shape of the line (see Figure 8.4).

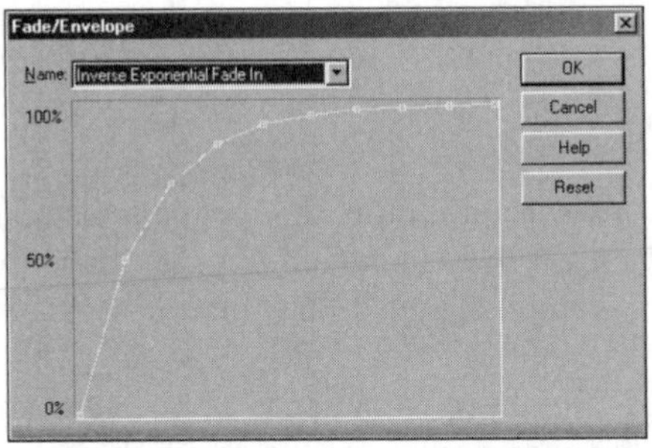

Figure 8.4
You can create some really complex fades by adding more Nodes.

4. After you've finished setting up the graph the way you want it, click on OK.

SONAR changes the volume of your audio data selection according to the fade you defined in the Fade/Envelope dialog box.

In addition to the Fade/Envelope feature (which allows you to apply destructive fades to your data), SONAR allows you to apply nondestructive fades. To apply a fade nondestructively, do the following:

1. If you want to create a fade-in for an audio clip, position your mouse in the upper-left corner of the clip until the shape of the mouse changes to a triangle. Then click and drag the mouse toward the right end of the clip to define the fade, as shown in Figure 8.5.

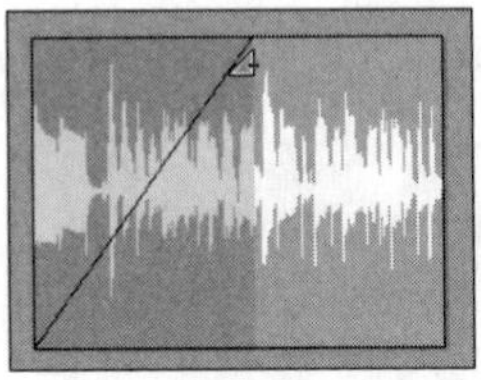

Figure 8.5
Apply a nondestructive fade-in to a clip by clicking in the upper-left corner of the clip and dragging toward the right.

2. If you want to create a fade-out for an audio clip, position your mouse in the upper-right corner of the clip until the shape of the mouse changes to a triangle. Then click and drag the mouse toward the left end of the clip to define the fade, as shown in Figure 8.6.

Figure 8.6
Apply a non-destructive fade-out to a clip by clicking in the upper-right corner of the clip and dragging toward the left.

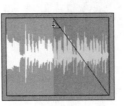

CHAPTER 8

TIP

The nondestructive fade feature doesn't allow you to define complex fades as with the Fade/Envelope feature, but you can apply nondestructive complex fades or volume changes to a clip (or an entire track) using envelopes. I'll talk more about envelopes in Chapter 12.

Crossfade

A *crossfade* is a special kind of fade that can be applied only to overlapping audio clips. This kind of fade can come in handy when you want to make a smooth transition from one style of music to another or from one instrument to another. It is especially useful when you're composing to video; you can change smoothly from one type of background music to another as the scene changes. Of course, it has many other types of creative uses as well.

When you apply a crossfade to two overlapping audio clips, it works like this: During playback as the Now time reaches the point at which the two audio clips overlap, the first audio clip fades out and the second audio clip fades in at the same time. You can apply a crossfade as follows:

1.   Select the two overlapping audio clips to which you want to apply the crossfade.

TIP

The two audio clips you select don't have to reside on the same track; they only have to overlap in time.

2.   Choose Edit > Audio > Crossfade to open the Crossfade dialog box (see Figure 8.7).

Figure 8.7
You can apply a crossfade to two overlapping audio clips by using the Crossfade dialog box.

3. Notice that the Crossfade dialog box looks almost exactly the same as the Fade/Envelope dialog box. It works almost exactly the same, too. You can choose from three preset fades, and you can manipulate the fade line with your mouse by adding, clicking, and dragging nodes. The only difference here is that an additional line appears on the graph. The darker line represents the second selected audio clip and can't be manipulated directly. As you make changes to the lighter line, the darker line mimics it. This feature ensures that the volumes of both audio clips are synchronized and provides a perfectly smooth crossfade. So, go ahead and make your changes as discussed earlier.

4. Click on OK.

SONAR applies the crossfade to the parts of the two audio clips that are overlapping. When you play back the audio, you hear the data from the first clip gradually fade out at the same time the data from the second audio clip gradually fades in.

In addition to the Crossfade feature (which allows you to apply destructive crossfades to your data), SONAR allows you to apply nondestructive crossfades. To apply a crossfade nondestructively, do the following:

1. Activate the Automatic Crossfade button located in the bottom right corner of the Track view (see Figure 8.8).

Figure 8.8
Activate the Automatic Crossfade feature by clicking the button in the bottom right of the Track view.

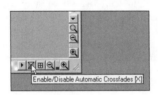

2. Click and drag one audio clip so that it overlaps another audio clip. Both clips must reside on the same track.

3. In the Drag and Drop Options dialog box, choose the Blend Old and New option.

4. Click OK. SONAR overlaps the clips and automatically applies a perfect crossfade to the overlapping sections, as shown in Figure 8.9.

Figure 8.9
SONAR automatically applies a crossfade to the overlapping sections of the clips.

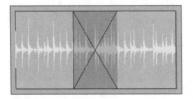

CHAPTER 8

Equalization (EQ)

You have a radio in your car, right? Maybe even a cassette or CD player, too? If so, then you've probably used equalization without even knowing it. Adjusting the bass and treble controls on your car radio is a form of equalization. Equalization (EQ) enables you to adjust the tonal characteristics of an audio signal by increasing (boosting) or decreasing (cutting) the amplitude of different frequencies in the audio spectrum.

NOTE

When a musical object (such as a string) vibrates, it emits a sound. The speed at which the object vibrates is called the *frequency*, which is measured in vibrations (or cycles) per second. This measurement is also called *Hertz* (Hz). If an object vibrates 60 times per second, the frequency would be 60 Hz. The tricky point to remember here, though, is that most objects vibrate at a number of different frequencies at the same time. The combination of all these different vibrations makes up the distinct sound (or *timbre*) of a vibrating object. That's why a bell sounds like a bell, a horn sounds like a horn, and so on with all other types of sounds.

Of course, we humans can't perceive some very slow and some very fast vibrations. Technically, the range of human hearing resides between the frequencies of 20 Hz and 20 kHz (1 kHz is equal to 1,000 Hz). This range is known as the *audio spectrum*.

Equalization enables you to manipulate the frequencies of the audio spectrum, and because sounds contain many of these frequencies, you can change their tonal characteristics (or timbre). Of course, this explanation is very basic. If you really want to learn more about acoustics, pick up a good book about sound recording, such as *Home Recording for Musicians* by Craig Anderton (Music Sales Corp., 1996, ISBN 0-8256-1500-3).

In other words, using EQ, you can bump up the bass, add more presence, reduce rumble, and sometimes eliminate noise in your audio material. Not only that, but you also can use EQ as an effect. You know how, in some of the modern dance tunes, the vocals sound like they're coming out of a telephone receiver or an old radio? That's an effect done with EQ.

SONAR provides two different types of EQ features: Graphic EQ and Parametric EQ. (Actually, five different EQ features are available, but I'll describe the other three in Chapter 11.) Both have their strengths and weaknesses.

Graphic EQ

You might already be familiar with graphic equalizers, because they are sometimes included on boom boxes and home stereo systems. SONAR's Graphic EQ feature simulates a hardware-based graphic equalizer. It even looks similar (see Figure 8.10).

Figure 8.10
The Graphic EQ feature resembles that of a real graphic equalizer.

The Graphic EQ feature provides ten different frequencies (called *bands*) you can adjust. Each band can either be boosted or cut by 12 dB. You simply drag the appropriate slider up (boost) or down (cut) to increase or decrease the amplitude of that frequency. But herein lies the weakness of Graphic EQ. Although it's very easy to use, you are limited by the frequencies you can manipulate. You can't change any of the frequencies below, above, or in between the ones provided. Still, Graphic EQ is very useful if you want to make quick equalization changes, and the frequencies provided are the most common ones. It works like this:

1. Select the audio data you want to change.
2. Choose Edit > Audio > Graphic EQ to open the Graphic EQ dialog box.
3. Adjust the sliders for the frequencies that you want to cut or boost.

CAUTION

Be careful when you're boosting frequencies, because doing so also increases the overall volume of the audio data. If you raise the volume too high, you could introduce clipping into the data.

4. Click on the Audition button to hear the first few seconds of the processed audio before you go ahead and accept the settings. That way, you can decide whether you like the way it sounds. By listening to a few seconds of the audio, you can test whether any clipping occurs. When you're done listening, click on Stop. By the way, SONAR includes the Audition button in many of its other features, too, and it always works in exactly the same way.

TIP

If clipping does occur, but you really want to boost some of the frequencies in your audio data, click on Cancel to exit the Graphic EQ dialog box without making any changes. Now, lower the volume of the audio data by using the 3dB Quieter feature. Then go back and try to apply the EQ again. By lowering the volume of the audio first, you can make enough room to allow more frequency boosting.

5. If you want to be able to use the same EQ settings again later without having to keep making the same slider adjustments, save them as a preset. You learned about presets in Chapter 5.

6. Click on OK.

SONAR processes the selected audio data, and when you play it back, it should sound the same way it did when you listened to it using the Audition feature.

TIP

By default, the Audition feature plays only the first few seconds of the selected data. You can adjust the Audition time by selecting Options > Global to open the Global Options dialog box. Under the General tab, set the Audition Commands For option to the number of seconds you want to use for the Audition feature. I usually like to keep this set anywhere between 5 and 10 seconds.

Parametric EQ

Parametric equalization, on the other hand, is much more powerful and flexible, but it's also a lot more complex and difficult to understand. With the Parametric EQ feature, you're not limited to specific frequencies. You can specify an exact frequency to adjust, and you can cut or boost by much larger amounts. You can also process a range of frequencies at the same time, such as cutting all frequencies above 10 kHz by 20 dB (which would reduce all the frequencies between 10 kHz and 20 kHz but leave the frequencies between 20 Hz and 10 kHz alone). I can explain the Parametric EQ feature a little better by showing you how it works:

1. Select the audio data you want to change.

2. Choose Edit > Audio > Parametric EQ to open the Parametric EQ dialog box (see Figure 8.11).

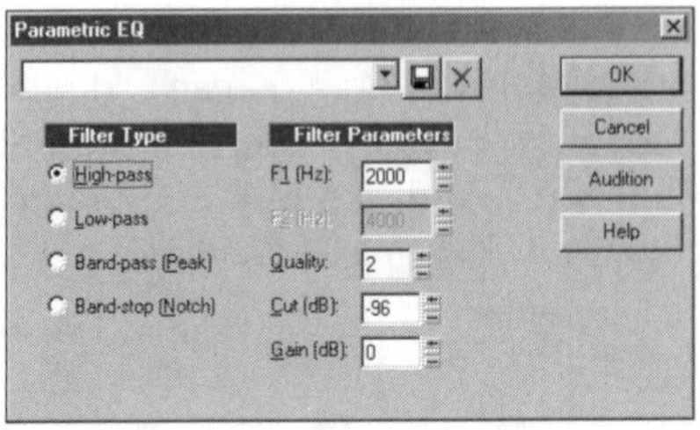

Figure 8.11
The Parametric EQ feature provides a lot more power, but it's also more difficult to use.

3. Choose one of the options in the Filter Type section: High-pass, Low-pass, Band-pass (Peak), or Band-stop (Notch). Then set the appropriate parameters in the Filter Parameters section. You can use the F1 and F2 parameters to set the frequencies you want to adjust. They work differently depending on the type of filter you choose (I'll talk more about this in a minute). The Cut parameter enables you to reduce the volume of the frequencies. To change this setting, just enter a negative number (such as 120) to cut by that number of decibels. The Gain parameter allows you to boost the volume of the frequencies. To change this setting, just enter a positive number (such as +20) to boost by that number of decibels. You can set the Quality parameter to determine how precise the Parameter EQ feature will be when processing your audio.

If you really want to zero in on a frequency or range of frequencies, use a higher value for the Quality parameter (200 being the highest). This setting gives you a sharper (for lack of a better word) sound. A low value (such as 2) allows the Parametric EQ feature to slightly process the other frequencies not defined specifically or outside the range, which gives you a smoother sound. It's a bit difficult to describe. Experiment with it a little, and you'll be able to hear the difference.

If you select the High-pass filter type, all the frequencies below the frequency that you set in the F1 parameter will be cut, and all the frequencies above it will be boosted, depending on how you set the Cut and Gain parameters. If you select the Low-pass filter type, all the frequencies above the frequency that you set in the F1 parameter will be cut, and all the frequencies below it will be boosted, depending on how you set the Cut and Gain parameters.

If you select either the Band-pass (Peak) or Band-stop (Notch) filter types, you have to set up a range of frequencies using both the F1 and F2 parameters. Use the F1 parameter to mark the beginning of the range and the F2 parameter to mark the end of the range. For the Band-pass (Peak) filter type, any frequencies outside the range are cut, and frequencies within the range are boosted, depending on how you set the Cut and Gain parameters. For the Band-stop (Notch) filter type, any frequencies outside the range are boosted and frequencies within the range are cut, depending on how you set the Cut and Gain parameters.

4. Click on the Audition button to hear the first few seconds of the processed audio before you go ahead and accept the settings. That way, you can decide whether you like the way it sounds. By listening to a few seconds of the audio, you can test whether any clipping occurs. When you're done listening, click on Stop.

5. If you want to be able to use the same EQ settings again later without having to keep making the same parameter adjustments, save them as a preset.

6. Click on OK.

SONAR processes the selected audio data, and when you play it back, it should sound the same way it did when you listened to it using the Audition feature.

Applications

Right about now, you might be saying to yourself, "Okay, EQ sounds pretty cool, but what can I do with it?" Well, you can use EQ in many different ways to process your audio. To begin with, you might want to try some of the presets that come included with SONAR. Not very many are provided for the Graphic EQ and Parametric EQ features, but you can find enough to give you a taste of what EQ can do. After that, you might want to try experimenting with some of the settings described in the following sections.

Fullness

To make your audio sound a little fuller, try boosting the range of frequencies between 100 and 300 Hz by 6 dB. To do so, use the Parametric EQ feature with the Band-pass (Peak) filter type and set the filter parameters to the following: F1 = 100, F2 = 300, Quality = 2, Cut = 0, and Gain = 6.

Punch

To add a little more punch to your audio, try boosting the range of frequencies between 800 Hz and 2 kHz by 6 dB. To do so, use the Parametric EQ feature with the Band-pass (Peak) filter type and set the filter parameters to the following: F1 = 800, F2 = 2000, Quality = 2, Cut = 0, and Gain = 6.

Noise Reduction

EQ can also be used as a simple means of reducing noise in your audio. This is especially true for high frequency hiss. Use the Parametric EQ feature with the Low-pass filter type and set the filter parameters to the following: F1 = 18000, Quality = 2, Cut = −96, and Gain = 0.

To get rid of buzzing or humming noises with EQ, use the Parametric EQ feature with the Band-stop (Notch) filter type and set the filter parameters to the following: F1 = 60, F2 = 60, Quality = 100, Cut = −96, and Gain = 0.

Specific Sounds

EQ is handy for molding specific types of sounds, such as stringed instruments like guitar and bass. For example, to give a bit of a different sound to an acoustic or electric guitar, try using the Graphic EQ feature with the following settings: 32 Hz = -12, 64 Hz = 0, 130 Hz = +4, 260 Hz = +7, 500 Hz = +6, 1 k = +3, 2 k = 0, 4 k = +4, 8.3 k = +7, and 16.5 k = 0.

For a bass guitar, trying using the Graphic EQ feature with the following settings: 32 Hz = -12, 64 Hz = 0, 130 Hz = +6, 260 Hz = +7, 500 Hz = +5, 1 k = +1, 2 k = 0, 4 k =0, 8.3 k = +6, and 16.5 k = +12.

And So On

I could go on and on with equalization applications, but that would fill a whole book on its own. Don't be afraid to experiment. The more you practice using the EQ features, the more skilled you will become at applying them. Keep one point in mind, though: With just the right amount of spices, a meal tastes great. Too many spices, and the taste starts taking a turn for the worse. The same goes for applying EQ to your audio. Too much EQ will make your projects sound amateurish.

Getting Rid of Silence

When you record an audio track in SONAR, even though there may be pauses in your performance (such as between musical phrases), your sound card still picks up a signal from your microphone or instrument, and that data is recorded. Although you might think that the data is just recorded silence, in actuality, it contains a very minute amount of noise that may come from your sound card itself or the microphone or instrument connected there. More often than not, you can't really hear this noise, because it's masked by the other music data in your project. And even during quiet passages, if you have only one or two audio tracks playing, the noise is probably still inaudible. With a large number of audio tracks, however, the noise can add up.

In addition, during playback, SONAR still processes those silent passages even though they don't contain any actual music. These passages take up valuable computer processing power and disk space. To remedy this problem, SONAR provides the Remove Silence feature. This feature automatically detects sections of silence in audio clips according to a loudness threshold that you set. Then, by first splitting long audio clips into shorter ones, it removes the resulting clips containing only silence. Thus, SONAR doesn't process that extra data during playback, and it doesn't save it to disk when you save your project.

To detect silent passages in audio, the Remove Silence feature uses a digital noise gate. Depending on the parameter settings you specify, this noise gate opens up when the Remove Silence feature comes upon a section in your audio that has an amplitude level greater than the one you set. It identifies this part of the audio as acceptable sound and lets it pass through. When the level of audio dips below a certain amplitude level that you set, the noise gate identifies that part of the audio as silence, and it closes to stop it from passing through. At that point, the Remove Silence feature splits the audio clip with one new clip containing just the music and another new clip containing just the noise. This process happens over and over until the whole initial audio clip is finished being scanned.

You use this feature as follows:

1. Select the audio data that you want to scan for silence.

2. Choose Edit > Audio > Remove Silence to open the Remove Silence dialog box (see Figure 8.12).

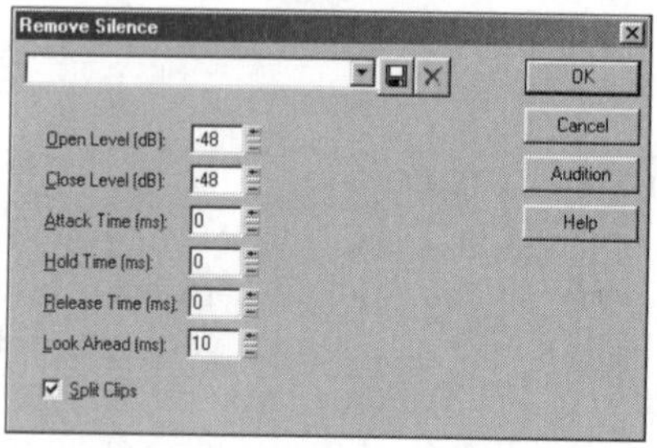

Figure 8.12
You can use the Remove Silence feature to clean up your audio tracks and make them more manageable.

3. Type a value for the Open Level parameter. This parameter determines how loud the audio data has to be to make the noise gate open, thus identifying the data as acceptable sound.

4. Type a value for the Close Level parameter. This parameter determines how soft the data has to be to make the noise gate close, thus identifying the data as silence.

5. Type a value for the Attack Time parameter. This parameter determines how quickly (in milliseconds) the noise gate will open to the amplitude set in the Open Level parameter. If the beginning of your audio data starts off soft (such as with a fade in), and its amplitude is below the Open Level setting, it could get cut off by the noise gate. For example, the beginnings of the words in a vocal part might be cut. To prevent this problem, you can set the Attack Time parameter so that the noise gate takes this kind of situation into consideration.

6. Type a value for the Hold Time parameter. This parameter determines how long the noise gate will remain open even when the amplitude level of the audio dips below the Close Level. This parameter is useful when the level of your audio goes up and down very quickly, which could make the noise gate react when it's not supposed to (such as during quick percussion parts). By setting a Hold Time, you can make sure that musical passages containing quick sounds don't get cut by mistake.

7. Type a value for the Release Time parameter. This parameter is the same as the Attack Time parameter but in reverse. It determines how quickly the noise gate will close after the amplitude of the audio reaches the Close Level. This feature is useful if your audio data gradually gets softer at the end, such as with a fade out.

8. Type a value for the Look Ahead parameter. This parameter determines how long (in milliseconds) the amplitude of the audio must stay above the Open Level before the noise gate will open. Basically, this setting lets you fine-tune how the noise gate determines whether the audio being scanned is acceptable sound or silence.

9. If you want SONAR to delete the audio clips that contain only silence, activate the Split Clips option. Otherwise, the silent portions of the audio won't be deleted; they will just be reduced to vacant space, but your clips will remain as they are.

10. You can save your settings as a preset, and you can use the Audition feature to hear the results of your settings if you'd like.

11. Click on OK.

SONAR scans the selected audio clip and then splits it up into pieces (and also removes the clips containing only silence) according to the settings that you specified.

TIP

Unless the musical passages and silent passages of your audio are separated pretty neatly, it can be difficult to get the right settings for the Release Time feature to perform accurately. You might find it easier and more precise if you simply split the audio clips by hand using the Split function. The process is a bit more time-consuming, though.

CHAPTER 8

Play It Backward

Assuming you're old enough to remember vinyl recordings, did you ever take a record and play it backward to see whether your favorite band had left some satanic messages in their songs or perhaps a recipe for their favorite lentil soup? Well, guess what? You can do the same thing with your audio data. SONAR lets you flip the data in an audio clip so that it plays in reverse.

This feature doesn't have much practical use, but combined with some other processing, it can render some cool effects. To use it, simply select the audio clip you want to change and choose Edit > Audio > Reverse. Now the data in that clip will play backward.

TIP

If you want to reverse the data in an entire track, make sure to combine all the audio clips in the track into one big audio clip first. If you don't, the data in each separate clip will be reversed, which is not the same as reversing the entire track. Try it, and you'll hear what I mean.

TIP

With the combination of the audio editing features discussed so far in this chapter and the audio effects features described in Chapter 11, there's no doubt that SONAR packs a lot of audio data editing power. But it still can't compare to dedicated audio editing applications such as Sonic Foundry's Sound Forge (**www.sonicfoundry.com**), Syntrillium's Cool Edit (**www.syntrillium.com**), and Steinberg's WaveLab (**www.steinberg.net**). Using these programs, you can edit your audio with surgical precision, and they provide many more processing features than can be found in SONAR. The people at Cakewalk are aware of this fact, so they included a little-known feature that enables you to access your favorite audio editing applications from within SONAR. I've tested the previously mentioned products, but there might be others that can use the feature as well.

To use your audio editing software from within SONAR, simply select the audio data that you want to edit. Then select the Tools menu. At the bottom of the menu, you should see your software listed there (SONAR automatically detects it during installation). Choose the program that you want to run. Your audio editing software then opens with the audio data you selected, ready to be processed. Make any changes you want and then close the audio editing software. Before closing, the program first asks whether you want to save the changes you made. Click on Yes. The program closes, and you return to SONAR. SONAR then tells you that the audio data has changed and asks whether you would like to reload it. Click on Yes. That's all there is to it. And now you have easy access to all the power of your audio editing software as well as SONAR. Isn't that cool?

The Edit Menu

Up until now, I've talked about editing features that pertain strictly to audio data. The remainder of SONAR's editing features are more diverse in their use, meaning some can be used with MIDI data, some with audio data, and some with both. The one aspect they all have in common is that they are accessed via the Edit menu. Click on the Edit menu, and you'll see them listed in the bottom half, starting with Deglitch and ending with Fit Improvisation. Because of their diversity, I'll go through each feature one by one, explaining what it does, along with how and why you would want to use it. Of course, I'll also let you know what kinds of data each feature works with.

Deglitch

Occasionally, you might find that, while you're playing your MIDI instrument, some unintended notes get recorded along with the legitimate musical material. This is especially true for people who play a MIDI guitar. The strings on a MIDI guitar can easily trigger notes when they're not supposed to. To help with this problem, SONAR provides the Deglitch feature. Using this feature, you can filter out any notes from your MIDI data that don't fall within the right pitch, velocity, and duration range for the music you're recording. It works like this:

1. Select the MIDI data from which you want to filter any unwanted notes.

2. Choose Edit > Deglitch to open the Deglitch dialog box (see Figure 8.13).

Figure 8.13
Using the Deglitch feature, you can filter out any unintended notes from your MIDI data by specifying acceptable pitch, velocity, and duration ranges.

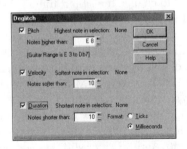

3. If you want to filter out notes by pitch, activate the Pitch option. Then, for the Notes Higher Than parameter, type the maximum note value allowed in your material. For example, if the highest note in your MIDI data should be C5, then you should set the Notes Higher Than parameter to C5. If the Deglitch feature finds any notes within the data that have a pitch higher than C5, it will delete them.

CHAPTER 8

4. If you want to filter out notes by velocity, activate the Velocity option. Then, for the Notes Softer Than parameter, type the minimum velocity value allowed in your material. For example, if the lowest velocity in your MIDI data should be 15, then you should set the Notes Softer Than parameter to 15. If the Deglitch feature finds any notes within the data that have a velocity lower than 15, it will delete them.

5. If you want to filter out notes by duration, activate the Duration option. Then, for the Notes Shorter Than parameter, type the minimum duration value allowed in your material. Also, be sure to specify whether the duration should be measured in ticks or milliseconds by choosing either the Ticks option or Milliseconds option via the Format parameter. As an example, if the lowest duration in your MIDI data should be 20 ticks, then you should set the Notes Shorter Than parameter to 20 and the Format parameter to Ticks. If the Deglitch feature finds any notes within the data that have a duration lower than 20 ticks, it will delete them.

6. Click on OK.

SONAR scans the selected MIDI data and removes any notes that fall within the criteria you set. By the way, you can scan for pitch, velocity, and duration all at once by having all the options activated if you'd like.

Slide

Remember back in Chapter 7, when I described how to move clips in the Track view by dragging and dropping them or by using the Clip Properties dialog box to change their Start times? Well, the Slide feature performs the same function. You can use it to move clips backward or forward within a track. So why does SONAR provide the same functionality more than once? Because the Slide feature has a few differences. Instead of just working with clips, you can use it with any kind of selected data from a group of MIDI notes to single events. And instead of having to specify an exact Start time (as in the Clips Properties dialog box), you can move data by any number of measures, ticks, seconds, or frames. In addition, the Slide feature doesn't give you the option of blending with, replacing, or sliding over existing events in a track. It simply moves the selected data so that it overlaps with any existing data. You use it as follows:

1. Using the appropriate view, select the MIDI data or audio clips that you want to move.

2. Choose Edit > Slide to open the Slide dialog box (see Figure 8.14).

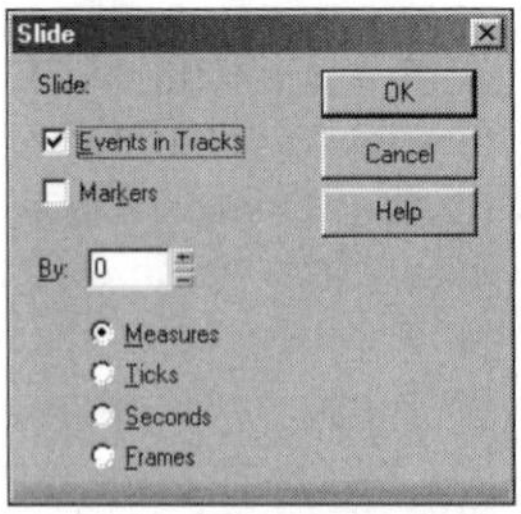

Figure 8.14
You can use the Slide feature to move any kind of data, not just clips.

3. If you want to move events, be sure the Events in Tracks option under the Slide parameter is activated. If you would also like to move any markers that happen to fall within the same time range as the selected data, activate the Markers option.

4. For the By parameter, type the number of units by which you want to move the selected data. If you want to move the data backward in time, enter a negative number. If you want to move the data forward in time, enter a positive number.

5. Choose the type of unit by which you want to move the selected data by activating the appropriate option. You can select Measures, Ticks, Seconds, or Frames.

6. Click on OK.

SONAR moves the selected data backward or forward in time by the amount you specified and the unit type that you chose.

Quantize

Even though you may be a great musician, you're bound to occasionally make mistakes when playing your instrument, especially when it comes to timing. No one I know can play in perfect time during every performance, and having to listen to a metronome while you play can sometimes be distracting. Instead of playing notes at the exact same time as the metronome sounds, you'll more than likely play some of them either a little ahead or a little behind the beat. You may even hold some notes a little longer than you're supposed to. Usually, if these timing errors are slight enough, they'll make your performance sound more "human" than anything else. But if the mistakes are large enough to stand out, they can make your performance sound sloppy. At this point, the Quantize feature can come in handy. It can help you correct some of the timing mistakes you make.

CHAPTER 8

To understand how to use the Quantize feature, you first have to know how it works. The Quantize feature scans the MIDI events in your selected data one by one, and it changes the Start time of each event so that it is equal to the nearest rhythmic value you specify. You specify this rhythmic value by using the Resolution parameter. So, if you want all the events in your data to be moved to the nearest sixteenth note, you can set the Resolution parameter to Sixteenth. The Quantize feature uses this value to set up an imaginary (for lack of a better word) time grid over your data. In this case, the grid is divided into sixteenth notes.

During the scanning process, the Quantize feature moves an imaginary pointer along the grid one division at a time. Centered around the pointer is an imaginary window, of which you can set the size using the Window parameter. As the Quantize feature moves its pointer and window along the grid, it looks to see whether any of your Events are in the vicinity. Any events that fall within the window have their Start times changed so that they line up with the current position of the pointer. Any events that fall outside the window are left alone. This procedure continues until the Quantize feature comes to the end of the data you selected. Actually, there's a little more to the procedure than that, but I'll explain the rest as I describe how to use the feature:

1. Select the data that you want to quantize. It can be anything from all the data in your project, to a single track or clip, or a selected group of events.

2. Select Edit > Quantize to open the Quantize dialog box (see Figure 8.15).

Figure 8.15
The Quantize dialog box provides a number of parameters you can set to determine exactly how you want your data to be corrected.

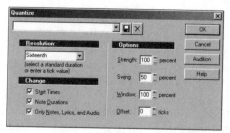

3. In the Resolution section, set the Resolution parameter. This parameter determines what rhythmic value will be used to set up the imaginary grid and what will be the nearest rhythmic value to which the events in your data will be aligned. It's best to set this parameter to the smallest note value found in your data. For instance, your data may contain quarter notes, eighth notes, and sixteenth notes. Because the smallest note value in your data is the sixteenth, you would set the Resolution parameter to Sixteenth.

4. In the Change section, activate the appropriate options for the types of events and the event properties you want to have quantized. You'll almost always want to have the Start Times option activated. Along with the Start Times of events, you can also quantize the durations of MIDI note events by activating the Duration option. You'll almost always want to have this option activated as well. If you don't, the ends of some notes may overlap the beginnings of others, which may not sound very good. You might not want to quantize the Start Times of Events but just the durations only if you want to create a staccato (separated notes) feel to your music. The Only Notes, Lyrics, and Audio option, when activated, makes it so only MIDI note, lyric, and audio events are quantized, leaving any other events (such as MIDI controller events) alone. You'll usually want to keep this option activated, too; otherwise, the Quantize feature will move controller events to the nearest grid point, which can actually screw up their timing.

TIP

Even though the Quantize feature can change the Start times of audio Clips, don't be confused into thinking that it can correct the timing of your audio data. It can't. Remember, audio data is different from MIDI data. The Quantize feature can move an entire audio clip to the nearest rhythmic value. However, if you record a sloppy performance as audio data, you cannot correct it except by doing the recording over again.

You can use one trick, however, to quantize a monophonic (one note at a time) melody or percussion part that was recorded as an audio clip. If you split the clip into smaller clips, each containing one note of the melody, then each note will have its own Start time, and you can use the Quantize feature to change the timing of each note.

5. In the Options section, set the Strength parameter. Quantizing your data so that all the events are aligned in perfect time with the grid can make your performance sound mechanical (like it is being played by a machine). So, instead of having the Quantize feature move an event to the exact current pointer position on the grid during the scanning process, you can have it move the event only slightly toward the pointer, thus taking the sloppiness out of the performance but keeping the "human" feel. You can do so by setting a percentage for the Strength parameter. A value of 100 percent means that all events will be moved to the exact grid point. A value of 50 percent means that the events will be moved only halfway toward the grid point. You'll have to experiment with this parameter to find the best-sounding setting.

CHAPTER 8

6. Set the Window parameter. This parameter tells SONAR how close to the current grid point an event has to be in order to be quantized. If the event falls inside the window, it is quantized. If it falls outside the window, it isn't. You set the Window parameter by using a percentage. A value of 100 percent means the window extends halfway before and halfway after the current pointer position on the grid. So, basically all events get moved; if they don't fall inside the window at the current pointer position, they will fall inside at the next position. A value of 50 percent means the window extends only one-quarter of the way before and after the current pointer position, meaning only half of the events in your selection will be processed.

7. Set the Offset parameter. This parameter is an extra setting thrown in to make the Quantize feature even more flexible (and complicated) than it already is. When the Quantize feature sets up its imaginary grid over your selected data, the grid is perfectly aligned to the measures and beats in your project. So, if your data selection started at the beginning of your project, the grid would be set up starting at 1:01:000 (measure, beat, tick). If you enter a value for the Offset parameter (in ticks), the grid is offset by the number of ticks that you enter. For example, if you enter an Offset of +3, the grid would be set up starting at 1:01:003 instead of 1:01:000. This means that if the current event being scanned was initially supposed to be moved to 1:01:000, it would be moved to 1:01:003 instead. Basically, you can use this parameter to offset the selected data from the other data in your project, in case you want to create some slight timing variations, and so on. It works similarly to the Time Offset parameter in the Track view, which you learned about in Chapter 4.

8. Set the Swing parameter, which is yet another parameter that makes the Quantize feature more flexible (and more difficult to understand). You might use it to work on a song that has a "swing" feel to it, similar to that of a waltz, where the first in a pair of notes is played longer than the second. It's difficult to explain, but essentially the Swing parameter distorts the grid by making the space between the grid points uneven. If you leave the parameter set at 50 percent, it doesn't have any effect. If you set it to something like 66 percent, the space between the first two points in the grid becomes twice as much as the space between the second and third points. This pattern of long space, short space gets repeated throughout the length of the grid, and your data is aligned according to the uneven grid points. You'll need to experiment with this parameter a bit to hear the effect it has on your data.

9. Click on the Audition button to hear how the quantized data will sound. Go back and make any parameter changes you think might be necessary.

10. If you want to use the same settings again later, save them as a preset.

11. Click on OK.

SONAR quantizes the selected data, and when you play it back, it should sound the same way it did when you listened to it using the Audition feature.

> **TIP**
> SONAR provides additional quantizing features with the Quantize MIDI Effect. See Chapter 11 for more information.

Groove Quantize

Not only can quantizing be used to correct the timing of your performances but also to add a bit of a creative flair. The Groove Quantize feature works in almost the same way as the Quantize feature, but it's slightly more sophisticated. Instead of using a fixed grid (meaning you can set the grid to use only straight rhythmic values such as sixteenth notes), it uses a grid with rhythmic values that are based on an existing rhythmic pattern called a groove pattern. This groove pattern can contain any kind of musical rhythm, even one taken from an existing piece of music.

Basically, the Groove Quantize feature works by imposing the timing, duration, and velocity values of one set of Events onto another set. For example, suppose you record a melody that comes out sounding a bit too mechanical, but your friend slams out this really kickin' MIDI bass line that has the exact "feel" you want. You can copy the bass clip data and use it as a groove pattern to groove quantize the melody clip data. By doing so, you impose the timing, duration, and velocity values (depending on your parameter settings) from the bass line on to the melody. Thus, the melody will have the same rhythm as the bass line but keep its original pitches.

The preceding example is just one of the many uses for the Groove Quantize feature. Just like the Quantize feature, the Groove Quantize feature provides Strength parameters to give you control over how much influence a groove pattern has over the data you're quantizing. You can define via percentages how much the timing, duration, and velocity values of the events will be affected, so you can use this feature for all kinds of editing tasks. You can correct off-tempo tracks, add complex beat accents to each measure of a tune, synchronize rhythm and solo tracks, align tracks with bad timing to one with good timing, and steal the "feeling" from tracks, as I explained in the preceding example.

As a matter of fact, groove quantizing has become so popular that companies now sell groove pattern files so that you can steal the "feeling" from tracks that have been recorded by professional keyboard, drum, and guitar players. It's almost like having Steve Vai play on your latest tune! Just look in any copy of *Electronic Musician* or *Keyboard* magazine, and you'll see advertisements for these types of products. Of course, you need to know how to use the Groove Quantize feature before you can make use of these groove pattern files, so let me tell you how:

1. If you want to grab the timing, duration, and velocity values from existing data, first select and copy that data so that it is placed into the Clipboard. Otherwise, you can use one of the groove patterns that comes included with SONAR (which I'll show you how to choose later).

2. Select the data that you want to groove quantize.

3. Choose Edit > Groove Quantize to open the Groove Quantize dialog box (see Figure 8.16).

Figure 8.16
The Groove Quantize dialog box provides a number of parameters you can set to determine exactly how you want your data to be groove quantized.

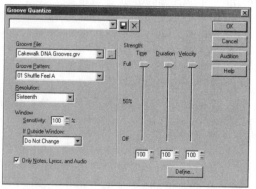

4. Set the Groove File parameter. If you're grabbing the values from existing data, as explained previously, then select Clipboard from the drop-down list and skip to Step 6. Otherwise, choose an existing groove file. SONAR ships with only one groove file (Cakewalk DNA Grooves.grv), so unless you've created your own groove files, you can leave this parameter as it is. If you have other groove files available, you can load them by clicking on the small button to the right of the Groove File parameter to bring up the Open Groove File dialog box. Just select a file and then click on Open.

5. Set the Groove Pattern parameter. Each groove file can contain any number of groove patterns. The groove file that comes with SONAR contains twelve different groove patterns. Choose the groove pattern you want to use.

6. The rest of the parameters for the Groove Quantize feature are the same as for the Quantize feature. You need to set the Resolution parameter; the Only Notes, Lyrics, And Audio; and the Window parameters. The Window Sensitivity parameter is the same as the Window parameter for the Quantize feature, but one additional Window parameter is available here. You can choose the If Outside Window parameter to have Groove Quantize change events even if they fall outside the window. If you select Do Not Change, then events outside the window are left alone (just as with the Quantize feature). If you select Quantize to Resolution, any events outside the window are moved to the nearest grid point as specified by the Resolution parameter. If you select Move to Nearest, then the Window Sensitivity parameter is ignored, and all events outside the window are moved to the nearest grid point as defined by the groove pattern. If you select Scale Time, SONAR looks at the events located right before and after the current event being scanned (as long as they are within the window), and it sets their relative timing so that they're the same. The Scale Time parameter is very difficult to explain, so you should try it out to hear what kind of effect it has on your music.

7. You also need to set the Strength parameters. They work the same as with the Quantize feature, but instead of just having one parameter for affecting the timing of events, three Strength parameters are provided to give you control over how the Groove Quantize feature will affect the time, duration, and velocity of each event. If you want the events to have the exact same timing, duration, and velocity of their counterparts in the groove pattern, then set all these parameters to 100 percent. Otherwise, you can make it so the events take on only some of the "feel" of the events in the groove pattern by adjusting the percentages of these parameters.

8. Click on the Audition button to hear how the quantized data will sound. Go back and make any parameter changes you think might be necessary.

9. If you want to use the same settings again later, save them as a preset.

10. Click on OK.

SONAR quantizes the selected data so that (depending on your parameter settings) the timing, duration, and velocity of the events sound exactly or somewhat like those in the groove pattern you used. By the way, if the groove pattern is shorter than the material you are quantizing, the Groove Quantize feature will loop through the groove pattern as many times as necessary to get to the end of your selected data. For example, if you use a groove pattern that is only one measure long, but your selected data is three measures, then the timing, duration, and velocity values of the groove pattern will be repeated over each of those three measures.

CHAPTER 8

Saving Groove Patterns

If you create your own groove pattern by grabbing the timing, duration, and velocity values from existing data, you can save it for later use as follows:

1. After you've gone through steps 1 through 4 in the preceding example on how to use the Groove Quantize feature and you've set the Groove File parameter to Clipboard, click on the Define button at the bottom of the Groove Quantize dialog box to open the Define Groove dialog box (see Figure 8.17).

Figure 8.17
Using the Define Groove dialog box, you can save your own groove patterns and groove files.

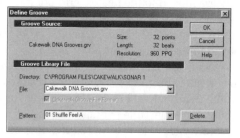

2. In the Groove Library File section, select an existing groove file via the File parameter. You can also type a new name to create your own new groove file.

NOTE

SONAR supports two types of groove files. One type is the DNA groove file, which contains only timing data but is compatible with other sequencing software. The groove files being sold by other companies are usually in this file format. SONAR also has its own proprietary groove file format that stores timing, duration, and velocity data. Unless you really need to share your groove files with others who don't own SONAR, I suggest you save your files in the SONAR format, because it provides more flexibility. To do so, be sure to activate the Cakewalk Groove File Format option in the Define Groove dialog box.

3. If you want to replace an existing groove pattern in the current groove file, just select one from the list via the Pattern parameter. If you want to save your groove pattern under a new name, type the name via the Pattern parameter.

TIP

You can also delete existing groove patterns in the current groove file. Just select the groove pattern you want to delete via the Pattern parameter and click on the Delete button. SONAR then asks you to confirm the deletion process.

4. Click on OK. If you're replacing an existing groove pattern, SONAR
    will ask you to confirm the replacement process.

SONAR saves your new groove pattern inside the groove file that you
selected (or created) under the name that you specified.

> **TIP**
>
> For examples of some cool applications for the Groove Quantize feature, look
> at the SONAR Help in the Editing MIDI Events and Controllers > Changing
> the Time of a Recording > Quantizing section.

Interpolate

Throughout the text of this book, I've mentioned the name SONAR quite
a few times. What if I want to change all those instances of the phrase to
SONAR 1.0 instead? Luckily, I'm using a word processing program on my
computer, so all I would have to do is use the search and replace feature
to have the program automatically make the changes for me. I mention
this point because the Interpolate feature is similar to the search and
replace feature you find in most word processing programs. The
difference is that the Interpolate feature works with event properties, and
in addition to simply searching and replacing, it can scale whole ranges
of event properties from one set of values to another set of values. This
means that you can easily transpose notes, change key signatures, convert
one type of controller message into another type of controller message,
and so on. It works like this:

1. Select the data that you want to change.

2. Choose Edit > Interpolate to open the Event Filter–Search dialog box.
    You learned about this dialog box and its parameters in Chapter 5.

3. Set all the available parameters so that SONAR can select the exact
    Events that you want to process.

4. Click on OK to open the Event Filter–Replace dialog box (see Figure
    8.18). This dialog box is also almost the same as the Event
    Filter–Search dialog box. It has the same settings, except some of the
    settings are not available, because here you need to enter only the
    values to which you want to change the original selected data. So,
    enter the replacement values in the appropriate parameters.

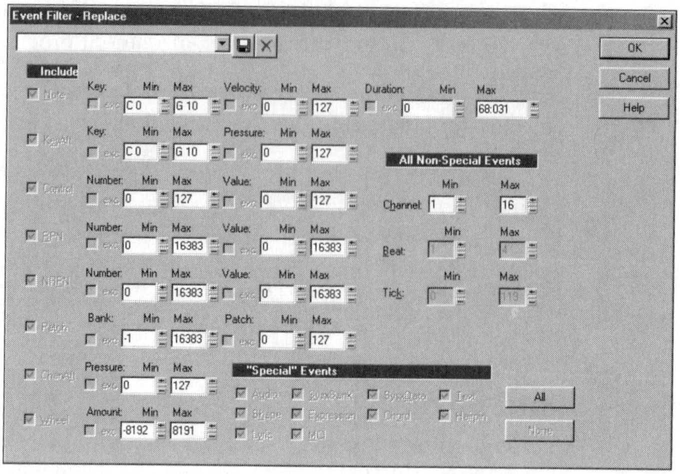

Figure 8.18
In the Event Filter–Replace dialog box, you can enter the replacement values only for the data you're trying to change.

5. Click on OK.

SONAR selects all the events in your initial selection according to the parameters you set the in Event Filter–Search dialog box. It then changes the values of those events according to the parameters you set in the Event Filter–Replace dialog box.

Interpolation Applications

You didn't think I was going to leave you high and dry trying to figure out such a complicated feature, did you? Actually, when you get the hang of it, using the Interpolate feature isn't too difficult, especially if you're just trying to make straight replacements of data. Anyway, the following sections describe some of the changes you can accomplish with this feature.

Straight Replacement

If all you want to do is replace one value with another, setting up the parameters in both dialog boxes is fairly easy. Say you want to change all the notes having a pitch of C#2 with notes having a pitch of D#7. To do so, set up the Event Filter–Search dialog box so that only the Note option is activated in the Include section. Then type C#2 for both the Key Min and Key Max parameters and click on OK. In the Event Filter–Replace dialog box, type D#7 for the Key Min and Key Max parameters and click on OK. All the C#2 notes are then changed to D#7 notes. Pretty easy, no? And you can use this approach with any of the data. Earlier, I mentioned changing one type of controller message to another. Just use the Control option along with the Number Min and Number Max parameters. as you did with the Note option and the Key Min and Key Max parameters.

TIP

You can also use wildcards when designating an octave number for the pitch of a note. In regards to the example, say you want to change all the C# notes to D notes, not just the ones in octave 2 to octave 7. Instead of using C#2, you can use C#?, and instead of using D#7, you can use D#?. The ? is the wildcard, which stands for any octave.

Scaling Values

When you're working with ranges of values, you can use the Interpolate feature to scale them from one range to another. This capability is useful in limiting certain values to keep them within a set of boundaries. For example, some of the note velocities in one of your MIDI tracks may be a bit high, and you want to quiet them down a bit. Usually, quieting them would mean having to use the Piano Roll view to change them all one by one. With the Interpolate feature, you can compress their range down in a couple of easy steps. To do so, set up the Event Filter–Search dialog box so that only the Note option is activated in the Include section. Then type 0 for the Velocity Min and 127 for the Velocity Max and click on OK. In the Event Filter–Replace dialog box, type 0 for the Velocity Min and 100 for the Velocity Max and click on OK. All the note velocities are then scaled down from a range of 0 to 127 to a range of 0 to 100. See how it works? You can use this approach with any of the other value ranges, too.

Inverting Values

You also can invert any of the value ranges by reversing the Min and Max parameters. For example, what if you want to make all the loud volume controller messages soft and the soft volume controller messages loud? To do so, set up the Event Filter–Search dialog box so that only the Control option is activated in the Include section. Then type 7 (the number for volume controller messages) for both the Number Min and Number Max parameters. Also, type 0 for Value Min and 127 for Value Max and click on OK. In the Event Filter–Replace dialog box, type 7 for both the Number Min and Number Max parameters. Also, type 127 for Value Min and 0 for Value Max and click on OK. All the loud sections of your selected data then become soft and vice versa. Again, you can use this technique for any of the other value ranges.

As a matter of fact, you can change a whole bunch of different parameters at once (even mix straight replacement, scaling, and inverting) by activating the appropriate parameters in the Event Filter–Search dialog box. For instance, you could easily set up all three of the preceding examples so that you would have to use the Interpolate feature only one time to process the same data. This feature is very powerful. You should experiment with it as much as possible because, in the long run, it can save you a lot of editing time.

CHAPTER 8

TIP

You also can find some other Interpolate application ideas in the SONAR Help file under the Editing MIDI Events and Controllers > Searching for Events > Event Filters section.

Length

The Length feature is one of the very simple but also very useful features provided in SONAR. Using it, you can change the size of a clip or group of selected data by specifying a percentage. It works like this:

1.   Select the data that you want to change.

2.   Choose Edit > Length to open the Length dialog box (see Figure 8.19).

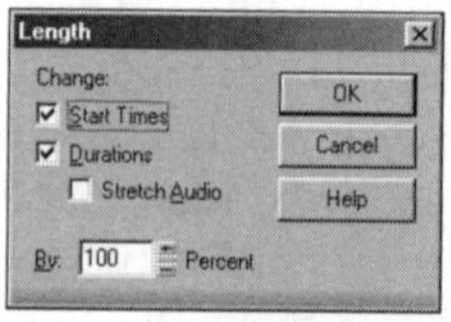

Figure 8.19
You can change the size of clips or selected groups of events by using the Length feature.

3.   Activate the Start Times, Durations, and/or Stretch Audio options. Activating the Start Times option makes the Length feature change the Start Times of the selected events so that the entire selection will change in size. Activating the Durations option makes the Length feature change the durations of the selected events. If you activate the Durations option without the Start Times option, the Length feature will change only the size of the durations of the selected events. This feature can be useful if you want to create a staccato effect for your notes. And if you want the length of your audio data to be changed, you can activate the Stretch Audio option.

4.   Enter a value for the By Percent parameter. A value of 100 percent doesn't make any changes at all. A value of 50 percent changes the selection to half of its original length. And a value of 200 percent changes the selection to twice its original length.

5.   Click on OK.

SONAR changes the size of the clip(s) or entire selection of events according to your parameter specifications.

TIP

For a more intuitive way to change the length of your data (meaning you can enter a length using an actual time value instead of a percentage), use the Fit to Time feature, which you'll learn about later in this chapter.

Retrograde

The Retrograde feature works similarly to the Reverse feature that you learned about earlier in this chapter. Instead of reversing the data in audio clips, however, the Retrograde feature reverses MIDI data. This means you can have your MIDI data play backward if you apply this feature. Just select the data you want to reverse and then select Edit > Retrograde. SONAR reverses the order of the selected events. In other words, if you were looking at the data via the Event view, the data is changed so that essentially the list is flipped upside down. That's about it.

Transpose

Transposition is a common occurrence when you're composing music, and SONAR's Transpose feature enables you to transpose quickly and easily. It works like this:

1. Select the data that you want to transpose.

2. Choose Edit > Transpose to open the Transpose dialog box (see Figure 8.20).

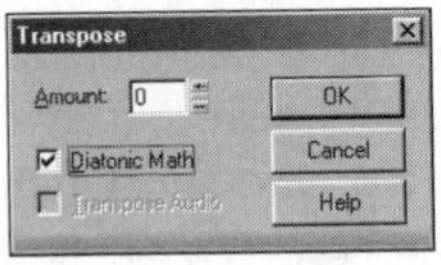

Figure 8.20
By entering a number of steps, you can transpose the pitches of note events up or down using the Transpose feature.

3. You can use the Transpose feature to transpose the pitches of your note events either chromatically so that they can be changed by half steps or diatonically so that they remain in the current key signature of your project. If you want to transpose chromatically, leave the Diatonic Math option deactivated. If you want to transpose diatonically, activate the Diatonic Math option.

4. If you have selected any audio data, you can opt to have its pitch changed as well. To do so, activate the Transpose Audio option.

5. Enter a value for the Amount parameter. A positive value transposes up, and a negative value transposes down. If you are transposing chromatically, this value corresponds to half steps. If you are transposing diatonically, the Transpose feature changes the pitches of your notes according the major scale of the current key signature. So, for example, if you enter a value of +1 and the key signature is D major, a D becomes an E, an E becomes an F#, and so on.

6. Click on OK.

SONAR transposes the pitches of the notes (or audio) in the selected data according to your parameter settings.

Scale Velocity

You learned about scaling the velocity values of events earlier in the description of the Interpolate feature. Using the Scale Velocity feature, you can do the same thing, but this feature has one extra option that enables you to scale the velocities by a percentage rather than enter exact values or a range of values. It works like this:

1. Select the data that you want to change.

2. Choose Edit > Scale Velocity to open the Scale Velocity dialog box (see Figure 8.21).

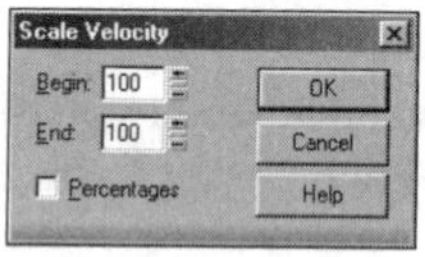

Figure 8.21
You can scale the velocities of note events by percentages if you use the Scale Velocity feature.

3. If you want to scale the velocities by percentages, activate the Percentages option. Otherwise, the values that you enter will be exact velocity values.

4. Enter values for the Begin and End parameters. For example, you can use the Scale Velocity feature to create crescendos and decrescendos. To create a crescendo, enter a small value (such as 0 or 50 percent) for the Begin parameter and a larger value (such as 127 or 150 percent) for the End parameter. Do the opposite for a decrescendo.

5. Click on OK.

SONAR scales the velocity values of the note events within the selected data according your parameter settings.

TIP
You can create crescendos and decrescendos with more precise control by drawing them with the Draw Line tool in the Controller pane of the Piano Roll view. You learned how to use this tool in Chapter 7.

Fit to Time

As I mentioned earlier, the Fit to Time feature works similarly to the Length feature: Using it, you can change the size of clips and selected groups of data. But instead of having to use a percentage, you can specify an actual time (according to the Time Ruler) at which the data will end. For example, if you have a clip that begins at 1:01:000 and ends at

4:02:000, the Start time of the clip remains the same, but you can change the End time of the clip so that it stops playing at the exact moment you specify. This feature is great when you need to compose music to a precise length such as for a radio commercial or a video. It works like this:

1. Select the data that you want to change.

2. Choose Edit > Fit to Time to open the Fit to Time dialog box (see Figure 8.22).

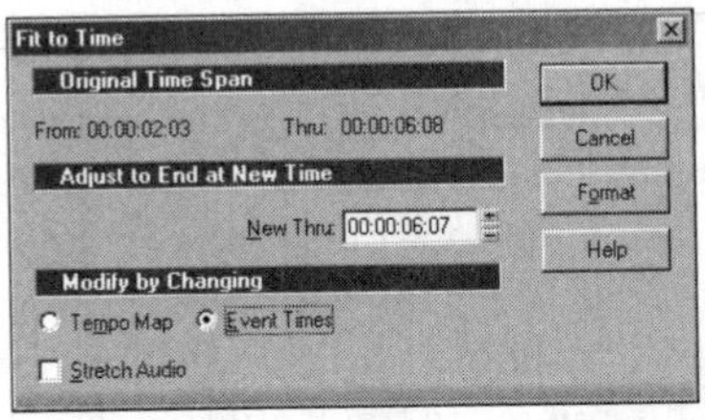

Figure 8.22

You can specify the exact length of clips or selected groups of events by using the Fit to Time feature.

3. The Original Time Span section shows the beginning and end times for the selected data. In the Adjust to End at New Time section, enter a new end time for the selected data. You can enter either hours, minutes, seconds, and frames or measures, beats, and ticks. To change the format, click on the Format button.

4. In the Modify by Changing section, activate either the Tempo Map option or the Event Times option. If you want the actual data to be changed (meaning the Start times of every event in the selection will be adjusted to accommodate the new end time), activate the Event Times option. If you would rather leave the data as it is and just have SONAR insert tempo changes into the project to accommodate the new end time, activate the Tempo Map option. The key difference here is that using the Tempo Map option affects the entire project, and all the data in all the tracks during the selected time will play at a different rate. If you want the data in only one track to be affected, you must use the Event Times option.

5. If you want to change the length of audio clips, you have to activate the Stretch Audio option.

6. Click on OK.

SONAR either changes the length of the selected data or inserts tempo changes into the project (depending on your parameter settings) to accommodate the new end time that you specify.

CHAPTER 8

Fit Improvisation

Having to play along with a metronome while recording in SONAR can be a nuisance sometimes. Depending on the type of music you are performing, using the metronome might not be conducive to your mood during the performance, which means you may end up with a less than acceptable recording. Some people just can't stand using a metronome. The problem is that, if you don't use the metronome while recording in SONAR, your data will not line up correctly to the measure, beat, and tick values along the Time Ruler. Therefore, editing your music can be a lot more difficult.

If you are one of those people who hates metronomes, then you're in luck. SONAR allows you to record your MIDI tracks without using the metronome but still line up your data correctly after the fact by using the Fit Improvisation feature. This feature works by adding tempo changes to your project according to an additional reference track that you must record. This reference track gives SONAR an idea of the tempo at which you were playing when you were recording your MIDI track without the metronome. The following is a more detailed version of how this feature works:

1. Record a MIDI track without using the metronome. For the most accurate results, try to play using as steady a tempo as possible.

2. Choose Options > Global to open the Global Options dialog box. Click on the MIDI tab. Be sure only the Notes option in the Record section is activated. It filters out any extraneous events when you're recording your reference track so that they don't mess up the timing. The more accurate your reference track, the better. After you're done recording it, you can go back to the Global Options dialog box and change the options back to the way they were.

3. Record a reference MIDI track. To do so, simply tap out the tempo of your initial MIDI recording by hitting a key on your MIDI instrument for every beat. So, if you recorded a track in 4/4 time, you would have to hit the key four times for every measure of music you recorded. Also, be sure that the first note in your reference track has a Start time of 1:01:000 so that it starts at the very beginning of the project. You can adjust it manually by using the Event view or Piano Roll view if you have to.

4. Select the reference track.

5. Choose Edit > Fit Improvisation.

SONAR scans your reference track, analyzing where the beats fall, and adds tempo changes to your project so that the data in your recorded track lines up with the measure, beat, and tick values on the Time Ruler. Now you can edit your data just as you would any other data that was recorded along with the metronome.

9

Composing with Loops

In addition to creating music by recording and editing your MIDI and audio performances, SONAR allows you to compose music with *sample loops*. Sample loops are short (though not always) audio recordings that you can piece together to create whole musical performances. Using them is a great way to add some acoustic audio tracks to your project without having to actually do any recording or having to know how to play an instrument. For example, you can buy a CD full of sample loops that contain nothing but acoustic drum beats. Not only can you buy drum loops, but you can also get real guitar solos, vocal chorus recordings, orchestral recordings, and more. You can create a whole project just by using sample loops, and SONAR even provides you with the tools to create your own loops. In this chapter, I'll tell you about all the loop-based features that SONAR provides, including the following:

▶ Groove clips

▶ Creating Groove clips

▶ The Loop Construction view

▶ Working with Groove clips

▶ The Loop Explorer view

▶ Project pitch and pitch markers

Groove Clips

In SONAR, sample loops are known as Groove clips. If you're familiar with Sonic Foundry's ACID software, you won't have any trouble with Groove clips, since they are Cakewalk's equivalent to Sonic Foundry's loops for ACID. Like loops for ACID, Groove clips automatically take care of the sometimes tedious chore of matching the playback tempo and pitch of each loop you use in a song. This is because Groove clips are sample loops with extra information stored within them that lets SONAR know their basic tempo, pitch, and playback properties. SONAR can then accurately shift the tempo and pitch of the Groove clips so that they match the tempo and pitch of the current project. Why is this important? Because not all sample loops are recorded at the same tempo and pitch, and in order to use them in the same song, they have to "groove" with one another, so to speak. Before loops for ACID or Groove clips came along, a musician would have to match the tempo and pitch of multiple loops manually, and let me tell you, it's not a fun task. Of course, not all sample loops contain the extra information I mentioned earlier. Plain sample loops need to be converted into Groove clips before you can use them within a SONAR project. But don't worry—it's not nearly as difficult as you might think.

Creating Groove Clips

As a matter of fact, any audio clip in SONAR can easily be converted into a Groove clip with a few clicks of your mouse. To convert a regular audio clip into a Groove clip, do the following:

1. Right-click on an audio clip in the Clips pane of the Track view and choose Clip Properties from the pop-up menu to open the Clip Properties dialog box.

2. Click on the Groove-Clips tab to display the Groove Clips parameters (see Figure 9.1).

Figure 9.1
Use the Clip Properties dialog box to convert an audio clip into a Groove clip.

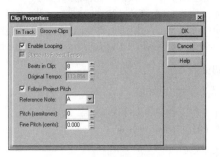

3. Activate the Enable Looping option. That's basically all you need to do, but there are some extra parameters that you need to deal with if you want some extra control on how SONAR will handle your new Groove clip.

TIP

Instead of opening the Clip Properties dialog box to enable looping for an audio clip, you can just right-click on the clip and choose Groove-Clip Looping from the pop-up menu. This method is quicker, but it doesn't give you access to the extra parameters.

4. When you activate the Enable Looping option for a clip, SONAR automatically activates the Stretch to Project Tempo parameter and makes a guess as to how many rhythmic beats are in the clip and the original tempo of the clip. If the beats are inaccurate, you can change the number of beats for the clip by entering a new number in the Beats in Clip parameter. These parameters must be accurate for SONAR to be able to change the playback tempo of the clip to follow the tempo of your project.

5. In addition to changing the tempo of the clip, SONAR can also change the pitch of the clip to follow the pitch of the project. This ensures that Groove clips stay in tune with one another within the same project. If you want SONAR to control the pitch of the clip, activate the Follow Project Pitch option.

TIP

Not all Groove clips should follow the pitch of the project. Why? Well, if you have a Groove clip that contains percussive data like a drum instrument performance, you don't want the pitch of that clip to change, because it will just make the drum performance sound strange. For these types of Groove clips, only the Stretch to Project Tempo option should be activated. The Follow Project Pitch option should be activated only for clips containing pitch-related performances such as guitar, bass, woodwinds, horns, strings, vocals, and the like.

6. When you activate the Follow Project Pitch option, you have to tell SONAR the original pitch of the material in the clip. SONAR doesn't automatically determine the pitch for you. To tell SONAR the original pitch of the clip, choose a pitch from the Reference Note drop-down list. For example, if the notes played in the clip are based on a C chord, choose C in the Reference Note drop-down list. How do you know the original pitch of the clip? You'll have to figure it out by listening to it.

7. If you want to transpose the pitch of the clip so that it plays differently from the project pitch, you can enter a value (measured in semitones) for the Pitch parameter. This parameter can come in handy if you are composing with orchestral instrument loops that need to be played in a different key.

8. If the pitch of the clip is slightly out of tune, you can adjust it by entering a value (measured in cents) for the Fine Pitch parameter.

9. Click OK.

SONAR will now treat your original audio clip as a Groove clip. If the tempo or pitch of the project changes (I'll talk more about this later), the Groove clip will be stretched and transposed accordingly. In addition, you'll notice that in the Track view, a regular audio clip is shown as a rectangle, but when a clip is converted into a Groove clip, it is shown as a rectangle with rounded corners (see Figure 9.2).

Figure 9.2
A Groove clip is indicated as a rectangle with rounded corners.

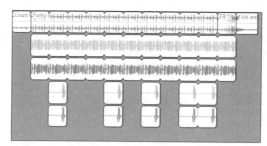

The Loop Construction View

Of course, there may be times when SONAR doesn't seem to stretch your Groove clips accurately. If this occurs, you'll hear slight anomalies in the audio when you change the tempo of your project. To correct this, you can try using the Loop Construction view to convert your audio clip. To utilize the Loop Construction view, do the following:

1. Right-click on the audio clip in the Clips pane of the Track view, and choose View > Loop Construction (or double click on the clip) to open the Loop Construction view (see Figure 9.3).

Figure 9.3
Instead of the Clip Properties dialog box, use the Loop Construction view to convert your clips.

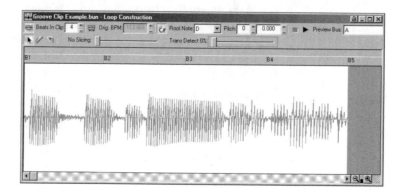

2. Along the top of the view, you'll see a toolbar containing all of the same parameters found in the Clip Properties dialog box. From left to right are the buttons for the Enable Looping option; the Beats In Clip parameter; the Enable Stretching option (which is the same as the Stretch to Project Tempo option); the Orig. BPM parameter (which is the same as the Original Tempo parameter); the Follow Project Pitch option; the Root Note parameter (same as the Reference Note parameter); and the Pitch parameters (same as the Pitch and Fine Pitch parameters. You can set these parameters as explained in the previous section.

3. The last three toolbar parameters are Stop Preview, Preview Loop, and Preview Bus. The Preview Loop and Stop Preview parameters let you listen to the loop currently displayed in the Loop Construction view. The Preview Bus parameter lets you choose which virtual main will be used to play the loop. I'll talk more about virtual mains in Chapter 12.

4. You'll also notice a second toolbar as well as the audio waveform of the loop currently displayed in the Loop Construction view. I'll talk more about the second toolbar in a minute. For now, notice that when you activate the Enable Looping option, SONAR automatically adjust two of the parameters in the second toolbar and adds vertical lines to the audio waveform (see Figure 9.4). These lines are slicing markers. Slicing markers designate a specific place in a loop where the timing data needs to be preserved when the timing of the loop is being stretched in order to fit the project tempo. The slicing markers make it so that a loop can be stretched without having its pitch change at the same time.

Figure 9.4
SONAR uses slicing markers to maintain the audio quality of a loop when it is stretched.

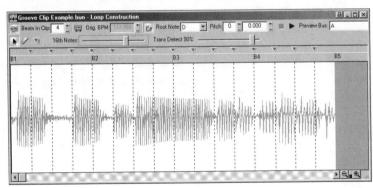

> **NOTE**
>
> Normally when you stretch (change the length of) audio data, the pitch is changed as well. Make the data shorter, and the pitch is raised. Make the data longer, and the pitch is lowered. By slicing the data into smaller pieces, the data can be stretched very accurately, preserving its original quality without changing its pitch. This slicing happens in real-time during playback, and it's non-destructive (meaning the original data is not changed).

5. To control the way that SONAR automatically adds slicing markers to your loop, you need to adjust the Basic Slicing and the Trans Detect (short for Transient Detection) sliders, which are located in the second toolbar. The Basic Slicing slider works by placing slicing markers at specific rhythmic locations in the loop according the Beats In Loop parameter (mentioned earlier). For example, if you set the Basic Slicing slider to Eighth Notes, slicing markers will be placed at every eighth note location in your loop. If your loop contains four beats, it will have seven slicing markers. You would think there should be eight slicing markers—since there are two eighth notes to every beat and two multiplied by four is eight—but the beginning of a loop never needs a slicing marker, so there is one fewer than expected. When adjusting the Basic Slicing slider, it's usually best to go with a note value equal to the smallest rhythmic value in your audio data performance. For example, if your loop contains sixteenth notes, try setting the Basic Slicing slider to 16th Notes. You can also try a setting that is one value lower, which in this case would be eighth notes. Just be aware that too few or too many slicing markers will introduce unwanted artifacts into the audio when your loops are being stretched.

6. When adjusting the Trans Detect slider, slicing markers are placed at the beginning of detected transients in the audio data of the loop. Transients are large spikes (big changes in volume) in the audio waveform. Because of this, the Trans Detect slider works best when working with percussive material. A setting of about 90 percent usually works well. And you'll usually want to use a combination of the Basic Slicing and Trans Detect sliders to get the optimum number of slicing markers set up in your loop.

7. If the Basic Slicing and Trans Detect sliders don't provide enough Slicing Markers or provide the wrong placement, you can use the Select, Erase Marker, and Default All Markers tools to create, erase, and adjust the slicing markers manually. The first three buttons in the second toolbar correspond to the Select, Erase Marker, and Default All Markers tools, respectively. Use the Select tool to move existing slicing markers by clicking and dragging the marker triangles in the marker area above the audio waveform display (see Figure 9.5). You can also use the Select tool to create your own slicing markers by simply double-clicking in the marker area. Manually made or changed markers are shown with a blue triangle.

Figure 9.5
Use the Select tool to create or move slicing markers.

8. To erase a slicing marker, just choose the Erase Marker tool and click on the triangle of the slicing marker that you want to erase.

9. If you moved any of the automatically created slicing markers and you want to put them back to their original positions, just click the Default All Markers button. If you created any slicing markers manually, those markers will remain untouched.

10. Once you are finished adjusting all the parameters for your new Groove clip, close the Loop Construction view.

You can usually rely on the automatic settings that SONAR provides, but just in case, it's good to know that you have total control on how your Groove clips are handled.

TIP
If you want to use your new Groove clip in a number of different projects, use the Export Audio feature to save the clip as a standard WAV file.

Working with Groove Clips

Once you've created your Groove clips, you can use them to compose music in a current project or to create an entirely new project altogether. Composing with Groove clips involves a combination of dragging and dropping to add clips to a project and slip editing to make the clips conform to music you are trying to create.

CHAPTER 9

The Loop Explorer View

If you have some Groove clips stored on disk in the WAV file format, you can use the Loop Explorer view to add them to your project. The Loop Explorer view lets you examine and preview your stored Groove clips as well as add them to your project via dragging and dropping with your mouse. To use the Loop Explorer view, do the following:

1. Choose View > Loop Explorer to open the Loop Explorer view (see Figure 9.6). The Loop Explorer view is very similar to the Windows Explorer.

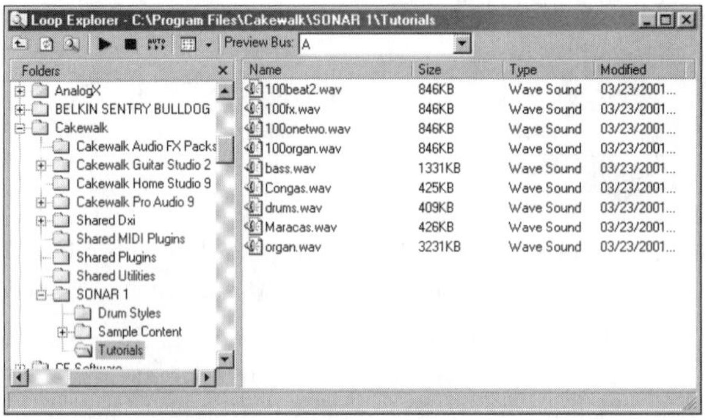

Figure 9.6
Use the Loop Explorer view to add existing Groove clips to your project.

2. In the Folders pane, navigate to the folder on your disk drive that contains your Groove clip files. Then select the folder. Its contents are then displayed in the File pane.

3. Your Groove clip files can be displayed as large or small icons, a list of file names, or a detailed list of file names. Just use the Views drop-down list to choose your option (see Figure 9.7).

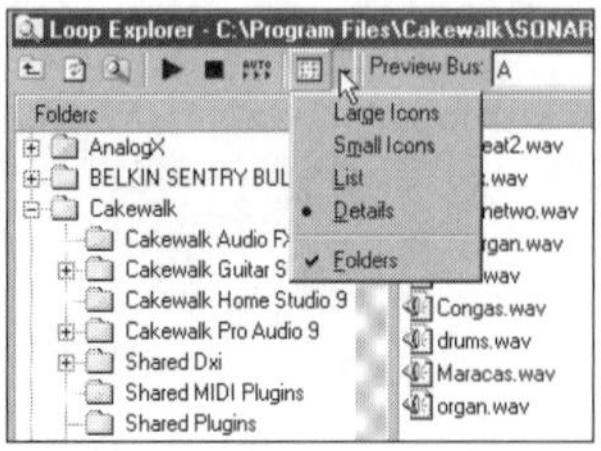

Figure 9.7
Use the Views drop-down list to choose the Groove clip file display option.

4. To preview a Groove clip, select its file in the File pane and then click the Play button in the Loop Explorer view toolbar. To stop playback, click the Stop button. If you would like a file to start playing automatically as soon as you select it, activate the Auto-Preview option (see Figure 9.8). As in the Loop Construction view, you can choose which virtual main to use for the loop playback. I'll talk more about virtual mains in Chapter 12.

Figure 9.8
Use the Play, Stop, and Auto-Preview options to preview a Groove clip file.

5. To add a Groove clip to a project, just drag and drop the clip from the Loop Explorer view into the clips pane of the Track view. If you drag the clip onto an existing track, the clip will be added to that track. If you drag the clip onto a blank area of the Clips pane, a new track containing the clip will be created for you. Also, depending on the horizontal position to which you drag and drop, the clip will be added to the track at the closest measure position in the track. For example, if you drag and drop the clip anywhere inside of measure two within the track, the clip will be added to the track with its beginning at the beginning of measure two.

6. You can keep the Loop Explorer view open for as long as you need to continue dragging and dropping Groove clips into your project.

After you've added your Groove clips, you can slip edit them to make them conform to the music you are trying to create. I talked about slip editing back in Chapter 7, but later in this chapter, I'll give you an example of how to use the technique with Groove clips.

TIP
You can also add Groove clips to a project by using the Import Audio feature. I talked about this feature back in Chapter 6.

Project Pitch

Controlling the pitch of the Groove clips in your project is extremely easy. The first thing you need to do is set the default pitch for the entire project. This is called the project pitch. To set the project pitch, do the following:

1. Make sure the Markers toolbar is visible by choosing View > Toolbars. Then activate the Markers option and click Close.

CHAPTER 9

2. In the Markers toolbar, use the Default Project Pitch drop-down list to set the initial pitch for your project (see Figure 9.9). For example, if you want the music in your project to start using a C chord, choose C in the Default Project Pitch drop-down list.

Figure 9.9
Use the Default Project Pitch drop-down list to set the initial pitch of your project.

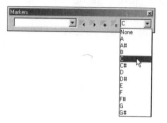

Pitch Markers

Once you've set the initial pitch for your project, all the Groove clips will automatically be transposed to play using that pitch until you change it. To change the project pitch at specified points within your project, you need to use pitch markers. I talked about markers back in Chapter 5, and while pitch markers work almost the same as regular markers, they do have a slight difference.

Create Pitch Markers

Creating pitch markers is essentially the same as creating regular markers. You simply set the Now time to the measure, beat, and tick at which you want to place the marker in the project, activate the Marker dialog box, and type in a name. But you also have to designate a pitch setting for that marker, which tells SONAR to change the project pitch at that point in the project. To create a pitch marker, just do the following:

1. Set the Now time to the measure, beat, and tick or the SMPTE time at which you want to place the marker in the object.

2. Select Insert > Marker to open the Marker dialog box (see Figure 9.10). You can also open the Marker dialog box in one of these ways: by pressing F11 on your computer keyboard; holding the Ctrl key on your computer keyboard and clicking just above the Time Ruler (the Marker section) in the Track, Staff, or Piano Roll views; right-clicking in a Time Ruler; clicking on the Insert Marker button in the Markers toolbar; or clicking on the Insert Marker button in the Markers view.

Figure 9.10
Using the Marker dialog box, you can create a pitch marker.

3. Type a name for the marker.

4. If you want the marker to be assigned to a measure/beat/tick value, you don't need to do anything more.

5. If you want the marker to be assigned to a SMPTE time, activate the Lock to SMPTE (Real World) Time option.

NOTE

If you use the Lock to SMPTE (Real World) Time value, your marker is assigned an exact hour/minute/second and frame value. It retains that value no matter what. So, even if you change the tempo of the project, the marker keeps the same time value, although its measure/beat/tick location may change because of the tempo. This feature is especially handy when you're putting music and sound to video and you need to have cues that always happen at an exact moment within the project.

By leaving a marker assigned to a measure/beat/tick value, however, you can be sure that it will always occur at that measure, beat, and tick even if you change the tempo of the project.

6. Assign a pitch to the marker using the Groove-Clip Pitch drop-down list.

7. Click OK.

When you're finished, your pitch marker (and its pitch) is added to the marker section (just above the Time Ruler) in the Track, Staff, and Piano Roll views.

TIP

Usually, you add markers to a project while no real-time activity is going on, but you can also add markers while a project is playing. Simply press the F11 key on your computer keyboard, and SONAR creates a marker at the current Now time. The new marker is automatically assigned a temporary name, which you can later change. You also need to add a pitch to each marker after you stop playback, because SONAR will not automatically assign pitches to markers.

Name Change

To change the name of a pitch marker, follow these steps:

1. Right-click on the marker in the Marker section of the Time Ruler in one of the views to open the Marker dialog box. Alternatively, select View > Markers to open the Markers view, and double-click on the marker in the list to open the Marker dialog box.

2. Type a new name for the marker.

3. Click on OK.

Time Change

Follow these steps to change the time value of a pitch marker numerically:

1. Right-click on the marker in the Marker section of the Time Ruler in one of the views to open the Marker dialog box. Alternatively, select View > Markers to open the Markers view and double-click on the marker in the list to open the Marker dialog box.

2. Type a new measure/beat/tick value for the marker. If you want to use an SMPTE value, activate the Lock to SMPTE (Real World) Time option and then type a new hour/minute/second/frame value for the marker.

3. Click on OK.

You can also change the time value of a pitch marker graphically by simply dragging the marker within the marker section of the Time Ruler in one of the views with your mouse. Drag the marker to the left to decrease its time value or drag it to the right to increase its time value. Simple, no?

Make a Copy

To make a copy of a pitch marker, follow these steps:

1. Hold down the Ctrl key on your computer keyboard.
2. Click and drag a pitch marker in the Marker section of the Time Ruler in one of the Views to a new time location.
3. Release the Ctrl key and mouse button. SONAR displays the Marker dialog box.
4. Enter a name for the marker. You can also change the time by typing a new value if you'd like. The time value is initially set to the time corresponding to the location on the Time Ruler to which you dragged the marker.
5. Click on OK.

Delete a Pitch Marker

You can delete a marker in one of two ways—either directly in the Track, Staff, or Piano Roll views or via the Marker view. Here's the exact procedure:

1. If you want to use the Track, Staff, or Piano Roll views, click and hold the left mouse button on the marker that you want to delete.
2. If you want to use the Markers view, select View > Markers to open the Markers view. Then select the marker that you want to delete from the list.
3. Press the Delete key on your computer keyboard.

TIP

To prevent your pitch markers from being edited, you can lock them into position. Just open the Markers view, select the marker or markers you want to lock, and click on the Lock button (the button with the picture of a little lock on it). To unlock a marker, the procedure is exactly the same.

A Groove Clip Exercise

Now that I've talked about how to create Groove clips and how to use them in a project, let's put that knowledge to practical use by working through a detailed exercise so that you can actually see Groove clips in action. Are you ready? Let's go:

1. Start SONAR. A blank new project should open automatically. If not, then choose File > New and choose the Normal template from the New Project File dialog box to create one.

2. If there are any tracks in the project, delete them. You should now have a totally blank Track view.

3. Set the Default Project Pitch to C and set the tempo for the project to 114 bpm. Also activate the Snap to Grid feature and, in the Snap to Grid dialog box, choose the Musical Time: Measure options and Move To mode.

4. Choose File > Open and open the demo project that comes with SONAR called SONAR Audio and MIDI Demo.bun.

5. If the Auto-Send Sysx dialog box appears, click Cancel. and close the File Info window. Choose Window > Tile In Rows so that you can see the Track views for both your new project and the demo project.

6. Drag-and-drop the first clip in Track 1 from the demo project into your new project. If the Drag and Drop Options dialog box appears, click OK.

   SONAR will automatically create a new track for the clip. Make sure the clip is positioned at the very beginning of the track (see Figure 9.11). Widen the track so that you can see the data in the clip.

Figure 9.11
Drag-and-drop the clip to beginning of the new track.

7. Drag-and-drop the clip in Track 1 at measure 6 from the demo project into Track 1 of your new project. Position the start of this clip at measure 2 and slip edit the clip so that its end extends to the beginning of measure 12 (see Figure 9.12).

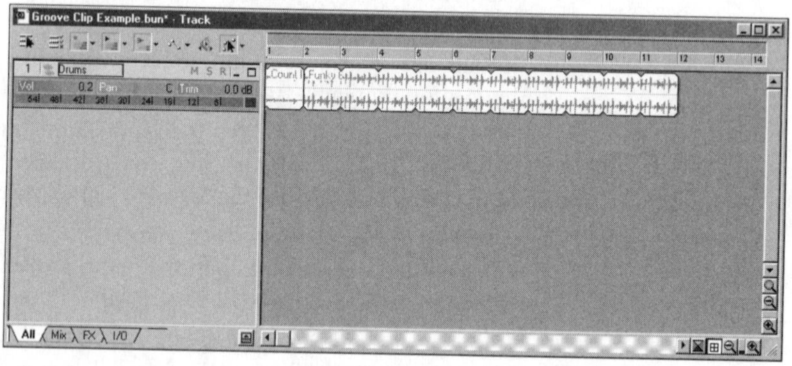

Figure 9.12
Slip edit the clip in Track 1 to extend its end to measure 12.

8. Drag-and-drop the clip in Track 1 at measure 13 from the demo project into Track 1 of your new project. Position the start of this clip at measure 12.

9. Drag-and-drop the clip (named Kick and Crash) in Track 1 at measure 37 from the demo project into Track 1 of your new project. Position the start of this clip at measure 13. Track 1 in your new project now contains all the drum parts (see Figure 9.13). Play the project to hear what it sounds like so far.

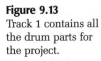

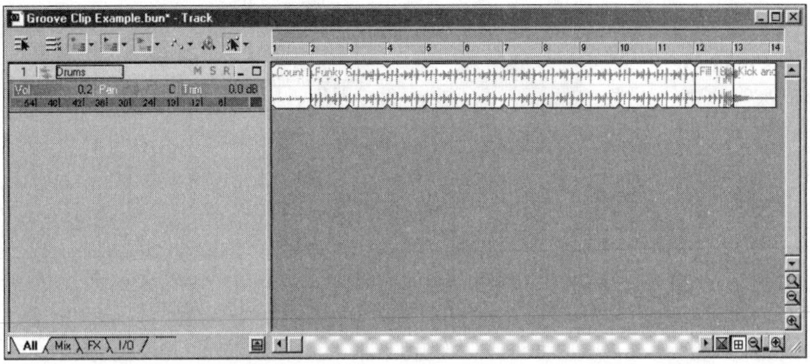

Figure 9.13
Track 1 contains all
the drum parts for
the project.

10. Close the SONAR Audio and MIDI Demo project. Then open another
    sample project that comes with SONAR called Riff Funk Audio and
    MIDI Demo.bun. Close the File Info window, as well as the Big Time
    and Staff views. Also, choose Window > Tile In Rows to reposition
    the Track views.

11. Drag-and-drop one of the clips in Track 2 (Guitar) from the demo
    project into your new project. Drop the clip somewhere underneath
    Track 1 in the new project so that SONAR will create a new track
    (Track 2, Guitar). Position the start of the clip at measure 2. Widen
    the track so that you can see the data in the clip. Also, if you need to,
    adjust the panning of the track so that it is panned at dead center.

12. Right-click on the new clip in Track 2 and choose Clip Properties to
    open the Clip Properties dialog box. Click the Groove-Clips tab. If it's
    not already, activate the Enable Looping option. Activate the Follow
    Project Pitch option. Choose D in the Reference Note drop-down list.
    Click OK.

13. Slip edit the clip in Track 2 so that its end goes to the beginning of
    measure 13. Play the song. Sounds kind of dull, huh? Okay, let's add
    some pitch markers.

14. Place pitch markers at the beginning of measures 6, 8, 10, 11 and 12.
    Give these markers the following pitches respectively: F, C, G, F, C.
    Your project should now look like what is shown in Figure 9.14.

CHAPTER 9

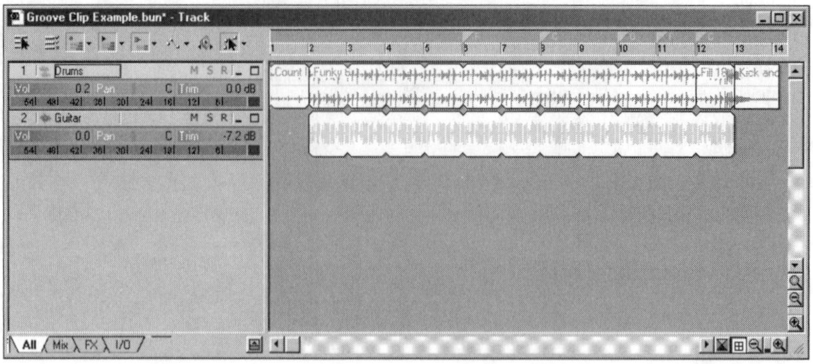

Figure 9.14
Place some pitch markers to make the project more interesting.

15. Play the project. Sounds better, right? The guitar doesn't sound quite right when it's transposed, though, does it? Select the guitar clip and choose View > Loop Construction to open the clip in the Loop Construction view. Adjust the Trans Detect slider to a value of 90 percent. Then adjust the Basic Slicing slider to a value of 16th notes. Close the Loop Construction view. Play the project. Ah, that's better.

16. Drag-and-drop one of the clips in Track 3 (Bass) from the demo project into your new project. Drop the clip somewhere underneath Track 2 in the new project so that SONAR will create a new track (Track 3, Bass). Position the start of the clip at measure 2. Widen the track so that you can see the data in the clip. Also, if you need to, adjust the panning of the track so that it is panned at dead center.

17. Right-click on the new clip in Track 3 and choose Clip Properties to open the Clip Properties dialog box. Click the Groove-Clips tab. If it's not already, activate the Enable Looping option. Activate the Follow Project Pitch option. Choose D in the Reference Note drop-down list. Click OK.

18. Slip edit the clip in Track 3 so that its end goes to the beginning of measure 13. Play the song.

19. The bass needs some adjusting, too. Select the guitar clip and choose View > Loop Construction to open the clip in the Loop Construction view. Adjust the Trans Detect slider to a value of 90 percent. Then adjust the Basic Slicing slider to a value of 16th notes. Close the Loop Construction view. Play the project. All right! Now it's starting to sound like a real song. There's still one thing missing, though.

20. Close the Riff Funk Audio and MIDI Demo project. Then open another sample project that comes with SONAR called Don't Matter Audio and MIDI Demo.bun. Close the File Info window, as well as the Staff view. Also, choose Window > Tile In Rows to reposition the Track views.

21. Drag-and-drop the first clip in Track 6 (Horns Left) from the demo project into your new project. Drop the clip somewhere underneath Track 3 in the new project so that SONAR will create a new track (Track 4, Horns Left). Position the start of the clip at measure 3. Widen the track so that you can see the data in the clip. Also, make sure that the panning for the track is set to 100 percent left.

22. Right-click on the new clip in Track 4 and choose Clip Properties to open the Clip Properties dialog box. Click the Groove-Clips tab. Activate the Enable Looping option. Activate the Follow Project Pitch option. Choose D in the Reference Note drop-down list. Click OK.

23. Select the Horns Left clip and choose View > Loop Construction to open the clip in the Loop Construction view. Adjust the Trans Detect slider to a value of 90 percent. Then adjust the Basic Slicing slider to a value of 16th Notes. Close the Loop Construction view.

24. Copy the Horns Left clip (using the Edit > Copy feature) and then paste (using the Edit > Paste feature) copies of the clip at the following measures: 6, 8, and 10. Now slip edit the clip in measure 10 so that its end extends to measure 12. The Horns Left track should look like Figure 9.15.

Figure 9.15
Copy and paste the clips in the Horns Left track.

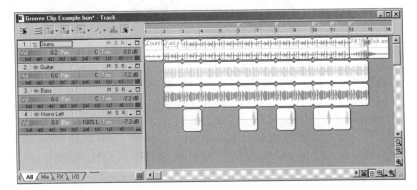

25. Drag-and-drop the first clip in Track 7 (Horns Right) from the demo project into your new project. Drop the clip somewhere underneath Track 4 in the new project so that SONAR will create a new track (Track 5, Horns Right). Position the start of the clip at measure 3. Widen the track so that you can see the data in the clip. Also, make sure that the panning for the track is set to 100 percent right.

26. Right-click on the new clip in Track 5 and choose Clip Properties to open the Clip Properties dialog box. Click the Groove-Clips tab. Activate the Enable Looping option. Activate the Follow Project Pitch option. Choose D in the Reference Note drop-down list. Click OK.

27. Select the Horns Right Clip and choose View > Loop Construction to open the clip in the Loop Construction view. Adjust the Trans Detect slider to a value of 90 percent. Then adjust the Basic Slicing slider to a value of 16th Notes. Close the Loop Construction view.

28. Copy the Horns Right clip (using the Edit > Copy feature) and then paste (using the Edit > Paste feature) copies of the clip at the following measures: 6, 8, and 10. Now slip edit the clip in measure 10 so that its end extends to measure 12.

The final version of your new project should look like what is shown in Figure 9.16.

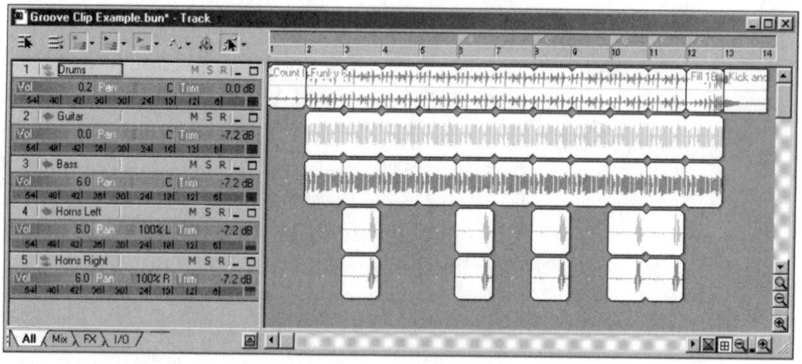

Figure 9.16
The final version of our example project should look like this.

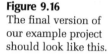

29. Play the project. Sounds cool, no?

Now you have a good working knowledge of how to use Groove clips.

You can add to this exercise by creating more tracks and inserting more clips. Don't forget that you can also change the mix by adjusting the volume and pan parameters for each track. Plus, since there are audio tracks, you can apply real-time effects as well. For more information on effects, read Chapter 11.

TIP

Change the tempo of the example project to 120 bpm. Play the project. Isn't that great? SONAR automatically adjusts the Groove clips so that they will play at the correct speed whenever you change the tempo of the project.

10

Software Synthesis

In Chapter 1, I talked about the differences between MIDI and digital audio. MIDI is simply performance data. MIDI data alone does not produce sound. In order to have sound produced from your MIDI data, you need a MIDI instrument. Usually, a MIDI instrument comes in the form of a MIDI synthesizer keyboard or module. These are hardware-based synthesizers. Today, however, personal computers have become so powerful that it is now possible to simulate a MIDI synthesizer via a computer software program. This process is known as software synthesis, and basically it has the power to turn your computer into a full-fledged MIDI synthesizer module. SONAR has built-in software synthesis features. In this chapter, I'll tell you all about the software synthesis features that SONAR provides, including the following:

▶ DX instruments

▶ Setting up and playing DX instruments

▶ The Virtual Sound Canvas

▶ The DreamStation

▶ The Tassman

▶ SoundFonts and LiveSynth Pro

DX Instruments

DX instruments (DXis for short) are a new technology developed by Cakewalk that is based on Microsoft's DirectX technology. DXis come in the form of plug-ins that can simulate any kind of hardware-based synthesizer module. As a matter of fact, many DXis have interfaces that look like on-screen versions of a hardware-based synth, with all kinds of knobs and switches that can be tweaked with your mouse. Because DXis are plug-ins, they can be used interchangeably within SONAR just like effects plug-ins (see Chapter 11 for more information about effects).

NOTE

In basic terms, a *plug-in* is a small computer program that by itself does nothing but when used with a larger application provides added functionality to the larger program. You, therefore, can use plug-ins to easily add new features to a program. In SONAR's case, plug-ins provide you with additional ways to produce music through the use of DXis.

What's more, DXis are based on standard computer code known as DirectX. SONAR enables you to use any audio plug-ins that are DirectX-compatible. DirectX is a special computer code built into Windows that controls all its multimedia functions, such as playing audio and video. This means that in addition to the DXis that come included with SONAR, many more will be available for purchase from other third-party vendors.

Using a DXi to generate music is just like using a hardware-based synth, except that because a DXi is software-based, it is run on your computer as an application from within SONAR. You control the settings of a DXi by tweaking on-screen parameters. You can generate sound with a DXi either in real-time, as you perform on your MIDI keyboard, or by using data from a pre-existing MIDI track. To use a DXi in your SONAR project, do the following:

1. Create a new project or open a pre-existing project.

2. Right-click in the Track pane of the Track view and choose Insert Audio Track to create a new audio track. Then widen the track to display its parameters.

3. Set the In parameter to None, and set the Out parameter to one of your sound card outputs.

4. Right-click in the Fx parameter of the audio track and choose DX Instruments > (name of the DXi you want to use) to set up a DXi for that track (see Figure 10.1). If you ever want to remove a DXi, just right-click on its name in the Fx parameter and choose Delete from the pop-up menu.

Figure 10.1
To use a DXi, add it to the Fx parameter of an audio track.

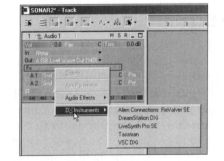

NOTE

Even though DXis are software-based, they still need to use a sound card output (which is hardware) in order to generate sound. Adding a DXi to an audio track allows the DXi to use the output of the track to generate sound. You can also add DXis to the aux bus and main Fx bins. For more information about aux buses and mains, read Chapter 12.

CHAPTER 10

5. After you add a DXi to the Fx parameter of the audio track, the window for that DXi appears showing the control interface of the DXi (see Figure 10.2). Using those controls, you can set up the DXi's parameters, such as the sounds it will produce, and so on. After you've finished setting the DXi's parameters, you can close the window to get it out of the way. If you need to access the DXi's controls again, just double-click on the name of the DXi in the Fx parameter of the audio track.

Figure 10.2
When added to the Fx parameter, a window appears showing all the controls available for the DXi that you chose.

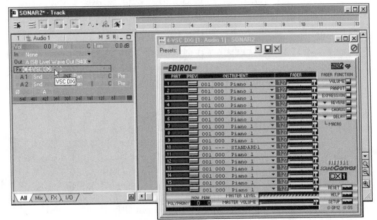

6. If you opened a pre-existing project that already contains MIDI tracks, you can skip this step. Otherwise, right-click in the Track pane of the Track view and choose Insert MIDI Track to create a new MIDI track. Then widen the track to display its parameters.

7. Set the In parameter to the MIDI channel which is being used to receive data from your MIDI keyboard. Then click on the Out parameter to display a list of available outputs. In addition to your MIDI interface outputs, the list will also show any DXis that you have previously set up (see Figure 10.3). Choose the DXi that you want to use.

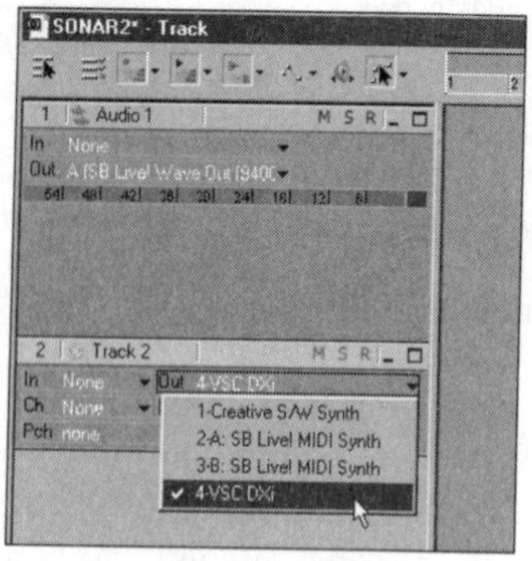

Figure 10.3
After you set up a DXi,
it will be displayed in
the Out parameter list
of your MIDI track.

8. Set the Ch (channel), Bnk (bank), and Pch (patch) parameters for
    the MIDI track. The settings you choose for these parameters depend
    on the DXi that you are using. For the Ch parameter, choose the
    same channel to which the DXi is set. The Bnk and Pch parameters
    automatically display different settings depending on the DXi. The
    parameters will show what sound presets the DXi has available.
    Choose the bank and patch that correspond to the sound that you
    want to use.

9. Either start performing some music on your MIDI keyboard or start
    playback of the project. Whichever action you choose, you should
    hear sound coming from the DXi.

NOTE

When you use a DXi in real-time by performing on your MIDI keyboard, you
might hear a delay between the time you press a key on your keyboard and
the time it takes for the DXi to produce sound. This is caused by sound card
latency. In order to prevent this delay, you need to use WDM drivers for your
sound card, and you also need to adjust the Latency slider to its lowest
possible setting. I talked about WDM drivers and latency in Chapter 2 and
Chapter 3.

Those are the basic steps you need to take in order to use DXis in your
projects. Don't worry if the instructions seem a bit generic. I'll provide
some more specific examples on how to use the DXis that come included
with SONAR.

The Virtual Sound Canvas

There are four DXis included with SONAR, one of which is the Virtual
Sound Canvas DXi (or VSC DXi for short). The VSC DXi simulates the
Roland Sound Canvas, which is a hardware-based MIDI playback
module. The VSC DXi is multitimbral (meaning it can play more than
one different sound at a time—up to sixteen), has a polyphony of 128

voices (meaning it can play up to 128 notes at a time), and comes with 902 built-in sounds as well as 26 different drum sets. The sounds in the VSC DXi can't be changed, and you can't create your own sounds, but the selection is quite varied, so I don't think you'll run out any time soon.

VSC DXi Basics

If you examine the main interface for the VSC DXi (see Figure 10.4), you'll notice that it provides sixteen parts, one part for each of the sixteen available MIDI channels. Part 1 corresponds to MIDI channel 1, Part 2 to MIDI channel 2, and so on. Each part provides a number of adjustable parameters. These parameters include the instrument, volume, panpot, expression, reverb, chorus, and delay.

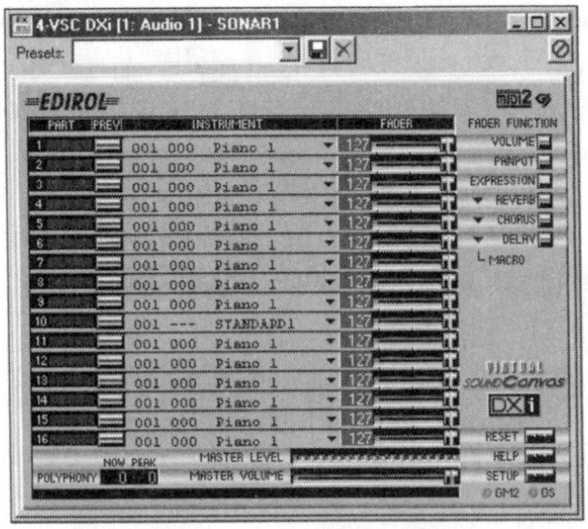

Figure 10.4

You can adjust the VSC DXi parameter settings using its main interface.

Selecting Instruments

Instruments refers to the sounds or programs or patches that the VSC DXi provides. To assign an instrument to a part, just click the Instrument drop-down list that corresponds to the part and choose an instrument from the pop-up menus (see Figure 10.5).

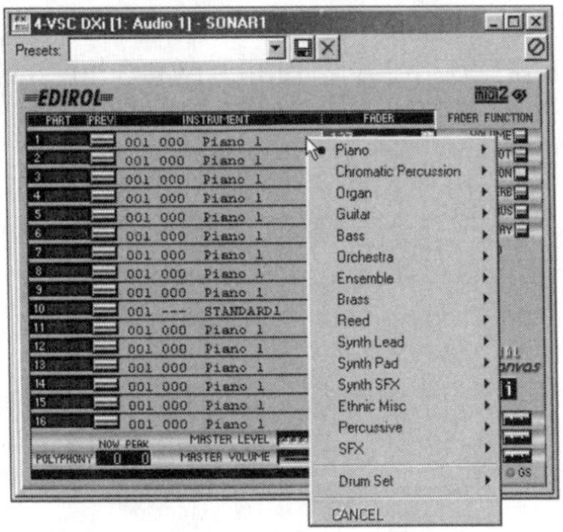

Figure 10.5

Choose an instrument for a part using the instrument drop-down list.

Preview the Instrument

To test the instrument and hear what it sounds like, click on the Prev (preview) button for the part (see Figure 10.6).

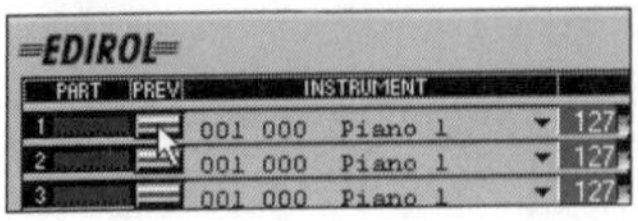

Figure 10.6

To test the sound of the instrument, click the part's Prev button.

Additional Instruments

The VSC DXi provides two different categories of instruments. One category is a set of GM (General MIDI)-compatible instruments. The other category is a set of GS (Roland GS format)-compatible instruments. The Roland GS format is similar to GM in that it provides a standardized set of rules for MIDI synths, but they usually pertain only to Roland MIDI devices. The GS format provides an expanded set of rules to include many more instruments as well as additional features not covered by GM. To switch between the GM and GS modes for the VSC DXi, click the Setup button at the bottom of the VSC DXi window to open the Setup dialog box. Then choose the GM2 or GS option for the Generator Mode parameter and click OK.

Adjusting Volume, Panpot, and Expression

To adjust the volume, panpot, and expression parameters for each part, do the following:

1. In the Fader Function section, choose the parameter you would like to adjust. To adjust volume, click the Volume button. To adjust panpot (panning), click the Panpot button. To adjust expression (velocity depth), click the Expression button.

2. When you click on a parameter button, it will light up with a green color (see Figure 10.7). This indicates that all the sliders in the Fader sections for each part now correspond to the parameter that you selected. For example, if you chose the Volume parameter, each slider would control the volume of its corresponding part.

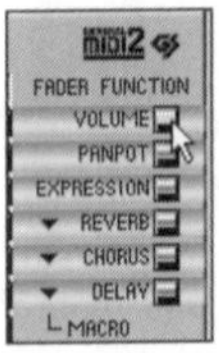

Figure 10.7

Activating a parameter makes it light up with a green color.

3. Click and drag the sliders in the Fader sections for each part to adjust the selected parameter (see Figure 10.8).

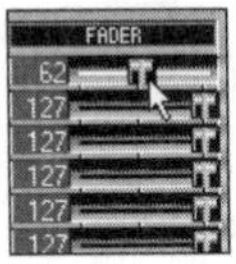

Figure 10.8
Click and drag the Fader sliders to adjust the chosen parameter for each part.

Applying Effects

In addition, the VSC DXi provides effects that can be applied to each part individually. This gives you a lot more flexibility than if you were to apply SONAR's effects because with the VSC DXi effects, each part can have a different amount of effects applied. With SONAR's effects, you would have to apply then to all the parts in the same amount because you would be assigning the effects to the audio track to which the VSC DXi is assigned. For more information about effects, read Chapter 11.

Assigning effects to parts works in exactly the same way as adjusting the volume, panpot, and expression parameters. Just click on the appropriate effect parameter button in the Fader Function section, and then adjust the Fader sliders for each part. The Fader sliders determine how much of the effect is applied to each part. For example, you could have a large amount of reverb on one part and a small amount of reverb on another part.

The only difference is that each effect provides a number of variations. Each part cannot have its own effect variation. All parts use the same effect variation. To change the variation of an effect, just click the Macro arrow next to the effect and choose a variation from the pop-up menu (see Figure 10.9).

Figure 10.9
Choose effect variations using the Macro arrows.

CHAPTER 10

TIP

Some of the VSC DXi parameters can be set by simply setting the corresponding MIDI track parameters. For instance, by the changing the Vol, Pan, Bnk, Pch, Chr, and Rev parameters of the MIDI tack driving one of the VSC DXi Parts, you can control the volume, panpot, instrument, chorus effect, and reverb effect parameters for that part. When you save your project, those parameters are stored along with it. But there is an advantage to adjusting parameters within the VSC DXi itself. You can save all the VSC DXi parameters as a preset using the Preset drop-down list and Preset Save and Delete buttons located at the top of the window. By saving a number of parameter configurations as presets, you can quickly switch between configurations to test out different instrumentation for the project you are working on.

VSC DXi Exercise

Now that I've covered all the boring parameter basics for the VSC DXi, what do you say we kick it up a notch? How about working through an exercise so that you can hear what the VSC DXi is really capable of?

To give you an idea of the amount of power that the VSC DXi provides, try this:

1. Choose File > Open and select the sample project that comes included with SONAR called "Orchestral.wrk." Click Open.

2. Click Cancel in the Auto-Send Sysx dialog box.

3. Close the File Info window and the Staff view. You won't need them.

4. Drag the bottom of the Track view to make it bigger in order to reveal all sixteen tracks in the project.

5. Right-click in the Track pane, and choose Insert Audio Track. Then widen the track to display its properties.

6. Right-click in the Fx parameter of the new audio track and choose DX Instruments > VSC DXi. You can either leave the VSC DXi window open or close it. If it's in the way of the Track pane in the Track view, move the VSC DXi window.

7. Select all sixteen MIDI tracks in the project by clicking and dragging your mouse over the track numbers. Don't select the audio track.

8. Choose Track > Property > Outputs to open the Track Outputs dialog box (see Figure 10.10).

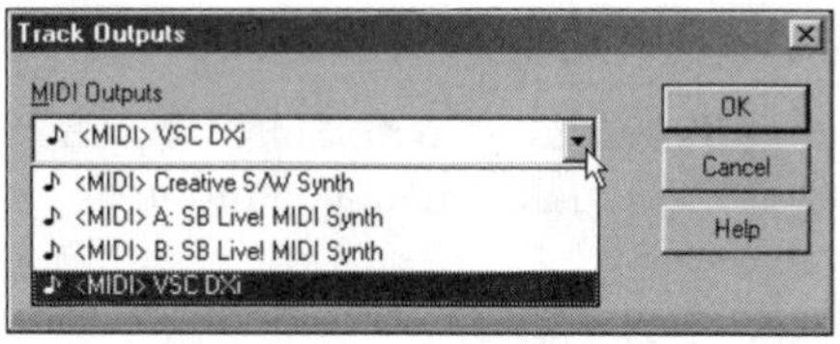

Figure 10.10
Use the Track
Outputs dialog box to
change the Out
parameters for multiple
tracks simultaneously.

Track Outputs

MIDI Outputs

♪ <MIDI> VSC DXi

OK
Cancel
Help

♪ <MIDI> Creative S/W Synth
♪ <MIDI> A: SB Live! MIDI Synth
♪ <MIDI> B: SB Live! MIDI Synth
♪ <MIDI> VSC DXi

9. In the MIDI Outputs drop-down list, choose the <MIDI > VSC DXi
    option. Then click OK. This changes the Out parameter of all the
    MIDI tracks simultaneously to the VSC DXi.

TIP

If you ever need to change the parameters for more than one track at a time,
just select the tracks that you want to adjust, then use the Track > Property
menu to change the properties for all of those tracks simultaneously.

10. Press the spacebar on your computer keyboard to start playback of
    the project. Then just sit back and listen.

Can you believe all of that sound is coming from one little software
synthesizer? Of course, there were no effects applied to any of the parts,
so it did sound a little dry.

TIP

In addition to adding effects within the VSC DXi itself, you can use the effects
provided by SONAR to liven up your DXis. Using the previous Orchestral
exercise, right-click in the Fx parameter of the audio track and choose Audio
Effects > Cakewalk > FxReverb to open the Cakewalk FxReverb dialog box.
Choose the Large Room–Bright Preset. Then try playing the project again.
What a sound, eh? The only problem with applying effects this way is that
they are applied to all the parts from the VSC DXi rather than individually.

TIP

One more thing about the VSC DXi is that even though some of the sounds
aren't the greatest, this DXi works wonderfully as a scratch-pad synth—
meaning you can use it to work out your musical ideas and then use some
more professional equipment for the final production. In addition, if you have
a songwriting partner (or team) and everyone is using SONAR, then everyone
has access to the VSC DXi. This means that you can use the VSC DXi to work
out your song ideas and you can be sure that the project will sound exactly
the same no matter if it is played on your computer or someone else's.

The DreamStation

Another of the DXis included with SONAR is the DreamStation. The DreamStation DXi simulates an analog modular synth (see Figure 10.11).

Figure 10.11
The DreamStation DXi puts the power of analog synthesis in your hands.

The DreamStation DXi provides three oscillator modules, an amplifier module, filter module, lfo (low frequency oscillator) module, envelope module, vibrato and portamento features, and controls pertaining to synth output, such as volume and panning. By adjusting the controls provided by each of the modules, you can create your own unique synthesizer sounds just as you would with a hardware-based analog synth.

Unfortunately, covering the topics of analog synthesis, as well as how to create your own sounds with the DreamStation DXi, would easily fill an entirely separate book. Instead, I'll show you how to load and save pre-existing sounds (called instruments) in the DreamStation DXi, and I'll provide an example of how you can use the DreamStation DXi in your SONAR projects.

NOTE

Although I won't be going into the subjects of analog synthesis or how to create your own sounds with the DreamStation DXi, you can find some good introductory synthesis information on the following Web sites: **http://tilt.largo.fl.us/faq/synthfaq.html** and **http://nmc.uoregon.edu/emi/emp_win/main.html**. And for more specific information about the DreamStation DXi (as well as some free downloadable instruments), check out this site: **http://hem.passagen.se/baloonia/baloonia.htm**.

TIP

There is one way you can create your own sounds with the DreamStation DXi automatically, and without having to know anything about analog synthesis. Just hold down the Shift key on your computer keyboard and then click on the CLR button at the top of the DreamStation DXi window. This makes the DreamStation DXi randomly set all of its parameters, thus automatically creating a new sound. Many of sounds may not be useable, but click enough times and you could come up with something very cool.

Loading and Saving Instruments

The DreamStation DXi sounds are called instruments. You can save and load instruments for your own use, and you can also share instruments with others. To load and save instruments for your own use, follow these procedures:

▶ To load an instrument, choose an instrument name from the Preset drop-down list at the top of the DreamStation DXi window. The DreamStation DXi comes with ninety-five pre-existing Instruments.

▶ To save an instrument, type a name for the instrument in the Preset parameter and then click the Save button (the one with the picture of a floppy disk shown on it). Your new instrument will show up in the Preset drop-down list.

▶ To delete an instrument from the Preset drop-down list, select the instrument from the list and then click the Delete button (the one with the large red X shown on it).

In addition to saving and loading instruments for your own use, you can save and load instruments as DSI files to share with other SONAR and DreamStation users. To use DSI files, follow these procedures:

▶ To load a DSI file, click the Load button at the top of the DreamStation DXi window. Choose your DSI file in the Open dialog box and then click Open.

▶ To save the current instrument as a DSI file, click the Save button. In the Save As dialog box, type in a name for the DSI file and then click Save.

A DreamStation DXi Exercise

Okay, now let's have some fun. To hear the DreamStation DXi in action, try the following exercise:

1. Choose File > Open and select the sample project file that comes included with SONAR called "DJ's in the House.wrk." Click Open.

2. Click Cancel in the Auto-Send Sysx dialog box.

3. Close the File Info window.

4. Right-click in the Track pane and choose Insert Audio Track.

5. Right-click in the Fx parameter of the new audio track and choose DX Instruments > DreamStation DXi.

6. In the DreamStation DXi window, choose Percussion: 03-Kick 2 in the Preset drop-down list. Then close the window.

7. Set the Out parameters for Tracks 1 and 2 to the DreamStation DXi that you just set up.

NOTE

One drawback to the DreamStation DXi is that it's "single" timbral rather than multitimbral. This means that it can play only one kind of sound at a time. Luckily, the DreamStation DXi doesn't take up much computer processing power, so you can set up multiple instances, each playing a unique sound.

8. Set up another audio track with another instance of the DreamStation DXi. In the DreamStation DXi window, choose Percussion: 10-Lazer Zap in the Preset drop-down list. Then close the window.

9. Set the Out parameters for Tracks 3 and 6 to the DreamStation DXi that you just set up. You will notice that each new instance of the DreamStation DXi will have a unique number display before it. Use that number to keep track of the different setups.

10. Set up another audio track with another instance of the DreamStation DXi. In the DreamStation DXi window, choose Percussion: 09-Hihats in the Preset drop-down list. Then close the window.

11. Set the Out parameters for Tracks 4 and 5 to the DreamStation DXi that you just set up.

12. Set up another audio track with another instance of the DreamStation DXi. In the DreamStation DXi window, choose Pad: 02-Warm in the Preset drop-down list. Then close the window.

13. Set the Out parameter for Track 7 to the DreamStation DXi that you just set up.

14. Set up another audio track with another instance of the DreamStation DXi. In the DreamStation DXi window, choose Effect: 10-Stick in the Preset drop-down list. Then close the window.

15. Set the Out parameter for Track 8 to the DreamStation DXi that you just set up.

16. Set up another audio track with another instance of the DreamStation DXi. In the DreamStation DXi window, choose Organ: 01-Electric in the Preset drop-down list. Then close the window.

17. Set the Out parameter for Track 9 to the DreamStation DXi that you just set up.

18. Set up another audio track with another instance of the DreamStation DXi. In the DreamStation DXi window, choose Bass: 15-Synth Bass 2 in the Preset drop-down list. Then close the window.

19. Set the Out parameter for Track 10 to the DreamStation DXi that you just set up.

20. Set up another audio track with another instance of the DreamStation DXi. In the DreamStation DXi window, choose 04-Square in the Preset drop-down list. Then close the window.

21. Set the Out parameters for Tracks 11 and 12 to the DreamStation DXi that you just set up.

22. Set up another audio track with another instance of the DreamStation DXi. In the DreamStation DXi window, choose Synth: 01-Solo 1 in the Preset drop-down list. Then close the window.

23. Set the Out parameter for Track 13 to the DreamStation DXi that you just set up.

24. Play the project.

That's a cool sound, isn't it? Of course, you can also liven things up even more by applying some effects. The nice thing about using multiple instances of the DreamStation DXi is that each instance can have different effects applied to it.

The Tassman

Like the DreamStation DXi, the Tassman DXi is a modular software synth, but rather than having a permanent set of modules, the Tassman allows you to create your own unique instruments by linking all kinds of different modules together (see Figure 10.12).

Figure 10.12
The Tassman DXi lets you create your own instruments via modular synthesis.

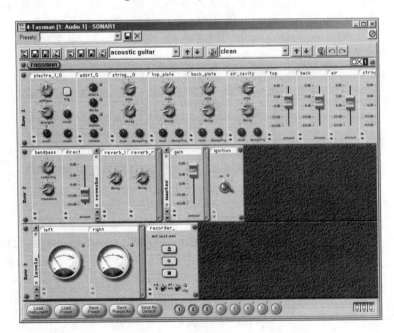

NOTE

If you purchased the basic version of SONAR, then you have only the Tassman DXi Special Edition, which doesn't let you build your own instruments. Only SONAR XL version owners get the full version of the Tassman DXi.

The Tassman DXi provides seventy-three different modules, which can be interconnected to produce almost any kind of sound imaginable. These modules represent different pieces of a synthesizer, such as an oscillator, an amplifier, an envelope, a mixer, and so on. This means that you can literally "build" your own virtual synth. But the Tassman DXi goes even further by providing modules that represent real-life sounds, such as a bowed string or a marimba bar. This means that you can create never-before-heard instruments such as a bowed marimba bar. Once you start using the DXi, you'll get a better picture of what I mean.

Like the DreamStation DXi, the Tassman DXi is very complex. As a matter of fact, the Tassman DXi is significantly more complex than the DreamStation DXi. Covering how to develop your own instruments with the Tassman DXi could easily fill one (if not two) entire books. So, instead, I'll show you how to load and save pre-existing sounds (called instruments) in the Tassman DXi, and I'll provide an example of how you can use the Tassman DXi in your SONAR projects.

NOTE

Although I won't be going into the subject of how to create your own instruments with the Tassman DXi, you can find a lot of good information in the manual that comes included with the DXi. The manual includes information about all the Tassman DXi modules, as well as four tutorials that walk you through how to build some simple instruments. In addition, you can find even more information (as well as free instrument downloads) on the Applied Acoustics Systems Web site: **http://www.applied-acoustics.com**.

Banks, Programs, Instruments, and Presets

You can work with sounds in the Tassman DXi in a number of ways. Sounds come in the form of instruments and presets. To get sound out of the Tassman DXi you must have an instrument and at least one preset loaded. But you can also group instruments and presets together as a program. A program is a single Instrument with multiple presets grouped together. In addition, you can store multiple programs in groups by using banks. Banks, programs, instruments, and presets can each be saved as different files, giving you all the flexibility you need to deal with sounds in the Tassman DXi.

Loading an Instrument

To load a single Instrument into the Tassman DXi, do the following:

1. Click the Load Instrument button in the toolbar at the bottom of the Tassman DXi window (see Figure 10.13).

Figure 10.13
To load an instrument, click the Load Instrument button.

2. Select an instrument file in the Load Instrument dialog box. Instrument files have an MOM extension. For example, BRASS.MOM would be an instrument file.

> **NOTE**
>
> The Tassman DXi includes a selection of instruments, which are located in the C:\Program Files\Cakewalk\Shared Dxi\AAS\Tassman DXi 2.0\synths folder.

3. Click Open to load the instrument.

The Tassman DXi loads the instrument file that you selected and displays the modules that make up that instrument. From here you can either play the instrument with its default preset (each instrument loads with one default preset); load additional presets from separate files; or adjust the module controls of the current instrument and save your own presets.

Loading and Saving Presets

To load additional presets for the current Instrument, do the following:

1. Click the Load Preset button in the toolbar at the bottom of the Tassman DXi window.

2. Select a preset file in the Load Preset dialog box. Preset files have a DXT extension. For example, MYHORN.DXT would be a preset file.

3. Click Open to load the preset. The Tassman DXi loads the preset and displays it in the Preset drop-down list in the toolbar at the top of the window (see Figure 10.14).

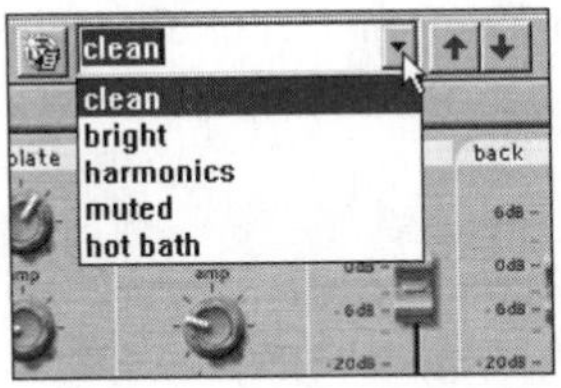

Figure 10.14
Currently loaded presets are shown in the Preset drop-down list.

If you would like to create and save a new preset, do the following:

1. Adjust the module controls for the current Instrument. You'll need to refer to the Tassman DXi manual in order to find out how each module and control works.

2. Click the New Preset button (see Figure 10.15). The preset is given a temporary name of Empty.

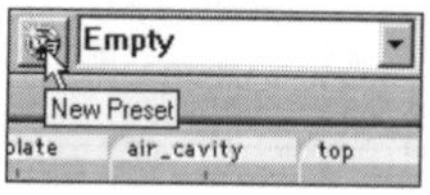

Figure 10.15
Click the New Preset button to create a new Preset.

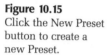

3. Type a name for the new preset in the Preset parameter (which is the same as the Preset drop-down list) in the toolbar at the top of the window.

4. To make your new preset the default preset for the current instrument, click the Save As Default button in the toolbar at the bottom of the window.

5. To save the preset as a file using its current name, click the Save Preset button and click Yes in the Save Preset dialog box.

6. To save the preset as a file using a different name, click the Save Preset As button, type a name for the file, and click Save.

You can also save groups of instruments along with all their presets into a program. Or you can load an existing program, which will replace the current instrument and presets.

Loading and Saving Programs

If you would like to load an existing program, do the following:

1. Click the Load Program button in the toolbar at the top of the Tassman DXi window (see Figure 10.16).

Figure 10.16
To load a program, click the Load Program button.

2. Select a program file in the Load Program dialog box. Program files have an FXP extension. For example, SECTION.FXP would be a program file.

NOTE

The Tassman DXi includes a selection of programs, which are located in the C:\Program Files\Cakewalk\Shared Dxi\AAS\Tassman DXi 2.0\Banks folder.

3. Click Open to load the program. The Tassman DXi loads the program and displays it in the program drop-down list in the toolbar at the top of the window.

To create and save a program, do the following:

1. Click the New Program button. The program is given a temporary name of Empty.

2. Type a name for the new program in the Program parameter (which is the same as the Program drop-down list) in the toolbar at the top of the window.

3. Load the instruments and presets that you would like to include in the program.

4. To save the program as a file using its current name, click the Save Program button and click Yes in the Save Program dialog box.

5. To save the program as a file using a different name, click the Save Program As button, type a name for the file, and click Save.

You can load multiple programs into the Tassman DXi and then save that group of programs as a bank. Or you can load an existing bank, which will replace the current group of programs.

Saving and Loading Banks

If you would like to load an existing bank, do the following:

1. Click the Load Bank button in the toolbar at the top of the Tassman DXi window (see Figure 10.17).

Figure 10.17
To load a bank, click the Load Bank button.

2. Select a bank file in the Load Bank dialog box. Bank files have an FXB extension. For example, SYNTH.FXB would be a bank file.

> **NOTE**
> The Tassman DXi includes a selection of banks, which are located in the C:\Program Files\Cakewalk\Shared Dxi\AAS\Tassman DXi 2.0\Banks folder.

3. Click Open to load the bank. The Tassman DXi loads the banks and displays the first program in the Program drop-down list.

To create and save a bank, do the following:

1. Click the New Bank button.

2. Load the programs that you would like to include in the bank.

3. To save the bank, click the Save Bank As button, type a name for the file, and click Save.

4. If you make any changes after you save the bank and you would like to quickly save it again using the same name, just click the Save Bank button and choose Yes in the Save Bank dialog box.

A Tassman DXi Exercise

Okay, now let's have some fun. To hear the Tassman DXi in action, try the following exercise:

1. Choose File > Open and select the sample project file that comes included with SONAR called "2-Part Invention #13 in A minor.wrk." Click Open.

2. Close the File Info window, the Staff view, and Big Time view.

3. Right-click in the Track pane, and choose Insert Audio Track.

4. Right-click in the Fx parameter of the new audio track and choose DX Instruments > Tassman.

5. In the Tassman DXi window, click the Load Instrument button.

6. In the Load Instrument dialog box, go to the C:\Program Files\Cakewalk\Shared Dxi\AAS\Tassman DXi 2.0\synths\polyphonic\Hammond folder.

7. Select the file called HAMM.MOM and click Open.

8. Close the Tassman DXi window.

9. Select Tracks 1 and 2 in the Track view.

10. Choose Track > Property > Outputs to open the Track Outputs dialog box.

11. Choose <MIDI > Tassman in the MIDI Outputs drop-down list, and click OK.

12. Right-click in the Fx parameter of the audio track and choose Audio Effects > Cakewalk > FxReverb to open the Cakewalk FxReverb window.

13. In the FxReverb window, choose Cathedral—Bright in the Presets drop-down list.

14. Close the FxReverb window.

15. Play the project.

Doesn't that sound glorious?

TIP

I know that the example was a bit basic, but, like the DreamStation DXi, the Tassman DXi is "single" timbral rather than multi-timbral, meaning it can play only one sound (instrument) at a time. And on top of that, the Tassman DXi uses **a lot** of computer processing power, so getting multiple instances of the DXi to run at the same time (even on a high-powered PC) is difficult. But there is a way you can get around this, and that is to record the output of the Tassman DXi to an audio track. That way you can build up multiple tracks of different Tassman DXi instruments using only one instance of the DXi. For information on how to record the output from a DXi, read Chapter 18.

SoundFonts

Last and somewhat least (I'll explain in a moment), SONAR includes the LiveSynth Pro DXi. This DXi allows you to use SoundFonts even if you don't have a SoundFont-compatible sound card. Unfortunately, the version of LiveSynth Pro DXi included with SONAR is only a trial version. You get full use of the DXi for 30 days, but after that, you are limited to using SoundFonts that are 1 MB or less in size. Most good SoundFonts are larger than that.

NOTE

Most modern MIDI instruments and sound cards use sample-playback to produce sounds. Sample-playback can produce some very realistic sounds. The reason for this realism lies in the fact that a sample-playback device plays samples, which are actually audio recordings of real-life instruments and sounds. When the sample-playback device receives a MIDI Note On message, instead of creating a sound electronically from scratch, it plays a digital sample, which can be anything from the sound of a piano note to the sound of a coyote howling.

A SoundFont is a special type of digital sample format, which works only with a SoundFont-compatible sound card. The SoundFont format was developed by Creative Labs, the makers of the ever-popular Sound Blaster line of sound cards. Most recent Sound Blaster-model sound cards are SoundFont compatible. For more information about Sound Blaster sound cards, check out **http://www.soundblaster.com/**. For more information about SoundFonts (as well as free SoundFont downloads), check out the following Web sites:

- ▶ **http://www.soundblaster.com/resources/ read.asp?ArticleID=12**
- ▶ **http://www.soundfonts.com/**
- ▶ **http://web.interpuntonet.it/soundfonts/**
- ▶ **http://thesoundsite.ismi.net/**
- ▶ **http://www.hammersound.net/**

Using the LiveSynth Pro DXi

To use the LiveSynth Pro DXi to play SoundFonts, do the following:

1. Create a new project or open a pre-existing project.

2. Right-click in the Track pane of the Track view and choose Insert Audio Track to create a new audio track. Then widen the track to display its parameters.

3. Set the In parameter to None and set the Out parameter to one of your sound card outputs.

4. Right-click in the Fx parameter of the audio track and choose DX Instruments > LiveSynth Pro. The LiveSynth Pro window opens (see Figure 10.18).

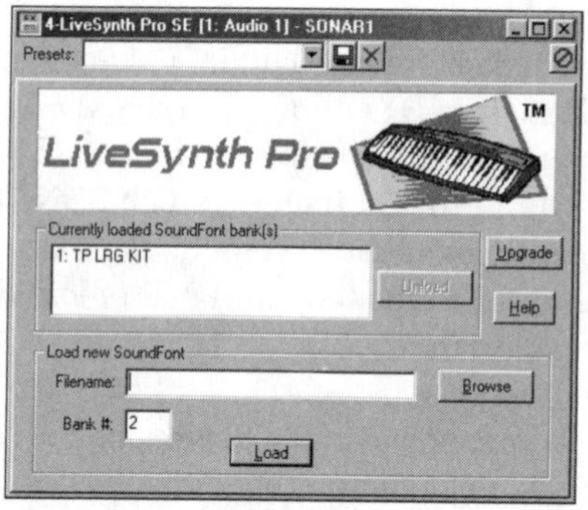

Figure 10.18

Use the LiveSynth Pro DXi to play SoundFonts with any sound card.

5. In the LiveSynth Pro window, click the Browse button and choose the SoundFont file you want to use. Click Open. The name of the SoundFont file appears in the Filename parameter.

6. Choose an unused bank number and type it into the bank parameter.

7. Click the Load button. LiveSynth Pro then loads your selected SoundFont into your selected bank. The Bank and SoundFont are listed in the Currently Loaded SoundFont Bank(s) list.

8. Repeat steps 5 through 7 to load additional SoundFonts. If you want to remove a SoundFont from the list, select the SoundFont and click the Unload button.

9. When you're finished loading SoundFonts, close the LiveSynth Pro window.

10. If you opened a pre-existing project that already contains MIDI tracks, you can skip this step. Otherwise, right-click in the Track pane of the Track view and choose Insert MIDI Track to create a new MIDI track. Then widen the track to display its parameters.

11. Set the In parameter to the MIDI channel which is being used to receive data from your MIDI keyboard and set the Out parameter to LiveSynth Pro.

12. Set the Ch (channel) parameter to the same MIDI channel as your MIDI keyboard. Set the Bnk (bank) parameter to the same bank containing the SoundFont you want to use for this MIDI track. Set the patch parameter to one of the patches available in the SoundFont. You'll see a list of available patches.

13. Repeat steps 10 through 12 to set up any additional new or pre-existing MIDI tracks.

After you record some data into your MIDI tracks or if the tracks already contained data, when you play the project, your MIDI tracks will drive the LiveSynth Pro, which will in turn play the appropriate sounds from the SoundFonts you have loaded.

Using SoundFonts with a Compatible Sound Card

If you have a SoundFont-compatible sound card (like the Sound Blaster Live), you can play SoundFonts with your sound card instead of the LiveSynth Pro DXi. The procedure for using a sound card to play SoundFonts is as follows:

1. Create a new project or open a pre-existing project.

2. Choose Options > SoundFonts to open the SoundFont Banks dialog box (see Figure 10.19).

Figure 10.19
Use the SoundFont Banks dialog box to load SoundFonts into your project.

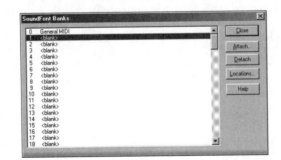

3. Select an empty bank, and click the Attach button to open the SoundFont File dialog box.

4. Choose the SoundFont file you want to load and click Open. The SoundFont you chose is loaded into the bank you selected.

5. Repeat steps 3 and 4 to load any additional SoundFonts.

6. To remove a SoundFont from your project, just select it in the list and click Detach.

7. Click Close when you're finished loading SoundFonts.

8. If you opened a pre-existing project that already contains MIDI tracks, you can skip this step. Otherwise, right-click in the Track pane of the Track view and choose Insert MIDI Track to create a new MIDI track. Then widen the track to display its parameters.

9. Set the In parameter to the MIDI channel which is being used to receive data from your MIDI keyboard and set the Out parameter to SoundFont Device.

10. Set the Ch (channel) parameter to the same MIDI channel as your MIDI keyboard. Set the Bnk (bank) parameter to the same bank containing the SoundFont you want to use for this MIDI track. Set the patch parameter to one of the patches available in the SoundFont. You'll see a list of available patches.

11. Repeat steps 10 through 12 to set up any additional new or pre-existing MIDI tracks.

After you record some data into your MIDI tracks or if the tracks already contained data, when you play the project, your MIDI tracks will drive your SoundFont-compatible sound card, which will in turn play the appropriate sounds from the SoundFonts you have loaded.

TIP

If you want to share your project with someone, and the project uses SoundFonts, be sure to send copies of the SoundFonts along with the project file. Of course, if you purchased the SoundFonts and they are copyrighted, the other person will have to purchase them as well. Sending copies of copyrighted SoundFonts to friends is a no-no. Thanks for respecting the rights of all the hard working musicians out there.

11

Effects:
The Really Cool Stuff

Just as adding spices to a recipe makes it taste better, adding effects to your music data makes it sound better. Effects can make the difference between a dull, lifeless recording, and a recording that really rocks. For example, you can apply echoes and background ambience to give the illusion that your song was recorded in a certain environment, such as a concert hall. You can also use effects to make your vocals sound rich and full. And the list goes on. SONAR provides a number of different effects features that you can use to spice up both your MIDI and audio tracks. Although applying these effects to your data isn't overly complicated, understanding what they do and how to use them can sometimes be confusing. So, this chapter covers the following topics:

▶ Plug-ins

▶ Offline and real-time processing

▶ Audio effects: Chorus, Equalization, Reverb, Delay, Flanging, Pitch Shifting, and Time/Pitch stretching

▶ MIDI effects: Quantization, Delay, Filtering, Arpeggio, Chord analyzing, Transposition, and Velocity

▶ The Session Drummer

CHAPTER 11

Offline or Real-Time?

SONAR's effects features are very similar to its editing features (which you learned about in Chapter 8), but they do have a couple of differences. One difference is that, although the Effects features come included with SONAR, they are not actually a part of the main application. Instead, they come in the form of plug-ins.

TIP
For a great source of DirectX plug-ins that you can download and use for free, check out **http://www.directxfiles.com/**.

Because the Effects features are plug-ins, not only do they add functionality to SONAR, but they also add more flexibility. Unlike the editing features, the Effects features can be used to process your data in two different ways: offline and real-time.

Offline Processing

You already know what offline processing is, because you've performed it while using SONAR's editing features. With offline processing, the MIDI and audio data in your clips and tracks are permanently changed. Therefore, offline processing is also called *destructive processing* because it "destroys" the original data by modifying (or overwriting) it according to any processing that you apply.

> **NOTE**
>
> As you know, you can remove any offline processing done to your data by using SONAR's Undo feature. You can also load a saved copy of your project containing the original data. But neither of these restoration methods is as convenient as using real-time processing, which I'll explain shortly.

The basic procedure for using effects in offline mode is essentially the same as when using any of SONAR's editing features. You just follow these steps:

1. Select the data that you want to change.
2. Choose the MIDI or audio effect feature that you want to use by selecting either Edit > Audio Effects or Edit > MIDI Effects.
3. Make the appropriate parameter adjustments in the dialog box that appears.
4. Click on the Audition button to test the current parameter settings. Make further adjustments if necessary.
5. If you're using an audio effect, click on the Mixing tab (see Figure 11.1). These parameters determine how your data will be processed. If you select the Process In-Place, Mono Result option, SONAR takes your originally selected data, processes it with the chosen effect, and then replaces it with the processed data. This means your original data is overwritten. If your original data was in stereo, it is converted into *mono* (or *monophonic*, meaning only one channel, whereas stereo has two channels, left and right). If you select the Process In-Place, Stereo Result option, SONAR takes your originally selected data, processes it with the chosen effect, and then replaces it with the processed data. Again, this means your original data is overwritten. Also, if your original data was in mono, it is converted into stereo. If you select the Create A Send Submix option, SONAR takes your selected data, mixes it all together into a stereo signal, processes it with the chosen effect,

and then places it into a new stereo track, which you designate by setting the Return Track parameter. In addition, if you activate the Keep Original Data option, your original data is left untouched. If you deactivate the Keep Original Data option, your original data is deleted.

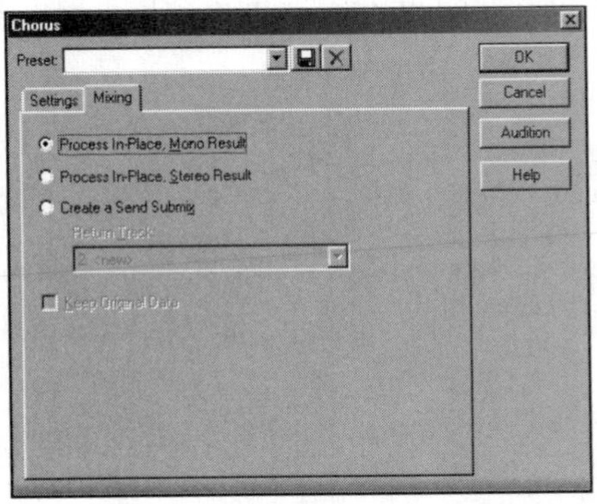

Figure 11.1
The Mixing parameters are available only when you're using an audio effect in offline mode.

6. Click on OK to close the dialog box.

SONAR processes the data by applying the effect according to the parameter settings you specified. It's very simple. Don't worry; I'll go over each individual effect and its corresponding parameters later in the chapter.

Real-Time Processing

On the other hand, real-time processing doesn't change the actual data in your clips and tracks. Instead, the Effects features are applied only during playback, letting you hear the results while leaving your original data intact. Therefore, real-time processing is also called *nondestructive,* because it doesn't apply any permanent changes to your data. By simply turning off the Effects features, you can listen to your data as it was originally recorded.

The basic procedure for using effects in real-time mode isn't any more difficult than using them in offline mode, although it is a little different, as you can see here:

1. In the Track view, right-click in the Fx field of the track to which you want to add an effect. A pop-up menu appears.

> **NOTE**
> You can also apply effects in real-time by using the Console view, but I'll talk about that approach in Chapter 12.

2.   Choose the effect you want to use from the pop-up menu. Depending on whether the track is for MIDI or audio, the list of effects is different. The effect you choose is added to the list in the Fx field.

3.   The corresponding window for the effect is opened automatically. You can also open an effect window by double-clicking the effect in the Fx field.

NOTE

In real-time mode, the parameters of an effect are displayed in a window instead of a dialog box. You therefore can access any of the other features in SONAR while still having access to the effect parameters. You also can use more than one effect at the same time, which I'll talk about in a moment.

4.   Make the appropriate parameter adjustments.

5.   Start playback of the project. You immediately hear the results of the effect being applied to the data in the track. While the project plays, you can make further parameter adjustments if necessary.

TIP

If you want to make a quick comparison between how the original data sound and how they sound with the effect applied, some of the effects provide a Bypass button. This button (located within the effect window) is available only when you're applying effects to audio tracks. When you activate the button, it bypasses (or turns off) the effect so that you can hear how the original data sound. When you deactivate the button, you can hear how the data sound with the effect being applied. You can also bypass an effect by clicking on the green box next to the name of the effect in Fx field.

NOTE

Notice that no Audition button is shown in the effect window. It isn't needed, because in real-time mode you can hear the results as the project plays. Also, notice that no Mixing tab is shown. In real-time mode, all mixing is handled via the Console view, which I'll talk about in Chapter 12. In addition, effects used in real-time mode don't provide a Cancel button. Instead, they provide a Reset And Cancel button, which still applies the effect to the track but with the default parameter settings. Any parameter settings that you changed are removed.

6.   If you want to add another effect to the same track (or add some effects to different tracks), go back to Step 1. You either can leave the effects windows open, or you can close them. It doesn't matter. You can also let the project continue to play as you add new effects. As soon as you add an effect to the Fx field, you hear the results according to the current parameter settings.

7. If you want to remove an effect, right-click on the effect you want to remove and select Delete from the pop-up menu.

TIP

If you apply more than one Effect to a track, the order in which the effects appear in the Fx field determines the order they are applied to the data in the track. For example, if you have the Chorus and Reverb effects added to the Fx field (in that order) of an audio track, SONAR first applies the Chorus effect to the data. It then takes the result of that application and applies the Reverb effect to it. This means that the order in which you apply effects to a track matters. If you apply effects in a different order, you get different results. This makes for some interesting experimentation. To change the order of the effects listed in the Effects bin, simply drag and drop the name of an effect left or right within the list.

You can simply go on using SONAR with the real-time effects in place. Remember that you will be aware of the results only during playback. The original data looks the same even if you examine it in the various views. Also, doing any editing to your original data doesn't change how the effects are applied to it. For example, if you have a track set up with some effects applied and you transpose the pitch of one of the clips within that track, during playback SONAR still applies the effects to the track in the same way. When the Now time reaches the point in the track containing the transposed clip, you simply hear the effect applied to the transposed data. This is one of the features that make real-time effects so flexible.

TIP

You can also apply real-time effects during recording. For example, this allows you to add some reverberation (which I'll explain later) to a vocal part to make it sound more appealing to the performer while his or her part is being recorded. This helps a performer get "in the groove" more, so to speak. In order to apply real-time effects during recording, you have to activate Input Monitoring, which I talked about in Chapter 6.

Advantages and Disadvantages

You might be asking yourself, "Why don't I just use real-time processing all the time, because it's so much more flexible?" Well, applying effects in real-time is very flexible, but in a couple of instances, you need to apply them offline. The first has to do with your computer's processing power. Most of SONAR's effects need to perform complex mathematical calculations to achieve their results. Applying effects in real-time means that not only does your computer have to deal with these calculations, but it also has to deal with SONAR playing back your MIDI and audio data. All these things going on at once can put a lot of strain on your computer's CPU. So, if you use too many effects in real-time at once, your computer might not be able to keep up. You may hear skips in playback or SONAR might stop playing altogether. If this ever happens, you need to apply some of the effects offline and keep only a few of them going in real-time. You lose a bit of flexibility in terms of being able to make changes to your data, but there's no limit to the number of effects you can apply to your data offline.

TIP

One thing you can do to make applying effects offline a little more flexible is to select the Create A Send Submix option and to activate the Keep Original Data option under the Mixing tab when you're applying an effect. Also, be sure to set the Wet parameter to 100 percent. This way, you can keep your original data intact and place only the output from the effect in another track. Although this approach doesn't allow you to change how the effect is applied, you can adjust how much of the effect you want to hear by adjusting the volumes of the two tracks. If you want to hear more of the original data, raise the volume on the original data track and lower the volume on the track that contains the processed data—and vice versa if you want to hear more of the processed data.

Applying effects offline also comes in handy when you want to process some specifically selected data. For example, if you want to process a short segment of data within a track or within a clip, you have to do it offline. In real-time, you can apply effects only to whole tracks.

Audio Effects

SONAR provides more than thirty different audio effects. If you choose either Edit > Audio Effects or Edit > Audio Effects > Cakewalk, you'll notice that some of these effects cover the same type of processing. Why would Cakewalk include multiple effects that accomplish the same tasks?

Well, some of the effects are designed to work with mono audio signals, and others are designed to work with stereo audio. They include parameters for both the left and right stereo channels. In addition, some of the effects process audio with a lower level of quality, and they include fewer parameter settings. So why include them? Because they provide one advantage: They don't take up as much computer processing power. This means you can apply more of the lower-quality effects to your tracks in real-time, especially if you have a slow computer system.

You also may have noticed that some of the effects mimic some of SONAR's editing features (as is the case with EQ). They mimic these effects so that you can process your data with these features in real-time.

SONAR's editing features can't be used in real-time because they aren't plug-ins. The Effects features, however, come with their own sets of parameters, so I'll go over them here for you step by step.

NOTE

Because I've already covered how to apply effects offline and in real-time, I'm just going to include the basic offline steps (along with parameter descriptions) in each of the following explanations. For detailed step-by-step procedures for applying Effects offline and in real-time, refer to the previous sections in this chapter.

Equalization

I talked about the how, what, and why of equalization back in Chapter 8. In addition to the two EQ editing features, SONAR provides four EQ effects for you to use. These are similar to the Parametric EQ editing feature.

2-Band EQ

As a matter of fact, the 2-Band EQ effect has the same exact parameters available as the Parametric EQ editing feature, but instead of one set of parameters, it has two. With these two parameters, you can apply two different types of equalization to your data at once. You use it as follows:

1. Select the audio data that you want to process.

2. Choose Edit > Audio Effects > Cakewalk > 2-Band EQ to open the 2-Band EQ dialog box (see Figure 11.2).

Figure 11.2
You can use the 2-Band EQ effect to apply two different types of equalization to your data at once.

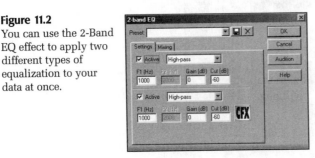

3. Under the Settings tab, activate one or both of the Active options to turn on each type of EQ.

4. Set the F1, F2, Gain, and Cut parameters. I explained these parameters in the Equalization section of Chapter 8.

NOTE

You've probably noticed that one parameter setting is missing: the Q (or Quality) parameter. It isn't here because the 2-Band EQ effect has a permanent Q parameter setting of 2. This is one of the factors that keeps this effect from taking up too much computer processing power. If you need more flexibility, use the Parametric EQ or FxEq effects, which are explained later.

5.   Click on the Audition button to test the current parameter settings. Make further adjustments if necessary.

6.   Set the appropriate options under the Mixing tab.

7.   If you want to use the current settings at a later time, save them as a preset.

8.   Click on OK.

SONAR processes the data by applying the effect according to the parameter settings you specified.

ParamEq

The ParamEq effect provides only one band of EQ and only three parameter settings, but it also takes up the least CPU processing power, so you can use many instances of the effect at once in real-time. Here is how it works:

1.   Select the audio data that you want to process.

2.   Choose Edit > Audio Effects > ParamEq to open the ParamEq dialog box (see Figure 11.3).

Figure 11.3

The ParamEq Effect provides a single band of parametric EQ.

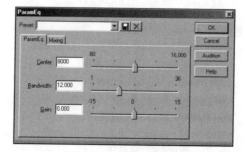

3.   Set the Center parameter. This sets the center frequency (80 Hz to 16 kHz) for the EQ, around which the frequencies will be boosted or cut.

4.   Set the Bandwidth parameter. This parameter is the same as the Q parameter mentioned earlier. It affects how many other frequencies around the center frequency will be affected. A low value means fewer frequencies around the center frequency will be affected. A high value means more frequencies around the center frequency will be affected.

5. Set the Gain parameter. This parameter determines whether the frequencies will be cut (use a negative value) or boosted (use a positive value), and by how much (–15dB to +15dB).

6. Click on the Audition button to test the current parameter settings. Make further adjustments if necessary.

7. Set the appropriate options under the Mixing tab.

8. If you want to use the current settings at a later time, save them as a preset.

9. Click on OK.

SONAR processes the data by applying the effect according to the parameter settings you specified.

Parametric EQ

Even though the Parametric EQ effect also provides parametric equalization, its parameters are a bit different from those previously mentioned. You use it like this:

1. Select the audio data that you want to process.

2. Select Edit > Audio Effects > Cakewalk > Parametric EQ to open the Parametric EQ dialog box (see Figure 11.4).

Figure 11.4
The Parametric EQ effect also provides parametric equalization but with slightly different parameter settings.

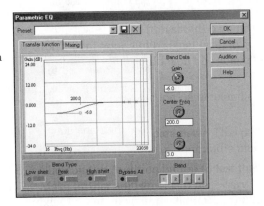

3. In the Band section under the Transfer function tab, select the number of the EQ band you want to modify. Like the 2-Band EQ effect, the Parametric EQ effect enables you to set up more than one equalization type at once. In this case, you can have up to four different equalization types set up to process your data at the same time. This way, you can do some very complex equalization processing.

4. You'll notice a couple of familiar parameters in the Band Data section: Gain and Q. They work just as they do in all the other EQ features. You can set the Gain from –24 to +24dB, and you can set the Q from 0.1 to 30. The Center Freq (short for frequency) parameter

works a bit differently depending on what type of equalization you choose in the Band Type section. Essentially, it determines the frequency below which other frequencies will be cut or boosted, above which other frequencies will be cut or boosted, or exactly where boosting or cutting will occur. You can set the Center Freq from 16 to 22050 Hz. Choose the settings for these parameters that you want to use.

5. In the Band Type section, choose the type of equalization you want to use. If you choose the Low Shelf option, any frequencies below the Center Freq are either boosted or cut depending on how you set the Gain parameter. If you choose the High Shelf option, any frequencies above the Center Freq are either boosted or cut depending on how you set the Gain parameter. If you choose the Peak option, the exact frequency designated by the Center Freq parameter is the frequency that is boosted or cut depending on how you set the Gain parameter.

TIP

You've probably noticed that in addition to the parameter settings, the Parametric EQ dialog box contains a graph display. This graph shows all the current equalization settings for all four types (bands). Along the left, it shows the amplitudes (gain), and along the bottom, it shows the frequencies. The shape of the line drawn on the graph shows you which frequencies in the audio spectrum are either boosted or cut, but that's not all. Four colored points on the graph represent each EQ band. Red is for band 1, blue for band 2, green for band 3, and purple for band 4. By clicking and dragging on these points, you can graphically change the Gain and Center Freq settings for each of the EQ types (bands), essentially "drawing" the EQ settings.

You still have to manually set the Band Type and Q settings, though.

6. If you want to set up more than one equalization type, go through steps 3 through 5 again.

7. Click on the Audition button to test the current parameter settings. Make further adjustments if necessary.

8. Set the appropriate options under the Mixing tab.

9. If you want to use the current settings at a later time, save them as a preset.

10. Click on OK.

SONAR processes the data by applying the effect according to the parameter settings you specified.

FxEq

Like Parametric EQ, the FxEq effect provides multiple EQ bands (with many of the same parameters) for you to adjust, but instead of four, you now have eight bands at your disposal, plus hi-shelf and lo-shelf filters. The FxEq effect is the most powerful of all the EQ effects provided, but it also takes up the most CPU processing power. Here is how it works:

1. Select the audio data that you want to process.

2. Choose Edit > Audio Effects > Cakewalk > FxEq to open the FxEq dialog box (see Figure 11.5).

Figure 11.5
The FxEq Effect provides eight bands of parametric EQ plus single hi-shelf and lo-shelf filters.

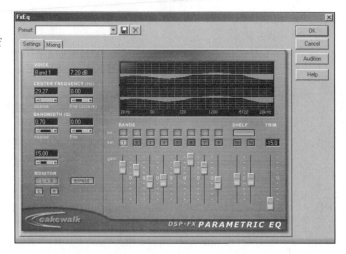

3. In the Bands section, click on the number of the EQ band you want to modify to select it. To turn a band on or off, click on the green button located just above the band number.

4. When you select a band, you'll notice that the Voice section displays the name of the selected band as well as the Gain setting for that band. To adjust the Gain, just drag the appropriate slider for the selected band up or down.

TIP

You can adjust the amplitude range for all the EQ bands by setting dB Scale control, which is located just above the Monitor section. Setting the dB Scale control limits the Gain range for each of EQ bands. For example, setting the dB Scale to 15 dB means that the Gain for each EQ band can only be adjusted from –15 dB to +15 dB.

5. Selecting a band also displays the Center Frequency and Bandwidth (Q) for that band in the sections of the same names. The Center Frequency and Bandwidth parameters work the same as they do for the Parametric EQ effect, which I explained earlier.

6. If you want to set up more than one EQ band, go through steps 3 through 5 again.

7. You can also set up a hi-shelf and/or a lo-shelf filter using the controls in the Shelf section. These parameters work just like the High Shelf and Low Shelf band types in the Parametric EQ effect, which I explained earlier.

8. To adjust the final output volume of the FxEq effect, use the Trim control.

9. You can also determine if the FxEq effect will process the left, right, or both channels of a stereo signal by using the controls in the Monitor section.

10. Click on the Audition button to test the current parameter settings. Make further adjustments if necessary.

11. Set the appropriate options under the Mixing tab.

12. If you want to use the current settings at a later time, save them as a preset.

13. Click on OK.

SONAR processes the data by applying the effect according to the parameter settings you specified.

Delay

You know what an echo is, right? It's a repeating sound that mimics an initial sound. For example, if you yell the word *hello* in a large enclosed area (such as a concert hall or a canyon), you hear that word repeated (or echoed) back over and over until it fades away. This effect is exactly what delay allows you to do to your audio data. You can create echoes that vary in the number of repeats and time between each repeat. SONAR includes four delay effects.

Delay/Echo (Mono)

The Delay/Echo (Mono) effect is pretty straightforward in terms of operation. This effect is intended to be used with monophonic audio rather than stereo. It works like this:

1. Select the audio data that you want to process.

2. Select Edit > Audio Effects > Cakewalk > Delay/Echo (Mono) to open the Delay/Echo (Mono) dialog box (see Figure 11.6).

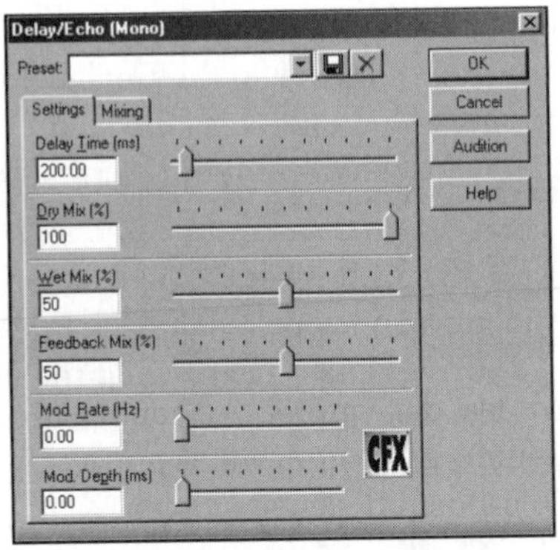

Figure 11.6
Using the Delay/Echo (Mono) Effect, you can add echoes to your audio data.

3. Under the Settings tab, set the Delay Time parameter. This parameter determines how much time (in milliseconds) occurs between each echo. You can set the Delay Time from 0.02 to 5000 milliseconds (which is equal to 5 seconds).

TIP

Many professional musicians use delay to synchronize the echoes with the music. For instance, you can have the echoes play in time with each quarter note, eighth note, sixteenth note, and so on. All that's required for this cool trick is a little simple math.

Begin by figuring the Delay Time needed to synchronize the echoes to each quarter note. To do so, just divide 60,000 (the number of milliseconds in one second) by the current Tempo (measured in beats per minute) of your project. So, for a Tempo of 120 bpm, you get 500 milliseconds. If you set the Delay Time to 500, the resulting echoes sound at the same time as each quarter note.

To figure out the Delay Time for other note values, you just need to divide or multiply. Because an eighth note is half the value of a quarter note, you simply divide 500 by 2 to get 250 milliseconds. A sixteenth note is half the value of an eighth note, so 250 divided by 2 is 125. See how it works? If you want to find out larger note values, just multiply by 2. Because a half note is twice as long as a quarter note, you multiply 500 by 2 to get 1,000 milliseconds, and so on.

4.   Set the Dry Mix and Wet Mix parameters. When you apply an Effect to your original data, you can determine how much of the effect and how much of the original data ends up in the final sound. This way, you can add a certain amount of effect without drowning out the entire original data. The Dry Mix parameter determines how much of the original data you will hear in the final signal, and the Wet Mix parameter determines how much of the effect you will hear in the final signal. You can set both of these parameters anywhere from 0 to 100 percent.

5.   Set the Feedback Mix parameter. With some effects, you can take their resulting signals and send them back through to have the effect applied again multiple times. That's what the Feedback Mix parameter does. The resulting sound can be different depending on the effect. For delay effects, the Feedback Mix controls how many echoes occur. You can set it anywhere from 0 to 100 percent. The lower the value, the fewer the number of echoes. The higher the value, the more echoes. Unfortunately, there's no way to determine exactly how many echoes will occur according to the percentage. You'll have to experiment with this one.

6.   Set the Mod Rate and Mod Depth parameters. These parameters are a bit difficult to describe. They enable you to add a "warble" type of effect to your audio data along with the echoes. The sound is also similar to that of the tremolo you hear on an electronic organ. To hear what I mean, check out the Fast Tremolo Delay preset. The mod rate determines the speed (in Hz or cycles per second) of the "warble," and the mod depth determines how much your audio data will be affected by it. This is just another one of those features that you have to experiment with to understand.

7.   Click on the Audition button to test the current parameter settings. Make further adjustments if necessary.

8.   Set the appropriate options under the Mixing tab.

9.   If you want to use the current settings at a later time, save them as a preset.

10. Click on OK.

SONAR processes the data by applying the effect according to the parameter settings you specified.

Echo

The Echo effect is similar to the Delay/Echo (Mono) effect, except that it works with stereo audio and some of its parameters are slightly different. Here is how it works:

1. Select the audio data that you want to process.

2. Choose Edit > Audio Effects > Echo to open the Echo dialog box (see Figure 11.7).

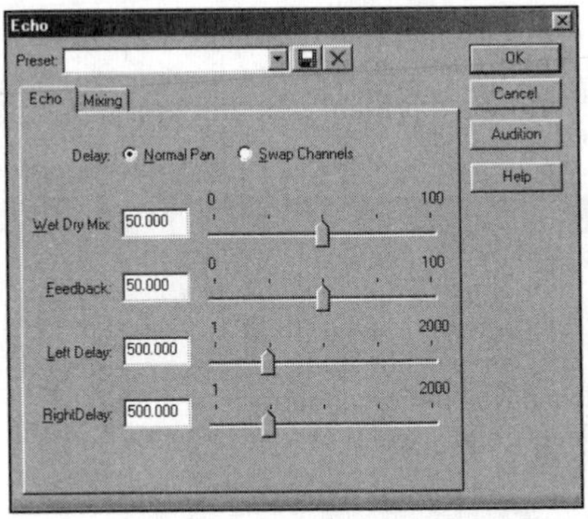

Figure 11.7
The Echo Effect is similar to the Delay/Echo (Mono) Effect, except that it works with stereo audio.

3. If you would like the echoes from each stereo channel added to themselves, choose the Normal Pan option for the Delay parameter. If you would like the echoes from the left stereo channel to be heard in the right stereo channel and vice versa, choose the Swap Channels option for the Delay parameter.

4. I've explained the Wet Dry Mix parameter before, but in this case there is only one parameter rather than two. Setting the Wet Dry Mix parameter to 50 percent gives you an equal balance between the original audio signal and the effect audio signal. Setting the Wet Dry Mix to 0 percent means you'll hear only the original audio signal. Setting the Wet Dry Mix to 100 percent means you will hear only the effect audio signal.

5. Set the Feedback parameter. This parameter works just like the Feedback parameter in the Delay/Echo (Mono) Effect.

6. Set the Left Delay and Right Delay parameters. These parameters work just like the Delay Time parameter in the Delay/Echo (Mono) Effect, except that here you get a separate setting for each stereo channel.

7. Click on the Audition button to test the current parameter settings. Make further adjustments if necessary.

8. Set the appropriate options under the Mixing tab.

9. If you want to use the current settings at a later time, save them as a preset.

CHAPTER 11

10. Click on OK.

SONAR processes the data by applying the effect according to the parameter settings you specified.

Delay

Very similar to Delay/Echo (Mono), the Delay effect has most of the same parameters. Because it works with stereo audio, however, there are two sets, plus a few extras. It works like this:

1. Select the audio data that you want to process.

2. Select Edit > Audio Effects > Cakewalk > Delay to open the Delay dialog box (see Figure 11.8).

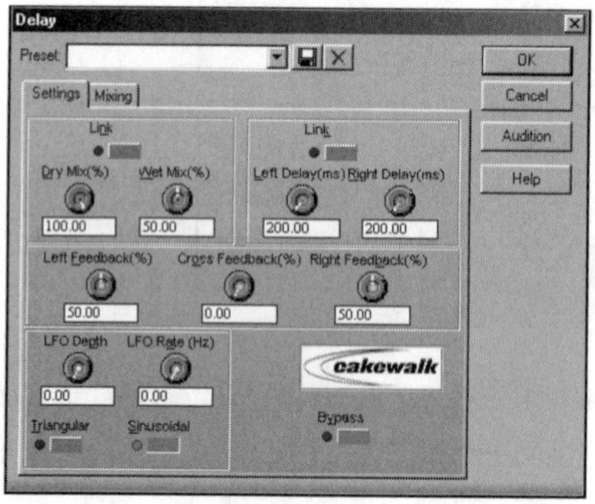

Figure 11.8
The Delay effect has a few additional parameters because it is designed to work with stereo audio.

3. Set the Left Delay and Right Delay parameters. These parameters work the same way as the Delay Time parameter in the Delay/Echo (Mono) Effect. In this case, separate controls are available for the left and right stereo channels. A Link option is also available. Activating this option links the Left Delay and Right Delay parameters together so that, if you change the value of one, the other is set to the exact same value. Most of the time, you should keep the Link option activated so that both stereo channels have the same amount of delay. However, setting different values for each channel can sometimes yield interesting results. Don't be afraid to experiment.

4. Set the Dry Mix and Wet Mix parameters. These parameters work the same way as the parameters of the same names in the Delay/Echo (Mono) effect. Separate controls are not available for each stereo channel in this case, but a Link option is available. Activating this option links the Dry Mix and Wet Mix parameters together, so if you increase the value of the Wet Mix, the value of the Dry Mix decreases and vice versa. This feature enables you to achieve a perfect balance between the original data and the effect.

5. Set the Left Feedback and Right Feedback parameters. These parameters work the same way as the Feedback Mix parameter in the Delay/Echo (Mono) effect. In this case, separate controls are available for the left and right stereo channels. A Cross Feedback parameter also is available. Using this parameter, you can take the resulting signal from the left channel and send it back through the right channel and the resulting signal from the right channel and send it back through the left channel. Essentially, this means that this parameter also provides control over the number of echoes that will occur and, at the same time, it helps to make the stereo field sound "fuller."

6. Set the LFO Depth and LFO Rate parameters. These parameters work the same way as the Mod Depth and Mod Rate parameters in the Delay/Echo (Mono) effect. In addition, two other options called Triangular and Sinusoidal are available. They determine the type of "warble" to be applied. The Triangular option creates a "coarse" or "sharp" sound, and the Sinusoidal option creates a "smooth" or "flowing" sound. You'll have to try them out to hear what I mean.

7. Click on the Audition button to test the current parameter settings. Make further adjustments if necessary.

8. Set the appropriate options under the Mixing tab.

9. If you want to use the current settings at a later time, save them as a preset.

10. Click on OK.

SONAR processes the data by applying the effect according to the parameter settings you specified.

FxDelay

The FxDelay effect allows you to create very complex echo effects by letting you set up multiple delays at once, such as setting up multiple Delay/Echo (Mono) effects at the same time to process your audio data. Here is how the FxDelay effect works:

1. Select the audio data that you would like to process.

2. Choose Edit > Audio Effects > Cakewalk > FxDelay to open the FxDelay dialog box (see Figure 11.9).

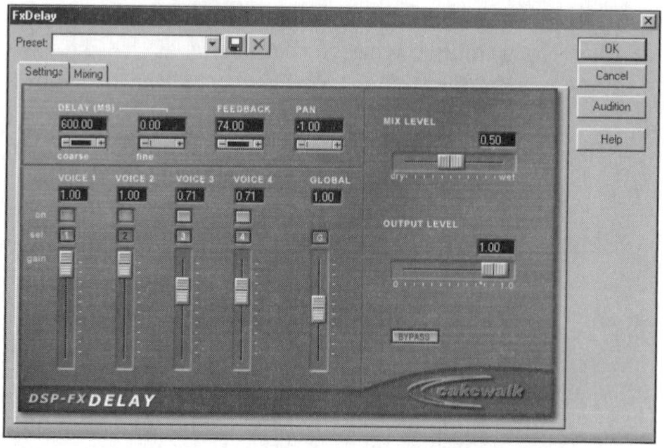

Figure 11.9

The FxDelay effect lets you create complex echo effects.

3. Set the Mix Level parameter. This parameter works just like the Wet Dry Mix parameter in the Echo effect.

4. Set the On options for each of the Voice parameters (1, 2, 3, and 4). The On options let you determine how many different delays you want to set up in your effect. You can have up to four different delays.

5. Each Voice (delay) comes with its own Gain, Delay, Pan, and Feedback parameters. This means that you can control the initial volume, echo time, panning in the stereo field, and feedback (number of echoes) of each Voice. To adjust the parameters for a voice, select the number of the voice via the Sel. options. Then, adjust the Gain, Delay, Feedback, and Pan parameters for that voice. You can do this for all four voices individually.

6. To adjust the Gain for all four voices simultaneously, use the Global parameter.

7. Set the Output Level parameter, which controls the overall volume level of the effect output.

8. Click on the Audition button to test the current parameter settings. Make further adjustments if necessary.

9. Set the appropriate options under the Mixing tab.

10. If you want to use the current settings at a later time, save them as a preset.

11. Click on OK.

SONAR processes the data by applying the effect according to the parameter settings you specified.

Chorus

Believe it or not, you'll find that SONAR's chorus effects (of which there are four) have many of the same parameters as its delay effects. Why? Because technically, chorus is a form of delay. Chorus uses delay and detuning to achieve its results. You don't hear echoes when using chorus, though, because the delay is extremely short. Instead, chorus makes your audio data sound "fatter" or "fuller." The name *chorus* comes from the fact that people singing in a chorus produce a full sound because each person sings slightly out of tune and out of time—not enough to make the music sound bad, but actually better. You can use SONAR's chorus effects to achieve similar results with your audio data. The following sections describe how to use them.

Chorus (Mono)

The Chorus (Mono) effect is designed to work with monophonic audio rather than stereo. To apply the Chorus (Mono) effect, you do the following:

1. Select the audio data that you want to process.

2. Select Edit > Audio Effects > Cakewalk > Chorus (Mono) to open the Chorus (Mono) dialog box (see Figure 11.10).

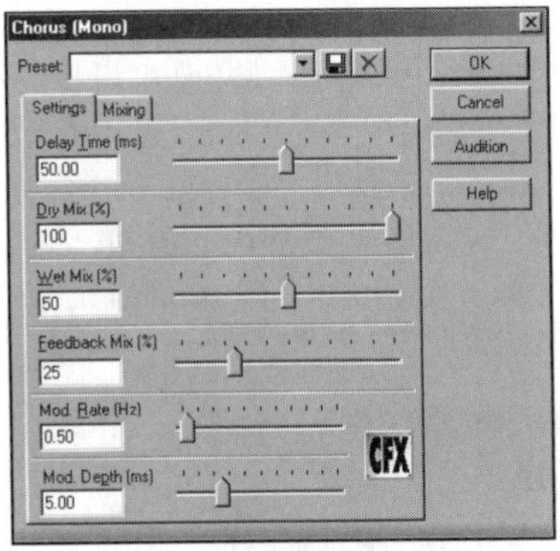

Figure 11.10
The Chorus (Mono) effect has the same exact parameters as the Delay/Echo (Mono) effect, although they provide different results.

3. Under the Settings tab, set the Delay Time parameter. The only difference between this Delay Time parameter and the same parameter in the Delay/Echo (Mono) effect is that this one has a range of only 20 to 80 milliseconds. If you set this parameter high enough, you can actually get some quick repeating echoes out of it. For adding chorus to your audio though, you should keep it set somewhere between 20 and 35.

4. Set the Dry Mix and Wet Mix parameters. I explained these parameters earlier.

5. Set the Feedback Mix parameter. Instead of setting the number echoes to occur (as in the Delay/Echo (Mono) effect), this parameter determines the "thickness" of the chorus. The higher the value, the "thicker" the chorus.

6. Set the Mod Rate and Mod Depth parameters. Instead of adding a "warble" to your audio (as in the Delay/Echo (Mono) effect), these parameters determine how detuning is added to the chorus. The Mod Rate determines how quickly the detuning occurs, and the Mod Depth determines the amount of detuning. A high Mod Depth setting makes your audio sound really out of tune (which isn't usually desirable), but a lower setting produces a nice chorusing.

7. Click on the Audition button to test the current parameter settings. Make further adjustments if necessary.

8. Set the appropriate options under the Mixing tab.

9. If you want to use the current settings at a later time, save them as a preset.

10. Click on OK.

SONAR processes the data by applying the effect according to the parameter settings you specified.

Chorus

Very similar to Chorus (Mono), the Chorus effect has most of the same parameters. Because it works with stereo audio, however, there are a couple differences. It works like this:

1. Select the audio data that you want to process.

2. Choose Edit > Audio Effects > Chorus to open the Chorus dialog box (see Figure 11.11).

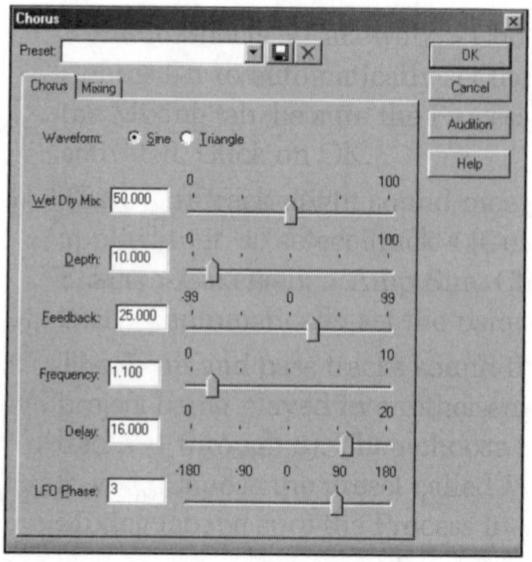

Figure 11.11
The Chorus effect is similar to the Chorus (Mono) effect, except that it works with stereo audio.

3. Set the Delay parameter. This parameter provides the same chorusing results as the Delay Time parameter in the Chorus (Mono) effect—but, of course, for stereo audio.

4. Set the Wet Dry Mix parameter. Set the value of the parameter low to hear more of the original audio data. Set the value of the parameter high to hear more of the effect audio data. Set the value of the parameter at 50 percent to hear an equal mix of the original and effect audio data.

5. Set the Feedback parameter. This parameter provides the same chorusing results as the Feedback Mix parameter in the Chorus (Mono) effect—but, of course, for stereo audio.

6. Set the Depth and Frequency parameters. They provide the same results as the Mod Depth and Mod Rate parameters in the Chorus (Mono) effect.

7. Set the Waveform parameter. The Sine and Triangle parameters determine the type of "warble" to be applied to the Chorus effect. The Triangle option creates a "coarse" or "sharp" sound, and the Sine option creates a "smooth" or "flowing" sound. You'll have to try them out to hear what I mean.

8. Set the LFO Phase parameter. This parameter allows you to change the sound of the "warble" (mentioned earlier) to give it a sort of "hollow" sound. You'll need to experiment to hear what I mean.

9. Click on the Audition button to test the current parameter settings. Make further adjustments if necessary.

10. Set the appropriate options under the Mixing tab.

11. If you want to use the current settings at a later time, save them as a preset.

12. Click on OK.

SONAR processes the data by applying the effect according to the parameter settings you specified.

Chorus

Yes, there are actually two chorus effects with the same exact name, but they are accessed and operated differently. To apply this Chorus effect (which provides more features and better sounding output), you do the following:

1. Select the audio data that you want to process.

2. Select Edit > Audio Effects > Cakewalk > Chorus to open the Chorus dialog box (see Figure 11.12).

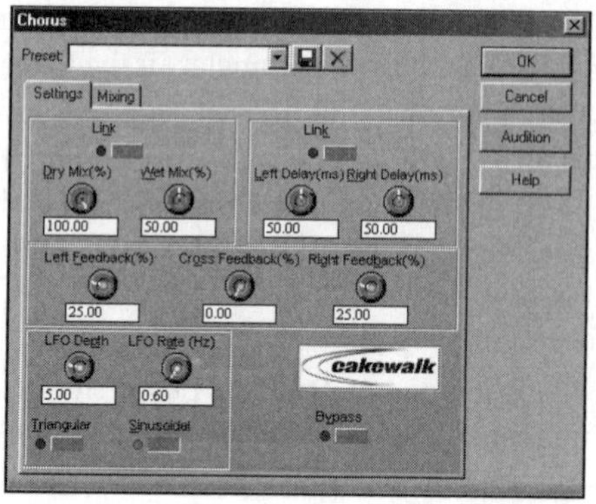

Figure 11.12
The Chorus effect has the same exact parameters as the Delay effect, although they provide different results.

3. Set the Left Delay and Right Delay parameters. They provide the same chorusing results as the Delay Time parameter in the Chorus (Mono) effect—but, of course, for the separate left and right stereo channels. You can also link these parameters together by activating the Link option.

4. Set the Dry Mix and Wet Mix parameters. I explained these parameters earlier.

5. Set the Left Feedback and Right Feedback parameters. They provide the same chorusing results as the Feedback Mix parameter in the Chorus (Mono) effect, but of course for the separate left and right stereo channels. Also, just as the Cross Feedback parameter in the Delay effect enhances the delay, this Cross Feedback parameter enhances the chorus.

6. Set the LFO Depth and LFO Rate parameters. They provide the same results as the Mod Depth and Mod Rate parameters in the Chorus (Mono) effect. I explained the Triangular and Sinusoidal parameters earlier in the "Delay" section.

7. Click on the Audition button to test the current parameter settings. Make further adjustments if necessary.

8. Set the appropriate options under the Mixing tab.

9. If you want to use the current settings at a later time, save them as a preset.

10. Click on OK.

SONAR processes the data by applying the effect according to the parameter settings you specified.

FxChorus

The FxChorus effect allows you to create very complex chorus effects by letting you set up multiple choruses at once, such as setting up multiple Chorus (Mono) effects at the same time to process your audio data. Here is how the FxChorus effect works:

1. Select the audio data that you would like to process.

2. Choose Edit > Audio Effects > Cakewalk > FxChorus to open the FxChorus dialog box (see Figure 11.13).

Figure 11.13

The FxChorus Effect lets you create complex chorus effects.

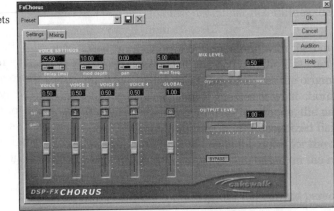

3. Set the Mix Level parameter. This parameter works just like the Wet Dry Mix parameter in the Echo effect.

4. Set the On options for each of the voice parameters (1, 2, 3, and 4). The On options let you determine how many different choruses you want to set up in your effect. You can have up to four different choruses.

5. Each voice (chorus) comes with its own Gain, Delay, Pan, Mod Depth, and Mod Freq parameters. This means that you can control the initial volume, chorus strength, panning in the stereo field, and depth and speed of the "warble" of each Voice. To adjust the parameters for a voice, select the number of the voice via the Sel. options. Then, adjust the Gain, Delay, Pan, Mod Depth, and Mod Freq parameters for that voice. You can do this for all four voices individually.

6. To adjust the Gain for all four voices simultaneously, use the Global parameter.

7. Set the Output Level parameter, which controls the overall volume level of the effect output.

8. Click on the Audition button to test the current parameter settings. Make further adjustments if necessary.

9. Set the appropriate options under the Mixing tab.

10. If you want to use the current settings at a later time, save them as a preset.

11. Click on OK.

SONAR processes the data by applying the effect according to the parameter settings you specified.

Flanging

Guess what? As with SONAR's chorus effects, you'll find that the program's flanger effects have many of the same parameters as its delay effects, too, because (yep, that's right) flanging is also a form of delay. Flanging produces a kind of "spacey" or "whooshy" type of sound. It does so by mixing a slightly delayed version of the original data with itself. As with chorus, you don't hear echoes because the delay occurs so quickly. It's difficult to describe what flanging sounds like, so you'll have to hear it for yourself. You can apply SONAR's flanging effects as described in the following sections.

Flanger (Mono)

The Flanger (Mono) effect is designed to work with monophonic audio, rather than stereo. To apply the Flanger (Mono) effect, you do the following:

1. Select the audio data that you want to process.

2. Select Edit > Audio Effects > Cakewalk > Flanger (Mono) to open the Flanger (Mono) dialog box (see Figure 11.14).

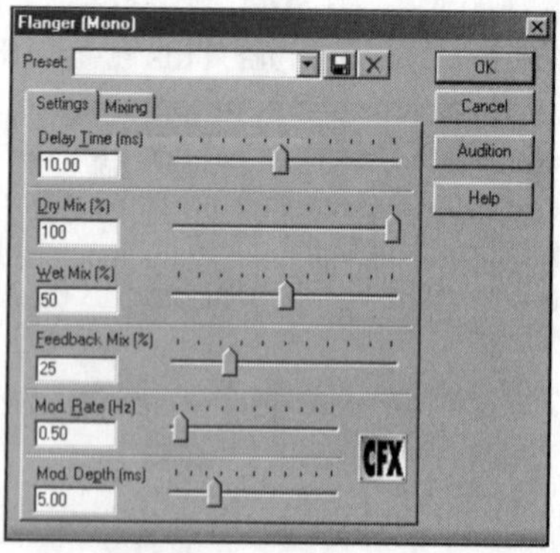

Figure 11.14
The Flanger (Mono) effect has the same exact parameters as the Delay/Echo (Mono) effect, although they provide different results.

3. Under the Settings tab, set the Delay Time parameter. The only difference between this Delay Time parameter and the same parameter in the Delay/Echo (Mono) effect is that this one has a range of only 1 to 20 milliseconds. If you set this parameter high enough, you can actually get some chorusing out of it. To add flanging to your audio, though, you should keep it set somewhere between 1 and 11.

4. Set the Dry Mix and Wet Mix parameters. I explained these parameters earlier.

5. Set the Feedback Mix parameter. Instead of setting the number of echoes to occur (as in the Delay/Echo (Mono) effect), this parameter determines the "thickness" of the flanging. The higher the value, the "thicker" the flanger.

6. Set the Mod Rate and Mod Depth parameters. Instead of adding a "warble" to your audio (as in the Delay/Echo (Mono) effect), these parameters determine the speed and amount of the flanging. The Mod Rate determines how quickly the flanging occurs, and the Mod Depth determines the amount of flanging. Check out some of the included presets to get an idea of what values to use for these parameters.

7. Click on the Audition button to test the current parameter settings. Make further adjustments if necessary.

8. Set the appropriate options under the Mixing tab.

9. If you want to use the current settings at a later time, save them as a preset.

10. Click on OK.

SONAR processes the data by applying the effect according to the parameter settings you specified.

Flanger

Very similar to Flanger (Mono), the Flanger effect has most of the same parameters. Because it works with stereo audio, however, there are a couple differences. It works like this:

1. Select the audio data that you want to process.

2. Choose Edit > Audio Effects > Flanger to open the Flanger dialog box (see Figure 11.15).

CHAPTER 11

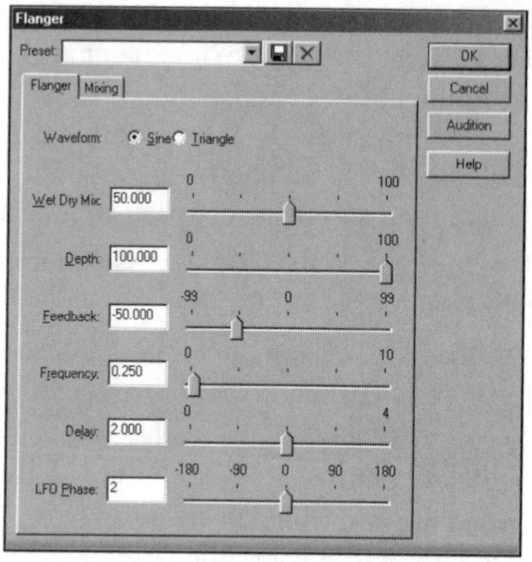

Figure 11.15
The Flanger effect is
similar to the Flanger
(Mono) Effect, except
that it works with stereo
audio.

3. Set the Delay parameter. This parameter provides the same flanging results as the Delay Time parameter in the Flanger (Mono) effect—but, of course, for stereo audio.

4. Set the Wet Dry Mix parameter. Set the value of the parameter low to hear more of the original audio data. Set the value of the parameter high to hear more of the effect audio data. Set the value of the parameter at 50 percent to hear an equal mix of the original and effect audio data.

5. Set the Feedback parameter. This parameter provides the same flanging results as the Feedback Mix parameter in the Flanger (Mono) effect—but, of course, for stereo audio.

6. Set the Depth and Frequency parameters. They provide the same results as the Mod Depth and Mod Rate parameters in the Flanger (Mono) effect.

7. Set the Waveform parameter. The Sine and Triangle parameters determine the type of "warble" to be applied to the Chorus effect. The Triangle option creates a "coarse" or "sharp" sound, and the Sine option creates a "smooth" or "flowing" sound. You'll have to try them out to hear what I mean.

8. Set the LFO Phase parameter. This parameter allows you to change the sound of the "warble" (mentioned earlier) to give it a sort of "hollow" sound. You'll need to experiment to hear what I mean.

9. Click on the Audition button to test the current parameter settings. Make further adjustments if necessary.

10. Set the appropriate options under the Mixing tab.

11. If you want to use the current settings at a later time, save them as a preset.

12. Click on OK.

SONAR processes the data by applying the effect according to the parameter settings you specified.

Flanger

Yes, there are actually two flanger effects with the same exact name, but they are accessed and operated differently. To apply this Flanger effect, you do the following:

1. Select the audio data that you want to process.

2. Select Edit > Audio Effects > Cakewalk > Flanger to open the Flanger dialog box (see Figure 11.16).

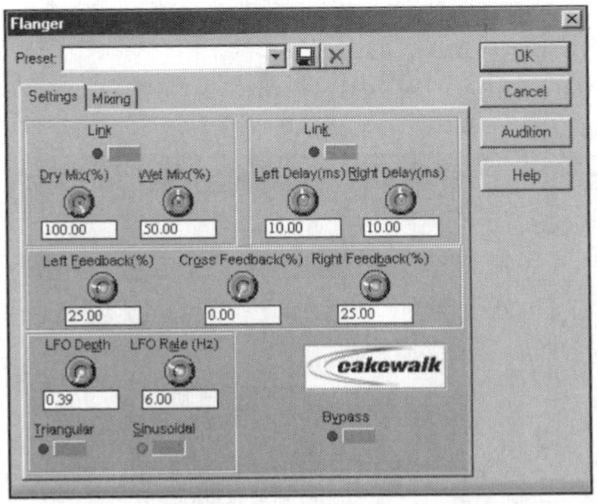

Figure 11.16
The Flanger effect has the same exact parameters as the Delay effect, although they provide different results.

3. Set the Left Delay and Right Delay parameters. They provide the same flanging results as the Delay Time parameter in the Flanger (Mono) effect, but for the separate left and right stereo channels. You can also link these parameters together by activating the Link option.

4. Set the Dry Mix and Wet Mix parameters. I explained these parameters earlier.

5. Set the Left Feedback and Right Feedback parameters. They provide the same flanging results as the Feedback Mix parameter in the Flanger (Mono) effect, but for the separate left and right stereo channels. Also, just like the Cross Feedback parameter in the Delay effect enhances the delay, this Cross Feedback parameter enhances the flanging.

6. Set the LFO Depth and LFO Rate parameters. They provide the same results as the Mod Depth and Mod Rate parameters in the Flanger (Mono) effect. I explained the Triangular and Sinusoidal parameters earlier in the "Delay" section.

7. Click on the Audition button to test the current parameter settings. Make further adjustments if necessary.

8. Set the appropriate options under the Mixing tab.

9. If you want to use the current settings at a later time, save them as a preset.

10. Click on OK.

SONAR processes the data by applying the effect according to the parameter settings you specified.

FxFlange

The FxFlange effect allows you to create complex flange effects by letting you set up multiple flanges at once, such as setting up multiple Flanger (Mono) effects at the same time to process your audio data. Here is how the FxFlange effect works:

1. Select the audio data that you would like to process.

2. Choose Edit > Audio Effects > Cakewalk > FxFlange to open the FxFlange dialog box (see Figure 11.17).

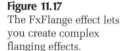

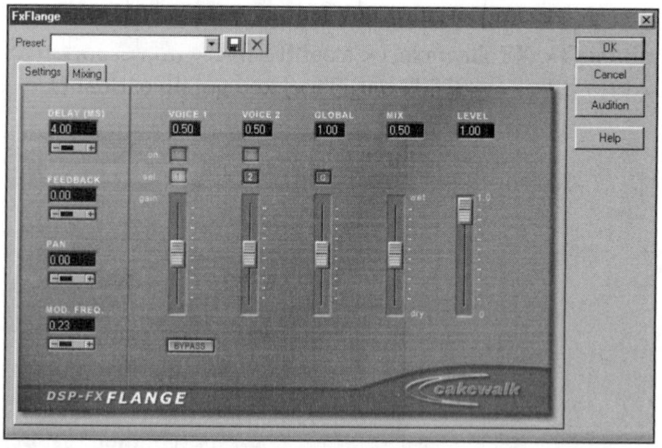

Figure 11.17
The FxFlange effect lets you create complex flanging effects.

3. Set the Mix parameter. This parameter works just like the Wet Dry Mix parameter in the Echo effect.

4. Set the On options for each of the voice parameters (1 and 2). The On options let you determine how many different flanges you want to set up in your effect. You can have up to two different flanges.

5. Each voice (flange) comes with its own Gain, Delay, Pan, Feedback, and Mod Freq parameters. This means that you can control the initial volume, flanging strength, panning in the stereo field, and depth and speed of the flanging of each voice. To adjust the parameters for a voice, select the number of the voice via the Sel. options. Then adjust the Gain, Delay, Pan, Feedback, and Mod Freq parameters for that voice. You can do this for both voices individually.

6. To adjust the Gain for both voices simultaneously, use the Global parameter.

7. Set the Level parameter, which controls the overall volume level of the effect output.

8. Click on the Audition button to test the current parameter settings. Make further adjustments if necessary.

9. Set the appropriate options under the Mixing tab.

10. If you want to use the current settings at a later time, save them as a preset.

11. Click on OK.

SONAR processes the data by applying the effect according to the parameter settings you specified.

Reverberation

Reverb (short for reverberation) is also a form of delay, but it's special because, instead of distinct echoes, reverb adds a complex series of very small echoes that simulate artificial ambience. In other words, reverb produces a dense collection of echoes that are so close together that they create a wash of sound, making the original audio data sound like it's being played in another environment, such as a large concert hall. Using SONAR's reverb effects, you can make your music sound like it's being played in all kinds of different places, such as in an arena, a club, or even on a live stage. SONAR includes five reverb Effects.

Reverb (Mono)

The Reverb (Mono) effect is designed to work with monophonic audio, rather than stereo. To apply the Reverb (Mono) effect to your data, you do the following:

1. Select the audio data that you want to process.

2. Select Edit > Audio Effects > Cakewalk > Reverb (Mono) to open the Reverb (Mono) dialog box (see Figure 11.18).

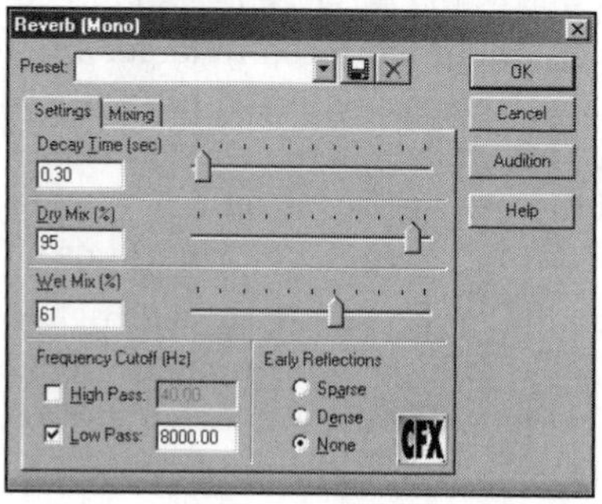

Figure 11.18
Using the Reverb (Mono) effect, you can add reverberation to your audio data.

3. Under the Settings tab, set the Decay Time parameter. When you're applying reverb to your data, you should imagine what type of environment you want to create. Doing so will help you in setting the effect parameters. Technically, the Decay Time determines how long it takes for the reverberation to fade away, but you can think of it as controlling how big the artificial environment will be. The lower the Decay Time, the smaller the environment. The higher the Decay Time, the larger the environment. You can set the Decay Time from 0.20 to 5 seconds. So, if you want to make your music sound like it's playing in a small room, a good Decay Time might be about 0.25. If you want to make your music sound like it's being played on a live stage, a good Decay Time might be about 1.50. Be sure to check out some of the included presets for more sample parameter settings.

4. Set the Dry Mix and Wet Mix parameters. I explained these parameters earlier in the chapter. One point you should note, however, is that in the case of reverb, the Dry Mix and Wet Mix parameters also make a difference on how the effect sounds. If you set the Dry Mix high and the Wet Mix low, your audio data will sound like it's positioned closer to the "front" of the imaginary environment. If you set the Dry Mix low and the Wet Mix high, your audio data will sound like it's positioned farther away. For example, if you want to simulate what it sounds like to be seated in the very back row of a music concert, you can set the Dry Mix low and the Wet Mix high. You need to experiment to get the exact parameter settings.

5. In the Early Reflections section, choose one of the following options: None, Dense, or Sparse. When you make a sound in any enclosed environment, some very quick echoes always occur because of the reflective surfaces (such as walls) that you are standing next to. These echoes are known as *early reflections*. To make your reverb simulations sound more authentic, SONAR provides this parameter so that you can control the density of the early reflections. If you select None, no early reflections are added to the effect. The Sparse option makes the reflections sound more like distinct echoes, and the Dense option makes the reverb effect sound "thicker." Early reflections are more pronounced in larger spaces, so if you want to simulate a really large space, you'll probably want to use the Sparse option. If you want to simulate a moderately sized space, you'll probably want to use the Dense option. And if you want to simulate a small space (such as a room), you should use the None option.

6. In the Frequency Cutoff section, set the High Pass and Low Pass parameters. If you think these parameters look like equalization settings, you're right. Using these parameters also helps to create more authentic environment simulations because smaller, closed environments tend to stifle some frequencies of the audio spectrum,

and larger environments usually sound brighter, meaning they promote more of the frequencies. The High Pass and Low Pass parameters work just like the EQ parameters I described earlier in the chapter. If you activate the High Pass parameter and set its frequency (in Hz), any frequencies above that frequency are allowed to pass and are included in the Effect, and any frequencies below that frequency are cut. If you activate the Low Pass parameter and set its frequency, any frequencies below that frequency are allowed to pass, and any frequencies above that frequency are cut. So, if you want to simulate a small room, you can leave the High Pass parameter deactivated, activate the Low Pass parameter, and set its frequency to around 8000 Hz. This setting would cut out any really high frequencies, making the room sound small and enclosed. For more examples on how to set these parameters, be sure to take a look at some of the included presets.

7. Click on the Audition button to test the current parameter settings. Make further adjustments if necessary.

8. Set the appropriate options under the Mixing tab.

9. If you want to use the current settings at a later time, save them as a preset.

10. Click on OK.

SONAR processes the data by applying the effect according to the parameter settings you specified.

Reverb

To apply the Reverb effect to your data, you do the following:

1. Select the audio data that you want to process.

2. Select Edit > Audio Effects > Cakewalk > Reverb to open the Reverb dialog box (see Figure 11.19).

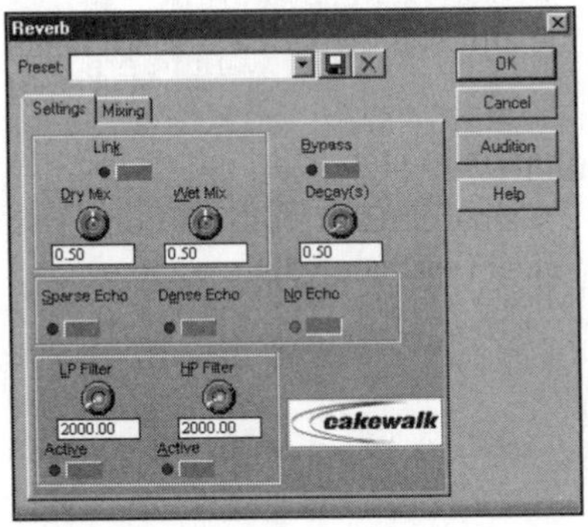

Figure 11.19
The Reverb effect parameters are exactly the same as the Reverb (Mono) effect except that they control both the left and right channels of the signal if your audio is in stereo.

3. Under the Settings tab, set the Decay(s) parameter. It is exactly the same as the Decay Time parameter in the Reverb (Mono) effect except that it controls both the left and right channels of the signal if your audio is in stereo.

4. Set the Dry Mix and Wet Mix parameters. They are exactly the same as the Dry Mix and Wet Mix parameters in the Reverb (Mono) effect except that they control both the left and right channels of the signal if your audio is in stereo. A Link option is also available, which I explained previously.

5. Choose an early reflections option. The No Echo, Dense Echo, and Sparse Echo options are exactly the same as the None, Dense, and Sparse options in the Reverb (Mono) effect, respectively.

6. Activate and set the frequency cutoff parameters. The LP Filter and HP Filter parameters are exactly the same as the Low Pass and High Pass filters in the Reverb (Mono) effect, respectively.

7. Click on the Audition button to test the current parameter settings. Make further adjustments if necessary.

8. Set the appropriate options under the Mixing tab.

9. If you want to use the current settings at a later time, save them as a preset.

10. Click on OK.

SONAR processes the data by applying the effect according to the parameter settings you specified.

WavesReverb

The WavesReverb effect is a simplified reverb effect that provides only four adjustable parameters. Because of this, however, it also takes up the least CPU processing power, so you can use multiple instances of the effect at once in real-time without bogging down your computer system. Here is how the WavesReverb effect works:

1. Select the audio data that you want to process.

2. Choose Edit > Audio Effects > WavesReverb to open the WavesReverb dialog box (see Figure 11.20).

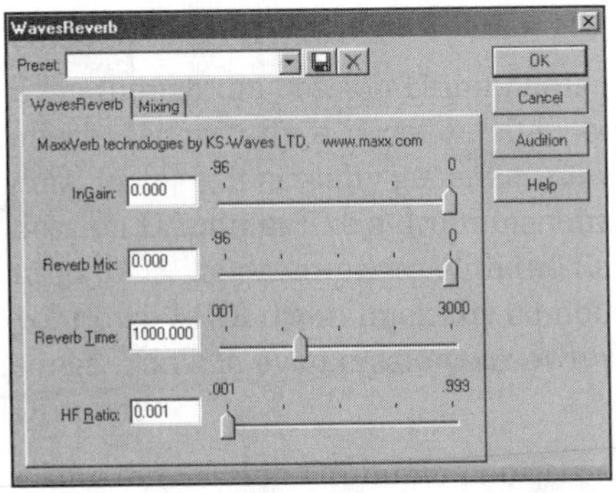

Figure 11.20
The WavesReverb effect provides reverb without taking up a lot of CPU processing power.

3. Set the InGain parameter. This parameter determines how loud the audio signal coming into the effect will be. More often than not, you'll want to keep this set at 0.

4. Set the Reverb Mix parameter. This parameter determines the balance between the original audio signal and the effect audio signal. Set it to 0 to hear the full reverberation effect.

5. Set the Reverb Time parameter. This parameter works just like the Decay Time parameter in the Reverb (Mono) Effect, except that it is limited to 3 seconds.

6. Set the HF Ratio. This parameter is similar to the Low Pass parameter in the Reverb (Mono) effect. Using a low value cuts out the high frequencies in the effect, and using a high value boosts the high frequencies in the effect.

7. Click on the Audition button to test the current parameter settings. Make further adjustments if necessary.

8. Set the appropriate options under the Mixing tab.

9. If you want to use the current settings at a later time, save them as a preset.

10. Click on OK.

SONAR processes the data by applying the effect according to the parameter settings you specified.

FxReverb

In contrast to the WavesReverb effects (as well as the other reverberation effects), the FxReverb effect provides the highest quality sound as well as the most adjustable parameters. Here is how it works:

1. Select the audio data that you want to process.

2. Choose Edit > Audio Effects > Cakewalk > FxReverb to open the FxReverb dialog box (see Figure 11.21).

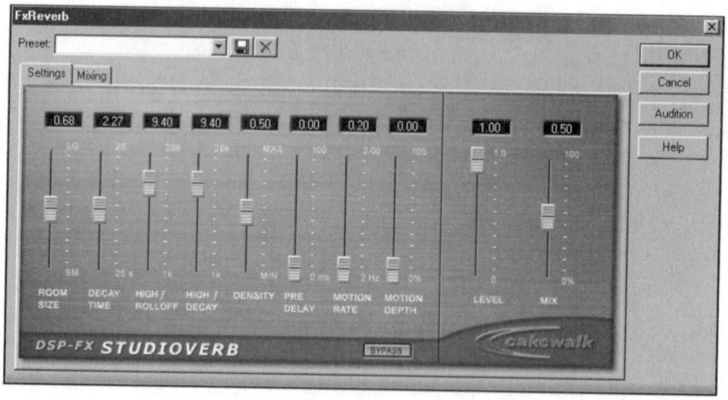

Figure 11.21
The FxReverb effect provides the best quality of all of SONAR's reverberation effects.

3. Set the Room Size parameter. This parameter determines the size of the environment you are trying to simulate.

4. Set the Mix parameter. I explained this parameter earlier in the chapter. It is similar to the Wet Dry Mix parameter used in other effects. One point you should note, however, is that in the case of reverb, the Mix parameter also makes a difference on how the effect sounds. If you set the Mix parameter low, your audio data will sound like it's positioned closer to the "front" of the imaginary environment. If you set the Mix parameter high, your audio data will sound like it's positioned farther away. For example, if you want to simulate what it sounds like to be seated in the very back row of a music concert, you can set the Mix parameter high. You need to experiment to get the exact parameter settings you desire.

5. Set the Decay Time parameter. When you're applying reverb to your data, you should imagine what type of environment you want to create. Doing so will help you set the parameters. Technically, the Decay Time determines how long it takes for the reverberation to fade away, but you can also think of it as controlling how big the artificial environment will be. It works in conjunction with the Room Size parameter. The lower the Decay Time, the smaller the environment, and vice versa. So, if you want to make your audio sound like it's playing in a small room, a good Decay Time might be about 0.5 seconds. If you want to make your audio sound like it's playing in a large area, a good Decay Time might be about 3 seconds.

6. Set the Pre Delay parameter. This parameter is similar to the Decay Time parameter, except that the Pre Delay determines the time between when your audio is first heard and when the reverb effect begins. This gives you even more control in determining your artificial environment. For small spaces, use a low setting (such as 1 millisecond). For large spaces, use a high setting (such as 70 milliseconds).

7. Set the High Frequency Rolloff and High Frequency Decay parameters. If you think these parameters look like equalization

settings, you're right. Using these parameters also helps to create more authentic environment simulations because smaller, closed environments tend to stifle some frequencies of the audio spectrum, and larger environments usually sound brighter, meaning they promote more of the frequencies.

When you set the High Frequency Rolloff parameter (in Hz), any frequencies below that frequency are allowed to pass and any frequencies above that frequency are cut. Setting the High Frequency Decay parameter determines how quickly the high frequencies above the High Frequency Rolloff are cut as the reverberation sounds. For examples on how to set these parameters, be sure to take a look at some of the included presets.

8. Set the Density parameter. This parameter determines the "thickness" of the reverberation. Experiment with it to hear what I mean.

9. Set the Motion Depth and Motion Rate parameters. In a real environment, reverberation is constantly changing as it sounds. It isn't static at all. The reverberant echoes actually move around the environment, which is what gives the environment a distinct sound. You can simulate this movement using the Motion Depth and Motion Rate parameters. The Motion Depth parameter determines how much movement there is and the Motion Rate parameter determines the speed of that movement. For examples on how to set these parameters, be sure to take a look at some of the included presets.

10. Set the Level parameter, which controls the overall volume level of the effect output.

11. Click on the Audition button to test the current parameter settings. Make further adjustments if necessary.

12. Set the appropriate options under the Mixing tab.

13. If you want to use the current settings at a later time, save them as a preset.

14. Click on OK.

SONAR processes the data by applying the effect according to the parameter settings you specified.

Dynamics

SONAR includes a number of effects that allow you to apply dynamic processing to your audio data, including compression and limiting. What does that mean? Well, one way to explain it would be to talk about taming vocal recordings. Let's say you recorded this vocalist who can really belt out a tune but doesn't have very good microphone technique. When he sings, he just stays in one place in front of the mike. Professional singers know that during the quiet parts of the song, they need to sing up close to the mike, and during the loud parts, they need to back away so that an even amplitude level is recorded. If a singer doesn't do this, the amplitude of your recorded audio will be very uneven. That's where compression and limiting comes in. Compression allows you to "squash" the audio signal so that the amplitude levels are more even. Limiting allows you to stop the amplitude of the audio signal from rising past a certain level to prevent clipping. This can happen if the performer sings too loudly. I'll talk about each of the available effects one at a time.

Compressor

The Compressor effect allows you to apply compression to your audio data. The effect works as follows:

1. Select the audio data that you want to process.

2. Choose Edit > Audio Effects > Compressor to open the Compressor dialog box (see Figure 11.22).

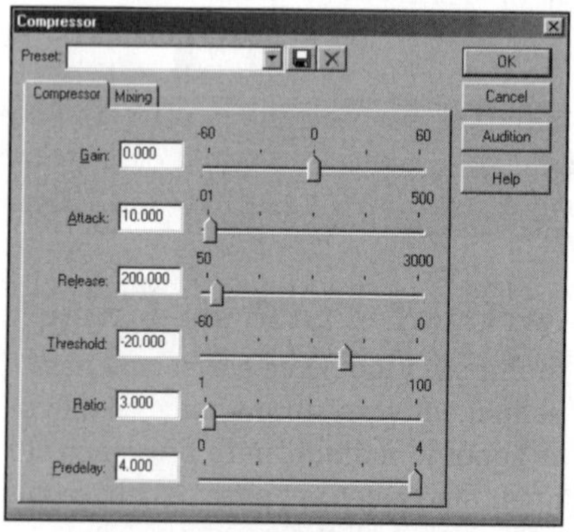

Figure 11.22
Use the Compressor effect to apply compression to your audio data.

3. Set the Threshold parameter. The Compressor effect uses a digital noise gate to identify the parts of your audio data that should be processed. The Threshold parameter determines at what amplitude level your audio data will start being compressed. When the amplitude of your audio data reaches the Threshold level, processing begins.

4. Set the Ratio parameter. This parameter determines how much processing is done to your audio data. A ratio of 1 means no processing is done. A ratio of 100 means that the audio is fully processed.

5. Set the Attack parameter. This parameter determines how quickly after the input level has reached the threshold that processing is applied. For example, if the input level reaches the threshold, it doesn't have to be compressed right away. A slow attack means the signal won't be compressed unless it lasts for a while. This is a good way to make sure fast, percussive parts are left alone, but long,

drawn-out parts are compressed. The Predelay parameter works in conjunction with the Attack parameter by delaying the processing when the input signal is first detected.

6. Set the Release parameter. This parameter determines how quickly after the input level goes below the threshold that processing is stopped (or the digital noise gate is closed). If you set the Release parameter too low, your audio could be cut off. A longer Release allows processing to sound more natural. You'll have to experiment to get to the right setting.

7. Set the Gain parameter. This parameter allows you to adjust the overall amplitude of your audio after it is processed.

8. Click on the Audition button to test the current parameter settings. Make further adjustments if necessary.

9. Set the appropriate options under the Mixing tab.

10. If you want to use the current settings at a later time, save them as a preset.

11. Click on OK.

SONAR processes the data by applying the effect according to the parameter settings you specified.

FX Compressor/Gate

The FX Compressor/Gate effect is similar to the Compressor effect, but it provides better quality processing and more features. Here is how it works:

1. Select the audio data that you want to process.

2. Choose Edit > Audio Effects > Cakewalk > FX Compressor/Gate to open the FX Compressor/Gate dialog box (see Figure 11.23). The dialog displays a graph. The right side of the graph shows output amplitude and the bottom of the graph shows input amplitude. Inside the graph is a line representing the input amplitude and output amplitude as they relate to each other. Initially, the line is drawn diagonally, and you "read" it from left to right. This shows a 1:1 ratio between input and output amplitudes, meaning as the input level goes up 1 dB, the output level also goes up 1 dB.

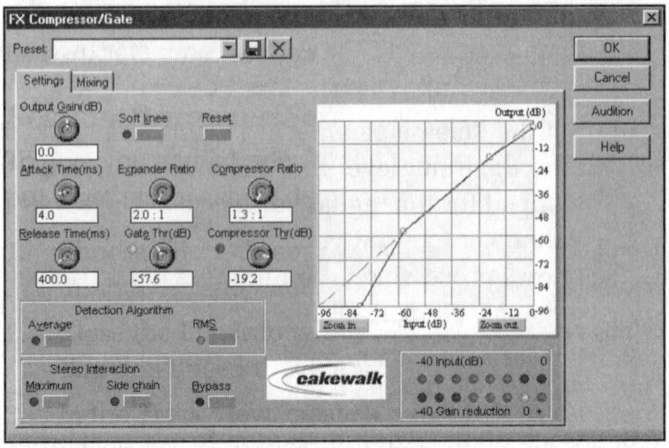

Figure 11.23
The FX
Compressor/Gate
provides high quality
compression with some
extra features.

3. Set the Compressor Thr (threshold) parameter. This parameter works the same way as the Threshold parameter in the Compressor effect.

4. Set the Compressor Ratio parameter. This parameter works the same way as the Ratio parameter in the Compressor Effect, except the values are numbered differently. A ratio of 1:1 means no processing is done. A ratio of 2:1 means that for every 2 dB increase in input amplitude, there is only a 1 dB increase in output amplitude. Thus, the amplitude is being compressed. If you set the Ratio parameter to its highest value (Inf:1), that causes limiting, so no matter how loud the input amplitude gets, it is limited to the level set by the Threshold parameter. I'll talk more about limiting later.

5. Set the Attack Time parameter. This parameter works the same way as the Attack parameter in the Compressor effect.

6. Set the Release Time parameter. This parameter works the same way as the Release parameter in the Compressor effect.

7. In addition to being able to compress audio data, the FX Compressor/Gate effect can cut out noises using a special noise gate (hence the name Compressor/Gate). By setting the Gate Thr (threshold) parameter, you can remove any unwanted noises that have an amplitude level that falls below the threshold. This is great for removing bad notes or string noise on guitar parts, for instance. Setting the Expander Ratio determines how soft the amplitudes below the Gate Thr will be made. For example, if you set the Expander Ratio to 100:1, then any sounds that fall below the Gate Thr will be cut out completely.

8. Set the Detection Algorithm parameter. This parameter establishes how the FX Compressor/Gate effect will determine the amplitude level of the incoming audio signal. Choosing the Average option tells the Effect to determine the average value of the input signal and use that to apply compression appropriately. Choosing the RMS (root mean square) option tells the Effect to determine the perceived loudness (as a listener would hear it over a period of time) of the input signal and use that to apply compression appropriately. The best method to use depends on the material being processed. You'll need to experiment to see which one works better.

9. Set the Stereo Interaction parameter. Choose the Maximum option to apply compression to both stereo channels equally. Choose the Side Chain option to apply compression only to the right channel of the stereo signal, while using the left channel signal to activate the threshold. This option can be used as a *ducking* effect, which can come in handy if you have music playing in the right channel and a voice-over playing in the left channel. As the voice comes in, the music is lowered so that listeners can hear the voice over the background music. For most applications, you'll want to use the Maximum option.

10. Activate the Soft Knee option to give a smoother transition as the input signal starts to be compressed.

11. Set the Output Gain parameter. This parameter allows you to adjust the overall amplitude of your audio after it is processed.

12. Click on the Audition button to test the current parameter settings. Make further adjustments if necessary.

13. Set the appropriate options under the Mixing tab.

14. If you want to use the current settings at a later time, save them as a preset.

15. Click on OK.

SONAR processes the data by applying the effect according to the parameter settings you specified.

FX Expander/Gate

Like the special noise gate option in the FX Compressor/Gate effect, the FX Expander/Gate effect allows you to cut out unwanted noises below a certain amplitude threshold. This effect takes less CPU processing power for those times when you don't need compression. Here is how it works:

1. Select the audio data that you want to process.

2. Choose Edit > Audio Effects > FX Expander/Gate to open the FX Expander/Gate dialog box (see Figure 11.24). The dialog box displays a graph. This graph is the same as the one in the FX Compressor/Gate effect.

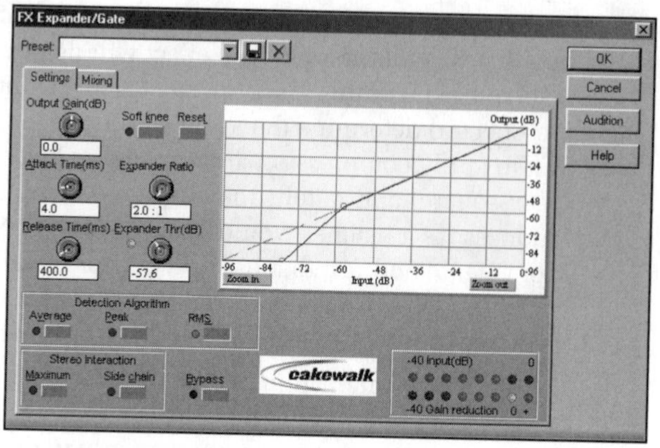

Figure 11.24
Use the FX
Expander/Gate effect to
remove low volume
noises from your audio
data.

3. Set the Expander Thr (threshold) parameter. This parameter works the same as the Gate Thr parameter in the FX Compressor/Gate effect.

4. Set the Expander Ratio parameter. This parameter works the same as the Expander Ratio parameter in the FX Compressor/Gate effect.

5. Set the Attack Time parameter. This parameter works the same as the Attack Time parameter in the FX Compressor/Gate effect.

6. Set the Release Time parameter. This parameter works the same as the Release Time parameter in the FX Compressor/Gate effect.

7. Set the Detection Algorithm parameter. This parameter works the same as the Detection Algorithm parameter in the FX Compressor/Gate effect, except there is one additional option. Choosing the Peak option tells the effect to determine the peak value of the input signal and use that to apply processing appropriately.

8. Set the Stereo Interaction parameter. This parameter works the same as the Stereo Interaction parameter in the FX Compressor/Gate effect.

9. Activate the Soft Knee option to give a smoother transition as the input signal starts to be processed.

10. Set the Output Gain parameter. This parameter allows you to adjust the overall amplitude of your audio after it is processed.

11. Click on the Audition button to test the current parameter settings. Make further adjustments if necessary.

12. Set the appropriate options under the Mixing tab.

13. If you want to use the current settings at a later time, save them as a preset.

14. Click on OK.

SONAR processes the data by applying the effect according to the parameter settings you specified.

FX Limiter

The FX Limiter effect allows you to stop an audio signal from getting any louder than a specified amplitude level. This effect can be put to good use during recording to prevent your input signal from getting too high and causing distortion or clipping. Here is how the effect works:

1. Select the audio you want to process.

2. Choose Edit > Audio Effects > Cakewalk > FX Limiter to open the FX Limiter dialog box (see Figure 11.25).

Figure 11.25
Use the FX Limiter effect to prevent an audio signal from getting too loud.

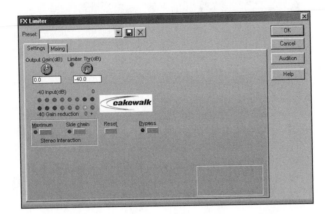

3. Set the Limiter Thr (threshold) parameter. This is the level that you don't want your audio signal level to go above. This means that the amplitude of the audio won't be able to get any higher than this value.

4. Set the Stereo Interaction parameter. I explained this parameter earlier.

5. Set the Output Gain parameter. This parameter allows you to adjust the overall amplitude of your audio after it is processed.

6. Click on the Audition button to test the current parameter settings. Make further adjustments if necessary.

7. Set the appropriate options under the Mixing tab.

8. If you want to use the current settings at a later time, save them as a preset.

9. Click on OK.

SONAR processes the data by applying the effect according to the parameter settings you specified.

FX Dynamics Processor

The FX Dynamics Processor effect (see Figure 11.26) combines all of the features of the previous dynamics effects into one. This means that this one effect can perform all of the functions of the FX Compressor/Gate, FX Expander/Gate, and FX Limiter effects. It also has the same parameter settings, which all work the same as in the previously described effects. Please review the previous sections in order to learn how to operate the parameters of this effect.

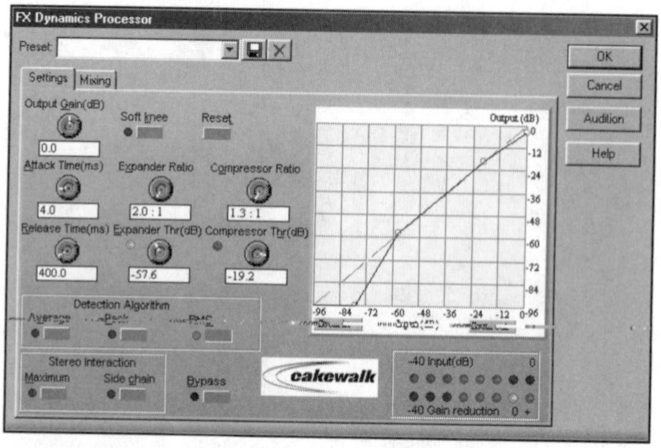

Figure 11.26
The FX Dynamics Processor combines all of the features of the other dynamics Effects.

Distortion

Most of the time, bad-sounding audio isn't something that you want. Distortion is something you usually try to avoid when recording audio data. But sometimes distortion can be a good thing (as Martha Stewart would say). For example, if you want to dress up a guitar part for a rock song, adding a bit of distortion can make it sound really cool. Or maybe you want to add a bit of "grit" to a vocal part. Using the Distortion effect, you can achieve these sounds, and here's how:

1. Select the audio data that you want to process.

2. Choose Edit > Audio Effects > Distortion to open the Distortion dialog box (see Figure 11.27).

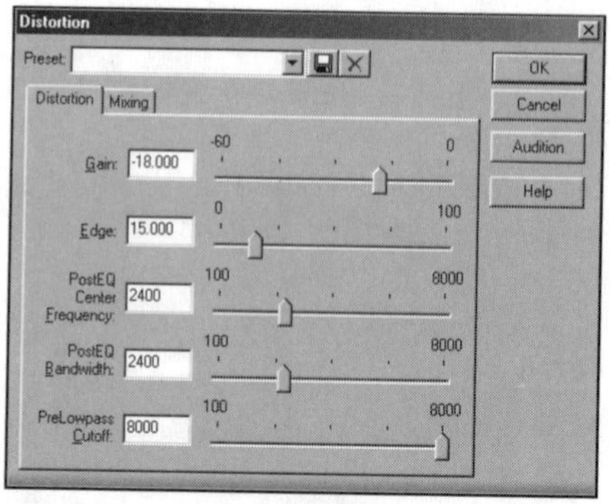

Figure 11.27
Use the Distortion effect to add distortion to your audio data.

3. Set the Edge parameter. This parameter determines by how much your audio data will be distorted. A low level means less distortion. A high level means more distortion.

4. Set the PostEQ Center Frequency and PostEQ Bandwidth parameters. These parameters allow you to apply equalization to the output signal of the Distortion effect. Using these parameters, you can achieve different sounding distortion effects. You'll need to experiment with them.

5. Set the PreLowpass Cutoff parameter. Any frequencies above the frequency you set for this parameter will be cut from the audio signal. You can use this to reduce the "harshness" that sometimes accompanies distorted audio so that you can achieve more of an effect rather than noise.

6. Set the Gain parameter. This controls the overall volume of the effect.

CAUTION

Don't set the Gain too high, because the distortion may damage your speakers (or ears, if you're using headphones). Start off with a nice low level when you are auditioning this Effect.

7. Click on the Audition button to test the current parameter settings. Make further adjustments if necessary.

8. Set the appropriate options under the Mixing tab.

9. If you want to use the current settings at a later time, save them as a preset.

10. Click on OK.

SONAR processes the data by applying the effect according to the parameter settings you specified.

Gargle

The Gargle effect provides something that is known as amplitude modulation. The effect modulates (or "vibrates") the amplitude (or volume) of your audio data. With this effect, you can achieve sounds such as the tremolo on an electronic organ. Here is how the Gargle effect works:

1. Select the audio data that you want to process.

2. Choose Edit > Audio Effects > Gargle to open the Gargle dialog box (see Figure 11.28).

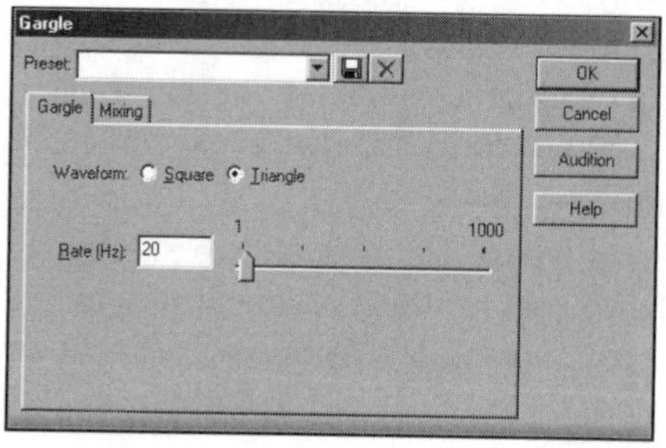

Figure 11.28
The Gargle effect lets you modulate the amplitude of your audio data.

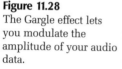

3. Set the Waveform parameter. Choose the Square option for a "harsh" sounding amplitude modulation. Choose the Triangle option for a "smooth" sounding amplitude modulation.

4. Set the Rate parameter. For a tremolo effect, use a low value, such as 7. For a very weird "ringing" effect, use a high value, such as 800.

5. Click on the Audition button to test the current parameter settings. Make further adjustments if necessary.

6. Set the appropriate options under the Mixing tab.

7. If you want to use the current settings at a later time, save them as a preset.

8. Click on OK.

SONAR processes the data by applying the effect according to the parameter settings you specified.

Changing Time and Pitch

In addition to the Length and Transpose editing features, SONAR provides the Pitch Shifter and Time/Pitch Stretch effects, which you also can use to change the length and pitch of your audio data. The effects, however, are more powerful and flexible. This is especially true of the Time/Pitch Stretch effect.

Pitch Shifter

The Pitch Shifter effect provides low quality, but it doesn't take up as much CPU processing power. In case you want to try out the Cakewalk FX Pitch Shifter, here's how it works:

1. Select the audio data that you want to process.

2. Select Edit > Audio Effects > Cakewalk > Pitch Shifter to open the Pitch Shifter dialog box (see Figure 11.29).

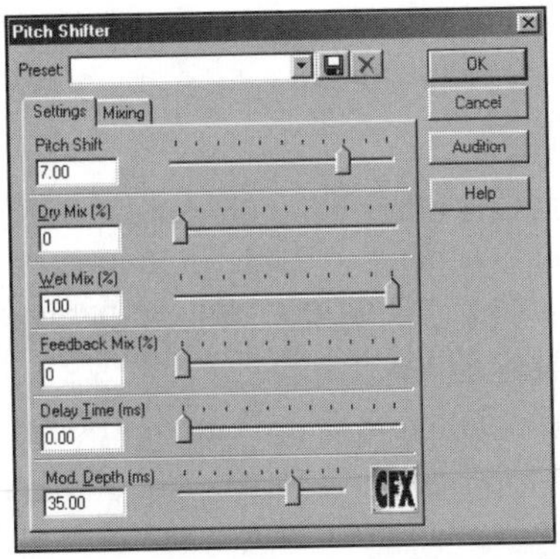

Figure 11.29
The Pitch Shifter doesn't provide very good sound quality. For better quality, use the Time/Pitch Stretch effect.

3. Under the Settings tab, set the Pitch Shift parameter. It is exactly the same as the Amount parameter in the Transpose editing function. You can use it to transpose the pitch of your audio data from −12 to +12 semitones (a whole octave down or up).

> **TIP**
> Normally, when you change the pitch of audio data, the length is altered, too. Raise the pitch and the data gets shorter, lower the pitch and the data gets longer. When this happens, though, the processed audio no longer plays in sync with the other data in your project. Luckily, you can use SONAR's pitch shifting effects to change pitch without changing the length of the audio data. The only problem to be weary of is that pitch shifting can produce unwanted artifacts if you use too large an interval. The famous Alvin & the Chipmunks were a product of this phenomenon. It's best to stay within an interval of a major third (four semitones) up or down if possible.

4. Set the Dry Mix and Wet Mix parameters. I explained these parameters earlier in the chapter, but in reference to pitch shifting, you should almost always keep the Dry Mix set to 0 percent and the Wet Mix set to 100 percent.

5. As far as the Feedback Mix, Delay Time, and Mod Depth parameters are concerned, they don't seem to have anything to do with the Cakewalk FX Pitch Shifter effect. Changing these parameters only introduces unwanted artifacts into the sound. My advice is to simply leave them set at their default values: Feedback Mix = 0, Delay Time = 0, and Mod Depth = 35.

6. Click on the Audition button to test the current parameter settings. Make further adjustments if necessary.

7. Set the appropriate options under the Mixing tab.

8. If you want to use the current settings at a later time, save them as a preset.

9. Click on OK.

CHAPTER 11

SONAR processes the data by applying the effect according to the parameter settings you specified.

Time/Pitch Stretch

The Time/Pitch Stretch effect is much more advanced and flexible, and it provides better quality than the Pitch Shifter effect. That doesn't mean it's difficult to use. Some of the more advanced parameters can be a bit confusing, but I'll go over them one at a time. The effect works like this:

1. Select the audio data that you want to process.

2. Select Edit > Audio Effects > Cakewalk > Time/Pitch Stretch to open the Time/Pitch Stretch dialog box (see Figure 11.30).

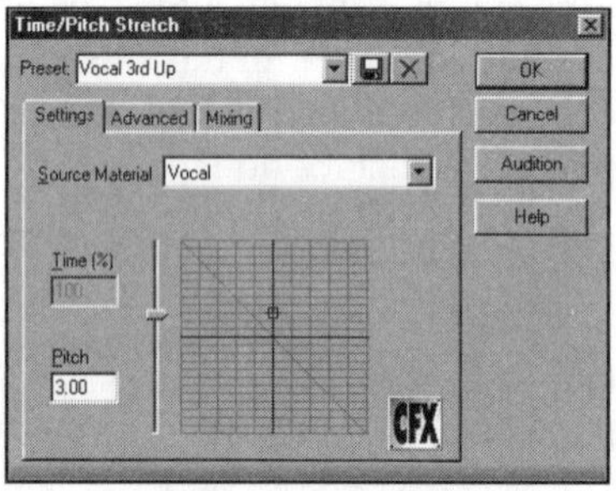

Figure 11.30
The Time/Pitch Stretch effect provides advanced time stretching and pitch shifting capabilities.

3. Under the Settings tab, set the Source Material parameter. One of the reasons the Time/Pitch Stretch effect provides better quality than the Pitch Shifter effect is that it takes into account the type of audio data you are processing. You should select the appropriate value for the Source Material parameter according to the type of data you want to process. For instance, if you are processing percussion data, you should set the Source Material parameter to Drums. If you can't find an appropriate setting in the supplied list, just set the Source Material parameter to Generic. This setting still usually provides good results.

4. Set the Time parameter. Using the Time parameter, you can change the length of your audio data as a percentage. If you want to make the data shorter, set the Time parameter to a percentage smaller than 100. For example, to make the data half of its original length, use a setting of 50 percent. If you want to make the data longer, set the Time parameter to a percentage larger than 100. For example, if you want to make data the twice its original length, use a setting of 200 percent. To change the Time parameter, just type a value or use the horizontal slider.

TIP

I mentioned earlier that, when you're transposing audio, it's best to stay within a major third (four semitones) up or down if possible, because audio doesn't react very well to higher values. Well, the same concept applies when you're changing the length of audio data. You should try to say within 10 percent longer or shorter if possible; otherwise, the results may not sound very good. This is another feature you have to experiment with.

5. Set the Pitch parameter. Using the Pitch parameter, you can transpose your audio data up or down one octave (in semitones). To change the Pitch parameter, just type a value or use the vertical slider.

TIP

Notice that a graph is shown in the Time/Pitch Stretch dialog box. Using this graph, you can change the Time and Pitch parameters by dragging the small blue square. Drag the square up or down to change the Pitch parameter. Drag the square left or right to change the Time parameter. Also, if you hold down the Shift key on your computer keyboard at the same time, the square automatically snaps to the exact grid points on the graph.

6. Under the Advanced tab, you'll see three parameters called Block Rate, Overlap Ratio, and Crossfade Ratio. These very advanced settings are used by the Time/Pitch Stretch effect to determine how your data will be processed. Luckily, you don't have to deal with them because they are automatically set to the appropriate values according to the setting you use for the Source Material parameter. So, basically, don't worry about them.

7. You'll also notice two other parameters under the Advanced tab: Accuracy and Algorithm. These parameters you do need to deal with. The Accuracy parameter determines the quality of the effect processing. If you set the Accuracy parameter to High, you'll get better quality out of the Effect, but it will also take longer to process your data. The Algorithm parameter is strictly for use when you're processing audio data containing vocals. If you're processing any other kind of material, you should leave the Algorithm parameter set to Normal. In the case of vocal material, though, setting the Algorithm parameter to Formant Preserving tells the effect to preserve the original vocal characteristics when transposing the pitch up or down. Without the Algorithm parameter set to Formant Preserving, transposing your vocal material up can make it sound like Alvin & The Chipmunks, and transposing it down can make it sound like Fat Albert.

8. Click on the Audition button to test the current parameter settings. Make further adjustments if necessary.

CHAPTER 11

9. Set the appropriate options under the Mixing tab.

10. If you want to use the current settings at a later time, save them as a preset.

11. Click on OK.

SONAR processes the data by applying the effect according to the parameter settings you specified.

Amplifier Simulation

For all you electric guitar players out there, SONAR provides the Amp Sim effect. Using this effect, you can simulate the sound of real-life guitar amplifiers, making your recorded guitar audio data sound like it's being played through different kinds of amps. To achieve this sound, the effect uses technology called *physical modeling*. In this technology, the characteristics of a real instrument or device are converted into a mathematical algorithm (called a *model*). The model can then be used to apply those same characteristics to your audio data to achieve more authentic sounding recordings. This explanation of the process is simplified, of course, but that's the gist of it. The Amp Sim effect works like this:

1. Select the audio data that you want to process.

> **TIP**
>
> Even though the Amp Sim effect was designed for guitar amplifiers, that doesn't mean you can't use it on other types of data. The distorted sounds the Effect produces also work well on vocals, especially if you're looking for that hard rock sound. Check out some of the music by Kid Rock to hear what I mean.

2. Select Edit > Audio Effects > Cakewalk > Amp Sim to open the Amp Sim dialog box (see Figure 11.31).

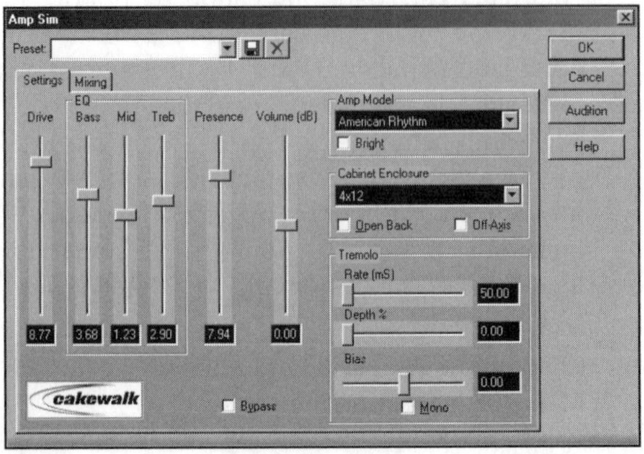

Figure 11.31
Using the Amp Sim effect, you can simulate your music being played through different kinds of guitar amplifiers.

3. Under the Settings tab in the Amp Model section, select the type of guitar amplifier you want to simulate. An additional parameter called Bright also is available in this section. It is similar to the Brightness switch found on many guitar amplifiers. It makes the effect sound brighter by boosting the high frequencies (everything above 500 Hz) of the audio spectrum.

4. In the Cabinet Enclosure section, select the type of cabinet you want to use for your virtual guitar amplifier. By setting this parameter, you can simulate different types of speaker enclosures. You have four options to choose from: No Speaker, 1×12, 2×12, 4×10 and 4×12. If you choose the No Speaker option, the effect sounds as though you plugged your guitar directly into the output of the amplifier and recorded the sound without using a microphone or the amplifier speakers. If you choose any of the other options, the effect sounds as though you played your guitar through an amplifier that has a certain number of speakers of a certain size and recorded the output by placing a microphone in front of the amp. For example, if you choose 4x12, the simulated amp would contain four speakers each at 12 inches in size. Also, when you select the other options, two other parameters become available: Open Back and Off-Axis. Activating the Open Back parameter makes the effect simulate a guitar amplifier that has a cabinet enclosure with an open (rather than a closed) back. Activating the Off-Axis parameter makes the effect sound as though you placed the virtual microphone (mentioned earlier) off to the side of the amplifier speaker rather than directly in front of it.

5. In the Tremolo section, set the Rate and Depth parameters. Setting these parameters allows you to add a "warble" type of sound to the effect. The Rate parameter controls the speed of the tremolo, and the Depth parameter controls how much tremolo is added. There is also a bias control (like that found on most guitar amps) that lets you determine if the tremolo will add to the volume level of the effect or subtract from the volume level of the effect. In addition, by activating the Mono option, the tremolo will produce a mono output rather than stereo.

6. Set the Bass, Mid, and Treb parameters in the EQ section. These parameters act similarly to the parameters in SONAR's Graphic EQ editing feature (which I discussed in Chapter 8). Each parameter enables you to cut or boost a specific frequency by −10 or +10 dB. The Bass parameter is set to 60 Hz, the Mid parameter is set to 600 kHz, and the Treb parameter is set to 6000 kHz.

7. Set the Drive parameter. This parameter basically controls how much distortion is added to the audio data being processing.

8. Set the Presence parameter. This parameter acts like a high-pass EQ with a permanent frequency of 750 Hz. You can use it to boost some of the higher frequencies of the effect, giving it more "presence."

9. Set the Volume parameter. This parameter controls the overall volume of the effect. No Dry Mix or Wet Mix parameters are available for this effect, so you hear only the totally processed signal through this one.

10. Click on the Audition button to test the current parameter settings. Make further adjustments if necessary.

11. Set the appropriate options under the Mixing tab.

12. If you want to use the current settings at a later time, save them as a preset.

13. Click on OK.

SONAR processes the data by applying the effect according to the parameter settings you specified.

TIP

SONAR provides a "lite" version of the Amp Sim effect, called Amp Sim Lite. The lite version provides the exact same features, except there is no tremolo processing available. The Amp Sim Lite Effect can be useful if you want to apply amplifier simulation in real-time but not use as much CPU processing power as the Amp Sim effect. Access the Amp Sim Lite effect by choosing Edit > Audio Effects > Cakewalk > Amp Sim Lite.

Analog Tape Simulation

Similar to the Amp Sim effect, the FX2 Tape SimeEffect uses physical modeling to simulate a realistic audio situation. But instead of simulating the sound of a guitar amplifier, the FX2 Tape Sim effect simulates the sound of your audio data being played off an analog tape deck. Why would you want to simulate old recording technology, especially when you have the clean and crisp sound of digital recording? Well, analog tape recording provides a sort of "warm" sound that can't be produced with digital recording, and that sound can be used to create authentic jazz or blues recordings. And some musicians just prefer the warm sound of analog as opposed to the crisp sound of digital. The FX2 Tape Sim effect lets you achieve that warm sound, and here is how it works:

1. Select the audio data that you want to process.

2. Choose Edit > Audio Effects > Cakewalk > FX2 Tape Sim to open the FX2 Tape Sim dialog box (see Figure 11.32).

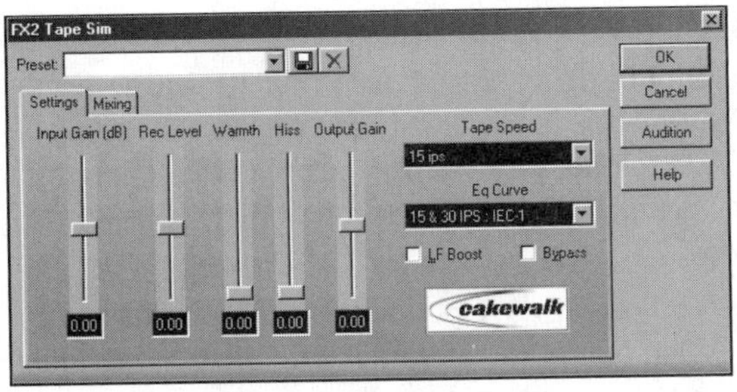

Figure 11.32
Use the FX2 Tape Sim effect to simulate the warm sound of analog tape recordings.

3. Choose the type of tape machine you would like to simulate by setting the Tape Speed and Eq Curve parameters. An additional parameter called LF Boost is available, which lets you add a small increase to the lower frequencies of the audio data, giving it an even "warmer" sound.

4. Set the Input Gain parameter. This parameter controls how loud the input signal into the effect will be. Usually, you'll just want to keep it set at 0 dB.

5. Set the Rec (short for Record) Level parameter. This parameter lets you control the level of the audio that would be recorded in an actual tape recording situation. Setting this parameter too high will cause distortion.

6. Set the Warmth parameter. This parameter controls that "warmth" sound I talked about earlier.

7. Set the Hiss parameter. As in an actual tape recording situation, you usually get tape hiss. If you want to be totally authentic in your simulation, you can use this parameter to add hiss to your audio data. A setting of 0 will turn the Hiss parameter off.

8. Set the Output Gain parameter. This parameter controls the overall volume of the effect. No Dry Mix or Wet Mix parameters are available for this effect, so you hear only the totally processed signal through this one.

9. Click on the Audition button to test the current parameter settings. Make further adjustments if necessary.

10. Set the appropriate options under the Mixing tab.

11. If you want to use the current settings at a later time, save them as a preset.

12. Click on OK.

SONAR processes the data by applying the effect according to the parameter settings you specified.

CHAPTER 11

An Effects Exercise

Before I begin talking about SONAR's MIDI effects, I thought it might be nice to work through a simple exercise on applying some of the audio effects to one of the sample projects that comes with SONAR. This way, you get a chance to hear some of the effects in action. Just follow these steps:

1. Choose File > Open, choose the Don't Matter Audio and MIDI Demo.bun file, and click on Open to open that sample project.

2. Close the File Info window and the Staff view. You don't need them right now.

3. In the Track view, select Tracks 1, 8, and 9. Then select Track > Delete to delete those tracks. They are MIDI tracks, and you don't need them for this exercise.

4. Add a little echo to the end of the horn tracks so that it trails off after the rest of the music stops playing. To do so, select the last clip in Track 5 (Horns Left) and the last clip in Track 6 (Horns Right). Then choose Edit > Audio Effects > Cakewalk > Delay. Choose the preset called 98bpm Delay to automatically set the parameters for the effect. Under the Mixing tab, be sure the Process In-Place, Mono Result option is activated. Click on OK.

> **TIP**
>
> If you want the delay effect on the horns to trail off at the end of the song, slip edit the ends of both of the clips that you just processed so that the ends of the clips extend to around the second beat in measure 9.

5. To make the horn tracks a little fuller, choose Edit > Select > None to get rid of the current data selection. Then select Tracks 5 and 6 entirely so that you can process all the data in the tracks. Choose Edit > Audio Effects > Cakewalk > Chorus. Choose the preset called Chorus Gtr to automatically set the parameters for the effect. Under the Mixing tab, be sure the Process In-Place, Mono Result option is activated. Click on OK.

6. The guitar track might sound nice with a bit of amp simulation applied to it, so select Track 4 (Guitar), and then choose Edit > Audio Effects > Cakewalk > Amp Sim. Choose the preset called American Lead to automatically set the parameters for the effect. Click on OK.

7. The drum and bass tracks sound fine, but you can simulate the entire project being played in another environment by selecting all the tracks (1 through 6). Then choose Edit > Audio Effects > Cakewalk > Reverb. Choose the preset called Vocal Med. Room. Under the Mixing tab, be sure the Process In-Place, Mono Result option is activated. Click on OK.

8. Play the project to hear what it sounds like.

The result is quite a bit different from the original, isn't it? Personally, I think the amp simulation effect on the guitar is too harsh, but that can easily be changed. As a matter of fact, you can do anything you want. Don't be afraid to experiment to see what the different effects sound like. With judicious application of effects, you can make your music sound more professional. Just remember not to go overboard. And as with everything else in life, the more you practice, the better you become.

MIDI Effects

SONAR provides one set of eight MIDI effects, a couple of which (Chord Analyzer and Session Drummer) are not really effects—but I'll get into that later. It also provides a few third-party plug-ins from MusicLab, Inc. (**http://www.musiclab.com/**) and NTONYX Ltd. (**http://www.ntonyx.com/**). Some of them are "lite" versions. You can buy the full versions and other MIDI plug-ins from these vendors, too.

Like the audio effects, some of the MIDI effects mimic some of SONAR's editing features. Again, they have this capability so that you can process your data with these features in real-time. You cannot use SONAR's editing features in real-time because they aren't plug-ins. In addition, the effects provide more power and flexibility, and they include additional parameters not found in the editing features, so I'll go over them here for you step by step.

NOTE

As I mentioned earlier, because I've already covered how to apply effects offline and in real-time, I'm just going to include the basic offline steps (along with parameter descriptions) in each of the following explanations. For detailed step-by-step procedures for applying effects offline and in real-time, refer to the previous sections in this chapter.

Automatic Arpeggios

In music, you can play the notes of a chord in a number of different ways. Most often, the notes are played all at once. You can also play them one at a time in sequence; this is called an arpeggio. SONAR's Arpeggiator effect automatically creates arpeggios for each note or chord in your selected MIDI data. Depending on how you set the parameters, however, you can achieve some very strange and interesting "melodies." This feature works as follows:

1. Select the MIDI data that you want to process.

2. Choose Edit > MIDI Effects > Cakewalk FX > Arpeggiator to open the Arpeggiator dialog box (see Figure 11.33).

CHAPTER 11

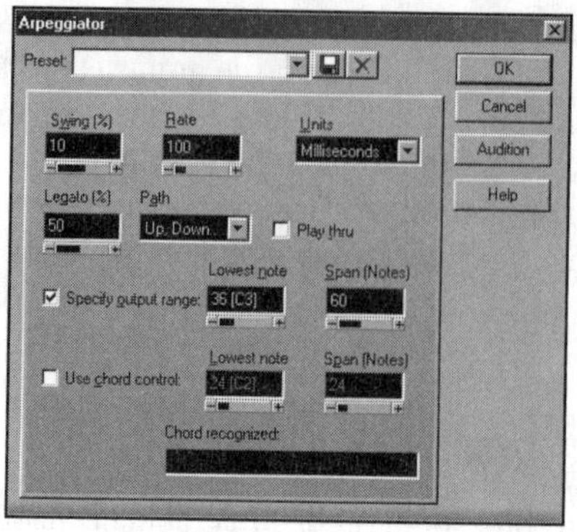

Figure 11.33

The Arpeggiator effect automatically converts your selected MIDI data into arpeggios.

3. Set the Swing parameter. This parameter works the same way as the Swing parameter in the Quantize editing feature (which I talked about in Chapter 8). The only difference is that of 50 percent being the normal setting (meaning no "swing" is applied); in this case, 0 percent is the normal setting. And you can set this Swing parameter from –100 to +100 percent. More often than not, you'll want to keep it set to 0 percent.

4. Set the Rate and Units parameters. These two parameters work together. The Rate parameter determines the amount of time between each note in the arpeggio. The Units parameter determines what units you want to use to set the Rate parameter. You can set the Rate parameter in notes, ticks, or milliseconds. By setting the Units parameter to Notes, you can easily synchronize the notes in the arpeggio to a certain note value so that you know they will play in sync with the rest of the music in your project.

5. Set the Legato parameter. This parameter determines the duration of the notes in the arpeggio. If you set the Legato parameter to 1 percent (the lowest value), the notes in the arpeggio are played with a very short duration (as in a staccato fashion in which the note is played and let go very quickly). If you set the Legato parameter to 99 percent (the highest value), the notes in the arpeggio are played with a very long duration. To be exact, each note plays until the start of the next note in the arpeggio.

6. Set the Path parameter. This parameter determines the direction in which the notes in the arpeggio will be played. If you select Up, Up, the notes in the arpeggio consecutively go up in pitch. If you select Up, Down, the notes in the arpeggio first go up in pitch and then come back down. If you select Down, Down, the notes in the arpeggio consecutively go down in pitch. If you select Down, Up, the notes in the arpeggio first go down in pitch and then come back up.

7. Set the Play Thru option. If you activate the Play Thru option, your original data remains intact and plays along with the new arpeggio data. If you deactivate the Play Thru option, only the arpeggio data remains, and your original data is removed.

8. Set the Specify Output Range option, along with the Lowest Note and Span (Notes) parameters. If you activate the Specify output range option, additional notes are added so that the arpeggio will play smoothly over each octave in the range you specify. Otherwise, only your original is used to create the arpeggio. The Lowest note parameter determines the lowest note that will be included in the arpeggio. The Span (Notes) parameter determines the number of half-steps in the range (from 12 to 127).

9. Set the Use Chord Control option, along with the Lowest Note and Span (Notes) parameters. If you activate the Use chord control option, the Arpeggiator effect first analyzes the original data that falls in the range you specify, and it guesses at what chord is being played. If you use the effect in real-time mode, the name of the chord that is guessed is shown in the Chord Recognized field. The effect uses the recognized chord to create the notes for the arpeggio (meaning the notes in the arpeggio are based on the recognized chord).

10. Click on the Audition button to test the current parameter settings. Make further adjustments if necessary.

11. If you want to use the current settings at a later time, save them as a preset.

12. Click on OK.

SONAR processes the data by applying the effect according to the parameter settings you specified.

I know the parameter settings for the Arpeggiator effect can be a bit confusing. Sometimes it's difficult to tell what the results will be after you apply the effect. Basically, they'll be different depending on the data that you process. You'll have to experiment. But just to give you a quick idea of what can be done with the effect, try the following example:

1. Select File > Open, select the file called Ballad #1.wrk, and click on Open to open that sample project.

2. Increase the Vel+ parameter for Track 3 (piano) to somewhere between 30 and 100. This setting makes it a bit louder so that you can hear the changes being made to it above the other instruments in the project.

3. Play the project to see what the original data in Track 3 sounds like.

4. Select Track 3.

CHAPTER 11

5. Choose Edit > MIDI Effects > Cakewalk FX > Arpeggiator.

6. Choose the preset called Bouncing.

7. Click on OK.

8. Play the project again.

Sounds cool, huh? SONAR has taken the original data in Track 3 and turned it into an arpeggio. By the way, this effect usually works best on this type of slow, chord-based data. Of course, you can try it out on faster, different kinds of data. Like I said, be sure to experiment with it.

Chord Analysis

Earlier, I mentioned that a couple of the MIDI effects aren't really effects at all. The Chord Analyzer is one of them. This effect doesn't do anything to your data, meaning it doesn't make any changes. The Chord Analyzer simply looks at your data and guesses what kind of chord is being played. Personally, I haven't found much use for it. If you don't already know the chords being used in your song, how are you writing the music?

But just in case you're interested, here's how the effect works:

> **NOTE**
>
> Although you can use the Chord Analyzer effect offline, it works best in real-time as your project is playing. Therefore, I'll go through the real-time procedure here instead of the offline procedure.

1. In the Track view, right-click in the Fx field of the track to which you want to add an effect.

2. Choose MIDI Effects > Cakewalk FX > Chord Analyzer to add the Chord Analyzer to the list.

3. The Chord Analyzer window opens (see Figure 11.34).

Figure 11.34
The Chord Analyzer is best used in real-time.

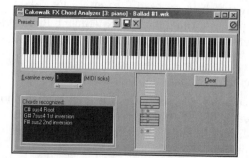

4. Set the Examine every parameter. Using this parameter, you can control how often the Chord Analyzer effect analyzes your data. The lower the number, the more accurate it is at guessing the names of the chords being played. This feature also requires more processing power from your computer, but I've never had any problems keeping this parameter set at 1 (the lowest setting). So, unless you have trouble with playback, I recommend that you just leave this setting at its default value.

5. Start playback of the project. As the project plays, the effect analyzes your data and displays the name of the chord it thinks is being played, along with how the chord looks in music notation and on a piano keyboard.

Actually, I stand corrected. This effect is useful as a learning tool, because it displays the chords being played on a piano keyboard and as music notation. Plus, it lists (in the Chord Recognized section) some possible alternatives you might want to try in place of the chord currently being used.

Echo Delay

Just as the delay effects enable you to add echoes to your audio data, the Echo Delay effect enables you to add echoes to your MIDI data. But because this effect works on MIDI data, some of the parameters are different, and some additional parameters are available as well. This feature works as follows:

1. Select the MIDI data that you want to process.

2. Choose Edit > MIDI Effects > Cakewalk FX > Echo Delay to open the Echo Delay dialog box (see Figure 11.35).

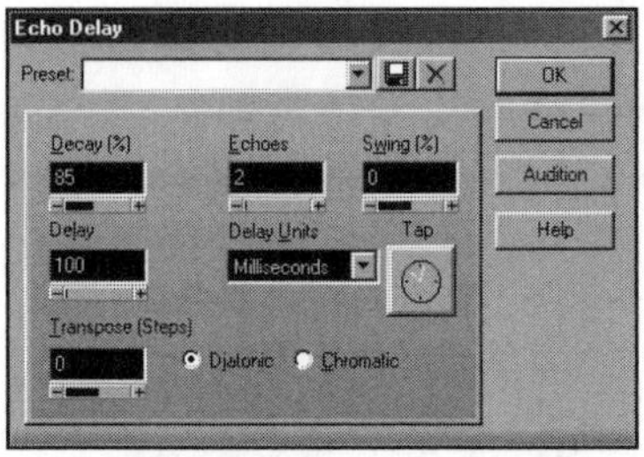

Figure 11.35
You can use the Echo Delay effect to add echoes to your MIDI data.

3. Set the Delay and Delay Units parameters. These two parameters work together. The Delay parameter determines the amount of time between each echo. The Delay Units parameter determines what units you want to use to set the Delay parameter. You can set the Delay parameter in notes, ticks, and milliseconds. By setting the

CHAPTER 11

Delay Units parameter to Notes, you can easily synchronize the echoes to a certain note value so that you know they will play in sync with the rest of the music in your project.

TIP

You can also set the Delay parameter by clicking on the Tap button in the Echo Delay dialog box. Clicking on the button at a certain tempo sets the Delay parameter to that tempo.

4. Set the Decay parameter. This parameter determines whether the echoes get softer or louder (and by how much). If you set the Decay parameter to a value below 100 percent, the echoes get softer. If you set the Decay to a value above 100 percent, the echoes get louder.

5. Set the Echoes parameter. This parameter determines how many echoes you will have.

6. Set the Swing parameter. This parameter works the same way as the Swing parameter in the Quantize editing feature (which I talked about in Chapter 8). The only difference is that of 50 percent being the normal setting (meaning no "swing" is applied); 0 percent is the normal setting. And you can set this Swing parameter from –100 to +100 percent. More often than not, you'll want to keep it set to 0 percent.

7. Set the Transpose (Steps) parameter. If you'd like, you can have each echo transposed to a different pitch value. This way, you can create some interesting sounds. You can set the Transpose (Steps) parameter from –12 to +12 steps. You determine the types of steps by choosing either the Diatonic (the pitches follow the diatonic musical scale) or the Chromatic (the pitches follow the chromatic musical scale) options.

8. Click on the Audition button to test the current parameter settings. Make further adjustments if necessary.

9. If you want to use the current settings at a later time, save them as a preset.

10. Click on OK.

SONAR processes the data by applying the effect according to the parameter settings you specified.

The Echo Delay effect is fairly easy to use, but just to give you a quick idea of what you can do with the effect, try the following example:

1. Select File > Open, select the file called Ballad #1.wrk, and click on Open to open that sample project.

2. Change the Vel+ parameter for Track 3 (piano) to 100. This setting just makes it a bit louder so that you can hear the changes being made to it above the other instruments in the project.

3. Play the project to see what the original data in Track 3 sounds like.

4. Select Track 3.

5. Choose Edit > MIDI Effects > Cakewalk FX > Echo Delay.

6. Choose the preset called Going Up.

7. Click on OK.

8. Play the project again.

Sounds sort of like an arpeggio, doesn't it? That's because of the Transpose parameter settings. You can achieve some pretty cool sounds by using this effect. As always, don't be afraid to experiment.

MIDI Event Filter

The MIDI Event Filter effect works almost exactly the same as the Select By Filter editing feature (which I talked about in Chapter 8). The only difference is that, instead of simply selecting the specified events, it deletes them. This feature gives you a quick way to remove specific kinds of MIDI data from your clips or Tracks. It works like this:

1. Select the MIDI data that you want to process.

2. Choose Edit > MIDI Effects > Cakewalk FX > MIDI Event Filter to open the MIDI Event Filter dialog box (see Figure 11.36).

Figure 11.36
Using the MIDI Event Filter effect, you can easily remove specific kinds of MIDI data from your clips and tracks.

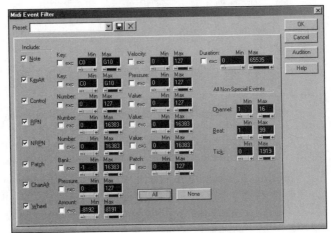

3. Set the appropriate parameters for the types of MIDI data that you want to remove. These settings are exactly the same as the settings for the Event Filter–Select Some dialog box (which I explained in Chapter 8).

4. Click on the Audition button to test the current parameter settings. Make further adjustments if necessary.

5. If you want to use the current settings at a later time, save them as a preset.

6. Click on OK.

SONAR processes the selected data and removes the types of MIDI data you specified via the effect parameter settings.

Quantize

The Quantize effect works almost exactly the same as the Quantize editing feature (which I talked about in Chapter 8). The only difference is that the effect provides a couple of additional parameters. It works like this:

1. Select the MIDI data that you want to process.

2. Choose Edit > MIDI Effects > Cakewalk FX > Quantize to open the Quantize dialog box (see Figure 11.37).

Figure 11.37
The Quantize effect works almost exactly the same way as the Quantize editing feature.

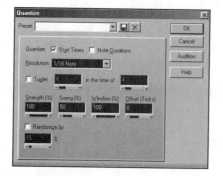

3. Set the Quantize parameter by activating/deactivating the Start Times and Note Durations options. These settings simply tell SONAR whether you want to quantize the start times and/or durations of each selected MIDI Event.

4. Set the Resolution parameter. This parameter works in exactly the same way as the Resolution parameter in the Quantize editing feature (which I talked about in Chapter 8).

5. Set the Tuplet option. Using this option, you can further define the Resolution parameter. For example, if you want to quantize your data according to an odd note value, activate the Tuplet option and set its related parameters to 5 and 4 (which would mean you want to quantize your data to the value of 5 notes occurring in the time of 4 notes).

6. Set the Strength, Swing, Window, and Offset parameters. These parameters work in exactly the same way as the Strength, Swing, Window, and Offset parameters in the Quantize editing feature (which I talked about in Chapter 8).

7. Set the Randomize By option. If you activate this option, a random time offset is applied to the timing of each quantized Event. You can use this option to achieve some very strange sounds. Do a little experimenting to hear what I mean.

8. Click on the Audition button to test the current parameter settings. Make further adjustments if necessary.

9. If you want to use the current settings at a later time, save them as a preset.

10. Click on OK.

SONAR processes the data by applying the effect according to the parameter settings you specified.

Transpose

Like the Transpose editing feature, the Transpose effect enables you to transpose your MIDI note data up or down by a number of half steps either chromatically or diatonically. However, the Transpose effect also provides some more advanced transposition methods. It works like this:

1. Select the MIDI data that you want to process.

2. Choose Edit > MIDI Effects > Cakewalk FX > Transpose to open the Transpose dialog box (see Figure 11.38).

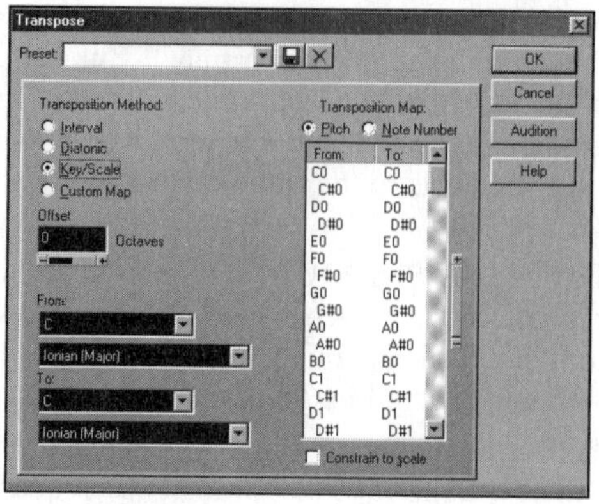

Figure 11.38
Using the Transpose effect, you can transpose your MIDI note data in a number of different ways.

3. If you want to transpose your data by a simple musical interval, choose the Interval option for the Transposition Method parameter. Then enter the number of half steps (–127 to +127) into the Offset parameter by which you want to transpose the data.

4. If you want to transpose your data diatonically so that the notes are changed according to degrees of a certain musical scale, choose the Diatonic option for the Transposition Method parameter. Then enter the number of scale degrees (–24 to +24) into the Offset parameter by which you want to transpose the data. Also, choose the musical scale you want to use by setting the Key parameter.

> **TIP**
>
> If you want any of the notes in your data that don't fit within the chosen musical scale to be transposed so that they will fit, activate the Constrain To Scale option. This feature works well for pop music. For something like jazz, though, in which many different non-scale notes are used in the music, it's best to keep this option deactivated. This option works for both the Diatonic and Key/Scale Transposition Methods.

5. If you want to transpose your data from one musical key and scale to another, choose the Key/Scale option for the Transposition Method parameter. In the From and To parameters, choose the musical keys and scales by which you want to transpose your data. You can also transpose the data up or down by a number of octaves at the same time by setting the Offset parameter.

6. To specify exactly how each note in the musical scale will be transposed, choose the Custom Map option for the Transposition Method parameter. Using this option, you can define your own Transposition Map. This means that you can set what note each note in the musical scale will be transposed to. To change the transposition value of a note in the musical scale, select the note in the From column of the Transposition Map. Then click on the plus or minus buttons to transpose that note up or down. This option is pretty tedious, but it gives you precise control over every musical note.

TIP

You can view notes in the Transposition Map either by note name or by MIDI note number. Simply select the appropriate option (Pitch or Note Number) located above the Transposition Map in the Transpose dialog box.

7. Click on the Audition button to test the current parameter settings. Make further adjustments if necessary.

8. If you want to use the current settings at a later time, save them as a preset.

9. Click on OK.

SONAR processes the data by applying the effect according to the parameter settings you specified.

Velocity

I'm tempted to compare the Velocity effect to the Scale Velocity editing feature (which I talked about in Chapter 8), but the effect not only enables you to scale MIDI velocity data, it also enables you to change it in many more advanced ways. As a matter of fact, you'll probably stop using the Scale Velocity editing feature when you get the hang of the Velocity effect, because you can use this effect as an editing tool as well. It works like this:

1. Select the MIDI data that you want to process.

2. Choose Edit > MIDI Effects > Cakewalk FX > Velocity to open the Velocity dialog box (see Figure 11.39).

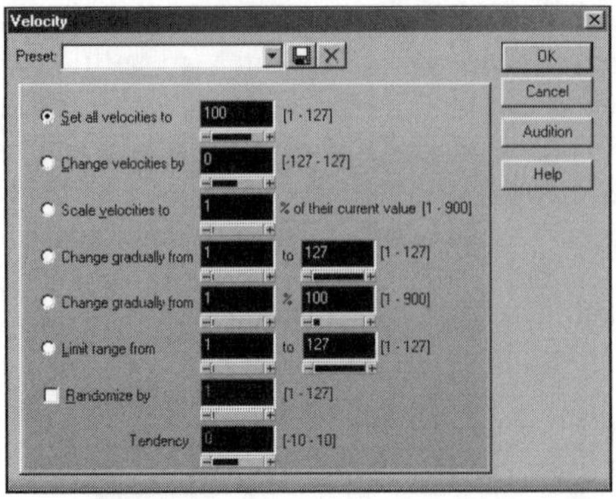

Figure 11.39
Using the Velocity effect, you can change your MIDI velocity data in many more ways than you can using the Scale Velocity editing feature.

3. To change all MIDI velocity values to an exact number, choose the Set all velocities To parameter, and type the value (1 to 127) you want to use.

4. To add or subtract a certain amount from each MIDI velocity in your selected data, choose the Change velocities by option and type the value (−127 to +127) you want to use.

5. To scale all MIDI velocity values by a certain percentage, choose the Scale velocities to option and type the value (1 to 900 percent) that you want to use.

6. The next two options also enable you to scale MIDI velocities, but from one value to another. If you choose the first Change gradually from option, you can scale MIDI velocities by exact values (1 to 127). If you choose the second Change gradually from option, you can scale MIDI velocities by a percentage (1 to 900 percent).

7. If you choose the Limit range from option, all the MIDI velocities in your selected data are changed to fit within the range of velocity values (1 to 127) you specify.

8. In addition to choosing one of the previous options, you can choose the Velocity effect's Randomize by option, which works in tandem with the others. By activating this option, you can add or subtract a random offset to each MIDI velocity in your selected data. You can enter a maximum value (1 to 127) to be used, and you can give priority over whether the random offset will be lower or higher (−10 to +10) than the maximum value that you specify.

9. Click on the Audition button to test the current parameter settings. Make further adjustments if necessary.

10. If you want to use the current settings at a later time, save them as a preset.

11. Click on OK.

SONAR processes the data by applying the effect according to the parameter settings you specified.

Session Drummer

Even though the Session Drummer is listed along with all the other MIDI effects, technically it is not an effect because it doesn't process existing data. Instead, it actually generates new MIDI data. You can think of the Session Drummer like a drum machine, a programmable MIDI instrument used to create drum parts. With the Session Drummer, you can compose your own MIDI drum tracks by combining existing rhythmic patterns into songs. You can even create your own patterns for use with the Session Drummer.

Using the Session Drummer consists of a number of multi-step processes, so I'll provide you with step-by-step procedures for each part of the process.

Opening and Setting Up

The best way to use the Session Drummer is in real-time, because you can use it to compose a drum track while listening to the existing tracks in your project. You can get started by following these steps:

1. Create a new project or open an existing one.

2. In the Track view, create a new MIDI track.

3. Set the Out and Ch parameters for the new track. The channel (Ch) should probably be set to 10, because that is the standard channel for General MIDI drums on most sound cards and synthesizers. Click on OK.

4. Add the Session Drummer effect to the Fx field of the new track by right-clicking in the Fx field and choose MIDI Effects > Cakewalk FX > Session Drummer.

5. The Session Drummer window opens (see Figure 11.40).

Figure 11.40
The Session Drummer window allows you to compose your own MIDI drum tracks by combining existing rhythmic patterns.

6. You'll see three different sections within the window: Style, Pattern, and Song. Just below the Style section is a row of buttons. These buttons control the different Session Drummer features. Click on the Plugin Settings button (the one with the picture of the yellow sprocket on it) to open the Settings dialog box (see Figure 11.41). Don't worry; I'll go over all the other Session Drummer features shortly.

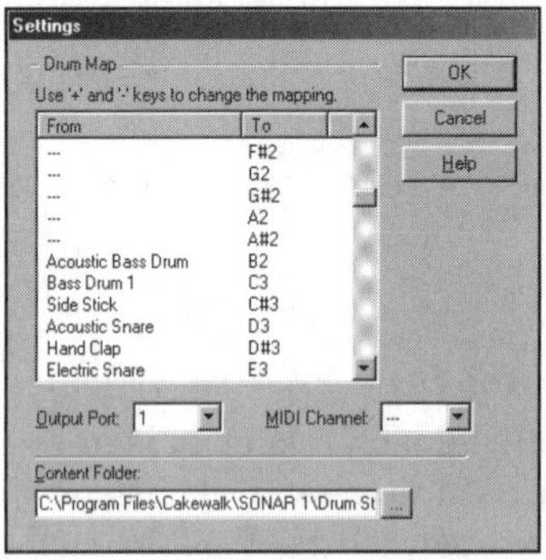

Figure 11.41

In the Settings dialog box, you can set the Session Drummer's Drum Map, Output Port, MIDI Channel, and Content Folder parameters.

7. All the drum patterns and styles included with SONAR are programmed to work with General MIDI. So, if you're using a General MIDI compatible synthesizer, you should be all set. If not, you can change the Drum Map parameter so that each drum instrument is mapped to a different MIDI pitch. To do so, click on the name of the drum instrument you want to change in the From column of the Drum Map. Then, to raise or lower the pitch for that instrument, press the plus or minus keys on the numeric keypad of your computer's keyboard, respectively.

8. Set the Output Port and MIDI Channel parameters to the same settings you used for the Out and Ch parameters you entered earlier.

9. All the drum styles and patterns included with SONAR are contained in special MIDI files. These files are initially located in the C:\Program Files\Cakewalk\SONAR 1\Drum Styles folder on your hard drive. If you want to change the location of the files, enter a new location in the Content Folder parameter. Be sure to remember to move any existing files from the old folder to the new folder.

10. Click on OK to close the Settings dialog box.

TIP

If you want to use these same settings again in the future, you can save them as a preset. The Presets parameter in the Session Drummer window saves only the parameter values from the Settings dialog box. Saving your Session Drummer songs requires a different procedure, which I'll talk about later.

Creating a Song

As I mentioned earlier, the Session Drummer window is divided into three sections: Style, Pattern, and Song. The Style section lists all the available drum style files currently in the Content Folder. Each file contains a number of different drum patterns. When you select a style from the list in the Style section, all the patterns contained in that style are listed in the Pattern section. By selecting patterns from the Pattern section, you can piece together a song. A song is an entire percussion performance that spans a certain number of measures, depending on how many patterns it contains and the length of each pattern used. The basic procedure for creating a song is as follows (I'm assuming you've already gone through the setup procedure, and the Session Drummer window is open and waiting to be used):

1. Select a style from the Style section.

2. In the Pattern section, you'll see all the patterns within the selected style. The name of each pattern and its length in measures is shown. To hear what a pattern sounds like, click on it to select it and then start your project playing. You can keep the project playing while you select different patterns. After you find a pattern you like, double-click on it (or click on the Add Pattern To Song button, the one with the picture of a plus sign on it) to add the pattern to the Song section.

3. In the Song section, the name, length, and the time (in measures, beats, ticks) of when the pattern will be played within the project is shown. You'll also see a Loop Count parameter for the pattern. It tells the Session Drummer how many times to play that pattern before moving on to the next pattern in the song. Set the Loop Count by double-clicking on it and typing a number.

4. Go back to Step 2 to add more patterns to the song.

5. If you want to remove a pattern from the song, select the pattern from the list in the Song section, and click on the Remove Pattern From Song button (the one with the picture of a minus sign on it). You can also remove all the patterns from the song by clicking on the Clear Song button (the one with the picture of a red X on it).

6. If you want to change the order of a pattern within the song, select the pattern. Then click on the Move Down button (the one with the picture of a downward-pointing arrow on it) to move the pattern toward the end of the song. Alternatively, click on the Move Up button (the one with the picture of an upward-pointing arrow on it) to move the pattern toward the beginning of the song.

7. To listen to the song, select the first pattern in the list and then start your project playing.

Saving and Loading Song Files

After you've finished creating your song, you can save it as a special Session Drummer Song file. This file type has an .SDX extension, and the files are stored in the same disk location as the styles. To save your song, follow these steps:

1. Click on the Save Song To File button (the one with the picture of a floppy disk shown on it) to open the Save As dialog box.
2. Type a name for the file and use an .SDX extension.
3. Click on Save.

To load your song for use in Session Drummer at a later date, do the following:

1. Click on the Load Song From File button (the one with the picture of a yellow folder shown on it) to open the Open dialog box.
2. Select the file you want to load.
3. Click on Open.

CAUTION

If you don't save your song, you'll lose it when you close the current project.

Applying the Song to Your Project

When you save a song, only the information that makes up the song is saved. In other words, only the names of each pattern, their locations in the song, and their number of loops are saved. The actual MIDI data is not saved. To save the MIDI data that is generated from a song into a track (I'm assuming you've already gone through the setup procedure, you've created a song, and the Session Drummer window is still open), follow these steps:

1. Go to the Track view and select the track that you set up previously.
2. Choose Edit > Apply MIDI Effects.
3. In the Apply MIDI Effects dialog box, activate the Delete The Effects From The Track Inserts option.
4. Click OK.

SONAR places the song data into the selected track. No matter where the Now time is currently set, the song data is always placed at the beginning of the project.

Creating Your Own Session Drummer Styles

Styles are stored as standard MIDI files. Therefore, you can easily create your own styles for use in Session Drummer. If you open one of the existing style files as a project in SONAR (see Figure 11.42), you'll notice that a style is made up of nothing more than a single track containing MIDI data composed specifically to be played by General MIDI drum sounds. The track is separated into sections with markers. Each marker designates a different drum pattern. The name of the style file is what shows up in the Style section of the Session Drummer, and the names of the markers are what show up in the Pattern section.

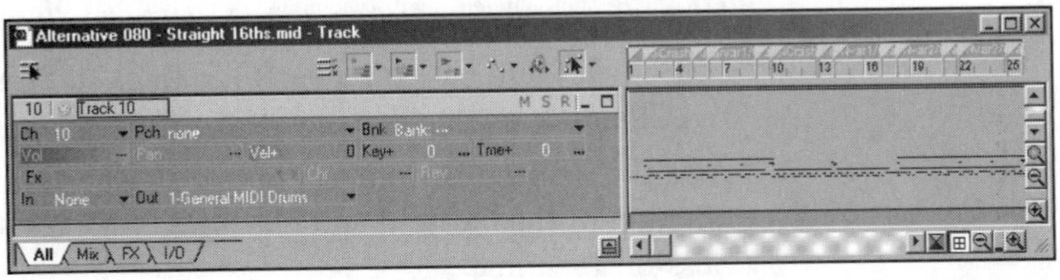

Figure 11.42

You can create your own Session Drummer Styles by recording your own drum patterns and placing them together as a single track.

After you've recorded your own drum patterns, you can easily create your own Session Drummer style by following these steps:

1. Open the project that contains the existing drum patterns that you recorded.

2. Create a new project and set a tempo for the project.

3. In the Track view of the original project, copy one of the drum patterns by using Edit > Copy.

4. Create 10 new MIDI tracks in the new project.

5. In the Track view of the new project, paste the drum pattern at the very beginning of Track 10. Track 10 is the standard track used for MIDI drum parts.

6. Set the Now time to the beginning of the project.

7. Choose Insert > Marker to open the Marker dialog box. Type a name. This is the name of the pattern, and it will appear in the Pattern section of the Session Drummer. Click on OK.

8. If you want to add more patterns, be sure to paste each new pattern at the end of the previous one. Each pattern should start at the beginning of a measure and should be at least one measure long.

9. Save the project as a style by choosing File > Save As to open the Save As dialog box. Type a name for the file. This is the name that will appear in the Style section of the Session Drummer. Also, be sure to choose MIDI Format 0 for the Save As Type parameter. And be sure to save the file to the same directory that you set in the Content Folder parameter of the Session Drummer Settings. Click on Save.

The next time you open the Session Drummer, your new style should be listed in the Style section.

Session Drummer Song Example

To give you a quick idea of the results you can get from the session, I've put together this short demonstration:

1. Choose File > Open, select the file called 2-Part Invention #13 in A minor.wrk, and click on Open to open the sample project.

2. Close the File Info window, along with the Staff and Big Time views. You don't need them.

3. In the Track view, create a new MIDI track (Track 3).

4. Set the Out and Ch parameters for Track 3. You should probably set the Channel to 10. Click on OK.

5. Add the Session Drummer Effect to the Fx field of Track 3 by right-clicking in the Fx field and choosing MIDI Effects > Cakewalk FX > Session Drummer.

6. The Session Drummer window opens.

7. Select the style named Alternative 080–Straight 16ths.

8. Add the following patterns to the song in the order listed:

    ▶ Crash/Kick/SN/Hat/Tamb–1 Loop

    ▶ SN/Tom fill1–2 Loops

    ▶ var1/Crash/Kick/SN/Hat/Tamb–1 Loop

    ▶ SN/Tom fill2–2 Loops

    ▶ Crash/Kick/SN/Hat–1 Loop

    ▶ SN/Tom fill3–2 Loops

    ▶ var1/Crash/Kick/SN/Hat–1 Loop

    ▶ SN fill1–2 Loops

    ▶ var2/Crash/Kick/SN/Hat–1 Loop

    ▶ SN fill3–2 Loops

9. At this point, you can save the song and apply it to the track if you'd like, but because this is just a demonstration, it's up to you.

10. Before you play the project, change the tempo to 100. The original tempo sounds too slow.

11. Play the project.

Sounds like one of those rearranged classical recordings like the ones on the CD called "BachBusters" by Don Dorsey, doesn't it? Have fun!

12

Mixing It Down

After you've recorded, edited, and added effects to your MIDI and audio data, it's time to mix down your project. It is called the *mixdown process* because you are taking all the MIDI and audio tracks in your project and mixing them together into a single stereo audio track. From there, you can put your music on CD, distribute it over the Internet, or record it onto tape. SONAR provides a number of different features that make the mixdown process as simple and intuitive as possible. Here's what I'll be covering in this chapter:

▶ Using the Console view and Track view for mixing

▶ Using the module and track managers

▶ Taking a snapshot

▶ Recording and editing automation

▶ Grouping

▶ Working with envelopes

The Console View

For mixing down the MIDI and audio tracks in your project, you can use either the Console view or the Track view. I've already covered many of the Track view features in earlier chapters. So, in this chapter, I'll tell you about the Console view and also let you know how the Track view fits into the mixdown process.

The Console view enables you to adjust the main parameters for each track in your project via on-screen buttons, knobs, sliders, and faders (vertical sliders). Similar in appearance to a hardware-based mixing board found in most recording studios, the Console view displays tracks as a collection of modules, each with its own set of adjustable controls.

CHAPTER 12

More precisely, the Console view consists of four major sections: the toolbar (located at the top of the view, containing some of the view's related controls); the MIDI and audio track modules (located in the main part of the view, displaying the controls for each MIDI and audio track in the project); the aux busses (located to the right of the MIDI and audio track modules, containing additional mixing controls, which I'll explain later); and the Mains (located to the right of the aux busses, also containing additional mixing controls, which I'll explain later).

Opening the Console View

To open the Console view, simply choose View > Console. The Console view then opens, displaying modules for every track in the current project. To see how it works, follow these steps:

1. Choose File > Open. In the Open dialog box that appears, select the file named Riff Funk Audio and MIDI Demo.bun and click on Open to open that sample project file.

2. Choose View > Console to open the Console view.

The Console view should look similar to the one shown in Figure 12.1.

Figure 12.1
When you open the Console view, it automatically displays a module for every track in the current project.

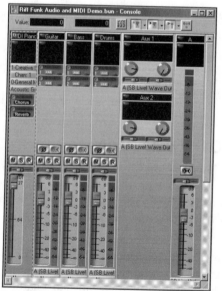

You'll also notice that one of the modules has a dotted outline around it. This dotted line indicates that the track corresponding to that module is currently the selected or focused track in the Track view.

The MIDI Track Modules

Each MIDI track module contains a number of different controls that enable you to manipulate many of its corresponding track parameters (see Figure 12.2).

Figure 12.2
A MIDI track module contains controls for adjusting the parameters of its corresponding track.

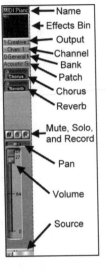

As matter of fact, all the controls are the equivalent of the track parameters shown in the Track pane of the Track view (all of which I have described in previous chapters). This means that if you change the value of a control in the Console view, the equivalent track parameter is also changed in the Track view. From top to bottom, the controls in a MIDI track module correspond to the controls described in the following sections:

Name

The Name control displays the name of the track represented by the MIDI track module. It is the equivalent of the Name parameter in the Track view. You can change the name by clicking on the control, typing some new text, and pressing the Enter key on your computer keyboard.

Effects Bin

You can use the Effects bin control to assign effects to the track represented by the MIDI track module. These effects are applied only in real-time. This control works in exactly the same way as the Fx field in the Track view (which I described in Chapter 11).

Output

Using the Output control, you can set the MIDI output of the track represented by the midi track module. It is the equivalent of the Out parameter in the Track view. You can change the output by clicking on the control and selecting a new MIDI port from the pop-up menu.

CHAPTER 12

Channel

The Channel control enables you to set the MIDI channel of the track represented by the MIDI track module. It is the equivalent of the Ch parameter in the Track view. You can change the channel by clicking on the control and selecting a new MIDI channel from the pop-up menu.

Bank

You can use the Bank control to set the MIDI patch bank of the track represented by the MIDI track module. It is the equivalent of the Bnk parameter in the Track view. You can change the bank by clicking on the control and selecting a new MIDI patch bank from the pop-up menu.

Patch

You can use the Patch control to set the MIDI patch of the track represented by the MIDI track module. It is the equivalent of the Pch parameter in the Track view. You can change the patch by clicking on the control and selecting a new MIDI patch from the pop-up menu.

Chorus and Reverb

Some MIDI instruments have built-in chorus and reverb effects. Some special MIDI controller messages even enable you to change the settings for these effects. Using the chorus and reverb controls, you can adjust the appropriate MIDI controller messages so that you can apply the chorus and reverb effects to your MIDI instrument. To adjust either control, simply click and drag the corresponding slider left or right. As you drag the slider, the Value parameter in the toolbar at the top of the Console view displays the current value of the control you are adjusting. If you drag the slider left, the value gets lower. If you drag the slider right, the value gets higher. Both the Chorus and Reverb controls can be adjusted from 0 to 127. The Chr and Rev parameters in the Track view are the equivalents of the Chorus and Reverb controls, respectively.

TIP

When you're adjusting sliders, knobs, or faders in the Console view or parameters in the Track view, a quick way to return them to their original positions is to double-click on them. When you do, the control snaps back to its default value. You can also change the default value for a control. To do so, set the control to the value you want to use as its default. Then right-click on the control and choose Set Snap-To = Current from the pop-up menu.

Mute, Solo, and Record Arm

The Mute, Solo, and Record Arm controls enable you to turn the Mute, Solo, and Record Arm (for recording) options on or off for the track represented by the MIDI track module. They are the equivalents of the Mute, Solo, and Record options in the Track view (which I described in Chapter 6). You can toggle these options on and off by clicking on them.

Pan

You can use the Pan control to set the MIDI panning of the track represented by the MIDI track module. It is the equivalent of the Pan parameter in the Track view. You can change the pan by clicking and dragging the slider left or right. As you drag the slider, the Value parameter in the toolbar at the top of the Console view displays the current value of the control. The value can range from 0 (all the way left) to 127 (all the way right). A value of 64 is dead center.

NOTE

In the Track view, the Pan parameter values range from 100 percent left to Center to 100 percent right, instead of the 0 to 64 to 127 in the Console view. But even though the values are shown differently, they are equivalent to each other—meaning a value of 0 in the Console view (which equals all the way left) is equal to a value of 100 percent left in the Track view (which also equals all the way left).

Volume

Using the Volume control, you can set the MIDI volume of the track represented by the MIDI track module. It is the equivalent of the Vol parameter in the Track view. You can change the volume by clicking and dragging the fader (vertical slider) up or down. As you drag the fader, the Value parameter in the toolbar at the top of the Console view displays the current value of the control. The value can range from 0 (lowest volume level) to 127 (highest volume level).

Source

The Source control enables you to set the MIDI input of the track represented by the MIDI track module. It is the equivalent of the In parameter in the Track view. You can change the source by clicking on the control and selecting a new source from the pop-up menu.

The Audio Track Modules

Like the MIDI track modules, the audio track modules contain a number of different controls that you can use to manipulate their corresponding track parameters (see Figure 12.3).

Figure 12.3
The audio track modules are very similar to the MIDI track modules in terms of the controls they provide.

As a matter of fact, almost all the controls are the same as those on the MIDI track modules. Included are the Name, Effects Bin, Mute, Solo, Record Arm, Pan, Volume, and Source controls. They all work in exactly the same manner as they do on the MIDI track modules, except, of course, they are controlling audio data instead of MIDI data. The one difference is with the Volume control. Instead of displaying its value as a MIDI volume controller number, its value is shown as decibels (dB).

Other than that, only four completely different types of controls are available on the audio track modules: Phase, Preferred Interleave, Output, and Aux Sends.

Phase

Sometimes phase cancellation can occur between the audio data of two different tracks. Phase cancellation occurs when one audio waveform increases in volume and the other decreases in volume at exactly the same time with the same amount. Because of this phenomenon, they cancel each other out, making the mixed audio sound "hollow." The Phase control allows you to invert the audio waveform of the data in an audio track around the zero axis. This can sometimes help eliminate phase cancellation. To invert the data in an audio track, just click the Phase control in the Console view. The Phase control is the equivalent of the Phase parameter in the Track view.

Preferred Interleave

There may be times when you want to hear a stereo track play in mono
(via one channel) or hear a mono track play in stereo (if stereo effects are
applied). Using the Preferred Interleave control in the Console view or
the Preferred Interleave parameter in the Track view, you can determine
how the data in a track will be played. By default, all Preferred Interleave
parameters for each track are set to Auto. The Auto setting means that
SONAR will automatically determine how a track will play according to
the data it contains. If a track contains mono data, it will play in mono.
If a track contains stereo data, it will play in stereo. If you click on the
Preferred Interleave control or parameter, it will cycle through the
options. A value of A means Auto. A single left speaker symbol means
Mono. And a double speaker symbol means Stereo.

Output

The Output control (located directly below the Volume control and
directly above the Source control) enables you to route the data from the
track represented by the audio track module to one of the mains (which
I'll explain later). This control is the equivalent of the Out parameter in
the Track view. You can change the Output by clicking on the control and
selecting a new main from the pop-up menu.

Aux Sends

The Aux Send controls (located directly below the Effects bin in the
Console view or directly below the Fx field in the Track view) enable you
to route (send) the audio data from the track represented by the audio
track module to one of the aux buses (which I'll explain later). You can
have up to sixteen aux sends for each audio track module, although, by
default, there are only two (I'll show you how to change this number
later). Each aux send has a number (1 to 16), which corresponds to the
number of the aux bus to which its data will be sent. Each aux send also
has three controls within it: an on/off button, a Send Level slider, and a
Pre/Post Fader button. The on/off buttons are located in the bottom-right
corner of each aux send. To toggle an aux send on or off, just click on its
on/off button. The Send Level slider controls the volume (or level) of the
audio data that will be sent to the aux bus. To adjust the slider, simply
drag it left or right. As you drag the slider, the Value parameter in the
toolbar at the top of the Console view displays the current value of the
send level. If you drag the slider left, the value gets lower. If you drag the
slider right, the value gets higher. The send level can be adjusted from
–INF (infinity, the lowest level setting) to +6 dB (the highest level setting).
The Pre/Post Fader button is located to the left of the on/off button. The
Pre/Post Fader button determines from what point in the audio track
module the audio data will be taken and sent to the aux bus. You can
toggle the Pre/Post Fader button by clicking on it. Initially, the button is
set to Pre (you can see this because the button says Pre on it). When you

click the button, it changes its name to Post. When you click it again, it changes its name back to Pre.

NOTE

As SONAR plays a project, it reads the data for each audio track from your hard drive. It then routes the data through the appropriate sections of the Console view, until it is finally sent to your sound card, and then to your speakers so you can hear it. The routing works as follows: The data for an audio track is read from your hard drive and routed through the corresponding audio track module. Within the module, the data first passes through the Effects bin (where any assigned effects are applied). The data is then sent through the Volume control (where its level can be adjusted), then the Pan control, and finally to the Output control. From here, it is sent out of the module and into the assigned main (which I'll talk about shortly). During this routing process, the data can be sent to an aux send either before or after it reaches the Volume control. If the Pre/Post Fader button is set to Pre, the data is routed to the aux bus after it goes through the Effects bin, but before it reaches the Volume control. This means that the Volume control will have no effect on the level of the signal being sent to the aux bus. If the Pre/Post Fader button is on set to Post, the data is routed to the aux bus after it goes through the Volume control. This means that the Volume control does affect the level of the signal being sent to the aux bus. For a graphical view of how audio signals are routed in SONAR, take a look at the diagram on pages 10-12 in the SONAR user's guide.

The on/off buttons are the equivalents of the A1 through A16 (depending on the number of aux sends available) parameters in the Track view. The Send Level sliders are the equivalents of the Snd parameters in the Track view. And the Pre/Post Fader buttons are the equivalents of the Pre/Post Fader parameters in the Track view.

NOTE

The aux sends shown in the Track view also provide Pan parameters. These Pan parameters are not provided in the Console view. So, if you want to apply panning to the audio data being sent to an aux bus, you'll need to adjust the parameters in the Track view, because there's no way to do it in the Console view.

The Aux Buses

The aux buses provide additional mixing control of your audio signals. Like the audio track modules, each aux bus contains Name, Effects Bin, and Output controls (see Figure 12.4).

Figure 12.4
Shown here in the Console view, the aux buses provide some of the same controls as the audio track modules.

You can also access the aux busses in Track view by clicking on the Show/Hide Mains and Aux Buses button located at the bottom of the Track view (see Figure 12.5).

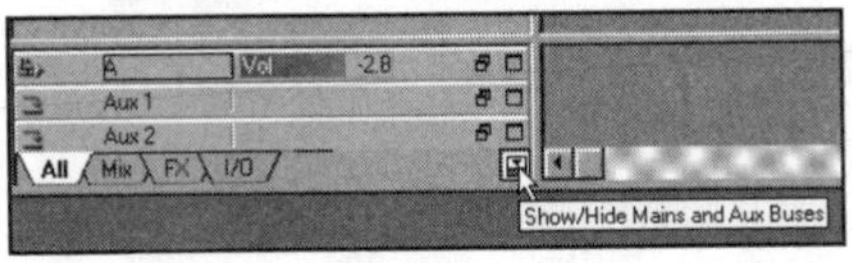

Figure 12.5
Access the aux buses in the Track view by clicking the Show/Hide Mains and Aux Buses button.

In addition to the Name, Effects Bin, and Output, each aux bus provides four other controls: Send Level, Send Balance, Return Level, and Return Balance.

Send Level

Although the name might be misleading, the Send Level control enables you to set the input level of the audio data coming into the aux bus. You can change the send level by clicking and holding down on the knob and then dragging up or down. As you drag your mouse, the Value parameter in the toolbar at the top of the Console view displays the current value of the control. If you drag up, the value gets higher. If you drag down, the value gets lower. The value can range from –INF to +6 dB. The Send Level control is the equivalent of the Snd parameter in the Track view.

Send Balance

Each aux bus works in stereo, so SONAR provides balance controls. Using the Send Balance controls, you can set the panning of the audio data coming into the aux bus. You can change the send balance by clicking and dragging the slider left or right. As you drag the slider, the Value parameter in the toolbar at the top of the Console view displays the current value of the control. The value can range from 0 (all the way left) to 127 (all the way right). A value of 64 is dead center. The Send Balance control is the equivalent of the Snd Bal parameter in the Track view.

CHAPTER 12

Return Level

The Return Level control works just like the Send Level control, except that it enables you to adjust the output level of the audio data going out of the aux bus. You can change the return level by clicking and holding down on the knob and then dragging up or down. As you drag your mouse, the Value parameter in the toolbar at the top of the Console view displays the current value of the control. If you drag up, the value gets higher. If you drag down, the value gets lower. The value can range from –INF to +6 dB. The Return Level control is the equivalent of the Rtn parameter in the Track view.

Return Balance

The Return Balance control works just like the Send Balance control, except that it enables you to adjust the panning of the audio data going out of the aux bus. You can change the return balance by clicking and dragging the slider left or right. As you drag the slider, the Value parameter in the toolbar at the top of the Console view displays the current value of the control. The value can range from 0 (all the way left) to 127 (all the way right). A value of 64 is dead center. The Return Balance control is the equivalent of the Rtn Bal parameter in the Track view.

What's It Good For?

One good use for the aux busses is to add the same effects to a number of different tracks. For example, say you have four audio tracks (1, 2, 3, and 4) containing the background vocals for your project, and you want to add some nice chorus to them. Without using an aux bus, you would have to set up a Chorus effect (each with identical parameter settings) in the Effects bins of each of the audio track modules for tracks 1, 2, 3, and 4. Not only is this approach cumbersome and tedious, it also puts extra strain on your computer because it has to process each of the four effects at the same time.

Using an aux bus, however, the process becomes much more streamlined. You can use Aux Bus 1 for this example. First, you activate Aux Send 1 in each of the four audio track modules (1, 2, 3, and 4). Then you set the send levels for each of the aux sends. In the Effects bin of Aux Bus 1, you set up the Chorus effect. Only one effect needs to be set up, because all four tracks are being sent to the aux bus. You then set the Send Level and Send Balance controls, along with the Return Level and Return Balance controls. Finally, you set the Pre/Post Fader buttons to Pre or Post. If you set the buttons to Pre, the data in each audio track module is sent to the aux bus before it's routed through each Volume control. This means that you can control the level of the effect (with the send level) and the level of the original data (with the Volume control) independently. If you set the Pre/Post Fader buttons to Post, the level of the effect goes up and down with the level of the original data via the Volume control.

The Mains

For every individual output on your sound card, a main is displayed in the Console view (see Figure 12.6).

Figure 12.6
A main looks similar to an audio track module.

So, if your sound card has only one output, only one main is displayed, and all the audio data from the audio track modules is sent to it. If your sound card has more than one output, more than one main is shown, and you can choose to which main the data from each audio track module and aux bus is sent.

> **TIP**
>
> Even if you have only one output on your sound card, you can have more than one main. By using more than one main, you can create subgroups of different mixes for your project. For example, you could send all your vocal tracks to one main, and all your drum tracks to another main. This would allow you to process each group of tracks with different effects. Also, if you have a sound card with only one output, but that output is stereo, you can set up one main to control the left channel and another main to control the right channel. To setup addition main modules, choose Options > Audio to open the Audio Options dialog box. Click the General tab. Then enter the number of mains you would like to set up in the Number Of Virtual Mains parameter. You can have up to 64 mains.

A main provides seven different controls. From top to bottom, the Name control initially displays a letter designating the sound card output assigned to the main. You can change it to something more recognizable if you'd like. Next is the Effects bin. Because the outputs from all the modules and busses are routed through the main, adding effects to its

Effects bin applies those effects to your entire final stereo signal. A good use for this control is to apply reverb to your entire mix. After the Effects bin comes the Main Meter, which shows the output level of your final stereo signal as SONAR plays the project. Levels are shown in decibels. Right-click on the Main Meter to change the decibel range that will be displayed. Next is the Preferred Interleave control, which works as I described earlier. Then comes the Main Balance control, which lets you set the panning for the main. The Volume control lets you adjust the output level of your final stereo signal, which is sent to your sound card output. And last is the Output control, which allows you to assign a main to a sound card output of your choice.

Configuring the Console and Track Views

Earlier, I mentioned that the number of aux busses shown in the Console view can be changed. Along with these changes, you can customize how the Console view looks and works in many other ways. These methods are described in the following sections.

Number of Aux Busses

Choose Options > Audio to open the Audio Options dialog box and click on the General tab (see Figure 12.7).

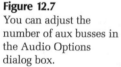

Figure 12.7
You can adjust the number of aux busses in the Audio Options dialog box.

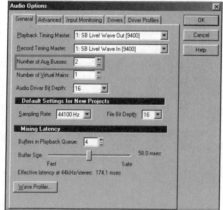

To designate the number of aux busses you want to be displayed in the Console view, just type a number in the Number Of Aux Busses parameter. Up to sixteen aux busses can be displayed.

> **TIP**
>
> If you know you won't need any aux busses during mixdown, you can enter a value of 0 in the Number of Aux Busses parameter. This setting helps keeps the Console view neat and compact.

When you adjust the number of aux busses, it also affects the number of aux busses displayed in the Track view.

The Track Managers

SONAR provides track managers for the both the Console view and the Track view, which allow you to hide modules, aux busses, and mains. What may seem a bit confusing, however, is that the track managers in the Console view and Track view work independently of one another. Meaning, if you hide a track in the Track view, its corresponding track module in the Console view is NOT hidden. Instead, you would have to hide the track module using the track manager in the Console view. In a way, this may seem a bit awkward at first, but it provides you with the flexibility to have the Track view and Console view set up differently.

The track mangers work as follows:

1. To open the Track view track manager, click on the Track Manager button located at the top of the Track view (see Figure 12.8).

Figure 12.8
Click the Track Manager button at the top of the Track view to open the track manager.

2. To open the Console view track manager, click on the Track Manager button located at the top of the Console view (see Figure 12.9).

Figure 12.9
Click the Track Manager button at the top of the Console view to open the track manager.

CHAPTER 12

3.   The Track Manager dialog box opens (see Figure 12.10). The track managers are identical, so the remaining instructions apply to both.

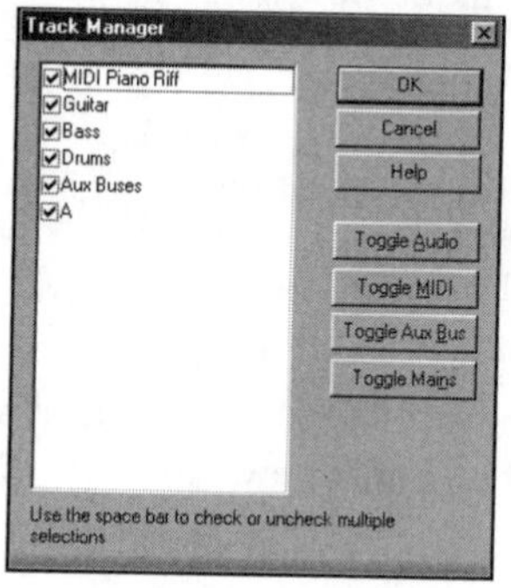

Figure 12.10
The track managers are identical.

4.   To hide an individual component, click to remove the check mark next to that component in the list. Then click on OK.

5.   To hide a group of components (such as all the MIDI track modules, all the audio track modules, all the aux busses, or all the mains), click on the appropriate button—Toggle Audio, Toggle MIDI, Toggle Aux Bus, Toggle Mains—to select the appropriate group. Then press the spacebar on your computer keyboard to remove the check marks. Finally, click on OK.

Of course, you can also make the components appear again by doing the opposite of the preceding procedures. These changes to the Console view and Track view are in appearance only. They don't affect what you hear during playback. For example, if you hide an audio track module that outputs data during playback, you still hear that data even if you hide the module. Hiding components of the Console view or Track view can come in handy when you want to work only on a certain group of tracks at a time and you don't want to be distracted or overwhelmed by the number of controls being displayed.

Changing the Meters

You can also change how the meters in the Console and Track views behave. While recording your audio tracks, you'll notice that the meters on the tracks that have their Arm controls activated will light up. These meters show the input level for the tracks (which I described in Chapter 6). To toggle these meters on or off, simply click on the Record Meters button in the toolbar at the top of Console or Track view (the first button to the right of the Track Manager button). You can do the same thing with the meters that are active during playback by clicking on the Playback Meters button (the second button to the right of the track manager button). And of course, you can also control the main meters by clicking on the Main Bus Meters button (the third button to the right of the track manager button).

The Console view provides one additional button: By clicking on the Peaks Only button (the fourth button to the right of the track manager button), you can control whether the meters will show the entire output level or just if the output level peaks (meaning it hits 0 dB).

NOTE

Like the track managers, the meters in the Console view and Track view work independently of one another. For instance, if you turn off the record meters in the Track view, this does NOT turn off the record meters in the Console view, and vice-versa.

TIP

If you ever need to lighten the load on your computer during recording or playback, you might want to try turning off some or all of the meters. The meters can take up quite a bit of your computer's processing power and affect SONAR's performance.

In addition to being able to turn the meters on and off, you can set various options to determine how the meters will work. If you click on the downward arrow next to one of the meter buttons, you'll see a pop-up menu with a number of options available. These options let you set how the meters will display the audio signal, how to measure the audio signal, the range of measurement, and various cosmetic options such as whether or not the decibel markings are shown. For detailed descriptions of each option, take a look at pages 10-21 in the SONAR user's guide.

Taking Snapshots

SONAR provides a number of different methods of mixdown, one of which is called snapshots. Using snapshots, you can take a "picture" of all the current control values in the Console and Track views and then store those values in your project at a specified Now time. For example, if your project is a pop song with a number of different sections (such as the intro, verse, chorus, and so on), you might want to change the mix each time a new section is reached by the Now time during playback. You can easily do so by creating a different snapshot at the beginning of each section of the song. During playback, as the Now time passes a point in the project where a snapshot is stored, the values for all the recorded controls are automatically changed to reflect the snapshot.

CHAPTER 12

NOTE

For automation purposes, the controls in the Console view and the parameters in the Track view work together rather than independently. This means that if you automate a control in the Console view, its corresponding parameter in the Track view is also automated and vice-versa.

To create a snapshot, just follow these steps:

1. Set the Now time to the point in the project where you want the snapshot to be stored.

2. Adjust the controls in the Console or Track view to values at which you want them to be set during that part of the project.

3. For all the controls you adjusted, right-click on each one and choose Arm For Automation from the pop-up menu.

TIP

Instead of having to arm each control one-by-one, you can also arm all the controls in a track by first selecting the track (click on the track number to select the track) and then choosing Track > Arm For Automation. You can also arm the controls in multiple tracks at once. Just select all the tracks whose controls you want to arm (use CTRL-click to select more than one track) and, again, choose Track > Arm For Automation.

NOTE

You'll notice that not all the controls/parameters can be automated. If a control/parameter can not be automated, the Arm For Automation option in the pop-up menu will be grayed out. Also, after a parameter in the Track view is armed for automation, it will have a red outline displayed around it.

4. Make sure the Automation toolbar is visible by choosing View > Toolbars, activating the Automation option, and clicking Close. The Automation toolbar is displayed (see Figure 12.11).

Figure 12.11
Use the Automation toolbar to take snapshots.

5. Click on the Snapshot button (the one with the picture of a camera shown on it) in the Automation toolbar.

6. Repeat steps 1 through 5 until you've created all the snapshots you need for your project.

7. When you're finished, click the Disarm All Automation Controls button (the first button to the right of the Snapshot button) in the

Automation toolbar to disarm all of the previously armed controls/parameters.

When you play your project, you'll notice the snapshots take effect as the Now time passes each snapshot point.

> **TIP**
>
> If you want to disable automation temporarily without changing or deleting any of the snapshots in your project, click the Enable/Disable Automation Playback button (the second button to the right of the Snapshot button) in the Automation toolbar.

Snapshot control values for each of the MIDI and audio track modules, as well as the aux bus and mains are stored as nodes on individual envelopes in the individual tracks represented by those modules. These envelope nodes can be edited, allowing you to change your recorded snapshot data. I'll talk more about envelopes later in the chapter.

Automating the Mix

Snapshots are great if you need quick control in value changing at certain points in your project, but most of the time, you'll want the controls to change smoothly over time as the project plays. To achieve this effect, you need to use SONAR's Record Automation feature. Using Record Automation, you can record the movements of any of the controls in the Console or Track views. You do so in real-time as your project plays.

You can record the values of the controls in the Console and Track views into your project by activating the Record Automation feature and manipulating the controls with your mouse as the project plays. This feature works like this:

1. Make sure the Automation toolbar is visible by choosing View > Toolbars, activate the Automation option, and click Close.

2. For the controls or parameters that you want to automate, right-click each one and choose Arm For Automation from the pop-up menu.

> **TIP**
>
> Instead of having to arm each control one by one, you can also arm all the controls in a track by first selecting the track (click on the track number to select the track) and then choosing Track > Arm For Automation. You can also arm the controls in multiple tracks at once. Just select all the tracks whose controls you want to arm (use CTRL-click to select more than one track) and, again, choose Track > Arm For Automation.

3. If your tracks don't already contain automation data, you can skip to
    Step 5. Otherwise, choose Transport > Automation Record Options to
    open the Automation Record Options dialog box (see Figure 12.12).

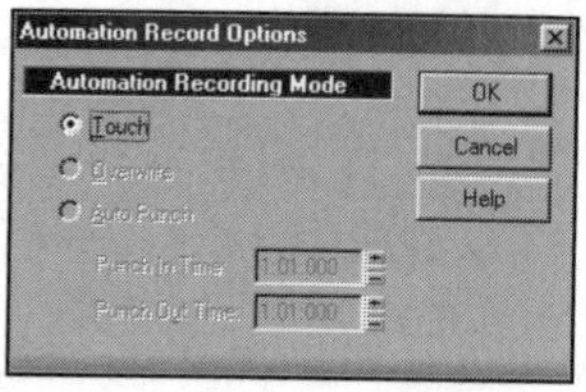

Figure 12.12
Set the automation
record mode using the
Automation Record
Options dialog box.

4. Set the automation recording mode. Use the Touch mode to record
    data only when you are manipulating a control or parameter with
    your mouse. Use the Overwrite mode to record over any pre-existing
    automation data. Use the Auto Punch mode to have SONAR
    automatically punch in and then punch out to record data during a
    specific range of time. The Auto Punch for automation works the same
    as it does for regular recording, which I talked about in Chapter 6.

5. Set the Now time to just before the point in the project where you
    want to start recording control changes.

6. Choose Transport > Record Automation to start the project playing
    and to start recording automation data.

7. When the Now time gets to the point in the project where you want
    to begin recording control changes, adjust the controls or parameters
    with your mouse.

8. When you're finished, choose Transport > Stop to stop playback of
    the project.

9. Because you're manipulating on-screen controls with your mouse,
    you can make only one change at a time. What if you want to have
    two different controls change at the same time? For every control that
    you want to have change in the same time frame, you must repeat
    steps 2 through 8.

TIP

Instead of starting and stopping playback each time you want to record
additional control changes, try setting up a loop so that SONAR will play the
project (or section of the project) over and over again. I described looping in
Chapter 6.

10. After you've finished recording all the control changes you need for
    your mix, click the Disarm All Automation Controls button (the first
    button to the right of the Snapshot button) in the Automation toolbar
    to disarm all of the previously armed controls/parameters.

When you play your project, you'll notice the automation taking effect as the Now time passes the sections where you recorded data.

Just as with snapshots, the control values for each of the MIDI and audio track modules, as well as the aux bus and mains, are stored as envelopes in the individual tracks represented by those modules. These envelopes can be edited, allowing you to change your recorded automation data.

Grouping

As I mentioned earlier, to change more than one control or parameter at once while you're recording automation data, you have to play through your project several times. To make things easier, you can connect a number of controls or parameters together so that, if you move one, the others will move with it. You do so by using SONAR's Grouping feature. With the Grouping feature, you can create groups of buttons, knobs, sliders, and faders whose movements are linked to one another.

Creating Groups

You can create up to twenty-four different groups, each of which is designated by a letter of the alphabet (A through X) and a color. The number of controls that can belong to a group is unlimited. To create a group, follow these steps:

1. Right-click on a control in the Console view or a parameter in the Track View and choose Group > A-X. Depending on what letter you choose, that control takes on the associated color.

2. Right-click on another control and choose Group > A-X. This time, choose the same letter as you did for the first control. This other control then takes on the same color.

3. Continue to add as many other controls to the group as you'd like. You can even create other groups. The same control, however, cannot belong to more than one group.

Now, if you move the first control, the second control will move, too, and vice versa. The values of both of these controls are also recorded if you have them grouped while recording automation data.

Ungrouping

To remove a control from a group, right-click on the control and then select Ungroup from the pop-up menu. The color of the control turns back to normal.

Group Properties

In addition to simple groups, in which you link different controls together so that they move identically, you can create some advanced control groups by manipulating the properties of a group. To change the properties of a group, right-click on one of the controls in the group and select Group Properties from the pop-up menu to open the Group Properties dialog box (see Figure 12.13).

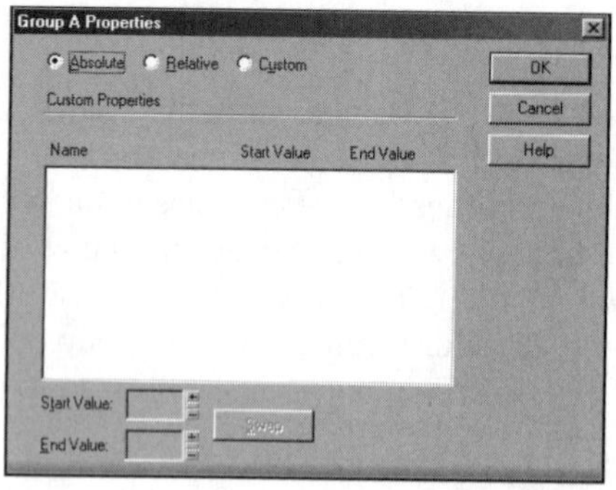

Figure 12.13

You can use the Group Properties dialog box to change the properties of a group.

By changing the properties of a group, you can change the way the controls in the group are related to one another in terms of the way they move. Controls in groups can be related absolutely, relatively, or via a custom definition.

Absolute

To make it so the controls in a group are related absolutely, select the Absolute option (which is the default setting when you create a new group) in the Group Properties dialog box and click on OK. Controls in a group that are related absolutely have the same range of motion. This means that if you move one control in the group, the others move by the same amount. This is true even if one control starts at one value and another control starts at a different value. For example, suppose you have two Volume controls on two different MIDI track modules linked together, and one of the Volume controls has a value of 10 and the other has a value of 20. If you move the first control up by 10, the other control moves up by 10, too. Now the first control has a value of 20, and the second control has a value of 30.

Relative

To make it so the controls in a group are linked relatively, select the Relative option in the Group Properties dialog box and click on OK. Controls in a group that are related relatively do not have the same range of motion. This means that if you move one control in the group, the others can move by different amounts. For example, suppose you have two Pan controls linked together, and one has a value of 0 (all the way left) and the other has a value of 64 (centered in the middle). If you move the first control so that it has a value of 64 (centered in the middle), the other moves so that it has a value of 127 (all the way right). Now if you move the first control to a value of 127 (all the way right), the second control remains at 127 (all the way right). The second control remains in this position because it can't go any higher, so it stays at that value, while the first control continues to be raised in value. I know this concept is a bit confusing, but if you fool with it awhile, you'll begin to understand it.

Custom

To make it so the controls in a group are related according to your own custom definition, select the Custom option in the Group Properties dialog box. All the controls in the group are listed in the dialog box (see Figure 12.14).

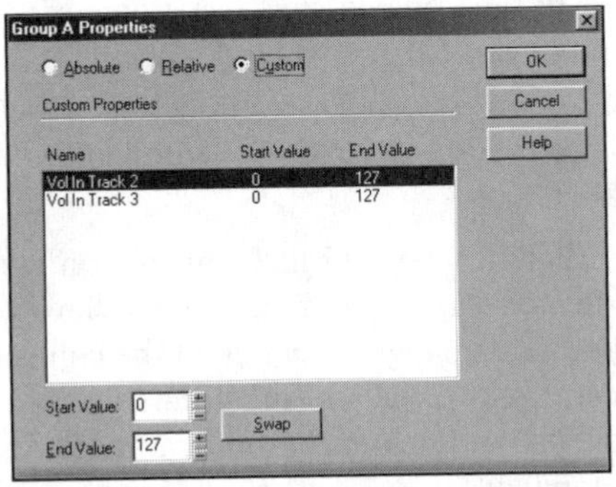

Figure 12.14
You can create complex relationships between controls in a group by using the Custom option.

Along with the names of each control, the Start and End values are also listed. By changing the Start and End values of each control, you can define some complex ranges of motion. For example, one good use of the Custom option is to create a "crossfade" motion between two Volume controls. Suppose you have one Volume control in a group with a Start Value of 0 and an End Value of 127, and you have another Volume control in the same group with a Start Value of 127 and an End Value of 0. As you move the first control up in value, the second control comes down, and vice versa. You can also set up more complex relationships simply by assigning different Start and End values to each control in a group.

To change the Start or End Value of a control in the list in the Group Properties dialog box, select the control and then type a value for either the Start Value or End Value parameters located at the bottom of the box. If you want to exchange the current Start and End values, click on the Swap button. After you've finished creating your custom definition, click on OK.

CHAPTER 12

TIP

You can also change the Start and End values of a control without having to open the Group Properties dialog box. Just set the control to the value that you want to set as the Start or End, right-click on the control, and select either Set Start = Current or Set End = Current.

Remote Control

Even with grouping, you still might find it cumbersome having to adjust on-screen controls with your mouse. To remedy this situation, SONAR provides a Remote Control feature. With the Remote Control feature, you can use an external MIDI device to control the movements of the on-screen controls in the Console view or parameters in the Track view. For example, if you have a MIDI keyboard, you can use a key on the keyboard to manipulate one of the button controls. Or if you have a pitch bend wheel on your keyboard, you can use it to manipulate one of the knob, slider, or fader controls.

By assigning different types of MIDI controller messages to the controls in the Console view or parameters in the Track view, you'll no longer have to use your mouse to change the value of the controls. You can use the actual button and keys or levers and sliders on your MIDI instrument or device. To activate the Remote Control feature for a control or parameter, just do the following:

1. Right-click on the control and select Remote Control from the pop-up menu to open the Remote Control dialog box (see Figure 12.15).

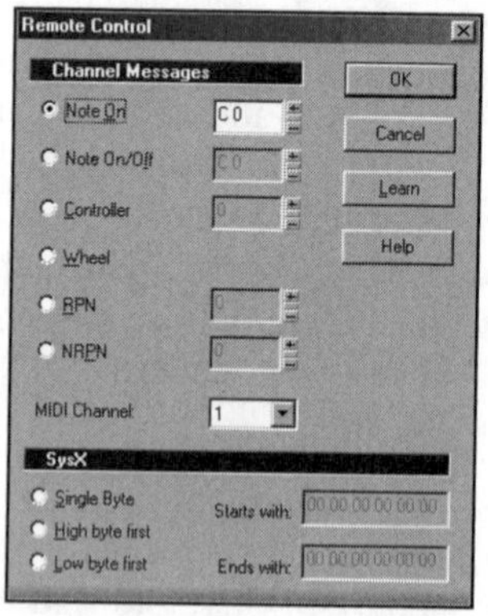

Figure 12.15
You can use the Remote Control dialog box to assign MIDI controller messages to controls in the Console view so that they can be changed via an external MIDI device.

2. If you want to use a key on your MIDI keyboard to manipulate this control, select either the Note On option or the Note On/Off option. Then enter the pitch of the key that you want to use. If you choose Note On, the value of the control is toggled on or off (for a button control) or to minimum value or maximum value (for knobs and sliders) each time you press the key. If you select the Note On/Off option, the value of the control is toggled on when you press the key and off when you let go of the key.

3. If you want to use a lever or slider on your MIDI keyboard to manipulate this control, select the Controller option. Then enter the value of the MIDI controller that you want to use. You can use this option to manipulate only knob, slider, and fader controls.

4. If you want to use the pitch bend wheel on your MIDI keyboard to manipulate this control, select the Wheel option.

5. If you want to use the special registered parameter number or non-registered parameter number MIDI messages to manipulate this control, choose either the RPN or NRPN option. Then enter the number of the parameter that you want to use.

6. If you want to use a Sysx message to manipulate this control, choose a Byte option. If the message contains a single byte of data that changes, while the rest of bytes in the message remain static, choose the Single Byte option. If the changing data contains two bytes with the first being the high byte, choose the High byte first option. If the changing data contains two bytes with the first being the low byte, choose the Low byte first option. Then enter into the Starts With parameter the bytes in the Sysx message that come before the changing data. And enter into the Ends with parameter the bytes in the Sysx message that come after the changing data.

7. Set the MIDI channel that your MIDI keyboard or device is using.

8. Click on OK.

TIP

Instead of having to figure out how the parameters for Remote Control need to be set, you can use the Learn feature to have it done automatically for you. First, move a control on your external MIDI device. Right-click on the control or parameter in SONAR that you want to manipulate and choose Remote Control from the pop-up menu. Then click the Learn button. The Remote Control parameters are set up for you automatically. Click OK.

Now you can manipulate the control from your MIDI keyboard or device, and you can do this while recording automation as well.

CHAPTER 12

Envelopes

In addition to the Snapshot and Record Automation features, SONAR provides one more method of automating its controls or parameters. I'm talking about the Envelope feature. Using this feature, you can "draw" control changes into individual clips or entire tracks within the Track view. In the following sections, I'll cover how to create and edit control changes using the Envelope feature.

Creating and Editing Envelopes

Earlier I mentioned that whenever you use the Snapshot or Record Automation features, SONAR stores the automation data as envelopes in the Track view. Well, you can also create (as well as edit) envelopes manually using the Envelope tool and your mouse.

Audio Envelopes

SONAR allows you to create envelopes for both audio and MIDI tracks, as well as the aux bus and main tracks in the Track view. Since the aux buses and mains deal with audio data, you automate them using audio envelopes. MIDI and audio envelopes are basically the same, but they have enough differences to require separate step-by-step procedures. To create and/or edit an audio envelope, do the following:

1. Activate the Envelope tool by clicking on the Envelope tool button in the Track view (see Figure 12.16).

Figure 12.16
Use the Envelope tool to create a new envelope.

2. If you want to create an envelope for an individual clip, right-click on that clip and choose Envelopes > Clip > (name of the parameter you want to automate). For individual clips, you can automate the gain (volume) or panning.

3. If you want to create an envelope for an entire track (including the aux bus and main tracks), right-click on that track in the clips pane and choose Envelopes > Create > (name of the parameter you want to automate). For tracks, you can automate the Mute, Volume, Pan, and Aux Bus Send Level/Pan controls. The aux bus and main tracks provide different parameters for automation (see the list in the pop-up menu).

NOTE

If you create an envelope for a clip inside of a track that already has an envelope for the same parameter, the clip envelope will be merged into the track envelope.

4. Initially, the envelope is shown as a straight, dotted line that runs from left to right in the clip or track. If it's a clip envelope, it will stop at the end of the clip. If it's a track envelope, it will continue past the right side of the Track view (see Figure 12.17). The vertical position of the envelope inside the clip or track indicates the current value for its associated parameter. For example, if you're automating the Vol (volume) parameter and its current value is 0, the envelope will be shown at the very bottom of the clip or track. If the Vol parameter value is 127, the envelope will be shown at the very top of the clip or track. And other values will be shown somewhere between the top and bottom of the clip or track.

Figure 12.17
A straight, dotted line in a clip or track represents a new envelope.

TIP

You can show and hide envelopes for easier editing purposes. If you don't see your new envelope, click on the black arrow next to the Envelope tool button and choose one of the options (such as Show All Envelopes) from the pop-up menu.

5. At the beginning of the envelope is a small square (called a n*ode*). To change the value of the envelope, click and drag the node up or down. As you drag the node, you will see the value of the parameter represented by the envelope displayed alongside your mouse cursor.

6. To make things more interesting, you can add more nodes to the envelope either by double-clicking anywhere on the envelope or by right-clicking on the envelope and selecting Add Node from the pop-up menu. You can add as many nodes as you need, which enables you to create some very complex parameter value changes. And in addition to dragging them up or down, you can also drag nodes left

CHAPTER 12

or right (to change their time/location within the project), so you can create any envelope shape you'd like (see Figure 12.18). You can also change the time and value of a node more precisely by right-clicking on it, choosing Properties from the pop-up menu, and then entering the new values in the Edit Node dialog box.

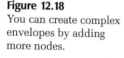

Figure 12.18

You can create complex envelopes by adding more nodes.

7. To make things even more interesting, you can change the shape of the line segments between two nodes. Right-click on a line segment and choose one of the following options from the pop-up menu: Jump, Linear, Fast Curve, or Slow Curve. If you want abrupt changes in the parameter values, choose Jump. For straight changes in the values, choose Linear. For fast but smooth changes in the values, choose Fast Curve. For slow and smooth changes in the values, choose Slow Curve. Depending on the option you choose, the shape of the line segment will change respectively.

8. If you need to delete a node, right-click on it and select Delete Node from the pop-up menu. And to delete all nodes, just right-click on the envelope and select Clear All from the pop-up menu.

9. If you need to reset a node to its original position, right-click on it and select Reset Node from the pop-up menu.

10. If you want to delete an entire envelope, right-click on it and select Delete Envelope from the pop-up menu.

MIDI Envelopes

To create and/or edit a MIDI envelope, do the following:

1. Activate the Envelope tool by clicking on the Envelope tool button in the Track view.

2. If you want to create an envelope for an individual clip, right-click on that clip and choose Envelopes > Clip > (name of the parameter you want to automate). For individual MIDI clips, you can automate the velocity.

3. If you want to create an envelope for an entire track, right-click on that track in the Clips pane and choose Envelopes > Create > (name of the parameter you want to automate). For MIDI tracks, you can automate the Mute, Volume, Pan, Chorus, and Reverb controls. In addition, you can automate any other MIDI controller messages by

choosing the Envelopes > Create > MIDI option, which opens the MIDI Envelope dialog box (see Figure 12.19). In the dialog box, choose the type of controller, the value of that controller, and the MIDI channel you want to use for the controller. Then click OK to create the new envelope.

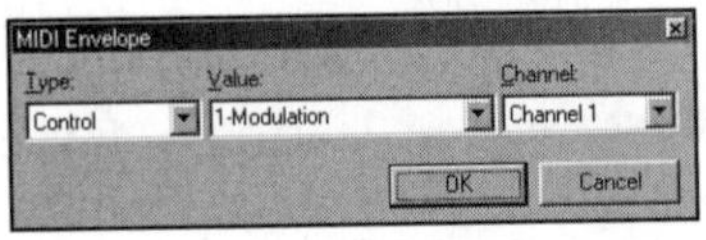

Figure 12.19
For MIDI tracks, you can create envelopes for any kind of MIDI controller messages.

TIP
If you think the parameters in the MIDI Envelope dialog box look familiar, you're right. They are the same parameters found in the toolbar at the top of the Piano Roll view, which are used to choose MIDI controllers for editing in the Controller pane. If a track contains MIDI controller messages and you create an envelope for that track with the same controller, they will contradict one another. In this case, you should select the track and choose Edit > Convert MIDI To Shapes. You'll see the Convert MIDI To Shapes dialog box, which is exactly the same as the MIDI Envelope dialog box. Choose the controller you want to convert and click OK. The controller messages in that track will be converted to envelopes.

4. Initially, the envelope is shown as a straight, dotted line that runs from left to right in the clip or track. If it's a clip envelope, it will stop at the end of the clip. If it's a track envelope, it will continue past the right side of the Track view. The vertical position of the envelope inside the clip or track indicates the current value for its associated parameter. For example, if you're automating the Vol (volume) parameter and its current value is 0, the envelope will be shown at the very bottom of the clip or track. If the Vol parameter value is 127, the envelope will be shown at the very top of the clip or track. And other values will be shown somewhere between the top and bottom of the clip or track.

5. At the beginning of the envelope is a small square (called a n*ode*). To change the value of the envelope, click and drag the node up or down. As you drag the node, you will see the value of the parameter represented by the envelope displayed alongside your mouse cursor.

6. To make things more interesting, you can add more nodes to the envelope either by double-clicking anywhere on the envelope or by right-clicking on the envelope and selecting Add Node from the pop-up menu. You can add as many nodes as you need, which enables you to create some very complex parameter value changes. And in addition to dragging them up or down, you can also drag nodes left or right (to change their time/location within the project), so you can

create any envelope shape you'd like. You can also change the time and value of a node more precisely by right-clicking on it, choosing Properties from the pop-up menu, and then entering the new values in the Edit Node dialog box.

7. To make things even more interesting, you can change the shape of the line segments between two nodes. Right-click on a line segment and choose one of the following options from the pop-up menu: Jump, Linear, Fast Curve, or Slow Curve. If you want abrupt changes in the parameter values, choose Jump. For straight changes in the values, choose Linear. For fast but smooth changes in the values, choose Fast Curve. For slow and smooth changes in the values, choose Slow Curve. Depending on the option you choose, the shape of the line segment will change respectively.

8. If you need to delete a node, right-click on it and select Delete Node from the pop-up menu. And to delete all nodes, just right-click on the envelope and select Clear All from the pop-up menu.

9. If you need to reset a node to its original position, right-click on it and select Reset Node from the pop-up menu.

10. If you want to delete an entire envelope, right-click on it and select Delete Envelope from the pop-up menu.

Now, when you play your project, the parameter values that you edited will follow the shape of the envelopes.

Additional Envelope Editing

Even though I've covered most of the editing procedures for envelopes in the previous sections, there are some additional ways in which you can edit envelopes.

Deleting Envelopes

Earlier I mentioned that to delete an envelope, you just need to right-click on the envelope and choose Delete Envelope from the pop-up menu. But if you want to delete more than one envelope or only part of an envelope, the procedure is a bit different:

1. Make sure the Select tool is activated by clicking on the Select tool button in the Track view (see Figure 12.20).

Figure 12.20
For normal data selection, use the Select tool.

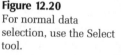

2. Select the data containing the envelope data you want to delete. This can be a single clip, an entire track, multiple tracks, or even part of a clip or track. To refresh your memory on how to select data in the Track view, go back to Chapter 7.

3. Choose Edit > Cut to open the Cut dialog box.

4. Depending on the data you selected in Step 2, either the Track/Bus Automation option or the Clip Automation option will be available (or maybe even both). Activate either one or both options.

CAUTION

If you don't want to delete any of the audio or MIDI data along with the envelope data, make sure to deactivate the Events In Tracks option in the Cut dialog box.

5. Click OK.

SONAR deletes your selected envelope/automation data.

Copying and Pasting Envelopes

You can also copy and paste an envelope (or part of an envelope) from one track to another. Why would you want to do that? Well, you might want the volume of one instrument in your project follow the volume of another instrument. You can do this by copying and pasting the volume envelope from the first instrument track to the other. Here is how it works:

1. Make sure the Select tool is activated by clicking on the Select tool button in the Track view.

2. Select the data containing the envelope data you want to delete. This can be a single clip, an entire track, multiple tracks, or even part of a clip or track. To refresh your memory on how to select data in the Track view, go back to Chapter 7.

TIP

If you are selecting clips in the Clips pane and you want the track envelope data for the track in which the clips reside to be selected, be sure to choose Edit > Select > Select Track Envelopes With Selected Clips.

3. Choose Edit > Copy to open the Copy dialog box.

4. Depending on the data you selected in Step 2, either the Track/Bus Automation option or the Clip Automation option will be available (or maybe even both). Activate either one or both options.

CAUTION

If you don't want to copy any of the audio or MIDI data along with the envelope data, make sure to deactivate the Events In Tracks option in the Cut dialog box.

CHAPTER 12

5. Click OK.

6. Select the track(s) and change the Now time to the position in the project at which you want to paste the envelope data.

7. Choose Edit > Paste to open the Paste dialog box.

8. Make sure the Blend Old and New option is activated in the What To Do with Existing Material section.

9. Click OK.

SONAR copies your selected envelope data and pastes it at the new location in the project.

Automating Effects and DXis

In addition to automating track parameters, SONAR lets you automate individual audio effect and DXi parameters. I talked about effects in Chapter 11, and about DXis in Chapter 10. The procedures for automating audio effects and DXis are essentially the same as for track parameters, but arming the parameters is a bit different.

Automating Effects Parameters

To automate effects parameters, you can follow the same procedures outlined in the "Taking Snapshots" and "Automating the Mix" sections of this chapter, which I discussed earlier. But when you get to the part of the procedure where you need to arm the parameter that you want to automate, follow these steps instead:

1. Right-click in the Fx field of the audio track to which you want to apply the real-time effect and choose Audio Effects > Cakewalk > (the name of the effect you want to use). You can choose from the five following effects: FxChorus, FxDelay, FxEq, FxFlange, and FxReverb.

> **NOTE**
>
> At the time of this writing, only five of the effects included with SONAR can be automated: FxChorus, FxDelay, FxEq, FxFlange, and FxReverb. This is because the technology for automating effects parameters is very new and most manufacturers have not yet updated their plug-ins to take advantage of it. In addition, only audio effects can be automated, not MIDI effects.

2. After the window for the effect appears, right-click on the name of the effect in the Fx field and choose Arm Parameter.

3. In the dialog box that appears, put a check mark next to each of the parameters in the Param Armed list that you would like to automate.

4. Click OK.

Now just follow the procedures in the "Taking Snapshots" or "Automating the Mix" sections of this chapter to record automation for your effect parameters.

As with track parameters, you can also use envelopes to automate effects parameters. The procedure is basically the same as outlined in the audio envelopes section of this chapter, which I discussed earlier. But only track envelopes can be used to automate effects parameters, and the procedure for initially creating the envelope is a bit different. To create an envelope to automate an effect parameter, do the following:

1. Right-click in the Fx Field of the audio track to which you want to apply the real-time effect and choose Audio Effects > Cakewalk > (the name of the effect you want to use). You can choose from the five following effects: FxChorus, FxDelay, FxEq, FxFlange, and FxReverb.

2. After the window for the effect appears, close it. Then right-click in the Clips pane of the track to which you applied the effect and choose Envelopes > Create > (the name of the effect to be automated).

3. In the dialog box that appears, put a check mark next to each of the parameters in the Envelope Exists list that you would like to automate.

4. Click OK.

Now just follow the procedures in the "Audio Envelopes" section of this chapter to finish creating the envelopes for your effect parameters.

Automating DXi Parameters

Unlike effect parameters, DXi parameters can be automated only by using envelopes. Here's how:

1. Set up a DXi in the Track view of your project. I went over this procedure in Chapter 10.

2. In the MIDI track that drives the DXi, right-click in the Clips pane and choose Envelopes > Create > MIDI to open the MIDI Envelope dialog box.

3. In the Type drop-down list, choose the Control, RPN, or NRPN options.

4. The Value drop-down list will show all of the parameters that the DXi offers for automation. Choose a parameter from the list.

5. In the Channel drop-down list, choose the MIDI channel of the current patch (program) being used in the DXi.

6. Click OK.

Now follow the procedures in the "MIDI Envelopes" section of this chapter to automate the DXi parameters.

A Mixdown Exercise

Of course, what would a chapter on mixing be without a sample mixdown session, right? Follow along as I show you how to use some of the features I described earlier in the chapter by mixing one of the sample projects included with SONAR:

1.   Select File > Open, choose the Don't Matter Audio and MIDI Demo.bun file, and click on Open to open that sample project.

2.   Close the File Info window and the Staff view. You don't need them right now.

3.   In the Track view, select Tracks 1, 8, and 9. Then choose Track > Delete to delete those tracks. They are MIDI tracks, and you don't need them for this exercise.

4.   Choose View > Console to open the Console view.

5.   Because Tracks 1 and 2 and Tracks 5 and 6 are stereo pairs, their Volume controls should be grouped together so that the drums and horns volume can be adjusted easily. Go ahead and group Tracks 1 and 2 together using Group A; then group Tracks 5 and 6 together using Group B.

6.   Set up a flanging effect on the guitar by adding the Flanger to the Effects bin in Track 4. Choose the Preset called Classic Flange; then change the Wet Mix parameter to 40 percent. The original setting adds a bit too much of the effect to the guitar. Remember, subtlety is the key to applying good-sounding effects.

7.   Set up a delay effect on the horns by activating the Aux Send 1 controls on Tracks 5 and 6. Then set both Send Levels to 0 dB and set both Pre Fader Enable buttons to Pre. In the Effects bin of Aux Bus 1, add the Delay effect. Open the effect and choose the Preset called 120bpm Delay. On Aux Bus 1, set the Send Level to 0 dB, the Return Level to –3 dB, and both the Send and Return Balances to 64. Now adjust the Volume controls for Tracks 5 and 6 to –3 dB.

8.   Set up a Reverb effect for the entire mix by activating the Aux Send 2 controls on all the tracks except Track 3 (reverb isn't usually applied to bass instruments). Then set the Send Levels for the drums (Tracks 1 and 2) to –8 dB; for the guitar (Track 4) to –8 dB; and for the horns (Tracks 5 and 6) to –10 dB. Set all the Pre Fader Enable buttons to Pre. In the Effects bin of Aux Bus 2, add the Reverb effect. Choose the Preset called Jazz Club. On Aux Bus 2, set the Send Level to 0 dB, the Return Level to 0 dB, and both the Send and Return Balances to 64. Now adjust the Volume controls for the drums to 4 dB; for the guitar to –3dB; and set the bass to 0 dB. Your Console view should now look similar to the one shown in Figure 12.21.

Figure 12.21
The initial settings for
the mixdown exercise
should look something
like the Console view
shown here.

TIP
You could use the Effects bin in a main to apply reverb to all the tracks, but
then you don't have the flexibility of leaving the effect off the bass and also
having varying degrees of the effect on the other instruments via the Send
Levels. Using the aux bus provides you with more choices in creating the
mix.

9. Play the project. Sounds pretty good, no? But I think it could be a
little more interesting. Set the Pan controls for the drums to 64. Set
the Now time to 1:01:000 (the beginning of the project). Be sure to
arm the Pan controls for automation. Now take a snapshot of all the
initial mix settings. Set the Now time to 1:04:000. Set the Pan
controls to 0 for Track 1 (Drums Left) and 127 for Track 2 (Drums
Right). Take another snapshot. Right in the beginning of the song, the
drums play in the very center of the stereo field. Then a few beats in,
they quickly spread to the far left and right. This arrangement gives
the mix a really powerful introduction.

10. Add a bit of movement to the guitar by first setting the Now time to
1:01:000 (the beginning of the project). Then arm the Pan control for
the guitar track for automation. Choose Transport > Record
Automation. Play the project. As the music plays, move the Pan
control for the guitar slowly back and forth between the values 30
and 98. Don't worry if you go a little past one of the values; just try to
move the control slowly so that the position of the guitar doesn't
change too quickly. When the project stops playing, deactivate

CHAPTER 12

Record Automation and activate the Enable/Disable Automation Playback feature. During playback, the guitar moves subtly from left to right and vice versa through the stereo field.

11. Play the project again from the beginning. Isn't that cool?

Feel free to add more changes or expand upon the mix a bit by applying other effects or maybe an envelope or two. Mixing music is an art form, but with a little practice, you'll find it's really not all that difficult. As always, don't be afraid to try new things. Just play with the mix, and if you like what you hear, great! If not, change it.

The Next Steps

After you've finished mixing all the data in your tracks together at just the right settings, it's time to create a final stereo track, which you can use to burn your project onto CD or get it ready for distribution in a multimedia project or on the Internet. Instead of including the information on how to do that here in this chapter, I've decided to break things up a bit. The next few chapters deal with some other important features found in SONAR, such as music notation and using StudioWare and CAL. If you would prefer to read these chapters later, you can skip to Chapter 18 to learn how to finish the mixing process and burn your music to a compact disc. For information on converting your project to a compatible format for multimedia or the Internet, read Appendix C, "Producing for Multimedia and the Web."

13
Making Sheet Music

In Chapter 7, I described how you can edit the data in your MIDI tracks graphically by using the Piano Roll view. SONAR also provides tools so that you can edit your MIDI data as standard music notation and guitar tablature. As a matter of fact, you can compose new music while working with notation by graphically adding, editing, and deleting notes. You can also add many of the symbols used in music notation, such as chord symbols, expression markings, and lyrics. And when you're ready, you can print your music as sheet music, complete with title, copyright notice, page numbers, and more by using the printer attached to your computer. To give you an idea on how to use all these wonderful features, in this chapter, I'll cover the following:

▶ Using the Staff view
▶ Editing music as notes and tablature
▶ Applying musical symbols
▶ Handling percussion
▶ Using the Lyrics view
▶ Printing your music

The Staff View

SONAR provides three different tools for editing MIDI data: the Event view, the Piano Roll view, and the Staff view. For really precise numerical editing, the Event view can't be beat. For precise graphical editing of both MIDI note and controller data, the Piano Roll view is the tool you'll want to use. (I described the Event and Piano Roll views in Chapter 7.) Many musicians, however, are used to composing and editing in standard music notation. The Staff view comes into play at this point.

Using the Staff view (see Figure 13.1), you can add, edit, and delete MIDI note data within your MIDI tracks. Looking similar to sheet music on a piece of paper, the Staff view represents notes as standard music notation and guitar tablature on musical staves with clefs, key signatures, time signatures, and many of the other symbols you might expect to see on a sheet of music.

Figure 13.1
Working in the Staff view is just like composing music on paper, but a lot easier.

More precisely, the Staff view consists of three major sections: the toolbars (located at the top of the view, containing all the view's related controls), the Staff pane (located in the center of the view, displaying the notes in the currently selected track[s]), and the Fretboard pane (located at the bottom of the view, displaying the notes currently being played as they would appear on a six-string guitar neck that uses standard tuning).

You'll also notice that the Staff view has scroll bars. They work just as they do in the other views. In addition, this view has a Snap to Grid function, which is represented by the Grid button in the first toolbar. Other similarities are the Marker area and the Time Ruler, which are located just above the Staff pane. The Staff view also has zoom tools, but they are located in the first toolbar rather than in the lower-right corner of the view. The reason for this placement is that, when you're zooming in the Staff view, it makes the notation grow larger both horizontally and vertically in equal proportions, so you don't need multiple zoom tools.

You can open the Staff view in two different ways:

▶ In the Track view, select the MIDI track(s) you want to edit and then choose View > Staff.

▶ In the Track view, right-click on a track or clip and choose View > Staff from the pop-up menu.

Whatever method you choose, SONAR then opens the Staff view and displays the data from the track(s) that you selected.

Changing the Layout

If you select more than one track to be displayed at once, the Staff view shows the data from each track on a separate stave.

> **TIP**
>
> Just like the other views, the Staff View provides a Pick Tracks button in the first toolbar. You can use it to change the tracks being displayed.

SONAR picks the clef (treble or bass) for each stave automatically by looking at the range of notes contained in the data. If a Track has notes that fall into both clefs, it shows the data on two connected staves, one with a treble clef and one with a bass clef.

> **NOTE**
>
> Up to twenty-four staves of notation can be displayed in the Staff view at once. This does not necessarily mean twenty-four tracks can be displayed, though. If the data from each track is shown on a single stave, then twenty-four tracks can be displayed at once. If, however, the data from each track is shown on a pair of staves (as previously mentioned), only twelve tracks can be displayed at once. Of course, you can also have some tracks shown with one stave and some shown with two, so the number of tracks will vary.

You can override these automatic stave settings though, if you'd like, by adjusting the Staff View Layout parameters. To adjust the way the data from your MIDI tracks is displayed in the Staff view, just do the following:

1. Right-click anywhere within the Staff pane and select Layout from the pop-up menu to open the Staff View Layout dialog box (see Figure 13.2).

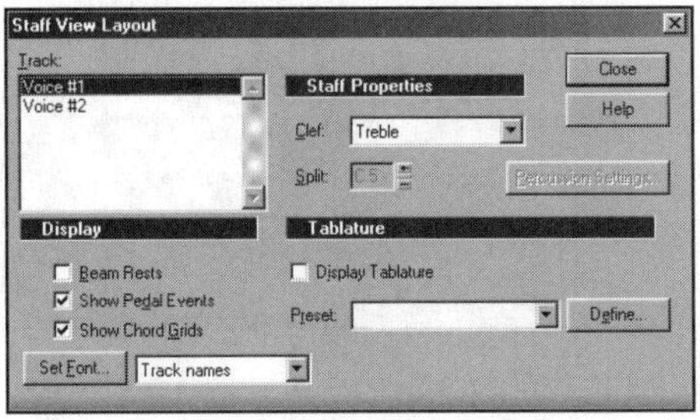

Figure 13.2
You can use the Staff View Layout dialog box to change the way your data is displayed in the Staff view.

2. From the list, select the name of the track that you want to change.

3. In the Staff Properties section, set the Clef parameter to the type of clef you want to use for that track. If you choose the Treble/Bass option, the track is displayed on two staves. To determine which notes will be shown on which stave, enter a note value for the Split parameter. Notes that are at or above the pitch that you enter are shown on the treble clef staff, and notes below are shown on the bass clef staff.

4. Click on Close.

The track is now shown with the stave settings you specified.

Percussion Tracks

If you open a MIDI track in the Staff view that has its Channel parameter set to 10 and you had previously set up your sound card ports to use the General MIDI instrument definitions (which you learned about in Chapter 3), the Staff view automatically displays that track as percussion notation in a percussion staff. It displays the track this way because, when you're using General MIDI, it is standard practice to put all percussion instruments on MIDI channel 10. If you want to override this automatic setting, you can do so as explained previously.

You can also change a number of other settings to customize the way your percussion staves appear. If you select your percussion track in the Staff View Layout dialog box, a new button (called Percussion Settings) becomes active. If you click on this button, the Percussion Notation Key dialog box appears (see Figure 13.3).

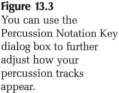

Figure 13.3
You can use the Percussion Notation Key dialog box to further adjust how your percussion tracks appear.

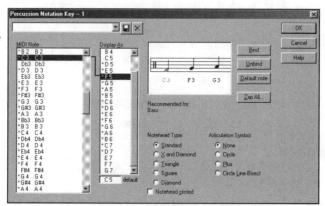

By manipulating the parameters in this dialog box, you can change the noteheads and articulation symbols used to display your percussion notes. You can also change which percussion sounds correspond to the different positions on the percussion staff. You do so as follows:

1. In the MIDI Note section, select the name of the instrument you want to change.

2. If you want to change the position on the percussion staff where that instrument will be shown, select the appropriate pitch in the Display As section. Then click on the Bind button to assign that staff position to the selected instrument.

3. If you don't want an instrument to have a specific staff position assignment, select the instrument and click on either the Unbind button or the Default note button. To remove all instrument assignments, click on the Zap All button.

NOTE

Any instruments that don't have a specific assigned staff position automatically use the default position, shown at the bottom of the Display As section. This means that those instruments are shown at that pitch position on the percussion staff. You can change the default position by typing in a new pitch value.

4. After you've bound an instrument to a position on the staff, you can designate the Notehead Type and Articulation Symbol it will use. Just select the appropriate options in those sections of the dialog box. When setting the Notehead Type, you can also opt to have the notehead circled or not by setting the Notehead circled parameter.

5. If you want to use these settings again later, save them as a preset.

6. Click on OK to close the Percussion Notation Key dialog box.

7. Click on Close to close the Staff View Layout dialog box.

Now the data in your percussion tracks is shown using the settings you specified.

TIP

SONAR displays ghost strokes (percussion notes played very softly for ornamentation) using the standard method of parentheses around the percussion notehead. It determines ghost strokes by testing to see whether the note velocity is lower than 32. This number is a fixed value that can't be changed. You can, however, change the note velocities of your data and then use the Vel+ Track parameter to trick SONAR into using a different determining value. For example, to stop notes from being shown as ghost notes, simply raise their velocity values. Then, so that the sound of the data isn't changed, set the Vel+ parameter so that it lowers the velocities to their original values during playback. Do the opposite to have notes shown as ghost notes.

Showing Pedal Events and Chord Grids

You also can control whether or not the Staff view will display Pedal Events or Guitar Chord Grids (I'll talk more about both of these symbols later). To do so, in the Display section of the Staff View Layout dialog box, set the Show Pedal Events and Show Chord Grids options.

Changing Text Fonts

You can also change how any of the text used in your data will be displayed. For example, you can change track names, measure numbers, lyric text, expression text, chord text, triplet numbers, and tablature fret numbers. To do so, just follow these steps:

1. Right-click anywhere within the Staff pane and select Layout from the pop-up menu to open the Staff View Layout dialog box.

2. In the Display section, choose the type of text you want to change by picking its designation from the Set Font drop-down list. For example, if you want to change how the track names look in your sheet music, select track names from the list.

3. Click on the Set Font button to open the Font dialog box (see Figure 13.4).

Figure 13.4
Using the Font dialog box, you can set how you want the text in your sheet music to appear.

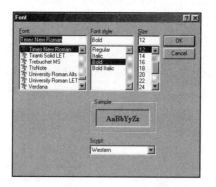

4. In the Font section, choose the font you want to use.

5. In the Font style section, choose a style for your text, such as Bold or Italic.

6. In the Size section, choose the size of the text you want to use.

NOTE

As you are changing these parameters, you can see a preview of how the text will look in the Sample section.

7. Click on OK to close the Font dialog box.

8. Click on Close to close the Staff View Layout dialog box.

Your text is now displayed according to the settings you specified.

Rhythmic Appearance

When converting your MIDI data into music notation, SONAR has to make some educated guesses about how to display the rhythmic values of the notes. It does so because, when you record your musical performance in real-time, instead of playing notes with perfect timing, you'll more than likely play some of them either a little ahead or a little behind the beat. You may also hold some notes a little longer than they should be held. Most often, these slight timing "errors" are desirable because they give your music a more "human" feel.

SONAR doesn't understand these slight rhythmic variations, however; it knows only exact note timing and durations. So, when it displays your data in the Staff view, the data may not always look like it's supposed to. That's why SONAR provides a number of parameters you can adjust to give it a better idea of how the music should be displayed.

Beaming Rests

When you're notating music with very complex rhythms, it's standard practice to lengthen the beams on beamed groups of notes to also include rests. Lengthening the beams makes it much easier for the person reading the music to pick out the right rhythms. For rhythmically simple music, however, it's usually best not to beam rests. In case you need this feature, though, you can turn it on and off by opening the Staff View Layout dialog box and setting the Beam Rests option in the Display section.

Setting the Display Resolution

For SONAR to make an educated guess as to how the rhythms in your music should be displayed, you have to give it a point of reference, which is called the Display Resolution. By setting this parameter, you are telling SONAR what is the smallest rhythmic note value used in your music. For example, if the smallest rhythmic value that can be found in your music is a sixteenth note, then you would set a sixteenth note value to be used for the Display Resolution. SONAR then rounds any start times and note durations to the nearest sixteenth note so that your music looks more like it should. This setting changes only the appearance of the music, not how it sounds. To set the Display Resolution, select a rhythmic value from the Display Resolution drop-down list located in the first toolbar (see Figure 13.5).

Figure 13.5
You can set the Display Resolution so that SONAR can make a better guess as to how your data should be displayed.

Filling and Trimming Durations

In addition to the Display Resolution parameter, SONAR provides two other options you can set to help it better understand how to display your music. The Fill Durations option rounds note durations up to the next beat or note (whichever comes first). For example, instead of showing two quarter notes tied together in the same measure, SONAR simply shows a single half note.

The Trim Durations option rounds note durations down so that they do not overlap one another. For example, if you have a note with a duration that extends past the start of the next note, the first note's duration is shortened so that you don't end up with something like a half note tied to a quarter note with an eighth note sitting in between the two.

Neither of these options changes the music in any way, just how it's displayed. The results vary depending on the music you are trying to display as notation, so you'll have to try either or both of these options to see whether they help "clean up" the rhythmic notation values. To turn the options on or off, just click on the Fill Durations and Trim Durations buttons (located in the first toolbar to the immediate left of the Display Resolution parameter).

Dealing with Notes

As you know, when you open a MIDI track in the Staff view, the notes in that track are displayed in the Staff pane as standard music notation. In addition to simply displaying the notes, the Staff View also enables you to edit and delete them, as well as add new ones.

You can add new notes to a track or edit the existing ones by using the tools represented by the first four buttons in the first toolbar (going from left to right on the left side of the Staff View).

Selecting

The first button in the toolbar represents the Select tool. Using this tool, you can select the notes for further manipulation, such as deleting, copying, moving, and so on. Essentially, you select notes the same way you would in the Piano Roll view. To select a single note, click on it. To select more than one note, hold down the Ctrl key on your computer keyboard while clicking on the notes you want to select. You know the rest. For more information, check out Chapter 7.

NOTE

When you select a note that is tied to another note, both notes are selected automatically because they are essentially the same MIDI note with its duration shown as two tied notes rather than one note with a larger rhythmic value.

Editing

After you've made a selection, you can copy, cut, paste, move, and delete the notes the same way you would in the Piano Roll view. You can also edit notes individually by using the Draw tool. The second button in the toolbar represents the Draw tool. Using this tool, you can add (which I'll talk about shortly) and edit the notes in the Staff pane.

To move a note to a different location within a staff, simply click on its note head and drag it left or right. This action moves the note to a different horizontal location within the staff and along the Time Ruler.

NOTE

If you have the Snap to Grid feature activated, the note snaps to the nearest note value set in the Snap To Grid dialog box.

To change the pitch of a note, simply click on its note head and drag it up or down within the same staff or into another staff. As you move the note, SONAR plays the different pitches so that you can hear what they sound like.

TIP

By default, SONAR uses note pitches that match the current diatonic key signature of the music. This means that as you drag a note to a new pitch, it automatically remains in the correct musical key. If you don't want the note to stay within the key, however, click the right mouse button after you've begun to drag the note to a new pitch. This way, you can change the pitch of the note chromatically in half steps.

Of course, you sometimes might want to make more precise changes to a note or change its duration. You can do so by using the Note Properties dialog box. With the Draw tool, just right-click on a note to open the Note Properties dialog box (see Figure 13.6).

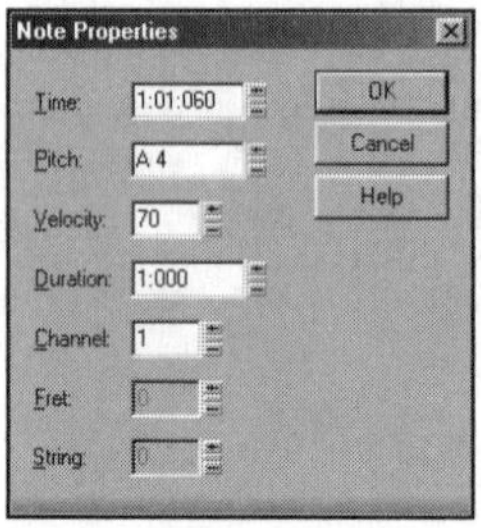

Figure 13.6
Using the Note Properties dialog box, you can make precise changes to a note in the Staff view.

In the Note Properties dialog box, you can make precise changes to the time, pitch, velocity, duration, and MIDI channel of an individual note by typing in numerical values. You can also specify the fret and string upon which the note will be played in the Fretboard pane (which I'll talk about later).

Drawing (or Adding)

In addition to editing, the Draw tool enables you to add notes to a staff by literally drawing them in. To do so, follow these steps:

1. Select the Draw tool by clicking on its toolbar button.

2. Select a duration for the new note(s). If you look at the second toolbar (just below the first one), you'll notice a number of buttons with note values shown on them. Clicking on these buttons determines the duration for your new note(s). For example, if you click on the Quarter Note button, the duration is set to a quarter note. This toolbar also contains two additional buttons: one representing a dotted note and another representing a triplet. If you want your notes to be dotted or part of a triplet, click on one of these buttons as well.

NOTE

When you create a triplet, SONAR places all three notes on the staff with the same pitch. Triplets have to be created with a full set of three notes without rests or ties. After you add the triplet, you can change the pitches of the notes to whatever you desire.

3. Click anywhere on a staff in the Staff pane to place the new note(s) at the start time(s) and pitch(es) you want.

TIP

It's a good idea to turn off the Fill Durations and Trim Durations options when you're entering new notes in the Staff pane. While you add notes, SONAR tries to change the way they are displayed, so you might find this confusing when you're trying to read the music.

Erasing

Even though you can select and delete notes (as described earlier), the Staff view includes an Erase tool for added convenience. To use it, just select the Erase tool and then click on any note(s) in the Staff pane that you want to delete. You can also click and drag the Erase tool over a number of notes to erase them all at once. By the way, the Erase tool is represented by the button in the toolbar with the picture of an eraser shown on it, located right next to the Draw tool.

Scrub and Step Play

When you're editing the data in a track, the procedure usually involves making your edits and then playing back the project to hear how the changes sound. But playing back very small sections can be a bit difficult, especially when you're working with a fast tempo. To remedy this situation, you can use the Scrub tool and the Step Play feature in the Staff view.

Scrub

Using the Scrub tool, you can drag over the notes in the Staff view to hear what they sound like. To use it, simply select the Scrub tool by clicking on its button in the first toolbar (the one with the small yellow speaker shown on it, located right next to the Erase tool). Then click and drag over the notes in the Staff pane. Dragging left to right plays the data forward (what would normally happen during playback), and dragging right to left enables you to hear the data played in reverse. This feature can be useful for testing very short (one or two measure) sections.

Step Play

The Step Play feature enables you to step through (play) the notes in the Staff view note by note. To use it, follow these steps:

1. Set the Now time to the point in the music where you want to begin stepping through the notes. You can do so by simply clicking in the Time Ruler.

2. To step forward through the notes, click on the Play Next button in the first toolbar (the third-to-last button, going from left to right). You can also press Ctrl plus the right-arrow keys on your computer keyboard.

3. To step backward through the notes, click on the Play Previous button in the first toolbar (the fourth-to-last button, going from left to right). You can also press Ctrl plus the left-arrow keys on your computer keyboard.

SONAR then moves the Now time cursor one set of notes at a time either to the right or left and plays the notes it lands on.

TIP

Instead of using the Scrub tool or the Step Play feature, you might want to try another useful technique for hearing what your changes sound like. Did you know that you can edit the data in your project as it's being played back? Of course, it's a bit difficult to edit anything while SONAR is scrolling the display as the project plays. What I like to do is work on a small section of a project at a time. I set up a section of the project to loop over and over, and as SONAR is playing the data, I make any changes I think might be needed. Because the data is being played back while I edit, I can instantly hear what the changes sound like. Using this approach is much easier than having to keep going back and forth, making changes, and manually starting and stopping playback. I described looping in Chapter 6.

Dealing with Symbols and Lyrics

In addition to notes, SONAR lets you add other markings to your notated music, including chord symbols, guitar chord grids, expression marks, and pedal marks. These markings, however, are only ornamental in nature; they have nothing to do with the data in your MIDI tracks. They also do not affect your music in any way, although there is one exception, which I'll explain later.

Essentially, SONAR provides these features so that you can create sheet music with a more professional look, but you have to enter the marks manually. The procedures are basically the same as when you're working with notes. You use the Draw tool to add the markings, and you can also select, copy, cut, paste, delete, and move them. To give you an idea on how to utilize them, I'll go through them one at a time.

Chord Symbols and Grids

Most sheet music sold to the public includes chord symbols with just simple chord names or with both names and guitar grids. SONAR gives you the flexibility to enter either one or both.

Adding and Editing

To add a chord symbol to your music, do the following:

1. Select the Draw tool.

2. Select the Chord tool by clicking on the Chord button in the second toolbar (the one with the letter *C* shown on it).

3. Position your mouse pointer above the staff to which you want to add the symbol.

> **NOTE**
> You can add chord symbols only in certain positions within your music. If a track is displayed as a single staff, you can place symbols above that staff. If a track is shown using a pair of staves (treble and bass clefs), you can place symbols above the top (treble clef) staff only.
>
> Also, chord symbols in music are usually lined up with the notes in the staff. SONAR allows you to place chord symbols in the same horizontal location above a note along the staff only (although there is an exception, which I'll explain later). As you move your mouse pointer along the top of the staff, the pointer changes to look like a pencil when you find a "legal" position to place a chord symbol.

4. Left-click to place the symbol above the staff. SONAR adds a copy of the most recently added chord (the default is C).

5. To change the name of the chord symbol, right-click on it to open the Chord Properties dialog box (see Figure 13.7).

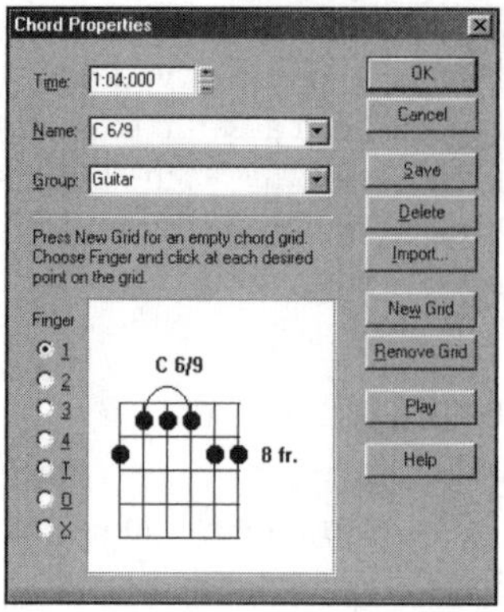

Figure 13.7
You can change the
name (and other assets)
of a chord symbol by
using the Chord
Properties dialog box.

6. Select the types of chords you want to choose from by selecting a group from the Group parameter drop-down list. SONAR includes only a single group of chords, called Guitar. You can, however, create your own groups and chord symbols, which I'll talk about shortly.

7. For the Name parameter, select a new name from the drop-down list. You'll notice that multiple chords in the list have the same name. They're named the same because some chords have guitar chord grids associated with them, and some don't. If a chord includes a grid, the grid is shown in the Grid section of the dialog box. You'll also find multiple chords with grids having the same name. This is to accommodate the different fingerings that can be used to play each chord on a guitar.

TIP

The list of chords is very long, and sometimes it can be tedious trying to scroll through it all just to find the chord you want. For a quicker way to navigate through the list, type the name of the chord you want to find in the Name parameter. Then click on the up- or down-arrow keys (depending on which way you want to move through the list) on your computer keyboard.

8. Earlier, I mentioned that SONAR allows you to place chords only at certain horizontal locations along the top of a staff. Although this is true when you are initially adding a chord, you can change the position of the chord by changing its start time. Just enter a new time (measures, beats, ticks) in the Time parameter of the Chord Properties dialog box. This way, chord symbols can be placed anywhere along the top of a staff. They don't have to line up with the notes.

9. Click on OK.

SONAR changes the name and position of the chord symbol and adds a grid to it according the new properties you specified.

The Chord Library

SONAR includes a large number of predefined chord symbols, which it stores as a Chord Library in a file named CHORDS.LIW. (This file is located on your hard drive in the folder named C:\Program Files\Cakewalk\SONAR 1). You can edit these chords or even add your own by using the Chord Properties dialog box.

To add a chord into a new or existing group, do the following:

1. Right-click on a chord symbol to open the Chord Properties dialog box.

2. To add a chord to an existing group, select the group from the Group parameter drop-down list. To add a chord to a new group, type the name of the new group in the Group parameter.

3. Type the name of the new chord in the Name parameter.

4. To add a grid to the new chord, click on the New Grid button. An empty grid is displayed in the Grid area (see Figure 13.8).

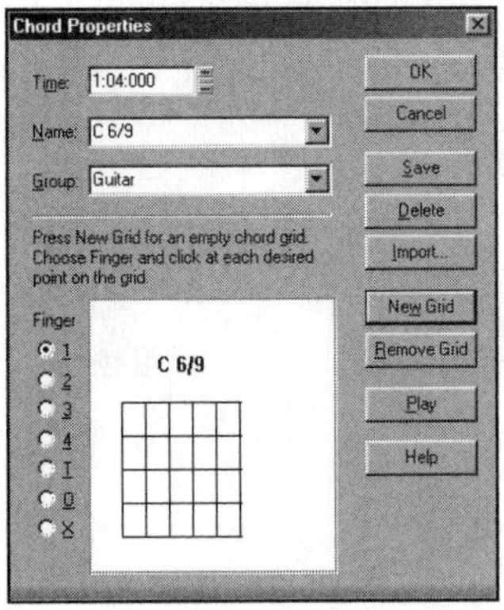

Figure 13.8
You can add a grid to a chord symbol by clicking on the New Grid button.

5. To place a dot on the grid, first choose a finger number from the Finger options and then click on the appropriate string and fret location on the grid. To assign an open string, select O for the finger number. To assign a muted string, select X for the finger number.

6. To insert a fret designation for the grid, click just to the right of the grid in the Grid section to open the Chord Fret Number dialog box. Then type a fret number and click on OK.

7. To hear what the chord sounds like, click on the Play button.

8. When you're satisfied with the new chord, click on the Save button to save it to the Chord Library.

9. Click on OK.

To edit a chord or group in the Chord Library, follow these steps:

1. Right-click on a chord symbol to open the Chord Properties dialog box.

2. To delete a group, select the group in the Group parameter drop-down list and click on the Delete button.

3. To edit a chord in an existing group, select the group from the Group parameter drop-down list.

4. To delete a chord, select the chord from the Name parameter drop-down list and click on the Delete button.

5. To edit a chord, select the chord from the Name parameter drop-down list and then type a new name.

6. If the chord has an accompanying chord grid, you can either delete it or edit it. To delete it, click on the Remove Grid button.

7. To edit the grid, change the finger assignment for a dot by clicking on the dot repeatedly to cycle through the Finger options.

8. To hear what the chord sounds like, click on the Play button.

9. When you're satisfied with the edited chord, click on the Save button to save it to the Chord Library.

10. Click on OK.

TIP

You can also import new chord definitions into the Chord Library by clicking on the Import button and selecting an .LIW file.

Expression Marks

Expression marks in music designate any kind of text that provides instructions on how the music should be played during different passages. These marks include tempo designations (such as *Allegro*), musical characteristics (such as *Play with feeling*), and dynamics instructions (such as *cresc.*, *ppp*, or *fff*). Essentially, expression marks are just simple text added to the sheet music.

Adding an Expression Mark

To add an expression mark to your music, do the following:

1. Select the Draw tool.

2. Select the Expression tool by clicking on the Expression button in the second toolbar (the one with the letter *f* shown on it).

3. Position your mouse pointer below the staff to which you want to add the mark.

NOTE

As with chord symbols, you can place expression marks only in certain positions within your music. If a track is displayed as a single staff, you can place the marks below that staff. If a Track is shown using a pair of staves (treble and bass clefs), you can place marks below the top (treble clef) staff only.

Also, as with chord symbols, marks are initially lined up with the notes in the staff (although you can change the way they're lined up by editing the marks and altering their start times). As you move your mouse pointer below the staff, the pointer changes to look like a pencil when you find a "legal" position to place a mark.

4.   Left-click to place the mark below the staff. SONAR opens an insertion box.

5.   Type the text that you want to use for the mark (see Figure 13.9).

Figure 13.9
Expression marks are just simple text that you type into the Staff pane.

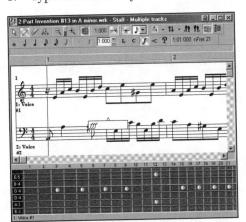

TIP

To leave a dangling hyphen at the end of an expression mark, type a space and a single hyphen after the text in the insertion box. Dangling hyphens are often used with expression marks in sheet music to show that the expression should be continued over a range of notes or measures until the next expression mark appears.

6.   Press the Enter key on your computer keyboard.

TIP

You can also press the Tab or Shift+Tab keys on your computer keyboard to move to the next or previous expression mark location, respectively.

SONAR then adds the expression mark to your music.

Editing an Expression Mark

To edit an expression mark, do the following:

1. Right-click on the expression mark to open the Expression Text Properties dialog box (see Figure 13.10).

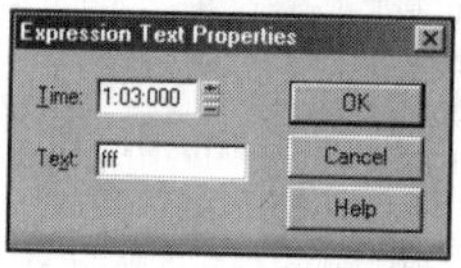

Figure 13.10
Using the Expression Text Properties dialog box, you can edit expression marks.

2. To change the position of the expression mark, enter a new start time (measures, beats, ticks) in the Time parameter.
3. To change the text of the expression mark, enter the new text in the Text parameter.
4. Click on OK.

The expression mark is then displayed in the new position showing the new text according to your settings.

TIP

You can also edit the text of an expression mark by clicking on it with the Draw tool to reopen the insertion box.

Hairpin Symbols

In addition to showing crescendos and decrescendos as text via expression marks, they can also be shown graphically via hairpin symbols. These symbols look like large "greater than" and "less than" signs (see Figure 13.11).

Figure 13.11
Crescendos and decrescendos can also be designated via hairpin symbols.

Adding a Hairpin Symbol

To add a hairpin symbol to your music, follow these steps:

1. Select the Draw tool.
2. Select the Hairpin tool by clicking on the Hairpin button in the second toolbar (the one with the "less than" sign shown on it).
3. Position your mouse pointer below the staff to which you want to add the symbol.

> **NOTE**
>
> As with expression marks, if a track is displayed as a single staff, you can place the symbol below that staff. If a track is shown using a pair of staves (treble and bass clefs), you can place the symbol below the top (treble clef) staff only.

4. Click to place the symbol below the staff.

SONAR then adds a copy of the most recently added hairpin symbol. To change the symbol, you can edit it by using the Hairpin Properties dialog box.

Editing a Hairpin Symbol

To edit a hairpin symbol, do the following:

1. Right-click on the hairpin symbol to open the Hairpin Properties dialog box (see Figure 13.12).

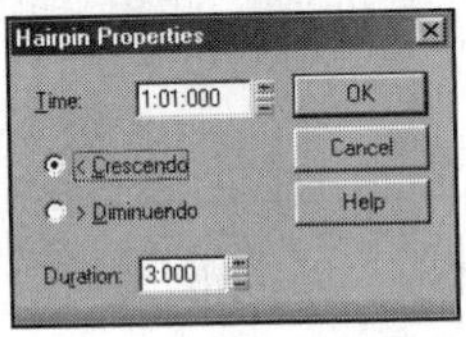

Figure 13.12
Using the Hairpin Properties dialog box, you can edit hairpin symbols.

2. To change the position of the hairpin symbol, enter a new start time (measures, beats, ticks) in the Time parameter.

> **TIP**
>
> You can also change the position of the hairpin symbol by dragging it.

3. To change the type of the hairpin symbol, choose either the Crescendo option or the Diminuendo (same as decrescendo) option.
4. To change the length of the hairpin symbol, enter a new value (beats, ticks) in the Duration parameter.
5. Click on OK.

The hairpin symbol is displayed in the new position, with the new type and duration according to your settings.

Pedal Marks

Earlier, I mentioned that there was one exception to the fact that markings do not affect the data in your MIDI tracks. That exception is pedal marks. On a sheet of music, pedal marks usually designate when the performer is supposed to press and let go of the sustain pedal on a piano. In SONAR, they mean essentially the same thing, but they refer to the sustain pedal attached to your MIDI keyboard (if it has one). More precisely, pedal marks in the Staff view designate MIDI controller number 64 (Pedal-sustain) messages in your MIDI tracks (which can also be edited in the Controller pane of the Piano Roll view). So, whenever you add or edit pedal marks in the Staff view, you are also editing the MIDI controller number 64 messages in that track.

Adding a Pedal Mark

To add a pedal mark to your music, follow these steps:

1. Select the Draw tool.

2. Select the Pedal tool by clicking on the Pedal button in the second toolbar (the one with the letter *P* shown on it).

3. Position your mouse pointer below the staff to which you want to add the mark.

NOTE

Similar to expression marks, if a track is displayed as a single staff, you can place the symbol below that staff. If, however, a track is shown using a pair of staves (treble and bass clefs), you can place the symbol below the bottom (bass clef) staff only.

4. Click to place the mark below the staff.

SONAR adds a pair of pedal marks (pedal down, which looks like an asterisk, and pedal up, which looks like a *P*) to your music. To edit the marks, you can use the Pedal Properties dialog box.

Editing a Pedal Mark

To edit a pedal mark, do the following:

1. Right-click on the pedal mark (either a pedal down mark or a pedal up mark; you can't edit them both at once) to open the Pedal Properties dialog box (see Figure 13.13).

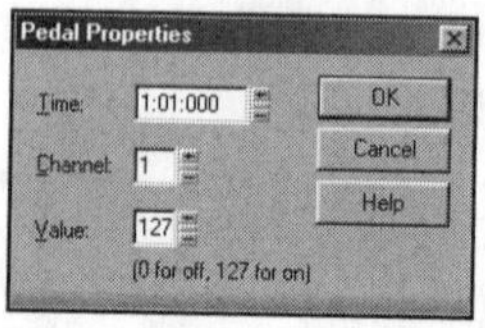

Figure 13.13
You can use the Pedal Properties dialog box to edit pedal marks.

2. To change the position of the pedal mark, enter a new start time (measures, beats, ticks) in the Time parameter.

> **TIP**
> You can also change the position of the pedal mark by dragging it.

3. To change the MIDI channel for the pedal mark, type a new channel number in the Channel parameter.

4. To change the type of the pedal mark, enter a new number in the Value parameter. Enter 0 to make it a pedal up mark. Enter 127 to make it a pedal down mark. Entering any numbers in between that range doesn't have any effect.

5. Click on OK.

The pedal mark is displayed in the new position, with the new type and MIDI channel according to your settings.

Lyrics

Just like any good notation software, SONAR enables you to add lyrics to your sheet music. Lyrics (like expression marks) are represented by simple text displayed below a staff. You can add lyrics to a track by using the Lyrics tool or the Lyrics view.

The Lyrics Tool

Follow these steps to add lyrics to your music with the Lyrics tool:

1. In the Staff view, select the Draw tool.

2. Select the Lyrics tool by clicking on the Lyric button in the second toolbar (the one with the letter *L* shown on it).

3. Position your mouse pointer below the staff, underneath the first note to which you want to add lyrics.

> **NOTE**
> If a track is displayed as a single staff, you can place the lyrics below that staff. If a Track is shown using a pair of staves (treble and bass clefs), you can place marks below the top (treble clef) staff only.
>
> Also, each word or syllable in the lyrics must be aligned with a note. SONAR automatically aligns the lyrics to the notes in the staff.

4. Click to place the lyric below the staff. SONAR opens an insertion box (just like when you add expression marks).

5. Type a word or syllable to be aligned with the current note.

6. To move forward and add a lyric to the next note, enter a space, type a hyphen, or press the Tab key on your computer keyboard. The insertion box moves to the next note waiting for you to enter text.

7. To skip over a note, don't type any text into the insertion box. Either enter a space or type a hyphen.

8. To move back to the previous note, press the Shift+Tab keys on your computer keyboard.

9. When you're finished entering lyrics, press the Enter key on your computer keyboard.

To edit lyrics by using the Lyrics tool, do the following:

1. Select the Draw tool.

2. Select the Lyrics tool.

3. Click on the word you want to change.

4. Edit the word.

5. Press the Enter key on your computer keyboard.

The Lyrics View

After you've entered some lyrics in the Staff view, you can display them in a separate window called the Lyrics view. This view is useful for providing a cue for performers while recording vocal tracks because you can make the lyrics appear in any size font that you would like (see Figure 13.14).

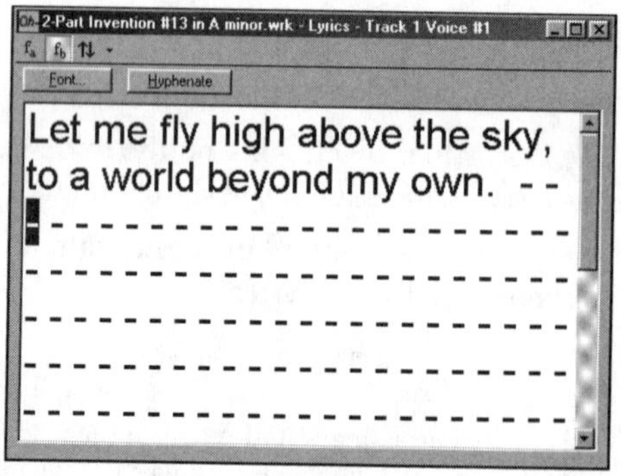

Figure 13.14
The Lyrics view is useful as a cue for vocal performers.

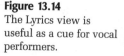

To open the Lyrics view, select a track in the Track view, then select View > Lyric. To change the size of the text, click on the fa or fb buttons. They provide two different preset font sizes. You can also use more specific font settings by clicking on the Font button to open the Font dialog box (which I described earlier). In this dialog box, you can change the font, style, and size of the text. The Lyrics view also has a Pick Tracks button that works just as in the other views.

Of course, you can also add and edit lyrics in the Lyrics view, but I don't recommend doing so. The process is not very intuitive, because you can't see what notes the words and syllables are being aligned with. If you want to use the Lyrics view for adding and editing, you can do so just as you would enter and edit text in the Windows Notepad. Each word that you type is automatically aligned to a note in the current track, and you can split words into syllables by entering hyphens either manually or automatically by pressing the Hyphenate button. That's all there is to it.

TIP

In addition to typing and editing lyrics in the Lyrics view, you can also select, cut, copy, paste, and delete text. Again, this procedure works just like in the Windows Notepad. What's nice about the Lyrics view is that if you already have some text saved in a text file, you can copy and paste it into this View to quickly add lyrics to a track. When you look at the lyrics in the Staff view, the words are automatically aligned to the notes in the staff. And if you want all or some of the words to be hyphenated automatically, just select all or some of the text in the Lyrics view and then click on the Hyphenate button. It's very quick and simple.

The Fretboard and Tablature

For all the guitar players out there, SONAR provides a couple of nice notation-related features just for you. The first one I'll describe is the Fretboard pane.

The Fretboard Pane

The Fretboard pane, located at the bottom of the Staff view, is both a visual aid and an editing tool. During playback, the Fretboard displays the notes at the current Now time in a selected track as they would be played on a six-string guitar using standard tuning. This makes the Fretboard a cool learning tool when you're trying to learn to play a new piece of music. It also displays notes when you use the Scrub tool or Step Play feature, which makes it even easier to pick out the fingerings. The color of the notes matches the color of the clip (from the Track view) in which they are stored.

Fretboard Properties

You can configure certain aspects of the Fretboard, such as its background style and the orientation of the strings. You can also turn it on or off.

To toggle the Fretboard on and off, click on the Fret view button located in the first toolbar. It's the second-to-last button, going from left to right.

To change the background style, right-click on the Fretboard and choose one of the following from the pop-up list: Rosewood Hi, Rosewood Lo, Ebony Hi, Ebony Lo, Maple Hi, or Maple Lo. The Hi and Lo designations have to do with the screen resolution you are using on your computer monitor. If you're using a high screen resolution, use one of the styles marked Hi. If you're using a low screen resolution, use one of the styles marked Lo. To be honest, the resolution you choose really doesn't make that much of a difference.

To change the orientation of the strings, right-click on the Fretboard and select Mirror Fretboard from the pop-up menu to invert the Fretboard so that the highest-sounding string appears at the bottom. To change it back, just select Mirror Fretboard again.

Adding Notes

In addition to using the Fretboard to display notes, you can add new notes to a track (staff) by clicking on the Fretboard. Just follow these steps:

1. Set the Now time so that the cursor rests at the point in the staff where you want to add the note(s). You can do so quickly by clicking in the Time Ruler.

2. Select the Draw tool.

3. Select a note duration by clicking one of the appropriate buttons in the second toolbar.

4. Click on the guitar strings in the Fretboard to enter notes on the staff. You can enter up to six notes (one per string).

5. Make the Now time cursor move forward by the same amount as the current note duration setting by pressing the Shift and right-arrow keys on your computer keyboard.

6. Repeat steps 3 through 5 to continue adding more notes.

Editing Notes

You can also edit existing notes in a track (staff) by using the Fretboard. You can change only the pitch of the notes, though. To do so, just follow these steps:

1. Set the Now time so that the cursor rests on top of the note(s) that you want to edit. You can do so quickly by clicking in the Time Ruler. You can also use the Step Play feature.

2. Select the Draw tool.

3. Drag the note(s) along the string(s) to a new fret (thus changing the pitch).

After you let go of the mouse button, SONAR changes the pitch of the note(s) in the staff.

Tablature

As a guitar or bass player, you might be more comfortable reading and working with tablature rather than standard notation. If that's the case, then you're in luck, because SONAR includes a number of features that enable you to display and edit your music as tablature.

Displaying Tablature

To display tablature for a track (staff), follow these steps:

1. Right-click in the Staff pane and select Layout from the pop-up menu to open the Staff View Layout dialog box.

2. Select the name of the track from the list for which you want to display tablature.

3. In the Tablature section, activate the Display Tablature option.

4. Select a tablature style from the Preset drop-down list.

5. Click on Close.

SONAR displays a tablature staff below the current staff, complete with tablature for each note in the track (see Figure 13.15).

Figure 13.15
Adding tablature to a track in the Staff view is very easy with SONAR.

NOTE
SONAR also offers another feature, called QuickTab, that lets you quickly generate tablature for a track, but it works only when you're displaying a single track in the Staff view. So, I recommend you simply use the previously mentioned method.

Defining a Tablature Style

While you're setting up a track to display tablature, you might not find a preset style that fits your needs. If that's the case, you can always create your own by doing the following:

1. Right-click in the Staff pane and select Layout from the pop-up menu to open the Staff View Layout dialog box.

2. Select the name of the track from the list for which you want to display tablature.

3. In the Tablature section, activate the Display Tablature option.

4. Click on the Define button to open the Tablature Settings dialog box (see Figure 13.16).

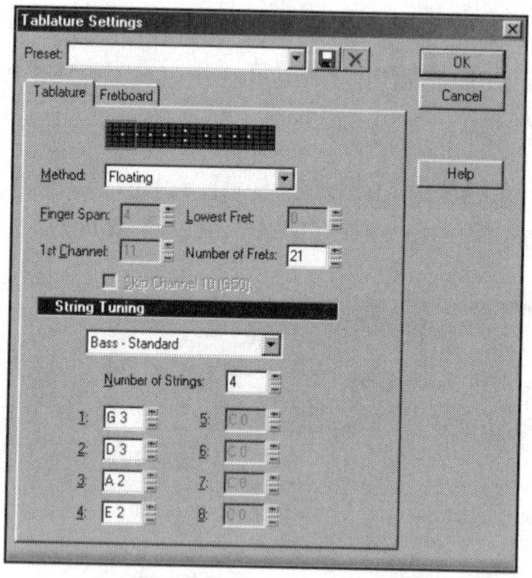

Figure 13.16

You can create your own tablature styles by using the Tablature Settings dialog box.

5. Under the Tablature tab, set the Method parameter. This parameter determines how the tablature will be displayed. If you select Floating, the notes can be shown anywhere on the Fretboard. If you select Fixed, notes are limited to a specific area on the neck of the guitar. To determine the size and position of that area, you must set the Finger Span parameter and the Lowest Fret parameter. The Finger Span parameter sets the size of the area in a number of frets. The Lowest Fret parameter sets the position of the area on the neck of the guitar by specifying the first fret upon which the area is based. The last tablature method (MIDI Channel) is useful if you record your guitar parts using a MIDI guitar and you use MONO mode so that each string is recorded using its own MIDI channel. If this is your situation, then select the MIDI Channel method and set the 1st Channel parameter to the lowest number channel used by your MIDI guitar.

6. In the Number of Frets parameter, enter the number of frets that the tablature should be based on.

7. In the String Tuning section, choose an instrument/tuning upon which to base the tablature.

8. Set the Number of Strings parameter to the number of strings the instrument provides.

9. The pitches of each string for the instrument appear in the parameters below the Number of Strings parameter. You can either leave them as is, or you can customize the pitches to your liking.

10. Save your settings as a preset.

11. Click on OK to close the Tablature Settings dialog box.

Your new tablature style should now appear in the Preset drop-down list in the Tablature section of the Staff View Layout dialog box.

Regenerating Tablature

You can use different tablature styles for different sections of the same tablature staff by following these steps:

1. In the Staff pane, select the notes or tablature numbers for which you want to use a different tablature style.

2. Right-click anywhere in the Staff pane and select Regenerate Tablature from the pop-up menu to open the Regenerate Tablature dialog box (see Figure 13.17).

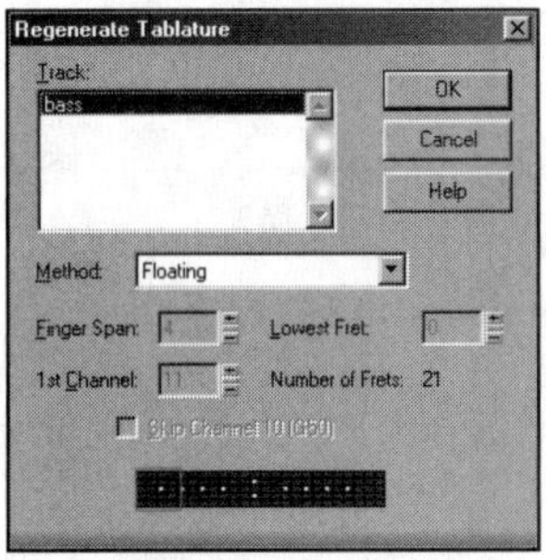

Figure 13.17
You can define different tablature styles for selected notes by using the Regenerate Tablature feature.

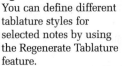

3. Set the Method, Finger Span, Lowest Fret, and 1st Channel parameters, if applicable. These parameters work the same way as described previously.

4. Click on OK.

SONAR changes the tablature style of the selected notes based on your parameter settings.

Adding Notes via Tablature

In addition to just displaying tablature, you can use a tablature staff to add notes to a track by doing the following:

1. Select the Draw tool.

2. Choose a note duration by clicking on the appropriate note duration button in the second toolbar.

3. Move the mouse pointer over the tablature staff. It changes its shape to a crosshair.

4. Position the crosshair within any measure and over a line in the tablature staff.

5. Click and hold the left mouse button. Now drag your mouse pointer up and down to select a fret number.

6. Release the mouse button to enter the note.

Editing Notes via Tablature

You can also edit notes via a tablature staff. To do so, just follow these steps:

1. Select the Draw tool.

2. To change the fret number of a note, right-click on it and select a new number from the pop-up menu.

3. To move a note to a different string (line) on the tablature staff, click and drag the note while pressing the Alt key on your computer keyboard. Drag the note up or down to move it. If the note is not supposed to play on a certain string, it will not be allowed to move there.

Exporting Tablature to a Text File

One last tablature feature that you might find useful is being able to save the tablature as a text file either for printing or distribution over the Internet. By saving the tablature this way, you can share your tablature with other guitarists even if they don't own SONAR. You use this feature as follows:

1. Select a MIDI track in the Track view.

2. In the Staff view, right-click anywhere in the Staff pane and select Export To ASCII TAB. The Save As dialog box opens.

3. Type a name for the file.

4. Click on Save.

SONAR saves the data in the MIDI track as tablature in a text file.

TIP

You might want to try quantizing the track before you save it as tablature. Doing so usually produces more accurate results.

Printing Your Music

After all is notated and done, you can print your music to paper if you have a printer connected to your computer. SONAR automatically sets up your music on separate pages, including the song title, composer, and other information, along with the notation. You can print your musical score like this:

1. Select File > Info to open the File Info window and fill out all the information you want to have included on your sheet music. You can use the Title, Subtitle, Instructions, Author, and Copyright parameters. For more information about the File Info window, see Chapter 4.

2. With the Staff view open, select File > Print Preview. SONAR goes into Print Preview mode (see Figure 13.18) and displays your music on virtual pages, letting you see how it will look before you print it.

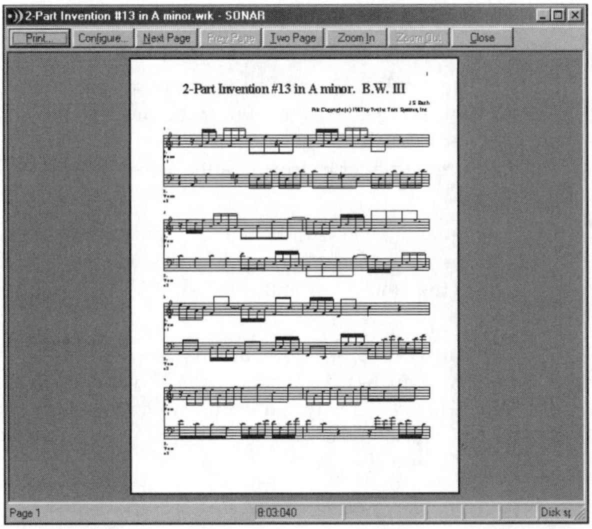

Figure 13.18
You can see how your music will look on paper before you print it by using the Print Preview mode.

3. To zoom the display in or out, click on the Zoom In or Zoom Out buttons.

4. Depending on the length of your song, SONAR usually shows two pages at once on the screen. If you would rather view only one page at a time, click on the One Page button.

5. If your song takes up more than two pages, you can navigate through them by using the Next Page and Prev Page buttons.

6. Before you print your music, you need to select a size for your score. To do so, click on the Configure button to open the Staff View Print Configure dialog box.

7. From the single drop-down list, choose the size you want to use. SONAR provides nine different sizes to choose from. They are standard music-engraving sizes used by professional music publishers. Each size is used for a different purpose. Size 0 (Commercial or Public) is usually used for wire-bound manuscripts. Size 1 (Giant or English) is usually used for school band music books or instructional books. Sizes 2 or 3 (Regular, Common, or Ordinary) are usually used for printing classical music. Size 4 (Peter) is usually used for folios or organ music. Size 5 (Large Middle) is usually used for ensemble music. Size 6 (Small Middle) is usually used for condensed sheet music. Size 7 (Cadenza) is usually used for pocket music editions. And Size 8 (Pearl) is usually used for thematic advertisement.

8. Click on OK. The music is redrawn using the new size.

9. Click on the Print button.

When the standard Windows Print dialog box opens, you can set up your printer and print your music.

TIP

Here's one final tip. If you like to compose your music from scratch using the Staff view, you can use one of the included templates listed in the New Project File dialog box when creating your new project. For example, if you want to compose for a string quartet, select the Classical String Quartet template.

The templates come with all the track parameters preset, but you might need to change a few of them to match your studio setup. After that, select all the tracks in the Track view and then select View > Staff to open them in the Staff view.

Everything is set up with the proper clefs, staff names, and more. The only settings you might need to adjust are the meter and key. Other than that, you have a blank slate ready and waiting to be filled with the music notation for your latest masterpiece.

14

Studio Control with StudioWare and Sysx

Most of today's modern appliances are computer controlled. Need to cook a meal? Push a few buttons on the stove, and it automatically sets the right time and temperature for your recipe. Need to wash your clothes? Yada, yada, yada… It's the same thing with modern recording studio gear—most everything is computer controlled, and the gear supports MIDI, too. I'm not just talking about MIDI instruments (such as synthesizer keyboards), but audio processing equipment and mixing boards as well.

Why would these products include support for MIDI? Because, like MIDI instruments, they have internal parameters that can be changed and stored. Because these products provide support for MIDI, their parameters become accessible to other MIDI devices, such as your computer. This means it is now possible to control just about every piece of equipment in your studio via your computer, provided the equipment supports MIDI and you have the right software. Lucky for you, you don't need to buy any additional software, because SONAR has some built-in features for controlling and storing the parameters for any outboard MIDI gear. All you have to do is connect your MIDI devices to your computer (just as you would any MIDI instrument), and they can "talk" to each other— which brings me to the topics I'm going to discuss in this chapter:

▶ Working with System Exclusive data

▶ Learning how to use the Sysx view

▶ Introducing StudioWare

▶ Taking snapshots with StudioWare

▶ Recording control movements in StudioWare

System Exclusive

MIDI devices (other than MIDI instruments) don't usually provide standard musical functions, so their internal parameters are not compatible with standard MIDI messages, such as Note On messages, for instance. Instead, they have to communicate using special MIDI messages called *System Exclusive*. I talked a little about System Exclusive messages in Chapter 3. System Exclusive messages give you access to any special functions that a manufacturer includes in a MIDI instrument or device.

Not only do you have access to these functions, but by utilizing System Exclusive messages, you can send all the data from the MIDI instruments and devices in your studio to SONAR to be stored in your projects. Why is this capability important? Because you can set up all your equipment with specific settings for a project, store the data in the project, and then send the data back to the devices at the beginning of your next recording session. This means that the next time you open the project, you can have all the equipment in your studio set up automatically, without your having to touch a single knob. Cool, no?

The Sysx View

SONAR gives you access to System Exclusive data via the Sysx view (see Figure 14.1). Using the Sysx view, you can store up to 8,191 banks, each of which can contain any number of System Exclusive messages (limited only by the amount of memory in your computer system). So, for example, you could dedicate a different bank to store the data for each separate piece of equipment in your studio. You could also store different sets of patch data for a single MIDI instrument in separate banks. Then, during different times in your Project, you could send specific Patch data to change the sounds in the instrument for that part of the song (you'll learn more about this topic later).

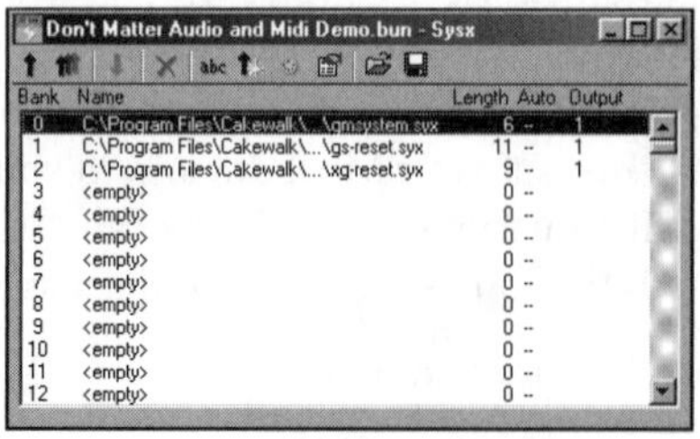

Figure 14.1
The Sysx View lets you store System Exclusive data within the current project.

Receiving System Exclusive Data

To store System Exclusive data in a bank in the Sysx View, you need to do a *data dump*. Essentially, the MIDI device from which you want to grab data dumps (or sends) it to your computer to be stored in one of the Sysx view banks.

NOTE

Be sure to check SONAR's Global MIDI Options to see whether the Record System Exclusive data setting is activated. To do so, select Options > Global to open the Global Options dialog box. Then select the MIDI tab. In the Record section, click on System Exclusive to place a check mark next to it. If this setting isn't turned on, SONAR will block all incoming System Exclusive data.

Creating a Data Dump

To do a data dump, follow these steps:

1. Choose View > Sysx to open the Sysx view and then click on a bank to highlight it for incoming System Exclusive data.

2. Click on the Receive Bank button (the one with the downward-pointing red arrow) to open the Receive System Exclusive dialog box (see Figure 14.2).

Figure 14.2
You use the Receive System Exclusive dialog box to request a data dump from your MIDI device.

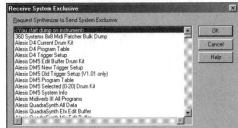

3. Choose a DRM (dump request macro) from the list. If you don't see your MIDI device listed, select the very first option: <You start dump on instrument>. Click on OK. Then start the data dump using the Control Panel on your device. (See the device's user guide for more information on how to use the Control Panel.)

NOTE

Dump request macros (DRMs) are special System Exclusive messages. Some MIDI devices support them, and some don't. If you have a MIDI device that supports DRMs, SONAR can send a DRM to the device, asking it to send back its parameter data. If you have a MIDI device that doesn't support DRMs, you have to initiate the data dump manually from the Control Panel on the device.

TIP

Just because your MIDI device isn't listed in the Receive System Exclusive dialog box doesn't mean the device doesn't support DRMs. You'll need to look in its user's guide to see whether it has DRMs available. If so, you can set them up to be used within SONAR. To do so, open the file C:\Program Files\Cakewalk\SONAR 1\cakewalk.ini using the Windows Notepad. Inside that file, you'll find instructions on how to add new DRMs to the list in the Receive System Exclusive dialog box.

4. If you do see your device listed, select the appropriate DRM and click on OK. The DRM may ask you for additional information. For instance, if the DRM requests that the device send the data for a single sound patch, you'll need to input the patch number you want it to send. This process is pretty straightforward; you can just follow the prompts.

5. Whichever method you use to initiate the data dump, SONAR ultimately displays the Sysx Receive dialog box when it's ready to receive the data (see Figure 14.3). The dialog box shows the number of bytes of data being received as the dump takes place.

Figure 14.3
The Sysx Receive dialog box displays a count of the System Exclusive data.

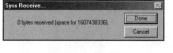

6. When the count stops, click on Done.

NOTE

If the number of bytes stays at zero more than a few seconds, then most likely something is wrong. Your MIDI device might not be hooked up properly, or you could have given the wrong answers for the additional DRM questions. Those answers differ depending on the MIDI device, so you'll need to consult its user's guide. In any event, if you have this problem, click on Cancel. Then check your connections and try the procedure again.

After the dump is complete, the Sysx view shows the bank you selected with a new name and length (in bytes).

Changing the Name of a Bank

If you want to change the name of a bank, follow these steps:

1. Select the bank.

2. Click on the Name button (the one with the lowercase *abc* shown on it) to open the Sysx Bank Name dialog box (see Figure 14.4).

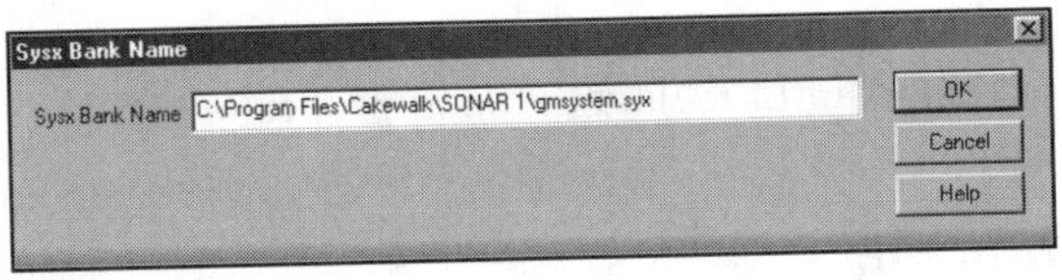

Figure 14.4
In the Sysx Bank Name dialog box, you can change the name of a bank.

3. Type a new name.
4. Click on OK.

> **TIP**
> You can also record System Exclusive data directly to a track, just as you would any other MIDI data. To do so, just set up your track parameters, start SONAR recording, and then manually initiate a data dump from your MIDI device. You should be aware of some limitations, though. When you're recording directly to a track, SONAR stores the data in Sysx data events instead of banks. Each Sysx data event can hold a single System Exclusive message of only 255 bytes in length. This means that if your MIDI device sends a message longer than 255 bytes, the message will get cut off, and it won't work when you try to send the data back. Plus, you won't get any warning that this has happened. It just won't work. So, essentially, you're better off using the Sysx view and banks to handle System Exclusive data. It's much easier, more efficient, and you can still send data back to a device during playback (I'll talk more about that in the next section).

Sending System Exclusive Data

After you set up your banks in a project, you can send the data back to your MIDI devices. Before you do, though, you should be sure that each bank being sent is first set to the appropriate MIDI output. Just as each track in the Track view can be set to send data to a particular MIDI output on your MIDI interface, each bank in the Sysx view can be set to a specific output as well. To do so, follow these steps:

1. Select the bank.
2. Click on the Output button (the one with the picture of a MIDI connection shown on it) to open the Sysx Bank Output dialog box (see Figure 14.5).

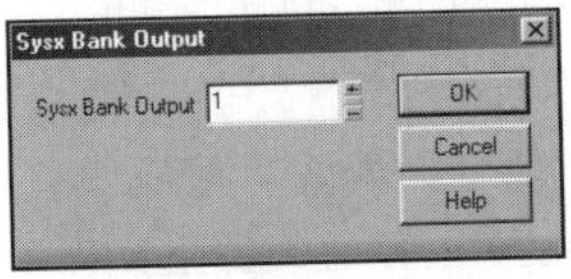

Figure 14.5
In the Sysx Bank Output dialog box, you can change the MIDI output assigned to a bank.

3. Type a new Output number. Remember that the data in this bank will be sent only to this MIDI output, so be sure the number is the same as the output number your device is connected to.
4. Click on OK.

After you assign the right output numbers to each of your banks, you can easily transmit the data to the appropriate MIDI devices in three different ways.

Manually

To send the data in a bank manually, just select the bank and click on the Send Bank button (the one with the single, black upward-pointing arrow shown on it). That's all there is to it. No muss, no fuss. You can also send all the data in every bank at once. You don't need to make any selections; just click on the Send All Banks button (the one with the three upward-pointing arrows shown on it).

Automatically

Each bank in the Sysx view has an option called Auto. If you activate this option for a bank, that bank will be sent automatically every time you open the project. For example, if you store all the parameter data from all your MIDI devices in a number of banks using the Sysx View and you set the Auto option on each of those banks, the next time you open your project, SONAR will send the System Exclusive data to your MIDI devices automatically. Your studio will then be ready to go, with all the correct settings for your project, without your having to do anything manually. To set the Auto option on a bank, just select the bank and click on the Auto Send Bank button (the one with the black, upward-pointing arrow and yellow star shown on it).

During Playback

Although using the Auto option is a very convenient way to send System Exclusive data, sometimes you might want to send a bank at a specific time during the playback of your project. For this purpose, SONAR provides a special Sysx bank event that you can place in any MIDI track in your project. Whenever SONAR encounters a Sysx bank event, it looks up the event's associated bank number in the Sysx view and then sends that bank.

To add a Sysx bank event to a MIDI track, you have to do so manually by using the Event view. Here's how:

1. Select a MIDI track in your project and choose View > Event List to open the Event List view for that track (see Figure 14.6).

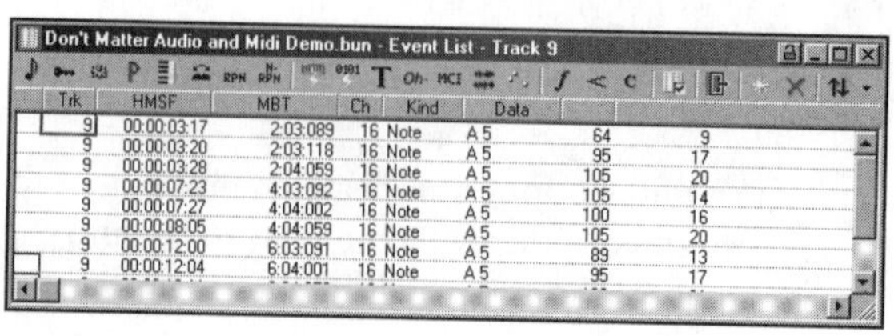

Figure 14.6
Using the Event List view, you can add Sysx bank events to your MIDI tracks.

2. Move the Now Time cursor to the point within the list where you want to insert the new Sysx bank event.

3. Click on the Insert Event button (the one with the yellow star shown on it) to insert a new event. Initially, the event will take on the characteristics of the event at which the Now time cursor was placed.

4. To change the event to a Sysx bank event, move the Now time cursor over to the Kind column and press the Enter key on your computer keyboard to open the Kind of Event dialog box (see Figure 14.7).

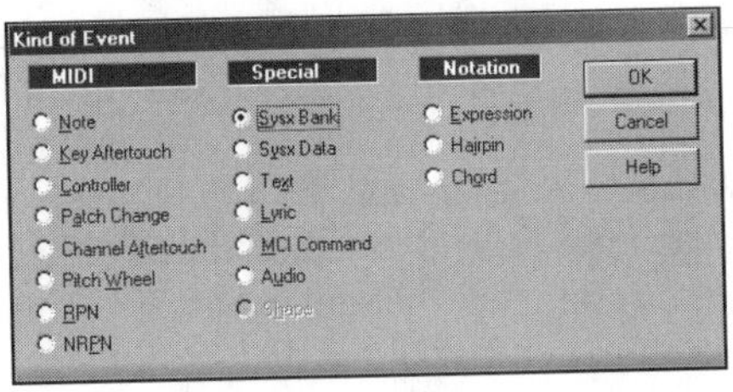

Figure 14.7
In the Kind of Event dialog box, you can change the type of the current event.

5. Select the Sysx Bank option in the Special section and click on OK.

6. Move the Now time cursor over to the Data column and press the Enter key on your computer keyboard. The number in the Data column becomes highlighted. Here, you enter the number of the bank you want to be sent.

7. Type a bank number and press the Enter key on your computer keyboard.

Now, during playback when SONAR encounters that Sysx bank event, it will send the appropriate System Exclusive data to your MIDI device.

CAUTION
MIDI is meant to transmit only one piece of data at a time. Of course, it transmits the data so fast that it sounds as if all the data in the tracks are playing simultaneously. But MIDI does have its limits, and if you try to transmit huge amounts of data in a short amount of time, playback will be interrupted. This happens quite often with System Exclusive data. So, if you're going to send banks of data during playback, try to send only one bank at a time throughout your project and also try to keep each bank short in length. You'll have to do a little experimenting, but if you keep each bank between 100 and 255 bytes, you shouldn't have any problems.

Editing Bank Data

The Sysx view provides a feature that allows you to edit the data in a bank. To edit this data, select a bank, and click on the Edit Data button (the one with a hand pointing to a piece of paper shown on it). Clicking on this button opens the Edit System Exclusive Bytes dialog box (see Figure 14.8).

CHAPTER 14

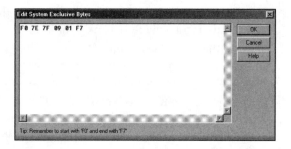

In the dialog box, you'll see a list of numbers. Each number represents one byte of System Exclusive data in hexadecimal format. You can change the numbers just as you would with text in a word processor. If the bank contains more than one System Exclusive message, the beginning of each message is designated by the number F0 and the end of each message is designated by the number F7. This way, System Exclusive data stays compatible with standard data in the MIDI language.

Whenever a MIDI device sees the number F0, it automatically knows that this number designates the beginning of a System Exclusive message. But that's as far as it goes in terms of identifying the data. All the bytes in a System Exclusive message that fall between the F0 and F7 are different, depending on which MIDI device they are associated with, so there's really not much else I can explain about this feature. If you want to learn more about the System Exclusive messages your MIDI device supports, consult the user's manual for that device.

If you ever want to delete a bank in the Sysx View, just select the bank, and click on the Clear Bank button (the one with the big red X on it). SONAR will ask whether you really want to delete. Be careful, because you cannot undo this procedure. When a bank is deleted, you cannot get it back without doing a data dump all over again.

Sharing with Friends

Even though all the data in the banks of the Sysx view are stored along with the data in your current project, you can also load and save banks individually in a special System Exclusive data file format. This file format is the same one used by the public-domain System Exclusive data dump software utility called MIDIEX. MIDIEX is such a popular program that its file format became a standard for storing System Exclusive data on disk. What's great about the file format is that SONAR and many other sequencers support it, so you can easily share your System Exclusive data with your friends. Of course, being able to share won't matter much if you don't own the same MIDI devices, but if you do, you can easily share sound patch data for your MIDI instruments, and so on.

Saving

To save the data in a bank, follow these steps:

1. Select the bank.
2. Click on the Save Bank To File button (the one with the floppy disk shown on it) to open the Save As dialog box.
3. Type a name for the file. The file should have an .SYX extension; SONAR should append this extension to the name automatically.
4. Click on Save.

Loading

To load data into a bank, follow these steps:

1. Select a bank.
2. Click on the Load Bank From File button (the one with the yellow folder shown on it).
3. If the bank you selected already has some data in it, SONAR will ask whether you want to append the data from the file to the existing data. Click on Yes to append the data, or click on No to replace the data. SONAR then displays the Open dialog box.
4. Select an .SYX file to load and click on Open.

The data from the file is loaded into the bank you selected, and the bank is named after the file. You can change the name of the bank, as you learned earlier.

> **TIP**
>
> There's no easy method for copying a bank either within the same project or from one project to another, but you can copy using the Save Bank and Load Bank features. Just save a bank to an .SYX file from the current project. If you want to have a copy of that bank in the current project, just load it into another bank. If you want to have a copy of that bank in another project, open the other project and then load the bank into the Sysx view of that project.

Intro to StudioWare

Being able to store all the parameter settings for your MIDI gear within a project is great. You can have your whole studio set up in a matter of seconds. To set those parameters initially, you still have to fiddle with the knobs and controls on the MIDI gear itself. Because some MIDI devices have a limited number of controls, the only way to change their parameters is to wade through an endless maze of menus on a small (and sometimes cryptic) LCD screen. SONAR provides a feature, called StudioWare, that lets you adjust all the parameters in your MIDI devices without ever having to leave your computer. And more importantly, it lets you access those less-than-accessible parameters in a very intuitive and easy manner.

Using StudioWare, you can create on-screen control panels that let you adjust the parameters in any of your MIDI devices remotely from your computer. Basically, you can have virtual buttons, knobs, and faders on your computer screen that represent each of the adjustable parameters in your MIDI devices. When you move a knob or fader on your computer screen, it changes the value of an assigned parameter in a MIDI device. So now, not only can you store MIDI device parameters, but you also can adjust them. Using the Sysx view and StudioWare, you may never have to touch your MIDI gear again (except maybe to turn it on). Plus, the adjustments you make to any on-screen controls can be recorded and then played back in real-time, which means you can automate parameter changes for a MIDI device as well.

The StudioWare View

Creating your own StudioWare panels may sound like a complicated task—and yes, it can be. You need to have a good understanding of MIDI and System Exclusive data, but that doesn't mean you can't get any use out of StudioWare. Besides, some basic panels are easy enough for anyone to put together, as I'll discuss in Chapter 15.

Getting started with StudioWare is actually very easy. As a matter of fact, for a really quick demonstration, you can have SONAR automatically create a panel for you from the track setup in your project. To see what I mean, do the following:

1. Select File > Open and load one of the sample projects included with SONAR. For this example, use the Don't Matter Audio and Midi Demo.bun project.

2. After the file loads, take a look at the Track view (see Figure 14.9). Notice that Tracks 2, 3, 4, 5, 6, and 7 are audio tracks, and Tracks 8 and 9 are MIDI tracks. Highlight all of them. (Forget about Track 1. It's blank.)

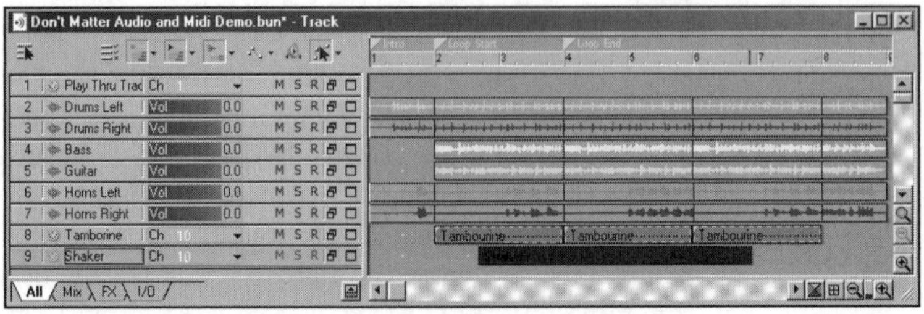

Figure 14.9
The Track view for Don't Matter Audio and Midi Demo.bun shows both audio and MIDI tracks.

3.   Select View > StudioWare to open the StudioWare view (see Figure 14.10).

Figure 14.10
The StudioWare view houses the virtual on-screen control panels.

As you can see in Figure 14.10, StudioWare has created a control panel representing all the tracks you selected in the Track view. Each track has its own set of controls, and, yes, they really work. If you don't believe me, go ahead and start playing the project. Then try changing one of the volume faders (by clicking and dragging it)—say, for the guitar track. See? Of course, you might be saying to yourself, "This view looks similar to the Console view, so why would I need it?" You're absolutely right. It mimics the same controls that are in the Console view, and you really don't need it. It's just a cool demonstration trick. StudioWare's real power lies in mimicking the control panels of your external MIDI devices.

Unfortunately, there's no quick trick for creating those types of panels, but SONAR does include a number of predesigned panels that you can use within your own projects. If you can't find a panel for your MIDI device, Cakewalk also provides a nice library of additional StudioWare panels on its Web site; you can download these panels for free. And you can even find other places on the Internet where you can download free panels written by other users (see Appendix D, "Cakewalk Resources on the Web").

Opening a StudioWare Panel

A StudioWare panel is either stored as part of a project file or as a separate StudioWare file with the extension .CakewalkStudioWare. If a project file contains a panel, the panel is automatically opened when you open the project. To open a StudioWare file, just do the following:

1.   Select File > Open to display the Open dialog box.

2.   Select StudioWare from the Files of Type drop-down list to display only StudioWare files.

3.   Choose a file.

4.   Click on Open.

SONAR then displays the StudioWare view containing the panel from the file you just opened. Because all panels are different, I can't really explain how each one works. Usually, a panel mimics the controls of a MIDI device, so if you own the corresponding MIDI device, you shouldn't have any trouble figuring out how to use its StudioWare counterpart.

After you've opened a panel, you can adjust the controls, take a snapshot, or record your control movements, and so on. Adjusting the controls is straightforward. The buttons, knobs, and faders in a StudioWare panel work the same way they do in the Console view (which you learned about in Chapter 12).

Taking a Snapshot

The snapshot function works almost the same way as with the Console view, too, but there are a few differences. Instead of recording the control data in separate tracks, the control data from a StudioWare panel is recorded into a single track. Most StudioWare panels include a knob control that allows you to set which track the control data will be recorded into. As an example, take a look at the General MIDI.CakewalkStudioWare panel. You'll see a knob labeled "Track." Adjusting that knob changes the track number for the panel. If you open some of the other sample panels, you'll notice the same type of track control. It might look a little different, but it functions in the same way. By the way, if a panel doesn't have a track control knob, either the panel wasn't designed to record data to a track (some of them don't), or the panel will automatically record its data to Track 1. So, when you're working with this kind of panel, it's a good idea to leave Track 1 dedicated to recording control data.

To take a snapshot of the controls in a StudioWare panel, do the following:

1.   Set the Now time to the point in the project where you want the snapshot to be stored.

2.   Adjust the controls in the StudioWare panel to the values at which you want them to be set during that part of the project.

3.   Click on the Snapshot button (the one with the picture of a camera shown on it) in the toolbar at the top of the StudioWave view (see Figure 14.11).

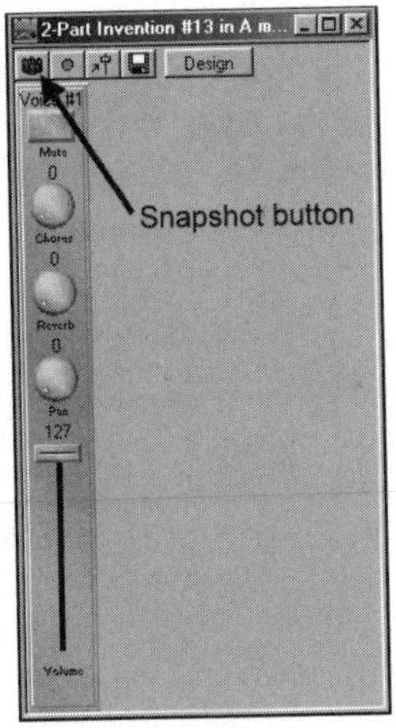

Figure 14.11
Click the Snapshot
button to take a
snapshot in the
StudioWare view.

Snapshot button

4. Repeat steps 1 through 3 until you've created all the snapshots that
    you need for your project.

Recording Control Movements

Recording the movements of the controls on a StudioWare panel is also
similar to the same procedure in the Console view, but as with taking a
snapshot, there are a few differences. The first difference is the track
number procedure I described in the preceding section.

The second difference is in grouping controls together. Just as you can do
in the Console view, you can group multiple controls together in a
StudioWare panel so that you can easily change more than one control
simultaneously. The differences here are in how controls are grouped and
in how single controls in a group are adjusted.

For grouping controls, instead of right-clicking on a control and assigning
it to a colored group, you simply select an initial control, hold down the
Ctrl key on your computer keyboard, and click on one or more additional
controls in the panel. Those controls are then grouped. Grouping controls
in a StudioWare panel is much less sophisticated. They don't have any
grouping properties like there are in the Console view either.

For adjusting a single control that belongs to a group, just hold down the
Shift key on your computer keyboard and then adjust the control. In the
Console view, the procedure is the same, except that you hold down the
Ctrl key.

All these techniques work with any StudioWare panel, even the ones you
design yourself, which you'll learn about in Chapter 15. There are also
differences in the actual recording of the control movements. The
procedure for recording control movements in the StudioWare view are
as follows:

CHAPTER 14

1. Turn on the Record Widget Movements function by clicking on the Record Widget Movements button (the button with the big red dot shown on it), located just to the right of the Snapshot button at the top of the StudioWare view (see Figure 14.12).

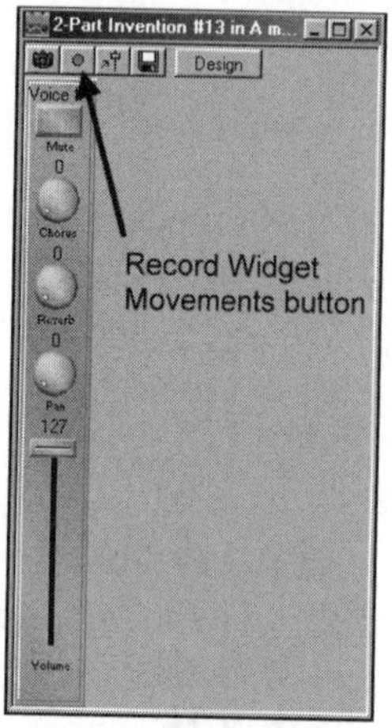

Figure 14.12
Click the Record Widget Movements button to activate the Record Widget Movements function.

2. Set the Now time to just before the point in the project where you want to start recording control changes.

3. Start the project playing.

4. When the Now time get to the point in the project where you want to begin recording control changes, adjust the controls in the StudioWare panel with your mouse.

5. When you're finished, stop playback of the project.

6. Because you're manipulating on-screen controls with your mouse, you can make only one change at a time. What if you want to have two different controls change at the same time? For every control that you want to have change in the same timeframe, you must repeat steps 2 through 5.

TIP
Instead of starting and stopping playback each time you want to record additional control changes, try setting up a loop so that SONAR will play the project (or section of the project) over and over again. I described looping in Chapter 6.

7. After you've finished recording all the control changes that you need, be sure to turn off the Record Widget Movements function.

TIP

If you want the controls in your StudioWare panel to move according to the changes you recorded, activate the Update Widget Values function by clicking on the Update Widget Values button (the button with the picture of a slider on it), located just to the right of the Record Widget Movements button at the top of the StudioWare view.

15

Advanced StudioWare Techniques

Chapter 14 ended with an introduction to StudioWare—what it is, what it does, and how you can use it to control your outboard MIDI devices from your computer with on-screen panels. That chapter also briefly touched on the topic of creating your own StudioWare panels. Initially, you might think that StudioWare should be left to the real techno-oriented musicians among us, but that's not true. Anyone can get some good use out of SONAR's StudioWare features. This chapter further describes StudioWare, covering the following topics:

▶ The basics of designing your own panels
▶ Widgets
▶ Widget properties and how to use them
▶ A step-by-step panel: Custom SONAR toolbars

Designing Basics

Designing your own StudioWare panels can get very involved, so Cakewalk has tried to make the process as intuitive as possible. Instead of making you wade through all kinds of complex computer programming code, SONAR lets you essentially drag and drop your way to creating a panel.

If you take a look at the StudioWare View (see Figure 15.1), you'll notice a button labeled Design at the top of the window.

Figure 15.1
The Design button puts StudioWare into Design mode.

Clicking on that button puts StudioWare into Design mode and, at the same time, reveals ten new buttons along the top of the window (see Figure 15.2).

Figure 15.2
In Design mode, ten new buttons become available in the StudioWare view.

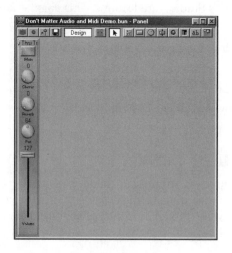

The first new button (the one with the grid shown on it) controls the Snap to Grid feature. It is similar to the Snap to Grid feature found in other areas of SONAR, which you learned about in Chapter 5. Instead of musical intervals, though, the grid is based on the pixels (dots) that make up your computer screen display. Clicking on the Snap to Grid button toggles that feature on or off. And if you click on the button while holding down the Shift key on your computer keyboard, the Snap to Grid dialog box is displayed. In this dialog box, you can set the size of the grid.

Clicking on the second button (the one with the mouse arrow shown on it) activates the Select tool. This tool allows you to select, move, and set the size of the widgets. The other eight buttons represent the widgets—

the elements that make up a StudioWare panel. (I'll describe the widgets in more detail later in this chapter.) Clicking on any of these buttons activates their associated widgets, allowing you to visually design a panel by placing objects (widgets) within the StudioWare view.

In other words, you can create a StudioWare panel by selecting different widgets and placing them within the StudioWare view with your mouse; for example, you can use the Button widget to add buttons to your panel. Then you can assign functions to each widget, making them perform different tasks. After you've finished your design, you can save the panel and then later use it within any of your projects. Using widgets isn't really very complicated, although assigning functions to widgets can get a bit confusing; I'll go over that topic later.

The basic procedure for designing a new StudioWare panel is as follows:

1. Either create a new project or open an existing one. StudioWare panels can be designed or used only while a project is open.

2. Select View > StudioWare to open the StudioWare view (see Figure 15.3). You can also open the StudioWare view by selecting File > New and choosing StudioWare panel from the New Project File dialog box.

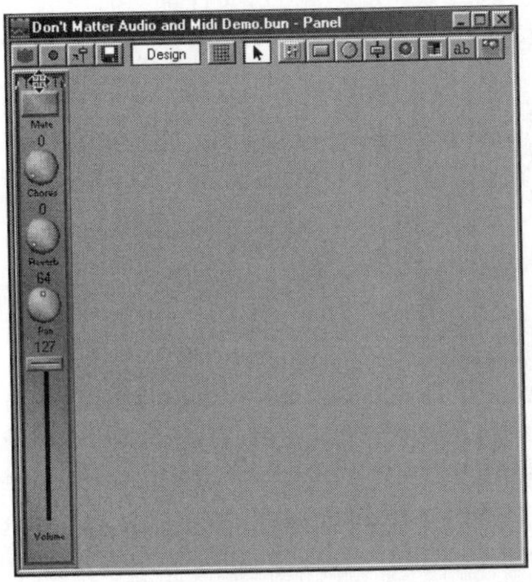

Figure 15.3
This new StudioWare panel contains the default set of controls.

3. Click on the Design button to put StudioWare into Design mode.

4. As you can see in Figure 15.3, whenever you create a new panel, SONAR automatically adds a set of controls for each track that's currently selected in the Track view. If no tracks are selected, just one set of controls is added for Track 1. But because you want to create your own panel from scratch, you should remove those default controls. To do so, click on each of the controls (widgets) one by one and press the Delete key on your computer keyboard.

TIP

You also can get rid of all the widgets simultaneously by clicking at the top of the set of controls, where you see the track number—for example, Track 1. Clicking here selects the Cluster widget (I'll explain this term in a moment), which contains all the other widgets. Then just press the Delete key on your computer keyboard to remove everything.

5. The StudioWare view should now look like the view shown in Figure 15.4. That vertical gray rectangle at the left is the blank slate that serves as the initial building block for your panel. This blank panel is actually a permanent cluster widget. You can't erase it. It will hold any other widgets you plan to add to the panel. Click on the cluster widget to select it and then drag the sides or corners with your mouse to change its size, thus setting the size of your panel.

Figure 15.4
The permanent cluster widget holds all the other widgets in your panel.

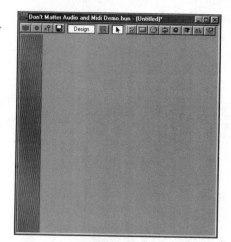

6. Add new widgets to your panel by clicking on one of the eight widget buttons at the top of the window to select it. Then click somewhere within the permanent cluster widget to place the new widget on your panel (see Figure 15.5). You can add as many widgets as you need (limited only by the amount of memory in your computer).

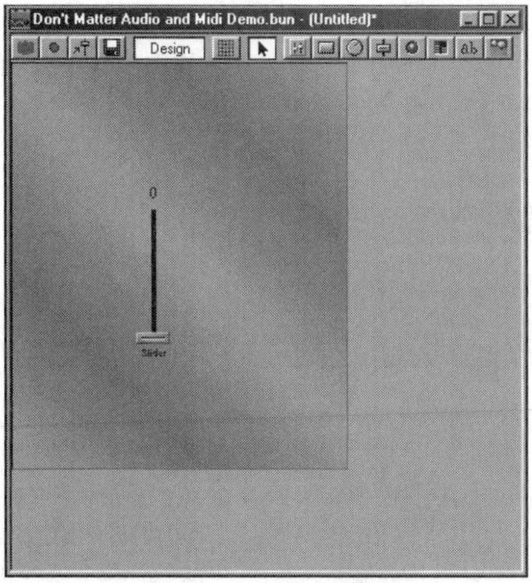

Figure 15.5
You just point and click to add a widget to your panel.

7. To change the position of a widget, select it and drag it to a new location within the panel. To change the size of a widget, select it and drag the highlighted sides or corners, just like you would a window. You can also copy, cut, and paste widgets as you would with anything else by using SONAR's Edit > Copy, Edit > Cut, and Edit > Paste menu commands.

8. Assign properties to each of the widgets in your panel. To do so, double-click on a widget to open the Widget Properties dialog box (see Figure 15.6). Adjust the relevant parameters and click on OK. (I'll explain widget properties in the next section of this chapter.)

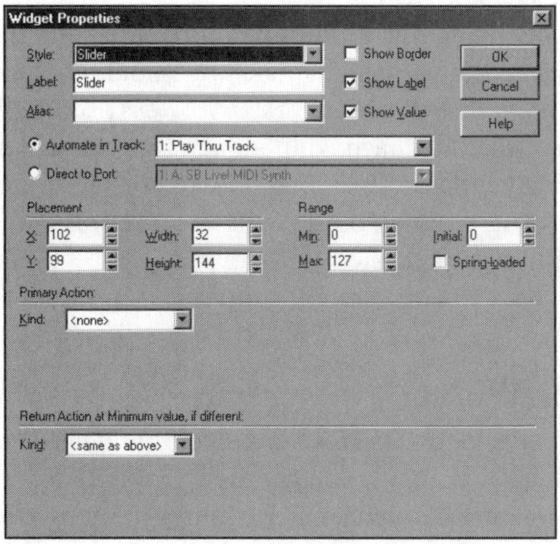

Figure 15.6
Using the Widget Properties dialog box, you can assign functions to each of the widgets in your panel.

9. After you finish making additions or changes to your new panel, you should save it. You either can save it along with the current project (you learned how to save projects in Chapter 4) or as a separate

CakewalkStudioWare file. To save it as a file, click on the Save button (the one with the floppy disk shown on it) to open the Save StudioWare dialog box (see Figure 15.7). There, type a name for the panel and click on OK.

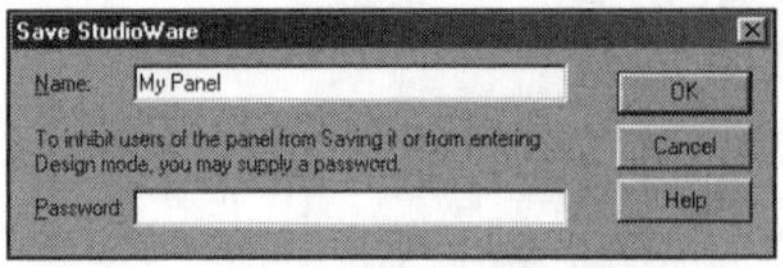

Figure 15.7
You can save your new panel by using the Save StudioWare dialog box.

Save StudioWare

Name: My Panel	OK
To inhibit users of the panel from Saving it or from entering Design mode, you may supply a password.	Cancel
Password:	Help

TIP

If you want to share your panel with friends, but you don't want them to be able to make any design changes to it, type a password in addition to a name in the Save StudioWare dialog box. The next time you open the StudioWare panel and click on the Design button, you will first be asked to enter the password. Don't forget your password, because you cannot make changes to your panel without it!

If you're sometimes forgetful—like Yours Truly—try encoding the password into the name of the panel. For example, you could use every other letter in the name of the panel as your password. So, for a panel named Special Proteus panel, the password would be seil poes pnl. It's doubtful that anyone will ever guess it, but you'll still have a quick and easy way to remember it.

Widgets and Their Properties

Graphically designing a StudioWare panel is one thing, but assigning properties to the widgets to make the panel work as you want it to is quite another. The basics are relatively easy to understand, and if you know the MIDI language well enough, you should get the hang of creating panels fairly quickly. Teaching how to create StudioWare panels could easily take up a whole book on its own, so instead, I'll just get you started by providing some basic information about each of the widgets—what they are, how to change their properties, and how to use them.

Cluster Widget

The cluster widget is a special widget that has but one purpose: to hold other widgets. Using it, you can design different sections of controls in your panel, just like what can be found in many real control panels on MIDI devices. For example, you could use one cluster widget to hold all the pitch-related controls for your device and another cluster widget to hold all the volume-related controls. You can also put cluster widgets inside each other so that you can divide your panel into additional subsections.

Name Change

Because a cluster widget doesn't provide any function other than acting as a "container" for other widgets, its only alterable property is its name. To change the name of a cluster widget, do the following:

1. Double-click on the cluster widget to open the Widget Properties dialog box.
2. In the field marked Label, type a name for the cluster widget.
3. Make sure the Show Label option is activated.
4. Click on OK.

By the way, you can change the name of other widgets in your panel using this same procedure.

Hidden Panel Sections

A cluster widget is good for one more thing: creating hidden sections of a panel. Why would you want to hide a part of your panel? Well, perhaps part of the panel should be accessible to the user only when certain conditions are met within another part of the panel. For example, you may have a very sophisticated MIDI device with a large number of alterable parameters—too many to fit nicely within the visible area of your panel. So, to keep things tidy, you could simply create a number of master buttons that, when clicked, would reveal their associated set of controls. Or you might just want to add a cool informational window containing author and copyright information about your panel. You do so as follows:

1. Click on the cluster widget button (the one with the dual faders shown on it) and then click anywhere within the panel to add a new cluster widget to the panel.
2. Resize the cluster widget so that it can fit the text of your name and perhaps a copyright notice.
3. Click on the Text/Numeric widget button (the one with the lowercase *ab* shown on it) and then click inside the new cluster widget to add a new Text/Numeric widget.
4. Double-click on the Text/Numeric widget to open the Widget Properties dialog box. Then, in the Label field, type Created by *Insert Your Name Here* and click on OK. You might have to resize the Text/Numeric widget so that your text will show correctly. At this point, your panel should look similar to Figure 15.8.

CHAPTER 15

Figure 15.8
Creating a hidden cluster widget is a fairly easy task, although it does involve quite a few steps.

5. Add another Text/Numeric widget and label it Copyright 2001 All Rights Reserved.

6. Change the name of the cluster widget to About this Panel..., but don't close the Widget Properties dialog box just yet. In the field named Alias, type HideAbout to assign a variable to the cluster widget.

NOTE

An *alias* is a variable that allows you to assign a numeric value to a widget. In other words, an alias lets a widget hold a number that can vary according to input from other widgets in the panel or from a user adjusting the widget's on-screen control. This programmable nature allows for some very sophisticated and complex panels.

In the case of a cluster widget, the value of its alias determines whether it will be visible. As soon as the alias surpasses a minimum value (that you set), the cluster widget becomes visible. As long as the alias remains less than the minimum value, however, the cluster widget stays invisible.

7. Under the Range section of the Widget Properties dialog box, type a Minimum value of 126 and an Initial value of 126. Also, make sure the Maximum value is 127.

8. Click on OK. The cluster widget will disappear. Don't worry; it's still there. You just can't see it.

9. To control the appearance of the cluster widget, you need to add a button to the panel. Click on the Button widget button (yeah, the one with a button shown on it) and then click inside the panel (preferably somewhere other than where the cluster widget is located).

10. Double-click on the Button widget and, in the Widget Properties dialog box, type HideAbout in the Alias field. Then make sure the Maximum value in the Range section is set to 127. Next, click on OK. (You can also give a name to the button, but I'll talk more about button widgets later.)

11. Remember to click on the Design button to exit Design mode.

Now try clicking on the button in your panel. The first time you click on the button, the About this Panel...Cluster Widget should appear. You see this panel because, when you click on the button, it changes the value of the "HideAbout" Alias to 127 (which is higher than the Minimum value). This makes the cluster widget become visible. Click on the button again, and the cluster should disappear. This time, the button changes the value of the "HideAbout" Alias back to 0 (which is lower than the Minimum value), thus making the cluster invisible again. What a neat trick, huh?

Text/Numeric Widget

The Text/Numeric widget is similar to the cluster widget in that it has a very simple nature; it enables you to add text to your panels. That's pretty much it. Text is useful for providing simple instructions on how to use the panel or for identification purposes, as I mentioned earlier. To change the text content of a Text/Numeric widget, just type some text in the Label field of the Widget Properties dialog box.

The Text/Numeric widget *does* have one advanced use, though. You can use it to display the numerical values of other widgets in the panel. You simply assign the same alias to the Text/Numeric widget as another widget, such as a button, knob, or slider. Then, when the value of the alias is changed by clicking on the button or moving the knob or slider, for example, the Text/Numeric widget will display the numerical value of the alias. You can set up a working example as follows:

1. If you don't already have a project open, do so now and set up a blank panel in the StudioWare view.

2. Click on the Slider widget button (the one with the single vertical fader shown on it) and then click somewhere inside the blank panel to add the slider widget to it.

3. Double-click on the Slider widget to open the Widget Properties dialog box.

4. Type SlideValue as the alias and click on OK. Don't worry about any of the other properties. The default values are fine.

5. Click on the Text/Numeric widget button (the one with the lowercase *ab* shown on it) and then click somewhere inside the panel to add the text/numeric widget to it.

6. Double-click on the Text/Numeric widget to open the Widget

CHAPTER 15

Properties dialog box.

7. Type SlideValue as the alias and type The Slider Value Is %d as the label.

> **TIP**
>
> In addition to the alias, StudioWare provides some special default variables that allow you to display the value of an alias via the Text/Numeric widget. By placing %d in the Label property of a Text/Numeric widget, you can show the value of that widget's alias as a decimal number. You can also display the value of an alias in hexadecimal form by using %x instead of %d. In addition, you can even specify the number of decimal digits that you want to see displayed by using the special variable %04d. In this case, if the alias were equal to 42, it would be displayed with four decimal places, like this: 0042.

8. Click on OK and turn off Design mode by clicking on the Design button. Your finished panel should look something like the one shown in Figure 15.9.

Figure 15.9
You can use the Text/Numeric widget like this to display the value of its alias.

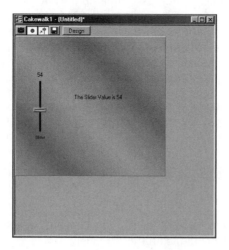

Now try dragging the slider control up and down. See how the text changes to reflect the value of the slider? When you move the slider up and down, it changes the value of its alias property (in this case, "SlideValue"). Because the Text/Numeric widget also has "SlideValue" as an alias, it is linked to the Slider widget. Plus, the special %d variable allows the value of the alias to be displayed in the Label property of the Text/Numeric widget.

Image Widget and Widget Appearance

To improve the look of your panels, you can use StudioWare to assign images to any of the widgets or place graphics directly in a panel using the Image widget. Actually, because StudioWare enables you to assign images to any of the other widgets, you probably won't use the Image widget very much. Perhaps, if you want to add a logo to your panel, you might use the Image widget, but then, you could also do so by simply assigning an image to a cluster widget. To see what you can do with images, take a look at some of the sample panels included with SONAR—in particular, the Line 6 POD.CakewalkStudioWare and the Roland JV-2080 Patch.CakewalkStudioWare files. They use images extensively to make the panels look very cool. By the way, these samples also use the hidden cluster widget technique I described earlier. Try clicking on some of the buttons, and you'll see what I mean.

Adding an Image Widget

If you ever need to use the Image widget, you follow these steps:

1. If you don't already have a project open, do so now and set up a blank panel in the StudioWare view.

2. Click on the Image widget button (the one with the picture shown on it) and then click somewhere inside the blank panel to add the Image widget to it.

3. Right-click on the Image widget and select Foreground Bitmap from the pop-up menu to open the Widget Bitmap file selector.

> **TIP**
>
> When you select Foreground Bitmap, the image you choose will be stretched to fill the Image widget. If you want to add a tiled background instead (the same thing you can do to the Windows Desktop), select Background Bitmap from the pop-menu.

4. Select a file and then click on Open. The image file has to be in the Windows bitmap (.BMP) image file format, or you won't be able to open it.

> **TIP**
>
> If you want to put the Image widget back to its original state (just a blank gray box), click on either the Default or the None buttons in the Widget Bitmap file selector.

Your new Image widget is then filled with the image you selected. If the image is bigger than the default Image widget size, the Image widget will expand to fit the entire image. As an example, take a look at Figure 15.10.

Changing Widget Appearance

Earlier, I mentioned that you can also simply assign an image to any of the widgets instead of having to use the Image widget. You do so in the same way you add an image to an Image widget, but with one small difference: The Foreground Bitmap and Background Bitmap options fill different parts of the widget with their images. For example, if you assign a background bitmap to a meter widget, the image fills the dark part of the meter display. If you assign a foreground bitmap, the image fills the lit part of the meter display. The Background and Foreground options work differently with each widget. To find out how, do a little experimenting.

NOTE

You must consider two exceptions when assigning images to widgets. First, the feature doesn't work at all with Text/Numeric widgets, for obvious reasons. Second, a cluster widget can accept only a background bitmap, and the image always fills the entire widget.

Instead of assigning an image to a widget, you can change its color. The procedure is the same as when you assign an image, except that you select either Foreground Color or Background Color from the pop-up menu and choose a color from the standard Windows Color Chooser dialog box.

Indicator Widgets

In addition to the Text/Numeric widget, two other widgets provide feedback on alias values. They are the LED and Meter widgets. Instead of textual or numeric feedback, though, the LED and Meter widgets provide graphical indications of alias values.

The LED Widget

The LED widget works similarly to the cluster widget in that it reacts whenever its alias becomes greater than the specified Minimum value. Instead of appearing or disappearing, however, the LED widget turns its "virtual light" on and off. You can use this widget for many different purposes; for example, you can use it to indicate when a button is pressed or not. Here's an example:

1. If you don't already have a project open, do so now and set up a blank panel in the StudioWare view.

2. Click on the Button widget button (the one with the button shown on it) and then click somewhere inside the blank panel to add the Button widget to it.

3. Double-click on the Button widget to open the Widget Properties dialog box.

4. Type LEDTest as an alias and click on OK.

5. Click on the LED widget button (the one with the red "light" shown on it) and then click somewhere inside the panel to add the LED widget to it.

6. Double-click on the LED widget to open the Widget Properties dialog box.

7. Type LEDTest as an alias and enter 126 for the Minimum and Initial values in the Range section. Then click on OK.

8. Turn off Design mode by clicking on the Design button. Your finished panel should look something like the one shown in Figure 15.11.

Figure 15.11

This panel example shows how to use an LED widget.

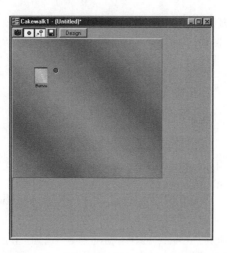

Now try clicking on the button in your panel. The first time you click on the button, the LED should light up (with the color red). It lights up because, when you click on the button, it changes the value of the "LEDtest" alias to 127 (which is higher than the Minimum value). This makes the LED widget light up. Click on the button again, and the LED should turn off. This time, the button changes the value of the "LEDtest" alias back to 0 (which is lower than the Minimum value), thus turning off the LED.

The Meter Widget

Instead of just a simple on/off indication, the Meter widget can display a whole range of values. This widget works well for graphically showing the value of the knob or slider widgets (which I'll talk about in a moment). Essentially, it works the same way as a Text/Numeric widget in that, if you assign the same alias to a knob or slider widget and the Meter widget, they are linked together and the Meter widget provides a graphical representation of the value of the alias. As an example, try the following steps:

1. If you don't already have a project open, do so now and set up a blank panel in the StudioWare view.

2. Click on the Slider widget button (the one with the single vertical fader shown on it), and then click somewhere inside the blank panel to add the Slider widget to it.

3. Double-click on the Slider widget to open the Widget Properties dialog box.

4. Type SlideValue as the alias, and click on OK. Don't worry about any of the other properties. The default values are fine.

5. Click on the Meter widget button (the one with the double bar meter shown on it) and then click somewhere inside the panel to add the Meter widget to it.

6. Double-click on the Meter widget to open the Widget Properties dialog box.

7. Type SlideValue as the alias.

8. Click on OK, and turn off Design mode by clicking on the Design button. Your finished panel should look something like the one shown in Figure 15.12.

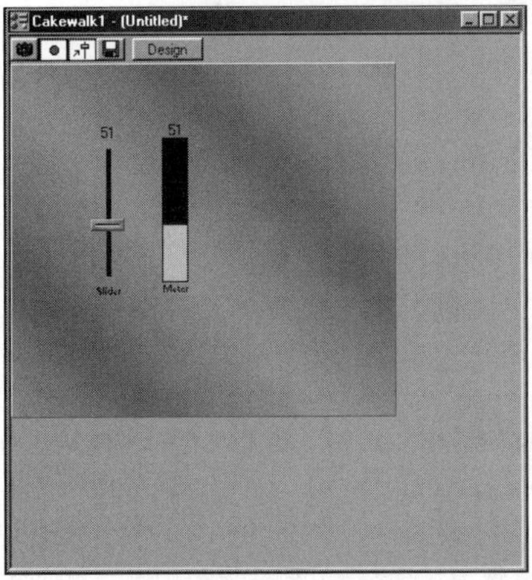

Figure 15.12
This example shows how to use the Meter widget to graphically display the value of its alias.

Now try dragging the slider control up and down. See how the meter changes to reflect the value of the slider? When you move the slider up and down, it changes the value of its alias property (in this case, "SlideValue"). Because the Meter widget also has "SlideValue" as an alias, it is linked to the Slider widget. So, when you move the slider up and down, the meter moves along with it.

Button Widget

As I've already demonstrated in a few of the previous examples, you can use the Button widget to make cluster widgets appear or disappear and to turn LED widgets on or off. You also can use it to send MIDI data (either to be recorded into a track or directly out to a MIDI port), run CAL programs (see chapters 16 and 17 for more information about CAL), and even activate functions within SONAR. You do so by using the other property settings in the Widget Properties dialog box.

More Widget Properties

If you open the Widget Properties dialog box (see Figure 15.13), you'll notice a number of other properties that you can apply to the widgets. These properties, which provide additional functionality to the button, knob, and slider widgets, are the real power behind StudioWare panels.

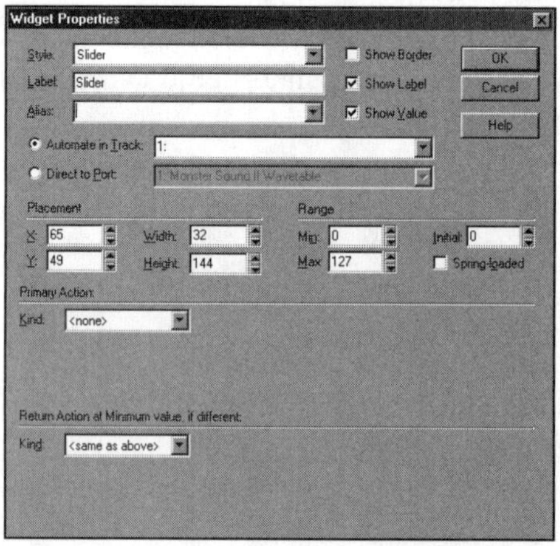

Figure 15.13
The additional property settings in the Widget Properties dialog box really give StudioWare panels their power.

Automate in Track and Direct to Port Properties

As you learned in Chapter 14, the movements of the controls on a panel can either be recorded to a track or sent directly out a MIDI port to be received by a MIDI device. What determines whether a widget's movements will be recorded or sent to a MIDI port are the Automate in Track and the Direct to Port properties.

Setting these properties is actually very simple. If you want the movements of a widget to be recorded to a track, you activate the Automate in Track property and select a track number from its drop-down list. If you want the movements of a widget to be sent directly out a MIDI port, you activate the Direct to Port property and select a port number from its drop-down list.

> **TIP**
>
> You can also use aliases with the Automate In Track and Direct To Port properties. This capability is useful if you want to be able to change the track or port number via another widget on the panel. For example, you can set up a Knob widget to act as a track number control. To do so, just assign the Knob widget an alias and then assign the same alias to the Automate in Track property of another widget. While you're using the panel, any adjustments you make to the knob affect which track is used to record the data from the other widget. Take a look at the sample panel called General MIDI.CakewalkStudioWare for a working demonstration. The track knob in that panel affects which track the data from all the other controls in the panel will be recorded on.

Primary Action Property

Of course, a widget also needs to be told what kind of data it's supposed to send, and that's where the Primary Action property comes in. The Primary Action property determines a widget's main function. Its function can be sending MIDI data (note, controller, patch change, pitch wheel, aftertouch, System Exclusive, and so on), running CAL programs, activating SONAR functions, or controlling track parameters, for example.

To set the primary action for a widget, you simply select the type of Action from the Primary Action Kind drop-down list. For each action, you must set additional associated parameters. For example, if you select Note from the list, you can set the MIDI channel, pitch, and velocity at which the note will be played when the widget is manipulated. I'm not going to go over all the primary actions available. If you know your MIDI, then most of them are self-explanatory. The SONAR Help file provides some basic reference information about actions in the Working with External Devices > Working with StudioWare > Functional Settings section, but as I mentioned earlier, it would take a whole book to show you how to really delve into StudioWare panel creation. Of course, I won't leave you without anything to ponder. To set up a button widget to send a Sysx Bank from the Sysx View, follow these steps:

1. Click on the Button widget button and then click somewhere inside your panel to add the button widget to it.

2. Double-click on the Button widget to open the Widget Properties dialog box.

3. Select Sysx Bank from the Primary Action Kind drop-down list.

4. Type the number of the Sysx bank you want to send in the Bank parameter box that appears.

5. Click on OK and then click on the Design button to exit Design mode.

Now, when you click on the button, the Sysx bank that you specified is sent. See how easy that is?

Return Action Property

Another property you should know about is the Return Action property. It is the same as the Primary Action property in that you can set it to execute the same types of actions. Instead of carrying out its function when a widget is first activated, however, it carries out the function in a secondary manner. In other words, if you set up a Return action for the preceding button example, when you first click on the button, the primary action is initiated. When you click on the button a second time (to return it to its original up position), the Return action is initiated. To see what I mean, assign a Return action to the button example I just talked about and then test it.

CHAPTER 15

Adjustable Widgets

Like Button widgets, the Knob and Slider widgets can be used to send MIDI data, manipulate track parameters, and so on. But instead of just a single value, the Knob and Slider widgets can send a whole range of values. Being able to send several values is great for sending MIDI controller data such as pitch change messages.

You can assign primary and return actions to Knob and Slider widgets in the same way you would with a Button widget, but to ensure the value of the widget is used when sending a range of data, you need to use an alias. You simply assign an alias to the knob or slider; then you type that same alias name into any of the Primary Action Kind parameters. For example, to set up a Knob widget that sends MIDI volume controller data, you can do the following:

1. Click on the Knob widget button (the one with the little knob shown on it) and then click somewhere inside your panel to add the Knob widget to it.

2. Double-click on the Knob widget to open the Widget Properties dialog box.

3. Type VolumeKnob as an alias.

4. Select Controller from the Primary Action Kind drop-down list.

5. For Channel, type the MIDI channel you want to use (1 to 16).

6. Select 7-Volume from the Number drop-down list.

7. Type the name of the alias (VolumeKnob) into the Value parameter.

8. Click on OK and then click on the Design button to exit Design mode.

Now, when you move the knob, it sends MIDI volume controller data to the MIDI channel you assigned.

Other Properties

Several other widget properties can come in handy when you're designing your panels. They include overlapping and precise sizing and positioning.

Widget Overlapping

When you place widgets on your panels, you can put them on top of one another. The last widget that you place will overlap any others that are underneath it. If you ever get into a situation in which you want a widget that's underneath to be on top instead, just right-click on it and select Bring to Top from the pop-up menu. Selecting this option brings that widget to the foreground on top of any of the other widgets. There is also a function for the opposite (Send to Bottom), which you access in the same manner.

Precise Sizing and Positioning

In the Widget Properties dialog box, you'll find a section called Placement. In that section, you can choose properties to specify the exact size and position of a widget right down to the pixel. This capability can be useful if you're trying to make things look really nice on your panel, and you want to make sure all the button widgets are the same size and so on.

The X and Y parameters specify the location of the top-left corner of the widget. Using these parameters, you can place the widget at any precise location within your panel. The Width and Height parameters do exactly what you would expect: They specify the exact width and height of the widget in pixels.

Custom Toolbars

If you invest enough time in learning how to use StudioWare, I guarantee you'll find that it makes many tasks a whole lot easier to deal with. The possibilities are numerous, so I really can't show them all to you. Of course, I couldn't end the chapter without at least giving you one nice example to try out.

Remember back in Chapter 3, when I mentioned that SONAR doesn't include any way for you to create your own custom toolbars? Well, I wasn't exactly telling the whole truth, because, by utilizing StudioWare, you can create panels that will function like your very own custom toolbars. And creating these kinds of panels is very easy, too. One of my personal favorites is a custom toolbar for SONAR's audio editing functions (which you can find by choosing Edit > Audio). You create it as follows:

1. If you don't already have a project open, do so now and set up a blank panel in the StudioWare view. Double-click on the blank panel to open the Widget Properties dialog box. Type Edit > Audio for the Label and activate the Show Label option. Then click on OK.

2. Click on the Button widget button and then click somewhere inside the blank panel to add the button widget to it.

3. Double-click on the Button widget to open the Widget Properties dialog box.

4. Type Normalize for the Label.

5. Select Binding from the Primary Action drop-down list.

6. Select Edit > Audio > Normalize from the Verb drop-down list.

TIP

If you want to have a button activate your own custom editing functions that you created with CAL (see chapters 16 and 17), select CAL Program as the primary action. Then, in the Program field, type (do(include "ProgramName.CAL")), where ProgramName.CAL is the name of the program you want to run.

7. Activate the Spring-loaded option in the Range section and click on OK.

NOTE

The Spring-loaded option in the Widget Properties dialog box makes the widget automatically snap back to its initial value after you move it. This capability is especially handy for creating single-click buttons. Normally, when you click on a button, it stays pressed until you click on it again to bring it back up to its original position. With the Spring-loaded option activated, the button "springs" back up, ready to be pressed again.

8. Repeat steps 2 through 7 until you have created buttons for all the Edit > Audio commands available.

9. Click on the Design button to exit Design mode and then save your new panel (or custom toolbar) as EditAudioToolbar.CakewalkStudioWare.

Now you can open the panel and use it within any project as a custom toolbar. To make things even easier, you might want to save the panel again, but this time save it inside your project so that it will be loaded automatically every time you open the project.

You're Not Alone

If you're still a little fuzzy about some of the information described in this chapter, don't worry. In time, you'll learn to master the full potential of StudioWare. And if you need some help along the way, you might turn to some of the other users out there who are still learning the software, just like you. There are plenty of places on the Internet where you can get in touch with your fellow users. Check out Appendix D. You may even find that you're satisfied with simply downloading existing panels that others have created. Either way, StudioWare will make your recording sessions easier and more productive.

16
CAL 101

One advantage that SONAR has over any other music sequencing product I've worked with is that it enables you to extend its functionality. If you find yourself in a situation in which you need to edit your MIDI or audio data in some way that is not possible with any of the current SONAR features—not a common occurrence, but it can happen—you can create a new editing function to take care of the task by using CAL. What is CAL, and how do you use it? Well, that's exactly what you'll learn in this chapter. This chapter covers the following:

▶ The definition of CAL

▶ How to run an existing CAL program

▶ Prewritten CAL programs

▶ Viewing CAL programs

What Is CAL?

CAL, which stands for Cakewalk Application Language, is a computer programming language that exists within the SONAR environment. You can use it to extend the functionality of SONAR by creating your own custom MIDI and audio data editing commands via CAL *programs* (also called *scripts*). A CAL program is a set of instructions written in the Cakewalk Application Language that tells SONAR how to perform a certain task. For example, if you want to change the volume of every other MIDI note in Track 1 to a certain value automatically, you can write a CAL program to do just that. And for future use, you can save CAL programs to disk as files with a .CAL extension.

NOTE

A *programming language* is a set of commands, symbols, and rules that are used to "teach" a computer how to perform tasks. By combining these language elements in different ways, you can "teach" a computer to perform any number of tasks, such as record and play music. The combination of elements for a certain task or set of tasks is called a computer *program*. For example, SONAR is a computer program, albeit a very complex one.

A number of different kinds of programming languages are in use, including BASIC, FORTRAN, C, LISP, and more. Each has unique characteristics. If you are familiar with C and LISP, you'll feel right at home with CAL; CAL derives many of its characteristics from these two languages.

You might be saying to yourself, "Um, well, that's nice, but I know nothing about computer programming, so what good is CAL going to do me?" Not to worry. Yes, CAL is a very complex feature of SONAR. If you really want to take full advantage of it, you have to learn how to use the language, but that doesn't mean CAL isn't accessible if you're a beginning user.

Included with SONAR are a number of prewritten CAL programs that you can use within your own projects. Cakewalk also provides a nice library of additional CAL programs on its Web site that you can download for free. And you can even find other places on the Internet where you can download free CAL programs that have been written by other users (see Appendix D). Let's talk about how you can use the existing CAL programs included with SONAR and any others that you might download from the Internet.

Running a CAL Program

Because all CAL programs are different, I can't explain how to use them in one all-encompassing way. When you run a CAL program, it usually asks you for some kind of input, depending on what the program is supposed to do and how it is supposed to manipulate your music data. But you can still follow this basic procedure to run a CAL program:

1.   Select the track or tracks (or data within the tracks) in the Track view that you want to be edited by the CAL program. This first step is not always necessary. It depends on the task that the CAL program is supposed to perform. It also depends on whether the CAL program was written to process only selected data in a project or all the tracks in a project. The only way to determine the function of a CAL program is to view it with the Windows Notepad, which you'll learn about later in this chapter.

2. Select Edit > Run CAL to display the File Open dialog box.

3. Choose the CAL program that you want to run and click Open.

That's all there is to it. Some CAL programs immediately carry out their tasks, whereas others first display additional dialog boxes if you need to input any values. The best way to begin using CAL (and to see how it works) is to try out some of the sample programs included with SONAR.

> **TIP**
>
> You can run CAL programs while a project is being played back. This means you can hear the results of the editing that the CAL program applies to your data at the same time your music is being played. If you don't like what the CAL program does, just choose Edit > Undo to remove any changes the program makes to your data. If you then decide that you actually like the changes, instead of running the CAL program again, just select Edit > Redo to put the changes back in place.

The CAL Files

To give you a better understanding of how CAL works and also how you can benefit from it, I'll describe the prewritten CAL programs included with SONAR in the following sections. I'll give you a brief description of what each program does and how to use it.

Dominant 7th Chord.CAL

The Dominant 7th Chord.CAL program builds dominant seventh chords by adding three notes with the same time, velocity, and duration to each selected MIDI note in a track. In other words, if you select a note within a track, and you run Dominant 7th Chord.CAL, the program treats the selected note as the root of a dominant seventh chord and adds a major third, a perfect fifth, and a minor seventh on top of it, thus creating a dominant seventh chord automatically.

Of course, if you know how to compose music, you probably won't get much use out of this CAL program. However, you might find it useful while working in the Staff view. While you're editing a MIDI data track in the Staff view, try highlighting a note and then running Dominant 7th Chord.CAL. It's cool to see those additional notes just appear as if by magic. This program can save you some time while you're inputting notes by hand, too.

Other Chord.CAL Programs

SONAR includes a number of other chord-building CAL programs that work the same way as Dominant 7th Chord.CAL, except they build different kinds of chords:

▶ **Major 7th Chord.CAL**—This builds major seventh chords by adding the major third, perfect fifth, and major seventh intervals to the selected root note or notes.

▶ **Major Chord.CAL**—This builds major chords by adding the major third and perfect fifth intervals to the selected root note or notes.

▶ **Minor 7th Chord.CAL**—This builds minor seventh chords by adding the minor third, perfect fifth, and minor seventh intervals to the selected root note or notes.

▶ **Minor Chord.CAL**—This builds minor chords by adding the minor third and perfect fifth intervals to the selected root note notes.

Random Time.CAL

If you overindulge yourself while using SONAR's quantizing features (see Chapter 8), your music can sometimes come out sounding like computer music, with a robotic or machine-like feel to it. In some cases, this sound can be desirable, but when you're working on a jazz or rhythm and blues piece, you don't want the drums (or any of the other instruments for that matter) to sound like a robot played them. In that case, Random Time.CAL may be of some help.

This CAL program takes the start times of each selected event in a track and adds a random number of ticks to them. To give you some control over this randomization, the program first asks you for a number of ticks to base its changes on. It then adds a random number to each Event time that is between plus or minus one-half the number of ticks that you input. For instance, if you tell the program to use six ticks, each event time will have one of the following numbers—chosen at random—added to it: −3, −2, −1, 0, 1, 2, or 3. Using this program is a great way to add a little bit of "human" feel back into those robotic-sounding tracks. To use Random Time.CAL, just follow these steps:

1. Select the track or tracks in the Track view that you want to process. You can also just select a single clip within a track, or you can select a specific range of events within one of the other views, such as the Piano Roll view or the Staff view.

2. Choose Edit > Run CAL to display the File Open dialog box.

3. Choose the Random Time.CAL file and click Open. The Random Time.CAL Program then displays a CAL dialog box (see Figure 16.1).

Figure 16.1
The Random Time.CAL Program asks for number of ticks upon which to base its event time processing.

4.   Enter the number of ticks you want to use and click OK.

You'll probably need to experiment a little with the number of ticks that you use, because too large a number can make your music sound "sloppy" or too far off the beat.

Scale Velocity.CAL

The Scale Velocity.CAL program is included with SONAR just to serve as a programming example; other than that, you don't really need it. SONAR already includes a Scale Velocity editing function, which provides even more features than Scale Velocity.CAL. For more information about Scale Velocity, see Chapter 8.

Split Channel to Tracks.CAL

If you ever need to share your music data with someone who owns a sequencing program other than SONAR, you can save your project as a Standard MIDI File (SMF). Standard MIDI Files are supported by most computer music software products on the market; thus, they allow musicians to work together on the same song without having to own the same software. But not all Standard MIDI Files are created equal. Actually, several types of files are available; one in particular is called Type 0. A Type 0 MIDI file stores all its data—which is all the MIDI data from all sixteen MIDI Channels—on one track. Type 0 files are sometimes used for video game composing, but hardly ever when composing for any other medium. Still, you might run across a Type 0 MIDI file, and Split Channel to Tracks.CAL can be useful in this situation. SONAR Automatically splits a Type 0 MIDI file to separate tracks.

Split Channel to Tracks.CAL takes the selected track and separates the data from it by MIDI channel into sixteen new tracks. For example, if the track contains data on MIDI Channels 1, 4, 5, and 6, Split Channel to Tracks.CAL creates sixteen new tracks (from the initial track), with the first track containing data from Channel 1, the fourth Track containing data from Channel 4, and so on. The remaining tracks that don't have corresponding channel data are just blank. You use it like this:

1.   Select a track in the Track view.

2.   If you want to split only a portion of the track, set the From and Thru markers to the appropriate time values.

3.   Choose Edit > Run CAL to open the File Open dialog box.

4. Choose the Split Channel to Tracks.CAL file and click Open. The Split Channel to Tracks.CAL Program then displays a CAL dialog box (see Figure 16.2).

Figure 16.2
The Split Channel to Tracks.CAL Program asks for the number of the track to start with when creating the new tracks.

5. Enter the number of the first track that you want Split Channel to Tracks.CAL to use when it creates the new tracks and click OK.

CAUTION
Be sure you have enough blank tracks (sixteen) below the one you select, because Split Channel to Tracks.CAL overwrites any existing data within the tracks that it uses.

After it's finished processing the original track, Split Channel to Tracks.CAL creates sixteen new tracks, starting with the track number you selected, each containing data from the sixteen corresponding MIDI channels. Now you can access and edit the music data more easily.

Split Note to Tracks.CAL

The Split Note to Tracks.CAL Program is similar to Split Channel to Tracks.CAL, except that, instead of separating the MIDI data from a selected track by channel, it separates the data by note. For example, if you select a track that contains notes with values of C4, A2, and G3, Split Note to Tracks.CAL separates that track into three new tracks, each containing all notes with only one of the available note values. So, in this example, a new track containing only notes with a value of C4 would be created, another new track containing only A2 notes would be created, and another new track containing only G3 notes would be created.

This program can be useful if you're working with a single drum track that contains the data for a number of different drum instruments. In MIDI, different drum instruments are represented by different note values because drums can't play melodies. So, if you want to edit a single drum instrument at a time, having each instrument on its own track would be easier. In that case, Split Note to Tracks.CAL can be put to good use. To apply Split Note to Tracks.CAL to your music data, follow these steps:

1. Choose Edit > Run CAL to open the File Open dialog box.

2. Choose the Split Note to Tracks.CAL file and click Open.

3. The Split Note to Tracks.CAL Program asks for the number of your Source Track (see Figure 16.3). It is the track that you want to split into new tracks. Enter a number from 1 to 256 and click OK.

NOTE

You'll notice this program is different from the other CAL programs in which you had to first select a track in the Track view. It's different because the person who wrote this CAL program did it differently from the rest. Why? I have no idea.

Figure 16.3

Here, you can enter the source track for the Split Note to Tracks.CAL Program.

4. The program then asks you for the number of the First Destination Track (see Figure 16.4). It is the number of the first new track that will be created. Enter a number and click OK.

Figure 16.4

Here, you enter the First Destination Track for the Split Note to Tracks.CAL Program.

5. The program then asks you for the number of the Destination Channel (see Figure 16.5). It is the MIDI channel that you want all the new tracks to be set to. Unless you want to change the channel, you should simply select the same channel that the source track is using. Enter a number from 0 to 16 and click OK.

Figure 16.5

Here, you can enter the Destination Channel for the Split Note to Tracks.CAL Program.

6. The program finally asks you for the number of the Destination Port (see Figure 16.6). It is the MIDI output that you want all the new tracks to be set to. Again, you should select the same output that the source track is using. Enter a number from 1 to 16 and click OK.

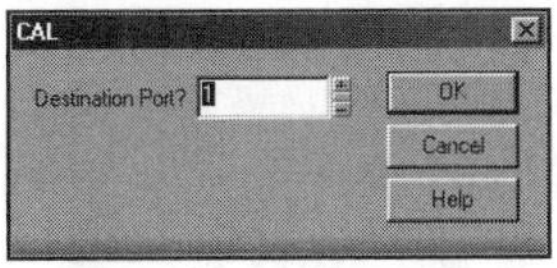

Figure 16.6

Here, you can enter the Destination Port for the Split Note to Tracks.CAL Program.

After you answer the last question, Split Note to Tracks.CAL processes the original track and creates a number of new tracks (depending on how many different note values are present in the original track), each containing all the notes for each corresponding note value.

Thin Controller Data.CAL

You use MIDI Controller data to add expressive qualities to your MIDI music tracks. For example, you can make a certain passage of music get gradually louder or softer (crescendo or decrescendo) by adding MIDI controller number 7 (Volume) to your MIDI Tracks. Sometimes, though, an overabundance of MIDI data can overload your MIDI instruments and cause anomalies such as stuck notes and delays in playback. If you have this problem, you can try thinning out the MIDI controller data in your tracks by using Thin Controller Data.CAL. This program allows you to decrease the amount of data being sent to your MIDI instruments by deleting only a select number of controller events—enough to reduce the amount of data without adversely affecting the music performance. It works like this:

1. Select the track or tracks in the Track view that you want to process. You can also just select a single clip within a track, or you can select a specific range of events within one of the other views, such as the Piano Roll view or the Staff view.

2. Choose Edit > Run CAL to display the File Open dialog box.

3. Choose the Thin Controller Data.CAL file and click Open.

4. The Thin Controller Data.CAL Program asks you for the number of the MIDI controller that you want to process (see Figure 16.7). For example, if you want to remove some of the volume data from a track, use MIDI controller number 7. Enter a number from 0 to 127 and click OK.

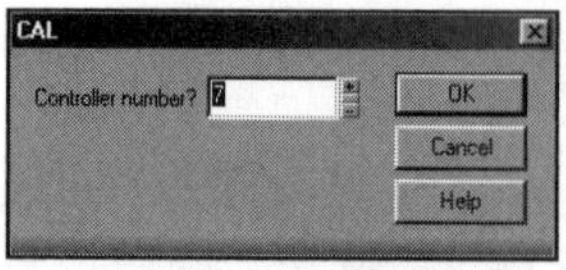

Figure 16.7
Here, you can enter the controller number for the Thin Controller Data.CAL Program.

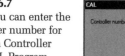

5. The program then asks you for the thinning factor (see Figure 16.8). For example, if you enter a value of 4, the program deletes every fourth volume event it finds in the selected track or tracks. Enter a number from 1 to 100 and click OK.

Figure 16.8
Here, you can enter the thinning factor for the Thin Controller Data.CAL Program.

After you answer the last question, Thin Controller Data.CAL processes the selected track or tracks and deletes all the MIDI controller events that correspond to the MIDI controller number and the thinning factor you entered. If this procedure doesn't clear up your MIDI playback problems, you can try thinning the data some more, but be careful not to thin it too much; otherwise, your crescendos and decrescendos (or other controller-influenced music passages) will start to sound choppy rather than smooth.

Other Thin.CAL Programs

Also included with SONAR are two other controller-thinning CAL Programs. These programs work almost the same way as Thin Controller Data.CAL, but each is targeted toward one specific type of controller. Thin Channel Aftertouch.CAL thins out channel aftertouch MIDI controller data, and Thin Pitch Wheel.CAL thins out pitch wheel (or pitch bend) MIDI controller data. To run these programs, you use the same procedure as you do with Thin Controller Data.CAL, but with one exception. The programs don't ask you to input the number of a MIDI controller, because they are each already targeted toward a specific Controller. Other than that, they work in the same manner.

Viewing CAL Programs

Unless a CAL program comes with some written instructions, you won't know what it is designed to do to the data in your project. This is especially true if you download CAL programs from the Internet. Many come with documentation, but many don't. Most programs, however, do come with a brief description (as well as instructions on use) within their source code.

NOTE
Source code (or *program code*) is the text of the programming language commands used for a particular program. You create a program by first writing its source code. A computer can then run the program by reading the source code and executing the commands in the appropriate manner, thus carrying out the intended task.

To read the source code of a CAL program, you need to use the Windows Notepad (or some other plain text editor). As an example, take a look at the source code for Major Chord.CAL:

1. Choose Start > Programs > Accessories > Notepad to open the Windows Notepad.

2. Choose File > Open and select the Major Chord.CAL file from the SONAR directory on your hard drive (or some other directory where your CAL files are stored). Click Open. Windows Notepad then opens Major Chord.CAL and displays its source code (see Figure 16.9).

Figure 16.9
You can use the Windows Notepad to examine and edit the source code of a CAL program.

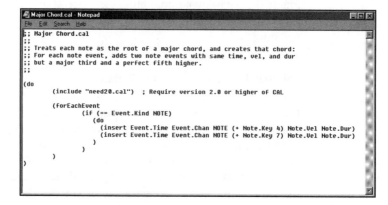

As you can see in Figure 16.9, the Windows Notepad allows you to see the source code of Major Chord.CAL and also allows you to read the brief description included there. You can do the same thing with any other CAL program to find out how it can be used and what task it's supposed to perform. But that's not all.

Using the Windows Notepad, you also can edit the source code for a CAL program, as well as create a CAL program from scratch. Since CAL programs are just plain text, you can use the same editing techniques as you do with any other text such as cut, copy, and paste text-editing procedures. I'll cover creating your own CAL programs, in Chapter 17.

17

Advanced CAL Techniques

In Chapter 16, you learned about the Cakewalk Application Language—what it is, what it does, and how you can run prewritten CAL programs to tackle some of the editing tasks that the built-in SONAR functions can't. I briefly touched on the topic of creating your own CAL programs. This chapter continues the CAL discussion and covers the following:

▶ Cakewalk Application Language programming basics

▶ Anatomy of a CAL program

▶ CAL functions reference

Intro to CAL Programming

Unfortunately, there is no easy way to create your own CAL programs. To tap the full power of its functionality, you need to learn how to create programs from scratch using the Cakewalk Application Language. The problem is that teaching a course in CAL programming would take up a whole book in and of itself. So instead, I'll just get you started by providing a brief introduction to the language. And the best way to do that is to walk you through the code of one of the CAL programs that comes included with SONAR.

To get started, open the Scale Velocity.CAL program (see Figure 17.1). The first thing you'll see is a bunch of lines that start with semicolons and contain some text describing the CAL program. These lines are called *comments*. Whenever you insert a semicolon into the code of a CAL program, SONAR ignores that part of the code when you run the program. This way, you can mark the code with descriptive notes. When you come back to the program at a later date, you will understand what certain parts of the program are supposed to accomplish.

Figure 17.1

The code for the Scale Velocity.CAL program provides a nice example for an explanation of the Cakewalk Application Language.

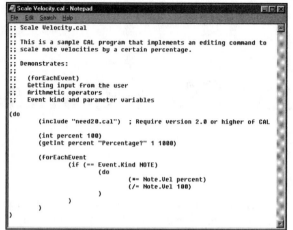

```
;; Scale Velocity.cal
;;
;; This is a sample CAL program that implements an editing command to
;; scale note velocities by a certain percentage.
;;
;; Demonstrates:
;;
;;   (ForEachEvent)
;;   Getting input from the user
;;   Arithmetic operators
;;   Event kind and parameter variables

(do

        (include "need20.cal")  ; Require version 2.0 or higher of CAL

        (int percent 100)
        (getInt percent "Percentage?" 1 1000)

        (forEachEvent
                (if (== Event.Kind NOTE)
                        (do
                                (*= Note.Vel percent)
                                (/= Note.Vel 100)
                        )
                )
        )
)
```

A little further down, you'll notice the first line of the actual code used when the program is run. The line reads (do. All CAL programs start with this code. The parenthesis designates the start of a function, and the do code designates the start of a group of code. As a matter of fact, a CAL program is just one big function with a number of other functions within it. You'll notice that for every left parenthesis, you'll have a corresponding right parenthesis. CAL programs use parentheses to show where a function begins and ends.

Include

The next line in Scale Velocity.CAL reads (include "need20.cal"). This is the Include function. This function allows you to run a CAL program within a CAL program. You might want to do so for a number of reasons. For instance, if you're creating a very large program, you might want to break it down into different parts to make it easier to work with. Then you could have one master program that runs all the different parts. You can also combine CAL programs. For example, you could combine the Thin Channel Aftertouch.CAL, Thin Controller Data.CAL, and Thin Pitch Wheel.CAL programs that come with SONAR by using the Include function in a new CAL program. Then, when you run the new program, it would run each of the included programs, one right after the other, so that you could thin all the types of MIDI controller data from your project in one fell swoop.

In Scale Velocity.CAL, the Include function is used to run the need20.cal Program. This program simply checks the version of CAL and makes sure that it is version 2.0 or higher. Some CAL programs check the version to avoid an error in case a very old version of CAL is being used.

Variables

After the <u>Include</u> function, the code for Scale Velocity.CAL shows <u>(int percent 100)</u>. This is a <u>Variable</u> function. In CAL programs, you can define variables to hold any values you might need while the program is running. In this instance, the variable <u>percent</u> is defined as an integer and is given a value of <u>100</u>. Variables can be used to store both number and text information. After you define a variable, you can refer to its value later in your code by simply using the variable name. That's what you see in the next line of code in Scale Velocity.CAL.

User Input

This next line reads <u>(getInt percent "Percentage?" 1 1000)</u>. Here, the program asks for input from the user. In English, this line of code translates to "Get an integer between 1 and 1000 from the user by having the user type a value into the displayed dialog box. Then store the value into the variable named <u>percent</u>." So, basically, when SONAR reaches this line of code in the program, it pauses and displays a dialog box (see Figure 17.2). Then it waits for the user to input a value and click on the OK button. It then assigns whatever the inputted value was to the variable <u>percent</u>. And then it continues running the rest of the program.

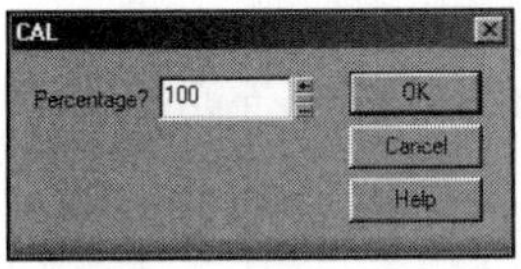

Figure 17.2
A CAL program gets input from the user by displaying dialog boxes.

ForEachEvent

The main part of the Scale Velocity.CAL program begins with the line of code that reads <u>(forEachEvent</u>. <u>ForEachEvent</u> is known as an *iterating* function. In this type of function, a certain portion of code is run (or cycled through) a specific number of times. In this case, for every event in the selected track or tracks, the code enclosed within the <u>forEachEvent</u> function is cycled through one time. So, in Scale Velocity.CAL, for every event in the selected track or tracks, this block of code is run through once:

```
(if (== Event.Kind NOTE)
        (do
                (*= Note.Vel percent)
                (/= Note.Vel 100)
        )
)
```

What does this code do? Let's talk about it.

Conditions

Within the <u>forEachEvent</u> function in Scale Velocity.CAL, every event in the selected track or tracks is tested using the <u>if</u> function. This function is known as a *conditional* function. Depending on whether certain conditions are met, the code enclosed within the <u>if</u> function may or may not be run. In Scale Velocity.CAL, every event is tested to see whether it is a MIDI Note event. This test is performed with the line of code that reads <u>(= = Event.Kind NOTE)</u>. In English, this line translates to "Check to see whether the current event being tested is a MIDI Note event." If the current event is a MIDI Note event, then the next block of code is run. If the current event is not a MIDI Note event, then the next block of code is skipped, and the <u>forEachEvent</u> function moves on to the next event in the selected track or tracks until it reaches the last selected event; then the CAL program stops running.

Arithmetic

The final part of Scale Velocity.CAL is just some simple arithmetic code. If the current event is a MIDI Note event, the Velocity value of the note is multiplied by the value of the <u>percent</u> variable, and the resulting value is assigned as the Note Velocity. Then the new Velocity value of the Note is divided by the number 100, and this resulting value is then assigned to be the final value of the Note Velocity. This way, the program scales the velocities of the notes in the selected track or tracks.

Master Presets

One of the most effective uses I've found for CAL is in creating what I like to call m*aster presets*. As I mentioned in Chapter 8, SONAR lets you save the settings for some of its editing functions as presets. This way, you can easily use the same editing parameters you created by simply calling them up by name, instead of having to figure out the settings every time you use a function. Presets are a real time-saver, but unfortunately, you can save presets for each of the individual functions only. What if you want to combine a few of the functions to create a certain editing process? For example, say you like to shorten your MIDI tracks before you quantize them. To do so, you first need to select the tracks, use the Length function, and then use the Quantize function to process your tracks. For each of the editing functions, you have to make the appropriate settings adjustments. If you create a CAL program to automatically run through the process for you, though, all you need to do is select your tracks and run the CAL program.

Shorten and Quantize Master Preset

To show you what I mean, I've cooked up a sample master preset that you can run as a CAL program and use in your projects. You need to do the following:

1. Open the Windows Notepad.
2. Type in the first few lines of code, as shown in Figure 17.3.

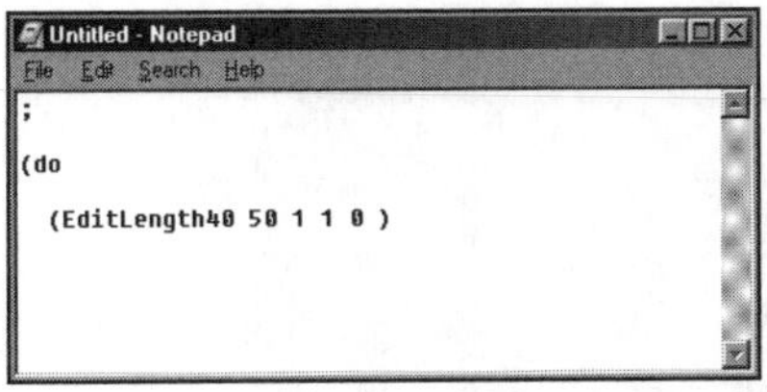

Figure 17.3
These are the first few lines of code in our new master preset.

```
;
(do

    (EditLength40 50 1 1 0 )
```

3. Examine the code. The first line is just a blank comment. The second line designates the beginning of the program. The third line tells SONAR to activate the Length function using the parameters as shown in Figure 17.4. In the source code, the command EditLength40 tells SONAR to activate the Length function. The number 50 corresponds to the Percent parameter in the Length dialog box. The numbers 1, 1, and 0 correspond to the Start Times, Durations, and Stretch Audio options, respectively. A 1 indicates that option is activated. A 0 indicates that option is not activated.

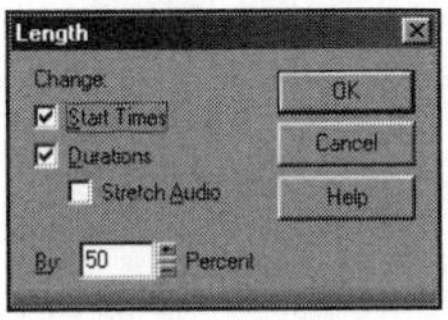

Figure 17.4
The first part of the CAL program shortens the selected MIDI tracks by 50 percent with the Length editing function.

```
Length
Change:                    OK
  ☑ Start Times
  ☑ Durations            Cancel
    ☐ Stretch Audio
                           Help
By: 50 ⬍ Percent
```

TIP

You may be wondering how to apply commands in CAL to the editing functions in SONAR and how to determine their corresponding parameters. To find out, take a look at the CAL Reference section of the SONAR Help file.

4. Now type in the last two lines of code as shown in Figure 17.5.

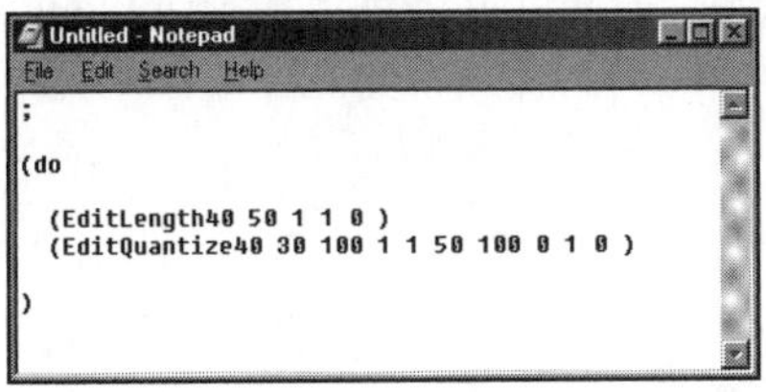

Figure 17.5
The final source code should look like this after you edit it.

```
;
(do

    (EditLength40 50 1 1 0 )
    (EditQuantize40 30 100 1 1 50 100 0 1 0 )

)
```

5. Examine the code. The command EditQuantize40 tells SONAR to activate the Quantize function using the parameters as shown in Figure 17.6. The numbers following that command designate the following parameter settings: Resolution, Strength percent, Start Times (on/off), Note Durations (on/off), Swing percent, Window percent, Offset, Notes/Lyrics/Audio option (on/off), and Stretch Audio (on/off).

Figure 17.6
The second part of the CAL program quantizes the notes in the selected MIDI tracks with the Quantize editing function.

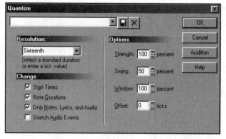

6. Save the new program with a file extension of .CAL.

Now, when you run this CAL program, it performs all the editing functions for you automatically with the same exact settings that you used. It's too bad that CAL doesn't support SONAR's MIDI or audio effects functions. I really wish that it did, because then you could create master presets to process your audio tracks, too. That capability would make CAL a hundred times more powerful than it already is. I hope that Cakewalk will add this functionality in a future version. In the meantime, you can still find plenty of uses for CAL.

CAL References

So, are you totally confused yet? If you've had some previous programming experience, you should have no trouble in picking up the Cakewalk Application Language. If you're familiar with the C or Lisp computer programming languages, CAL is just a stone's throw away in terms of functionality.

Really, the best way to learn about CAL is to study the code of existing CAL programs. As I mentioned earlier, you can also read the reference material included in the SONAR Help file. A couple of references cover all the CAL functions and data types, describing what they are and how they work. You can find the references in the CAL Reference section of the Help file.

If, even after this discussion, you still find yourself lost in all this technical jargon, you can utilize CAL by using prewritten programs. As I mentioned before, this part of SONAR has a lot of power, and it would be a shame if you let it go to waste. CAL can save you time and even let you manipulate your music data in ways you may never have thought of. Don't be afraid to experiment. Just be sure to back up your data, in case things get a bit messed up in the process.

TIP

For more information about programming with CAL, check out some of the Web sites I've listed in Appendix D.

18

Take Your SONAR Project to CD

Congratulations! You've made it to the final chapter of the book. Your project has been recorded, edited, mixed, and now you can share it with the rest of the world. To be able to share it, you need to create your very own CD. So, in this chapter, I'll cover the basics of creating a custom audio CD, including the following:

▶ Purchasing a CD recorder (CD-R)

▶ Preparing your project for CD audio

▶ Using the popular Easy CD Creator software

▶ Taking advantage of advanced Easy CD Creator options

Purchasing a CD Recorder

A CD recorder (or CD-R drive) is similar to a CD-ROM drive except that, in addition to reading CDs, it can write to them, too. Just a short while ago, CD-R drives were available only to the privileged few who could afford them and needed to create their own CDs. These people, however lucky to be early adopters of recordable CD technology, also had to deal with unreliable drives. The creation of unreadable discs was very common.

Today, after several drive generations, prices have come down and reliability has gone up. In fact, many new computer systems shipping from the likes of Gateway and Dell include CD-R drives as standard components. But despite these incentives, you still might be one of the few computer musicians who hasn't purchased a CD-R drive. Before you run out to the store to spend your hard-earned cash, you should know a little bit about CD-ROM technology and how to get a drive.

CHAPTER 18

A Little Bit About CD-R Drives

You should consider a number of points when purchasing a drive. The first is whether you want a CD-R or CD-RW. CD-R stands for CD-Recordable. These drives were the first ones created. They are essentially write-once drives. Once data is written using these drives, you can't erase or write over the data.

Most drives today are CD-RW, or Read-Write drives. These drives allow you to rewrite to a CD as many as 1,000 times before the disc is worn out. The problem with CD-RW drives is that their discs can be read only by multiread CD-ROM drives, which aren't as common as regular CD-ROM drives. You should also know that audio CD players can't handle CD-RW discs; they can play only CD-R discs. But because a CD-RW drive can create both CD-R and CD-RW discs, your purchasing decision is pretty much a given here.

The other major issue to consider is external versus internal. If you're not the type of person who finds it easy to open your computer and install new equipment, then you should get an external drive. Although many external drives require you to install a card in your system, installing a card is easier than installing the entire drive, which requires you to hook up the power and data cables and screw the drive into place. The process isn't really very difficult, but it's not for the novice user either. The easiest drives to install are those that simply connect to the USB (universal serial bus) port on the back of your computer. Be careful when choosing this type of drive, though, because they tend to transfer data a lot slower than internal or card-based external drives. If you want the best performance, you should get an internal or card-based drive.

Your next decision is whether you should choose between an IDE/EIDE or SCSI drive. The difference is the interface that connects the drive to your computer. IDE/EIDE is the standard for PCs, and it's a lot cheaper than SCSI. But it's also slower. SCSI is more important for Macintosh machines, because they use the SCSI interface exclusively. To attach a SCSI drive on a PC, you have to install a separate SCSI adapter card inside your machine. For IDE/EIDE, all you need to do is plug in and install the drive; no card is required. And to be honest, you don't need the extra speed that SCSI provides. Most IDE/EIDE drives provide excellent performance.

Speed is important, however, when it comes to the speed of the drive itself. Each new generation of recordable drives gets faster and faster, just as the read-only CD-ROM drives have been doing. Right now, it's common to find 6-10x drives. By the way, when you're shopping, be sure to look at the write speed of the drive, not the read speed. CD-R drives write much slower than they read. Also, look at a drive's overall throughput when writing. Just because the drive spins the disc really fast doesn't necessarily guarantee it's as fast as similar drives.

Some people avoid buying the fastest drives, because newer, faster drives can be a bit unreliable in creating CDs that other drives will be able to read. However, these faster drives can be made to run slower when writing to a disc, so this aspect shouldn't concern you too much.

I recommend that you look into the drives offered by Hewlett-Packard or Ricoh. I'm currently using the CD-Writer Plus 8200i from Hewlett-Packard on my desktop computer and the MP8040SE from Ricoh on my laptop computer. Both products are excellent performers, although they may be a bit outdated by the time you read this book.

Where to Look

The best place currently on the Web to find any computer hardware for purchase is at one of the two major hardware purchasing Web sites: **Computers.com** or **Computershopper.com**. At these sites, you can easily enter some criteria for the type of drive you want and narrow it to a model and a location within driving distance. For example, on Computershopper.com (see Figure 18.1), you can enter basic speed, interface, and pricing criteria.

Figure 18.1
On Computershopper.com, you can specify the type of drive you want and then search for available makes and prices.

CHAPTER 18

On Computers.com (see Figure 18.2), you can enter that criteria as well as sort it by product name and price.

Figure 18.2
On Computers.com, you can sort the drive listings by product name and price.

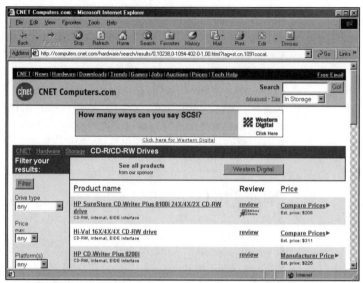

On average, drives run (at the time of this writing) between $200 and $500, depending on features such as writing speed, external versus internal, and reading speed. You can even find some of the lower-end drives for as little as $150, but it's better to spend a little extra and get a quality drive; otherwise, you may regret your choice later.

Preparing a Project for CD Audio

A project can't be laid down as audio tracks on a CD as is. Instead, you have to convert all your MIDI tracks in a project to audio tracks. Then you have to export those audio tracks to a .WAV file so that your CD recording software can write the file to your CD. To do so, you need to follow a number of steps.

Convert Your MIDI Tracks

The first step is to convert any MIDI tracks that use your sound card's built-in synthesizer for playback to audio tracks as follows:

1. Insert a new audio track and assign the input for the track to your sound card's stereo input. For instance, if you have a Sound Blaster Live card, set the Track to the Stereo SB Live Wave In input.

2. Mute all the tracks in your project except the one you just created and the MIDI tracks you're going to convert.

3. Open your sound card's mixer controls (see Figure 18.3) by double-clicking on the small speaker icon in the Windows Taskbar.

Figure 18.3
This window shows the sound card mixer controls for the Sound Blaster Live.

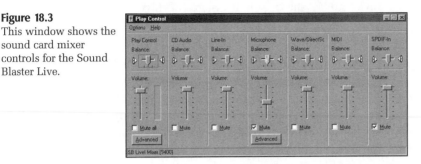

4. Select Options > Properties and click on Recording in the Adjust Volume For section of the resulting Properties dialog box. Then click on the OK button to bring up the recording mixer controls, as shown in Figure 18.4.

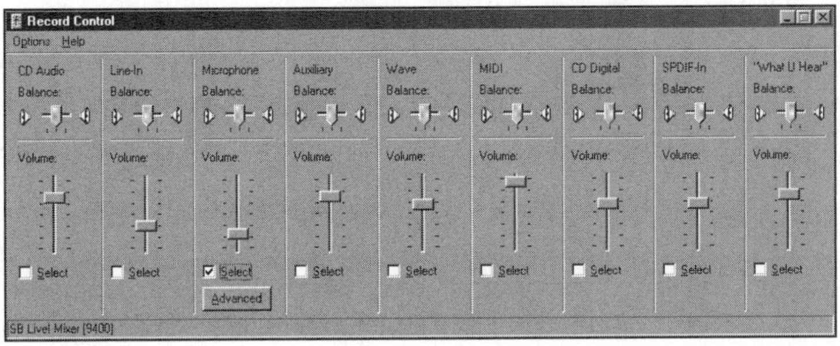

Figure 18.4
This window shows the recording mixer controls for the Sound Blaster Live sound card.

5. Activate the recording source for your sound card's synth by clicking on the appropriate Select option (see Figure 18.5).

Figure 18.5
You need to activate your sound card's synth before you can record its output.

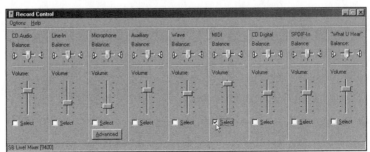

6. Click on the Record button on the toolbar in SONAR, and your MIDI tracks are recorded to the stereo audio track.

Next, you need to convert any MIDI tracks that use external MIDI instruments for playback to audio tracks, as shown in the following steps. If you don't have any MIDI tracks of this kind, you can skip this section.

1. Insert a new audio track and assign the input for the track to your sound card's stereo input. For instance, if you have a Sound Blaster Live card, set the track to the Stereo SB Live Wave In input.

2. Mute all the tracks in your project except the one you just created and the MIDI tracks you're going to convert.

3. Open your sound card's mixer controls by double-clicking on the small speaker icon in the Windows taskbar.

4. Select Options > Properties, and click on Recording in the Adjust Volume For section of the resulting Properties dialog box. Then click on the OK button to bring up the recording mixer controls.

5. Activate the recording source for your sound card's line input(s) by clicking on the appropriate Select option (see Figure 18.6).

Figure 18.6
You need to activate your sound card's line input(s) before you can record any external MIDI instruments.

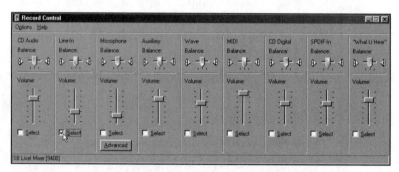

6. Be sure the audio outputs from your external MIDI instrument are connected to the line input(s) of your sound card. If you have more than one MIDI instrument and you're using a mixing board, connect the stereo output(s) of your mixing board to the line input(s) of your sound card.

7. Click on the Rewind button on the toolbar in SONAR so that recording will begin at the beginning of the song. Then click on the Record button on the toolbar in SONAR, and your MIDI tracks are recorded to the stereo audio track.

After you're finished, you should have two new audio tracks representing your sound card's built-in synthesizer and your external MIDI instruments.

Convert Your DXi Tracks

You also need to convert any MIDI tracks that use DXis for playback. To do so, just follow these steps:

1. Mute all the tracks in your project except the MIDI and audio tracks pertaining to your DXis.

2. Choose Edit > Bounce To Tracks to open the Bounce To Tracks dialog box. I talked about the Bounce To Tracks function in Chapter 7.

3. Choose New Track in the drop-down list for the Destination parameter.

4. Choose Mix To Single Track Stereo Event(s) in the drop-down list for the Format parameter.

5. In the Source Bus(es) section, choose the output of your sound card you would like SONAR to use when recording your DXis.

6. In the Mix Enables section, make sure all the options are activated.

7. Click OK.

SONAR creates a new stereo audio track containing all the music from your DXis.

Convert Your Audio Tracks

After all your MIDI tracks are converted to audio tracks, you need to mix and export all your audio tracks down to a .WAV file. SONAR provides a very convenient feature expressly for this purpose, called Export Audio. This feature takes any number of original audio tracks—preserving their volume, pan, and effects settings—and mixes them into a single stereo .WAV file. Here's how to use it:

1. Mute all the MIDI tracks in your project and any audio tracks that you don't want included in the .WAV file.

2. Choose File > Export Audio to open the Export Audio dialog box, as shown in Figure 18.7.

Figure 18.7
You use the Export Audio dialog box to mix and export your tracks.

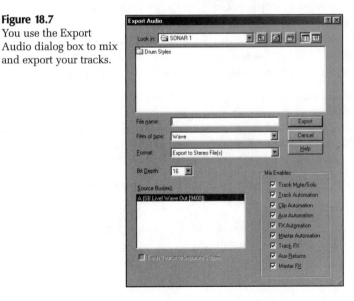

CHAPTER 18

3. From the Look In list, select the folder you want to save the .WAV file into. Then type a name for the file in the File Name field.

4. Choose the type from the Files of Type drop-down list. In this case, use the Wave option.

5. Select the Format you want to use. You can mix your audio tracks to a single stereo file, two mono files (that, when combined, create a stereo file), or a single mono file. You can also set the bit depth using the Bit Depth parameter. I explained bit depth in Chapter 6.

6. Choose the sound card(s) you want to use to process your audio tracks from the Source Bus(es) field.

7. Leave the Each Source To Separate Submix option deactivated.

8. Leave all the Mix Enables options activated to ensure that your new .WAV file will sound exactly the same when played back as the original audio tracks.

9. Click on the Export button, and SONAR mixes all your audio tracks down to a new .WAV file.

When you're done, you should have a .WAV file that you can use along with your CD recording software to create an audio CD.

Using Easy CD Creator

When it comes to CD recording software, almost 90 percent of the drives on the market include a "lite" version of Easy CD Creator from Roxio (formerly known as Adaptec). Also, an upgrade offer is usually included for the full version of the software. Because of its popularity, I'll discuss how to use Easy CD Creator to burn your own CDs. If you have some other CD recording software, the process should be similar.

NOTE

Because a laser is used to heat up the blank CD and write the information to it, recording a CD is also referred to as *burning* a CD.

You can just follow these basic steps to create an audio CD:

1. Start Easy CD Creator.

2. Choose File > New CD Project > Music CD to create an untitled music CD project (see Figure 18.8).

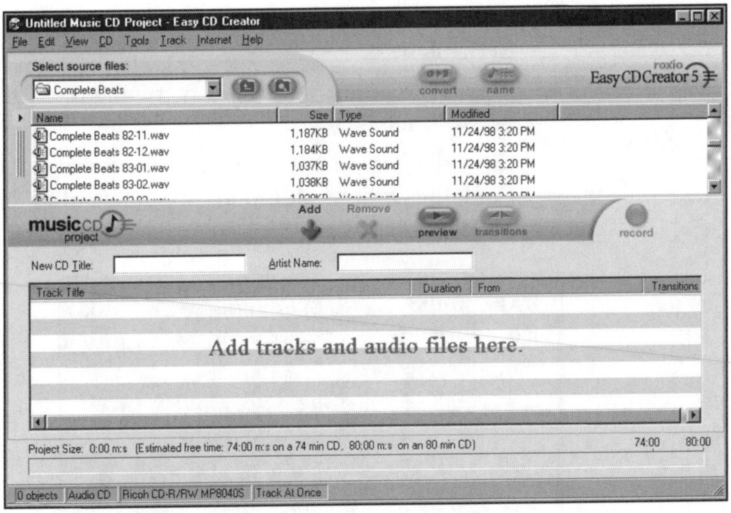

Figure 18.8
You can create a music
CD using Easy CD
Creator's main interface.

3. In the Select Source Files drop-down list, choose the drive containing the WAV files you want to burn to CD.

4. In the file list below the Select Source Files drop-down list, select the WAV file(s) you want to burn to CD.

5. To preview the file(s), click the Preview button.

6. Click the Add button to add the selected file(s) to your music CD project. The file(s) are added to the music CD project list in the bottom half of the Easy CD Creator window (see Figure 18.9).

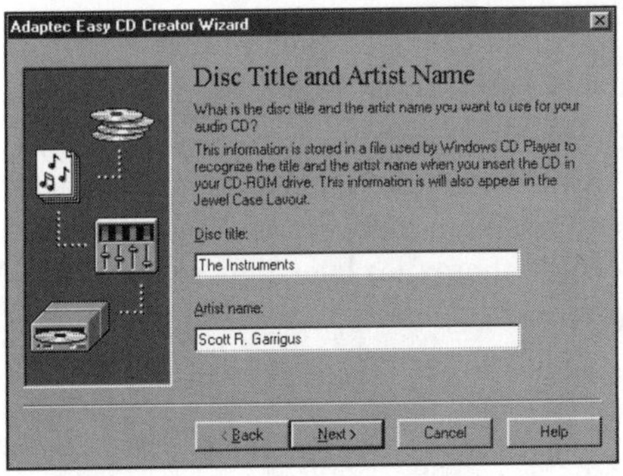

Figure 18.9
The files for your music
CD project are listed in
the bottom half of the
Easy CD Creator
window.

7. To remove a file from the project list, select it and click the Remove button.

8. Repeat steps 3 through 7 until you've finished adding all your files to the project.

TIP
You don't have to fill the entire CD at this point. As long as you don't finalize the CD, you can add to it over time until it is filled.

9. Add a title to your project by typing the name of the CD in the New CD Title field.

10. Add an artist to your project by typing the name of the artist in the Artist Name field.

11. Click the Record button to open the Record CD Setup dialog box. Click the Options button to reveal the entire dialog box (see Figure 18.10).

Figure 18.10
Record your project to CD using the Record CD Setup dialog box.

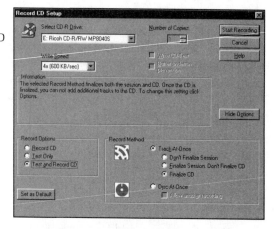

12. Choose your CDR drive using the Select CD-R Drive drop-down list.

13. Choose the write speed for your drive using the Write Speed drop-down list.

14. Choose the number of copies you want to make by typing a number into the Number of Copies parameter.

15. Decide whether you want to add more files to the CD later. If you want to add more files later, choose the Track-At-Once and Don't Finalize Session options in the Record Method section. If you don't want to add more files later, choose the Track-At-Once and Finalize CD options.

TIP

If you plan on having your audio CD duplicated professionally, you should have all your songs gathered together and burn them to the CD all at once using the Disc-At-Once option. This option writes and closes a CD in one move, without turning the writing laser on and off between tracks. If you use the Track-At-Once option to burn your CD, the writing laser is turned on and off between tracks and multiple sessions to create "links" between them. These "links" will show up as errors when the duplication service tries to create a master copy from your CD-R.

16. When you're creating a CD, it helps to first have your system do a test. Testing ensures the best quality and improves your chances for a successful burn. although testing nearly doubles the time required to create a CD, Roxio recommends testing at least the first few times you use the program. After that, you can probably skip it. Choose the Test and Record CD option in the Record Options section.

17. To burn your CD, click the Start Recording button.

> **TIP**
>
> To avoid glitches in the burning process—especially for audio CDs—you should leave your computer alone until the process is complete. If it gets bogged down while burning, you could end up with a ruined CD. Of course, you can just go ahead and burn another one, but then you'll be wasting both your time and money.

Working with Advanced CD Creator Options

Creating a music CD with Easy CD Creator is a fairly easy process, but you might want to know about some advanced program features.

Previewing Songs, Changing Names, and Rearranging the Order

After you've created a project you like, you can do several things before recording the CD. Right-click on a song in the project list to bring up a menu. Choosing Rename from this menu lets you rename the song. Choosing Properties from the menu opens that file's properties. To preview any song, double-click on it. To change the order of a song, just drag and drop its track number anywhere within the list.

Saving and Loading a Project

Sometimes you might want to save a good project to use again at a later date. If you've made a particularly good mix of songs and want to burn it for friends from time to time, it is a good idea to save the final project. That way, you don't have to re-create it every time you want to create another copy of the CD.

To save a project, select File > Save Project List. You can load previously saved projects by choosing File > Open CD Project.

Other Easy CD Creator Features

If you have the Platinum version of Easy CD Creator, you'll no doubt notice that you have access to a number of other advanced features such as CD Copier (which lets you make copies of existing CDs), CD Label Creator (which lets you create custom CD labels and jewel case inserts), and more. Since Easy CD Creator comes with a comprehensive user's guide, I won't be covering those additional features here.

Appendix A
Sample Project Roadmap: From Recording to Mixdown

Throughout this book, you've learned about everything you need to know to create a project from start to finish in SONAR. This information includes how to set up a project, record your tracks, edit your MIDI and audio data, mix your tracks down to stereo, and burn the final recording to CD. But just to give you a brief overview of the whole process, I've put together this outline of all the steps you need to take to record a song using SONAR.

Set Up Your Project

1. Create a new project. If you use a template other than Normal to automatically set the parameters for your project, you can skip the rest of this section. Otherwise, move on to Step 2.
2. Add a title and other descriptive information to your project using the File Info window.
3. Set the types of MIDI data to be recorded in the Global Options dialog box under the MIDI tab.
4. Set the Clock, Metronome, MIDI Input, and MIDI Out parameters in the Project Options dialog box.
5. Set the tempo for the project by using the Tempo toolbar.
6. Set the meter and key for the project by using the Meter/Key view.
7. Set the bit depth and sampling rate (if you're going to record audio) for the project on the General tab in the Audio Options dialog box.

For more information, refer to Chapter 4, "Working with Projects."

Record Your Tracks

1. Create a new track and set it up, typing in a name and choosing an input and output in the Track view.
2. Input initial values for the Volume and Pan parameters, if you need them.

3. If the track is for audio, you can skip this step; otherwise, for a MIDI track, choose values for the Channel, Bank, and Patch parameters.

4. Set the record mode using the Record Options dialog box.

5. Arm the Track and set your input signal level.

6. Click the Record button and start your performance.

7. If you need to add data to only a certain part of the track, use the Auto Punch Record mode and set the Punch In and Punch Out times. You can also use the Loop toolbar to set loop points and have SONAR loop a certain section of the song for recording in only that section.

8. Repeat steps 1 through 7 for every track you need to complete your song.

9. Save your project as a work (.WRK) file if it contains only MIDI data; otherwise, if it contains audio data, save it as a bundle (.BUN) file.

For more information, refer to Chapter 6, "Recording and Playback."

Edit Your Data

1. Use the Track view to make any arrangement changes to your song. For example, you can move clips from one part of the song to another part. You can also mute any tracks that you don't want to use in the final mix. Also, adjust the Key+, Vel+, and Time+ parameters at this time.

2. If you need to do any precise editing to your MIDI tracks, use the Piano Roll and Event views. You use these views for tasks such as changing the pitch and velocity of different notes or correcting the timing of your performance using quantizing. You can also use the Staff view for certain tasks if you feel more comfortable using standard music notation. If you want to add any permanent MIDI effects to your data, do so at this time. Otherwise, you can add effects in real-time during mixdown.

3. For precise editing of your audio tracks, use the Track view. Cut, copy, or paste sections of audio and make adjustments to the volume if you need to. Add any EQ or permanent effects at this point, too. Otherwise, you can wait to add effects in real-time during mixdown, if your computer system can handle it.

4. Save your project as a work (.WRK) file if it contains only MIDI data; otherwise, if it contains audio data, save it as a bundle (.BUN) file.

For more information, refer to Chapter 7, "Editing Basics," and Chapter 8, "Exploring the Editing Tools."

Mix Down Your Project

1. Open the Console view and set initial values for the volume and panning for each track in the project.

2. Set the chorus and reverb settings for the MIDI tracks.

3. Set the Aux Send settings for the audio tracks.

4. Add any real-time effects you want to use for the individual MIDI and/or audio tracks.

5. Add any real-time effects you want to use on the aux send(s).

6. Add any real-time effects you want to use on the mains.

7. Take a snapshot of the current console setup in case you want to come back to it later.

8. Perform a test run of the mix by playing the song and adjusting the parameters during playback.

9. Record your mix movements using the Record Automation feature. If you find that you need to make two different value changes at once during a mix, just make multiple Record Automation passes.

10. Save your project as a work (.WRK) file if it contains only MIDI data; otherwise, if it contains audio data, save it as a bundle (.BUN) file.

For more information, refer to Chapter 11, "Effects: The Really Cool Stuff," and Chapter 12, "Mixing It Down."

Burn to CD

1. Export your project to a stereo audio WAVE (.WAV) file.

2. Use Easy CD Creator to record your WAVE file to CD.

For more information, refer to Chapter 18, "Take Your SONAR Project to CD."

Appendix B
Backing Up Your Project Files

At the end of every recording session, I back up my project files. It doesn't matter whether I'm running late or whether I'm so tired that I can barely keep my eyes open. I always back up my files. Why? Because there once was a time I didn't really think much of making backups. I would do it occasionally—just to be safe—but I never thought I'd run into any trouble. Then one day I went to boot up my PC, and *poof!* My hard drive crashed, taking a lot of important files with it, including a project that I spent weeks working on. Believe me, after that experience, I never took file backups for granted again, and you shouldn't either.

Backing up your files really isn't difficult, and it doesn't take up very much extra time. This is especially true if your project includes only MIDI data. Work (.WRK) files containing only MIDI data are usually very small, and you can make backups of them by simply copying them to a floppy disk, just like you would any other small files. Bundle (.BUN) files—project files that contain audio data—on the other hand, need to be handled a little differently because of their large size. Most bundle files do not fit on a floppy disk, but if you have an Iomega Zip disk drive (or similar "super floppy" drive), you might be able to make a quick backup copy that way.

Back Up with Easy CD Creator

If you have a bunch of files to back up, you need a much larger storage format such as a tape or a CD-recordable drive. In Chapter 18, "Take Your SONAR Project to CD," you learned about using Easy CD Creator to create an audio CD from your SONAR project. Well, in case you didn't know it, you can also use Easy CD Creator along with your CD-R drive to back up data files. The procedure is similar to creating an audio CD, and you can use the Easy CD Creator Wizard to step through the process like this:

1. Start Easy CD Creator.
2. Choose File > New CD Project > Data CD to create an untitled data CD project.

3. In the Select Source Files drop-down list, choose the drive containing the file(s) you want to burn to CD.

4. In the file list below the Select Source Files drop-down list, select the file(s) you want to burn to CD.

CAUTION

If you've set up your SONAR file folders the way I discussed in Chapter 3, "Customizing SONAR," you should be able find your project files in the My Documents/Cakewalk SONAR/Project Files folder. If you use video in your project, not only do you have to back up the work or bundle file for the project, but the individual video file, too. SONAR does not save video data along with project data, not even in a bundle file. For more information about SONAR's video features, read Appendix C, "Producing for Multimedia and the Web."

5. Click the Add button to add the selected file(s) to your data CD project. The file(s) are added to the data CD project list in the bottom half of the Easy CD Creator window (see Figure B.1).

Figure B.1
When you're creating a data CD, you can select any file or files from any of the storage drives connected to your computer system.

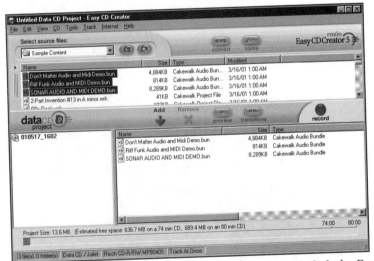

6. To remove a file from the project list, select it and click the Remove button.

7. Repeat steps 3 through 6 until you've finished adding all your files to the project.

8. Click the Record button to open the Record CD Setup dialog box. Click the Options button to reveal the entire dialog box.

9. Choose your CDR drive using the Select CD-R Drive drop-down list.

10. Choose the write speed for your drive using the Write Speed drop-down list.

11. Choose the number of copies you want to make by typing a number into the Number of Copies parameter.

12. Decide whether you want to add more files to the CD later. If you want to add more files later, choose the Track-At-Once and Don't Finalize Session options in the Record Method section. If you don't want to add more files later, choose the Track-At-Once and Finalize CD options.

13. When you're creating a CD, it helps to first have your system do a test. Testing ensures the best quality and improves your chances for a successful burn. Although testing nearly doubles the time required to create a CD, Roxio recommends testing at least the first few times you use the program. After that, you can probably skip it. Choose the Test and Record CD option in the Record Options section.

14. To burn your CD, click the Start Recording button.

Back Up with Windows

If you don't have a CD-recordable drive or you would rather back up your files to a tape drive or other removable format, you can use the Backup utility that comes with Windows. By default, Windows doesn't install the Backup utility during setup, so you might have to install it yourself. To do so, follow these steps:

1. Click the Start button and select Programs > Accessories > System Tools. If you see the Backup utility listed there, you're all set. If not, you have to install it from your original Windows CD.

2. To install Backup, open the Windows Control Panel, and double-click on the Add/Remove Programs icon to open the Add/Remove Programs Properties dialog box (see Figure B.2).

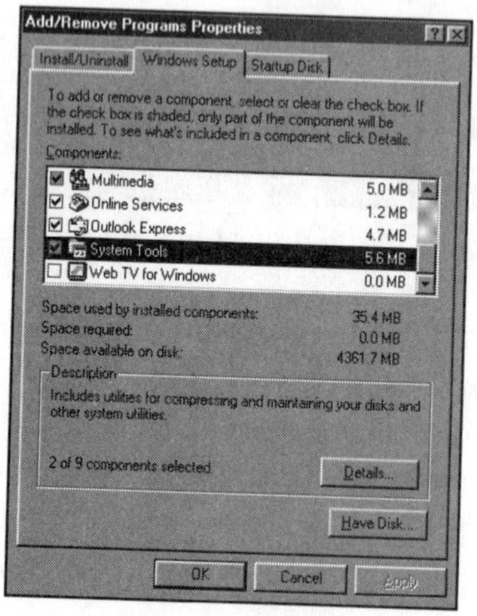

Figure B.2
You can install the Windows Backup utility by using the Add/Remove Programs Properties dialog box.

3. Select the Windows Setup tab.

4. Select System Tools in the Components list and click the Details button to open the System Tools dialog box (see Figure B.3).

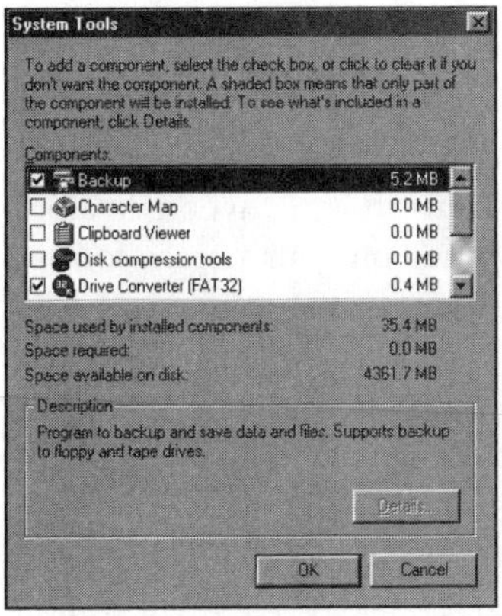

Figure B.3
You can install all the utilities included with Windows via the System Tools dialog box.

5. Find Backup in the Components list, and put a check mark next to it.

6. Click the OK buttons to close both dialog boxes.

7. Insert your original Windows CD when Windows asks for it and click OK. The Backup utility is then installed.

When Backup is installed, you can use it to back up all your important files. Just follow these steps:

1. Click the Start button and select Programs > Accessories > System > Backup to run Backup.

2. When the Backup Wizard asks you what you would like to do, choose Create A New Backup Job and click OK.

3. The wizard then asks whether you want to back up everything on your computer or just the files or folders that you select. Because you need to back up just your My Documents folder, choose the Back Up Selected Files, Folders And Drives option, and click Next.

4. The wizard then asks you to select the files, folders, or drives you want to back up (see Figure B.4).

Figure B.4
Here, you can select the files and/or folders that you want to back up.

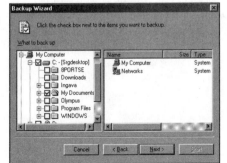

5. Click the + (plus) sign next to your hard drive (C:) to see a list of folders there. Put a check mark next to the My Documents folder, and click Next.

6. When you're asked what types of files to back up—all or only new and changed files—choose the All Selected Files option, and click on Next.

7. The wizard then wants to know where to store your backup files. Your response depends on your storage format, so just select the drive you want to use.

TIP

You can probably use Backup with your CD-R drive. Most CD-R drives ship with a software program called DirectCD. (Once known as Adaptec DirectCD, the company that makes this product is now known as Roxio.) This software lets your computer "see" your CD-R drive as just another storage device. So, you can copy files to it just like you would to a floppy disk, and Backup works with it, too. Refer to the documentation that came with your CD-R drive to see whether the product includes DirectCD.

8. Tell the wizard whether it should compare the original files to the backup files after the backup process is done to make sure that they contain the same data. (I like to keep this option activated to be extra safe.)

9. Choose whether you want your data compressed. If you're short on space, having this feature available is nice, but otherwise keeping the data uncompressed is a little safer.

10. Give your new backup job a name, so that the next time you run Backup, all you need to do is select the job by name and start the process. The program will remember all your previous option choices.

11. Click Start, and your files are then backed up.

Now, don't you feel better already? You can rest easy knowing that all your hard recording work won't be lost even if your computer does decide to give up on you one of these days. Believe me, it's not a fun experience.

Appendix C
Producing for Multimedia and the Web

In addition to regular music production, SONAR includes a number of features to help you in creating music for multimedia and the Internet. You can import a video file into a SONAR project and then compose music to it. You can also export video files along with your synchronized music. And you can export your music files to a number of popular Internet audio file formats, including RealAudio, Windows Media Format, and MP3. In essence, these capabilities round out SONAR's full set of features, allowing you to use the program for most— if not all—of your music production needs.

Importing Video Files

If you're ever asked to compose music for film, video games, or some other visually based task, SONAR's File > Import Video File command will come in very handy. Using this command, you can include an AVI, MPEG, or QuickTime video in your project and edit the existing audio track or tracks or add new ones.

NOTE
AVI, MPEG, and QuickTime are special digital video file formats specifically designed for working with video on computers. Each format uses its own unique compression scheme to achieve video quality as good as possible in a file size as small as possible. AVI (Audio Video Interleaved) is a Windows-based format, which means that any computer running Windows can play AVI files. QuickTime is a Mac-based format, which means that any Macintosh computer can play QuickTime files. With special player software, a computer running Windows can play QuickTime files, too, which is why the format is supported by SONAR. MPEG (Motion Pictures Expert Group) is a more advanced format that sometimes requires special hardware for playback. Therefore, MPEG video files are usually of much better quality than AVI or QuickTime, and they are also smaller in size.

To add a video file to your project, follow these steps:

1.   Select File > Import Video File to open the Import Video File dialog box (see Figure C.1).

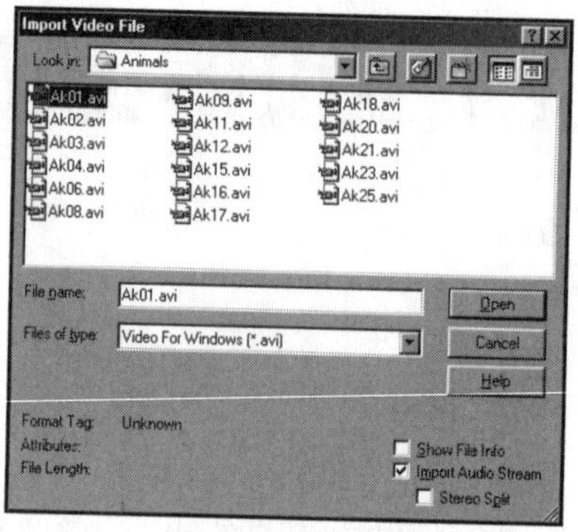

Figure C.1

Here, you can select a video file to add to your project.

2.   Choose the type of video file (AVI, MPEG, or QuickTime) you want to add from the Files of type drop-down list and select a file.

3.   If the video file contains audio data, you can import that data, too, by activating the Import Audio Stream option at the bottom of the box. If the audio is in stereo, you can import it as a single stereo audio track or a pair of audio tracks containing the left and right channels of the stereo signal by deactivating or activating the Stereo Split option respectively.

4.   Click on Open.

SONAR then loads the video file and displays the first video frame along with the current Now time in the Video view (see Figure C.2). If you imported audio along with the video, the new audio track or tracks are inserted into the project above the currently selected track.

Figure C.2

The Video view displays the video along with the current Now time.

Initially, when you play the project, the video starts playing back at the beginning, but you can change where the video starts by adjusting the Start Time, as well as the Trim-in time and Trim-out Time. Using these parameters, you can adjust when within the project the video will start and end playback. To change these parameters, follow these steps:

1. Right-click within the Video view and select Video Properties from the pop-up menu to open the Video Properties dialog box.

2. Under the Video Settings tab, input the new values for Start Time, Trim-in Time, and Trim-out Time. The Start Time uses measures, beats, and frames for its value; and the Trim-in and Trim-out times use hours, minutes, seconds, and frames just as with SMPTE Time Code.

3. Click on OK.

The video now starts and stops playing back within the project at the times you specified. You also can adjust a number of other parameters for the Video view, and you access all of them via the right-click pop-up menu. For instance, if you want to remove the video from your project, just select the Delete command. If you want to temporarily disable video playback, select the Animate command. You can even change the size of the video display by using the Stretch Options command.

> **TIP**
>
> If you choose Full Screen under the Stretch Options command, the video display covers the entire computer screen and you cannot access SONAR with the mouse (although keyboard commands still work). To get back to the normal display, just press the Esc (Escape) key on your computer keyboard.

Exporting Video Files

After you've imported a video file into your project, and either edited its existing audio or added new audio tracks to it, you can export the file so that other people can see and hear your work. Follow these steps to export the file:

1. Select File > Export Video to AVI to open the Export Video to AVI dialog box (see Figure C.3).

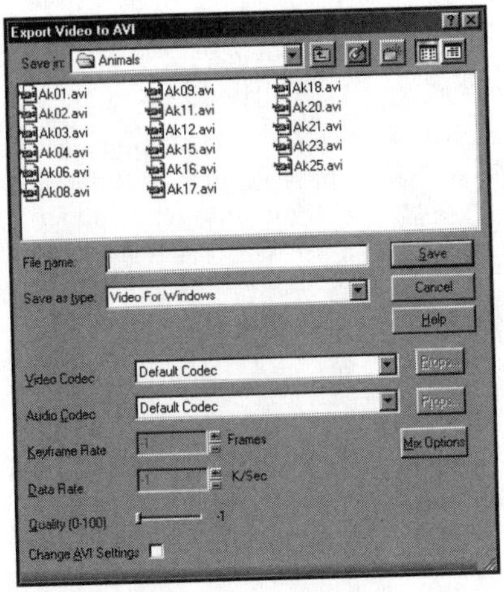

Figure C.3
You can use the Export Video to AVI dialog box to export video files.

2. Type a name for the file in the File Name area. You don't need to select a file type because SONAR allows you to save your video to the AVI format only. You can't save to MPEG or QuickTime.

3. Click on Save, and the video file is saved with its original parameter settings. If you want to dabble with the method of compression used in the file, along with other video-related parameters, you can set them in the lower half of the dialog box.

TIP

For more information about multimedia and video-related parameters, you should consult a dedicated book on the subject. I've found *Multimedia: Making It Work with CD-ROM, Fourth Edition* (Osborne Publishing, 1998, ISBN 0078825520) by Tay Vaughn to be very informative.

When you save your video file, any audio tracks in your project are mixed down and saved along with the video.

Exporting Audio Files

In addition to exporting your audio tracks as WAVE (.WAV) files for the purpose of burning to CD (as you learned in Chapter 18, "Take Your SONAR Project to CD"), you can also export them as RealAudio, Windows Media Format, and MP3 files for distribution over the Internet.

NOTE

Just as AVI, MPEG, and QuickTime are special digital video file formats, RealAudio, Windows Media, and MP3 are special audio file formats specifically designed for distributing audio over the Internet. Each format uses its own unique compression scheme to achieve the best possible sound quality in the smallest possible file size. All three formats are very popular, and all three support streaming audio as well. This means that you can listen to the audio as you download it rather than having to wait for the whole audio file to be downloaded before you can play it. In terms of quality, the order from highest to lowest goes like this: Windows Media, MP3, RealAudio.

However, this order depends on who's listening, because everyone has his or her own opinions on the subject. For more information about RealAudio, visit **www.real.com/devzone/**. For more information about Windows Media, visit **www.microsoft.com/windows/windowsmedia/**. For more information about MP3, visit **http://help.mp3.com/help/**.

Exporting to RealAudio

Do the following to mix and save your audio tracks as a RealAudio file:

1. Select the track or tracks you want to export in the Track view.

2. Choose File > Export Audio to open the Export Audio dialog box (see Figure C.4).

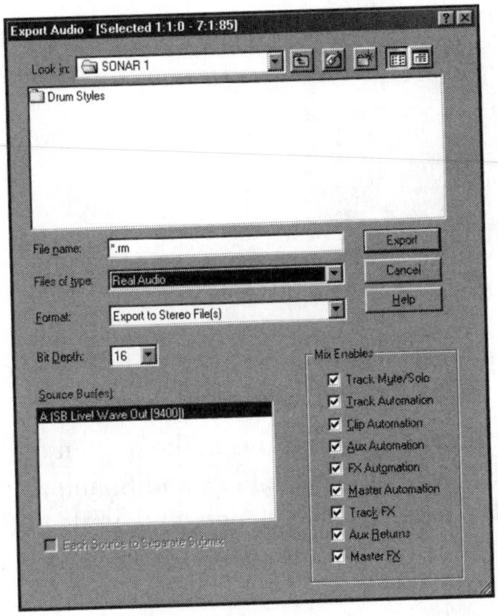

Figure C.4
You can use the Export Audio dialog box to export to RealAudio.

APPENDICES

3. From the Look In list, select the folder you want to save the RealAudio file into. Then type a name for the file in the File Name box.

4. Choose a file type from the File of Types list. In this case, use the RealAudio option.

5. Select the format you want to use. You can mix your audio tracks to a single stereo file, two mono files (that, when combined, create a stereo file), or a single mono file.

6. Choose the sound card or cards you want to use to process your audio tracks from the Source Bus(es) list.

7. Leave all the Mix Enables options activated to ensure that your new RealAudio file will include the same effects and mix automation that you used on the original audio tracks.

8. Click on Export to open the RealAudio Settings dialog box (see Figure C.5).

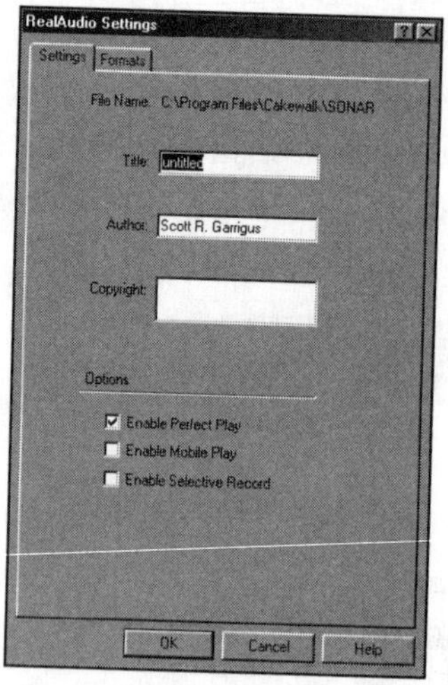

Figure C.5

In the RealAudio Settings dialog box, you can adjust specific parameters for the RealAudio file.

9. Under the Settings tab, you can enter title, author, and copyright information for the RealAudio file.

10. Choose from the three options at the bottom of the dialog: Enable Perfect Play, Enable Mobile Play, and Enable Selective Record. Enable Perfect Play requires the listeners to download the entire RealAudio file before hearing it rather than being able to stream the file. This option ensures uninterrupted playback, but your listeners will also have to wait for the download. Enable Mobile Play gives listeners a choice between downloading and streaming a file. Enable Selective Record lets listeners save the file to their hard drive for later. If you don't want people to be able to keep a copy of the file, make sure Enable Mobile Play and Enable Selective Record are not activated.

11. Under the Formats tab (see Figure C.6), you can select the modem speeds that you want your RealAudio file to be optimized for. It's really best to just select them all so that your listeners can hear the best quality at their own specific modem speed. For example, someone using a 56 Kbps modem will hear a better version of your file than someone listening with a 28 Kbps modem. Otherwise, everyone would hear just the same low-quality file.

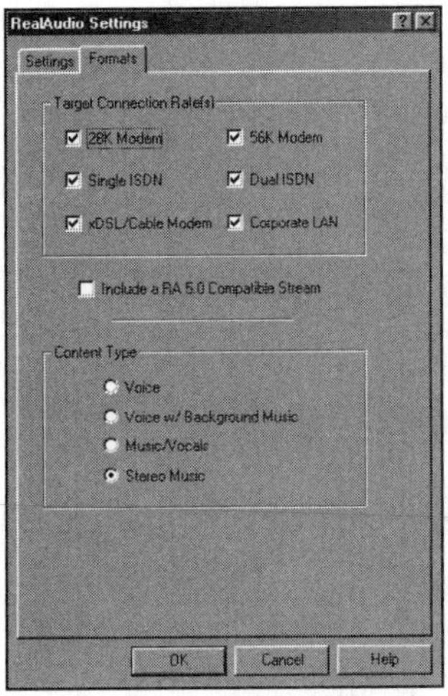

Figure C.6

You can set modem speeds on the Formats tab of the RealAudio Settings dialog box.

12. If you want your file to be compatible with the older 5.0 version of RealAudio, select the Include A RA 5.0 Compatible Stream option. This option makes your file a little bigger, but it's worth the extra size just in case someone using the old RealAudio Player software tries to listen to your file.

13. If you want to optimize the RealAudio file for certain types of content, select the type of music that you've recorded in your project in the Content Type section. Most of the time, you'll probably use the Stereo Music option.

14. Click on OK, and your audio is saved as a RealAudio file with an .RM extension.

Exporting to Windows Media

To mix and save your audio tracks as a Windows Media file, just follow these steps:

1. Select the track or tracks you want to export in the Track view.

2. Choose File > Export Audio to open the Export Audio dialog box.

3. From the Look In list, select the folder you want to save the Windows Media file into. Then type a name for the file in the File Name box.

4. Choose the type of file from the File of Types list. In this case, use the Windows Media option.

5. Select the format you want to use. You can mix your audio tracks to a single stereo file, two mono files (that, when combined, create a stereo file), or a single mono file.

6. Choose the sound card or cards you want to use to process your audio tracks from the Source Bus(es) list.

7. Leave all the Mix Enables options activated to ensure that your new Windows Media file will include the same effects and mix automation that you used on the original audio tracks.

8. Click on Export to open the Microsoft Audio Encode Options dialog box (see Figure C.7).

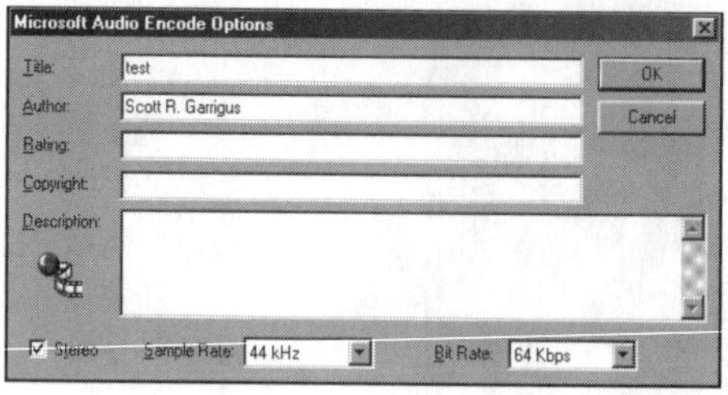

Figure C.7

In the Microsoft Audio Encode Options dialog box, you can adjust specific parameters for the Windows Media file.

9. Enter Title, Author, Rating, Copyright, and Description information for the Windows Media file.

10. Choose from the three other settings: Stereo, Sample Rate, and Bit Rate. Stereo determines whether the Windows Media file will be in stereo. You learned about sampling rates in Chapter 1, "Understanding MIDI and Digital Audio." Sample Rate lets you set the sampling rate for the Windows Media file. The higher the rate, the better the file will sound, but the bigger the file size will be. Bit Rate lets you target the modem speed for the Windows Media file. For example, if you want the file to be able to play over a 28.8 Kbps modem, select the 22 Kbps bit rate. This bit rate will play over any modem speed 28.8 Kbps and higher. If you want to produce a higher quality file, you can select a higher bit rate, but the file won't play on a 28.8 Kbps modem. A bit rate of 48 Kbps or lower should play on a 56 Kbps modem, but you are better off with a 40 Kbps or lower setting because the Internet can be slow at times.

11. Click on OK, and your audio is saved as a Windows Media file with a .WMA extension.

Exporting to MP3

To mix and save your audio tracks as an MP3 file, follow these steps:

1. Select the track or tracks you want to export in the Track view.

2. Choose File > Export Audio to open the Export Audio dialog box.

3. From the Look In list, select the folder you want to save the MP3 file into. Then type a name for the file in the File Name box.

4. Choose the type of file from the File of Types list. In this case, use the MP3 option.

5. Select the format you want to use. You can mix your audio tracks to a single stereo file, two mono files (that, when combined, create a stereo file), or a single mono file.

6. Choose the sound card or cards you want to use to process your audio tracks from the Source Bus(es) list.

7. Leave all the Mix Enables options activated to ensure that your new MP3 file will include the same effects and mix automation that you used on the original audio tracks.

8. Click on Export to open the Cakewalk MP3 Encoder dialog box (see Figure C.8).

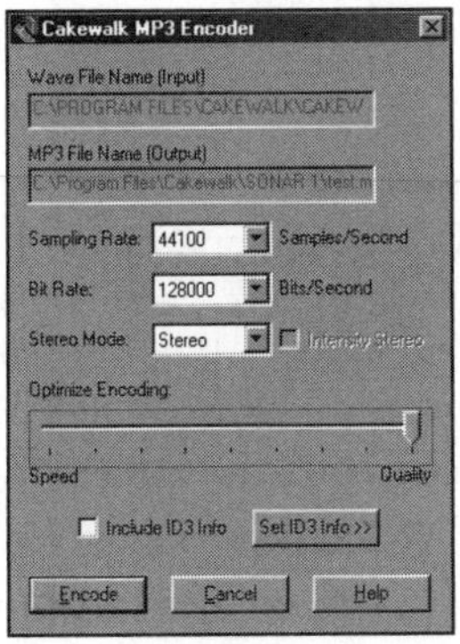

APPENDICES

Figure C.8
In the Cakewalk MP3 Encoder dialog box, you can adjust specific parameters for the MP3 file.

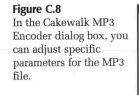

9. Just as with Windows Media, you can select a sampling rate, bit rate, and Stereo mode. The only difference is Joint Stereo mode, which lets you create smaller MP3 files by comparing the left and right audio signals and eliminating any material that is the same in both channels. Using this option usually degrades the audio quality, though, so I advise against choosing it unless you really need smaller MP3 files.

10. Use the Optimize Encoding setting to adjust how long it takes to encode your MP3 file. If you set the slider toward the left, encoding will go faster; to the right, encoding will go slower. But the more time spent on encoding, the better the quality of the file. So, I recommend you leave the slider set all the way to the right. Encoding a file doesn't take very long anyway.

11. If you want to include some information about the file, select the Include ID3 Info option. To enter the information, click on Set ID3 Info to open the ID3 Info dialog box. Here, you can enter Title, Artist, Album, Year, Track Number, Comment, and Genre information. Click on OK when you're done.

12. Click on Encode, and your audio is saved as an MP3 file with an .MP3 extension.

TIP

If you want to include the music from the MIDI tracks of your project in your RealAudio, Windows Media, or MP3 files, read the "Convert Your MIDI Tracks" section of Chapter 18, "Take Your SONAR Project to CD."

Appendix D
Resources on the Web

Although I've made every effort to include as much information as possible about SONAR within this book, someone will always have that one question that goes unanswered. And, as I mentioned earlier in the book, some of the topics could fill up tomes all on their own. But that doesn't mean I'm going to leave you out in the cold with nowhere to turn.

I spent some time searching the Internet and found that it provides a number of resources you can use to locate any additional information you might need. I've tried to be sure to list all the quality sites that are available, but I may have missed a few. If you know of a great Cakewalk-related Web site that's not on this list, please drop me a note at **www.garrigus.com** so that I can be sure to include the site in the next edition of this book.

SONAR Power!
http://www.garrigus.com/scott/work/sonarpower.html

This is one of the first sites that you should visit. I have a created a site exclusively for the *SONAR Power!* book. There is a Discussion area, where you can post your questions and get them answered directly by me. There is also a Live Chat area, where I hold scheduled chat sessions. You can also get a free subscription to my monthly music technology newsletter, which includes more tips and techniques that you won't find in this book. Plus, as a subscriber you are eligible to win free music products each month. Be sure to stop by and meet all of the other *SONAR Power!* readers out there!

APPENDICES

Cakewalk Technical Support Homepage

http://www.cakewalk.com/Support/

The Cakewalk Technical Support Homepage is also one of the first places you should look for answers. Cakewalk provides a large selection of materials, including answers to the most frequently asked questions (FAQs), product updates, and technical documents. You also can find lessons, tips, and tricks, as well as additional helpful publications and resources. And, of course, you can get in touch with Cakewalk's Tech Support people if you need to.

Official Cakewalk Newsgroups

http://www.cakewalk.com/Support/newsgroups.html

Another place you can look for help is the Official Cakewalk Newsgroups. The Cakewalk newsgroups not only provide you with direct access to Cakewalk Technical Support, but also to other users. You can find specific topics on SONAR, digital audio, and MIDI FX, as well as dedicated groups for general information and beginners.

AudioForums.com

http://www.audioforums.com/

AudioForums.com is yet another Web site where you can find discussions about Cakewalk products. You won't find anything overly special about this site, but you can find some good information here, so I thought I should include it. This site also includes discussion areas for audio-related topics such as PC Audio Hardware, Mac Audio Hardware, Studio Gear, and more.

Cakewalk Users Guild

http://www.shatterproof.net/cakewalk/

Unfortunately, what could be one of the best unofficial Cakewalk resources on the Web—-the Cakewalk Users Guild—isn't updated on a regular basis. But this site still contains plenty of useful information. You can find answers to frequently asked questions (FAQs), file downloads, Projects by other users for download, and so on.

Li'l Chips Cakewalk Area

http://www.lilchips.com/cakewalk/index.asp

The Li'l Chips Cakewalk Area provides free Instrument Definition files and free StudioWare panels for download. Most of them pertain to Roland MIDI products, but you still can find a nice collection that could be useful to you.

The Secrets of Cakewalk's CAL Programming

http://www.cal.pyar.com/

If you want to delve more deeply into the Cakewalk Application Language (CAL), you should not miss this site. It has a full tutorial that teaches you how to program using CAL. Subjects include Programming Fundamentals, The Syntax of CAL, Techniques and Work-Arounds, and there are sample programs for download.

The Ultimate Cakewalk CAL Web Page

http://www.geocities.com/sunsetstrip/cabaret/5721/cal/

Another nice CAL resource, The Ultimate Cakewalk CAL Web Page is more like a compilation of links to other CAL resources. You can find basic CAL site links, as well as links to information on how to use CAL. The best part of the site, however, is the extensive list of CAL scripts available for download. More than 70 scripts are available, covering a wide variety of useful editing functions.

Synth Zone

http://www.synthzone.com/

Although not a dedicated Cakewalk site, the Synth Zone is an excellent MIDI, synthesizer, and electronic music production resource guide. You can find links to a ton of information, such as patches and associated software, for just about any synthesizer product from just about any manufacturer. You can also find links to discussion groups, classifieds ads and auctions, music and audio software downloads, and more.

ProRec

http://www.prorec.com/

Another excellent non-dedicated Cakewalk site, ProRec is one of the best audio recording resources for musicians. Updated regularly, the site provides industry news, articles, and reviews. Sifting through all the information on this site will take a while, but it's definitely worth the time and effort.

Index

Italicized page numbers refer to illustrations and charts or Tip, Caution, and Note boxes.

INDEX

MUSKA&LIPMAN

Order Form

Postal Orders:
Muska & Lipman Publishing
P.O. Box 8225
Cincinnati, Ohio 45208

Online Orders or more information:
http://www.muskalipman.com
Fax Orders:
(513) 924-9333

Title/ISBN	Price/Cost
Sound Forge Power! 1-929685-10-6	
Quantity _____	
	× $29.95
Total Cost _____	
CD Recordable Solutions 1-929685-11-4	
Quantity _____	
	× $29.95
Total Cost _____	
Online Broadcasting Power! 0-9662889-8-X	
Quantity _____	
	× $29.95
Total Cost _____	

Title/ISBN	Price/Cost
MP3/FYI 1-929685-05-X	
Quantity _____	
	× $14.95
Total Cost _____	
Subtotal _____	
Sales Tax _____ (please add 6% for books shipped to Ohio addresses)	
Shipping _____ ($6.00 for US and Canada $12.00 other countries)	
TOTAL PAYMENT ENCLOSED _____	

Ship to:

Company _____

Name _____

Address _____

City _____ State _____ Zip _____ Country _____

E-mail _____

Educational facilities, companies, and organizations interested in multiple copies of these books should contact the publisher for quantity discount information. Training manuals, CD-ROMs, electronic versions, and portions of these books are also available individually or can be tailored for specific needs.

Thank you for your order.